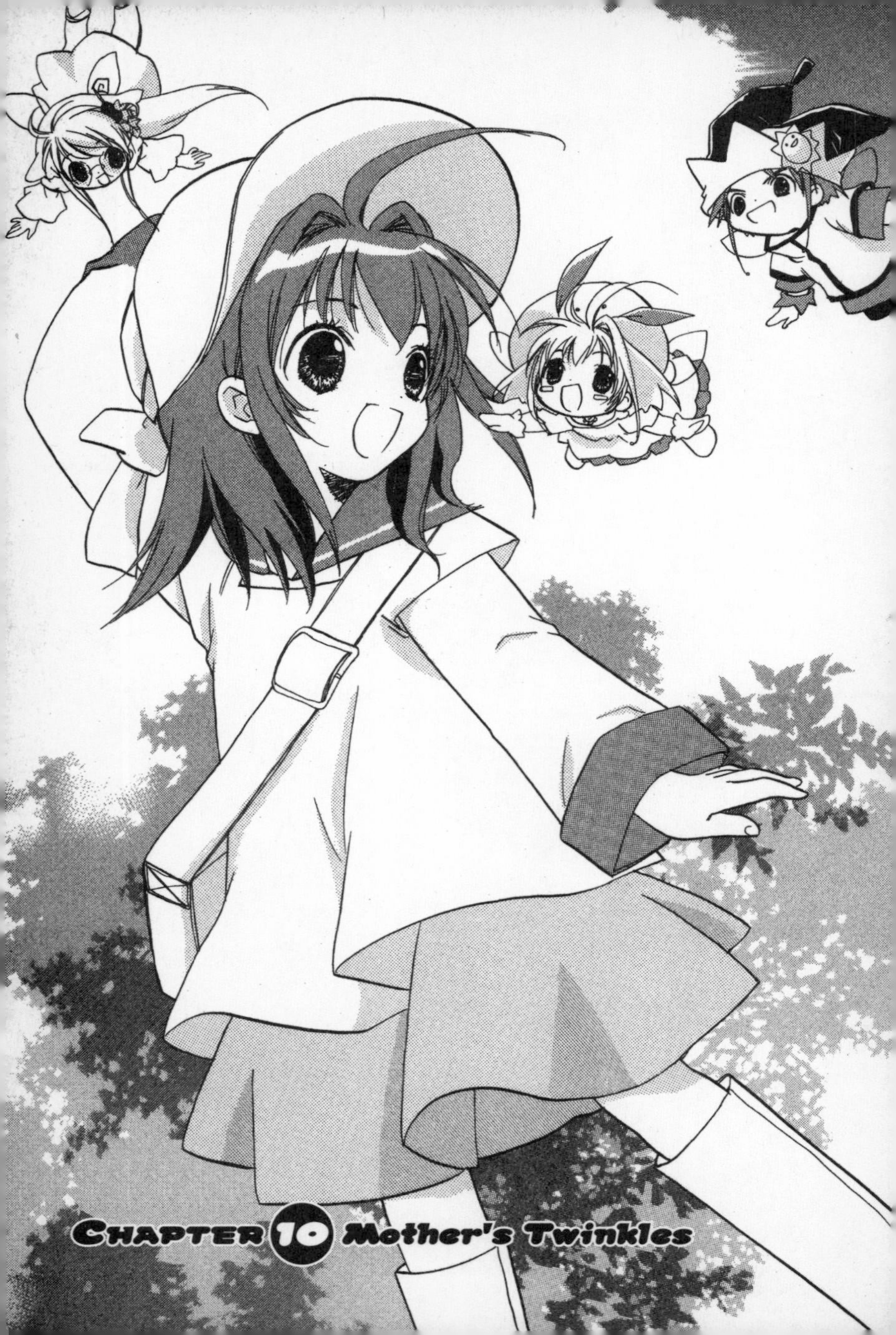
CHAPTER 10 Mother's Twinkles

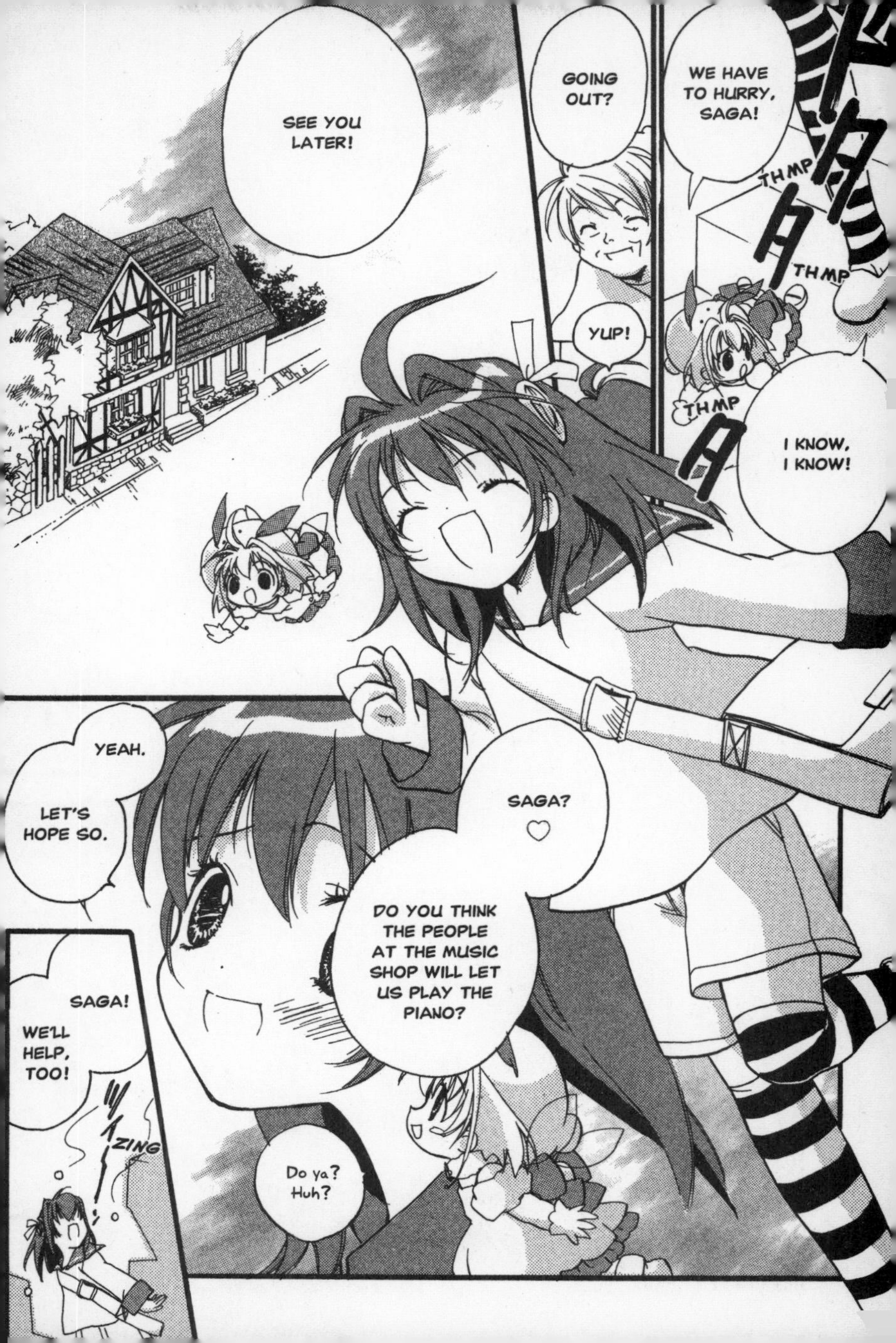
WE HAVE TO HURRY, SAGA!
THMP
THMP
THMP
I KNOW, I KNOW!
GOING OUT?
YUP!
SEE YOU LATER!
SAGA? ♡
DO YOU THINK THE PEOPLE AT THE MUSIC SHOP WILL LET US PLAY THE PIANO?
Do ya? Huh?
YEAH.
LET'S HOPE SO.
SAGA!
WE'LL HELP, TOO!
ZING

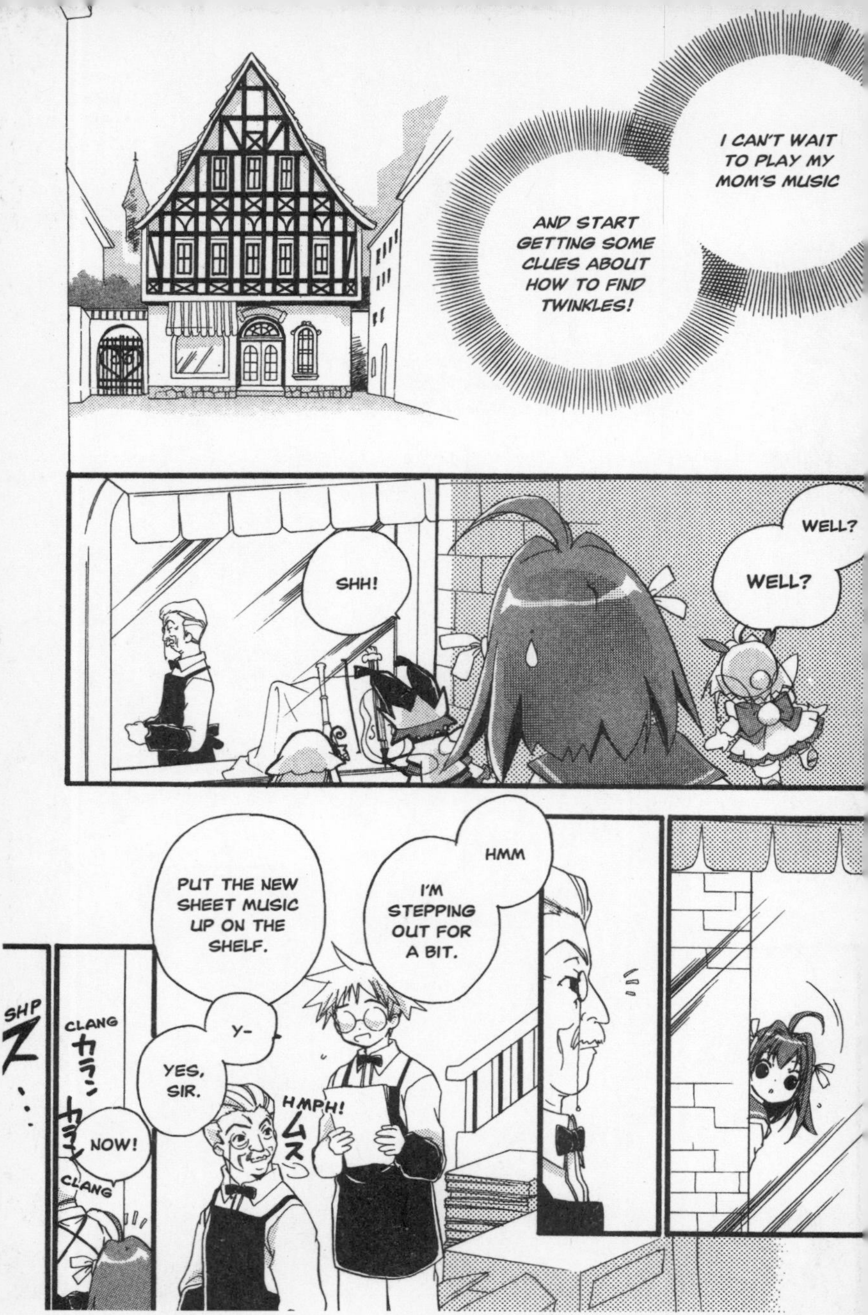
I CAN'T WAIT TO PLAY MY MOM'S MUSIC
AND START GETTING SOME CLUES ABOUT HOW TO FIND TWINKLES!
WELL?
WELL?
SHH!
HMM
I'M STEPPING OUT FOR A BIT.
PUT THE NEW SHEET MUSIC UP ON THE SHELF.
Y-
YES, SIR.
HMPH! ムス
NOW!
CLANG カラン
カラン CLANG
SHP

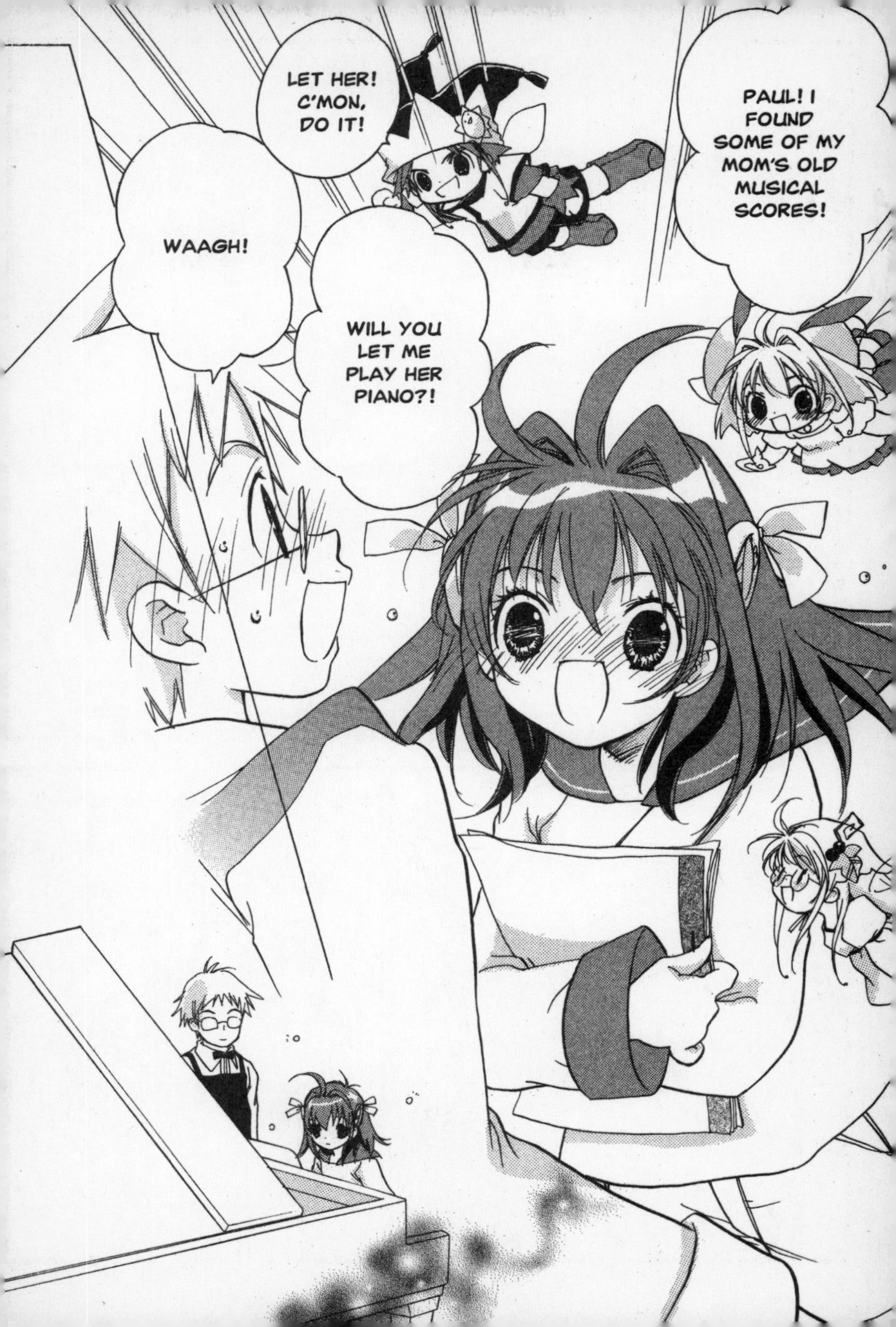
PAUL! I FOUND SOME OF MY MOM'S OLD MUSICAL SCORES!
WILL YOU LET ME PLAY HER PIANO?!
WAAGH!
LET HER! C'MON, DO IT!

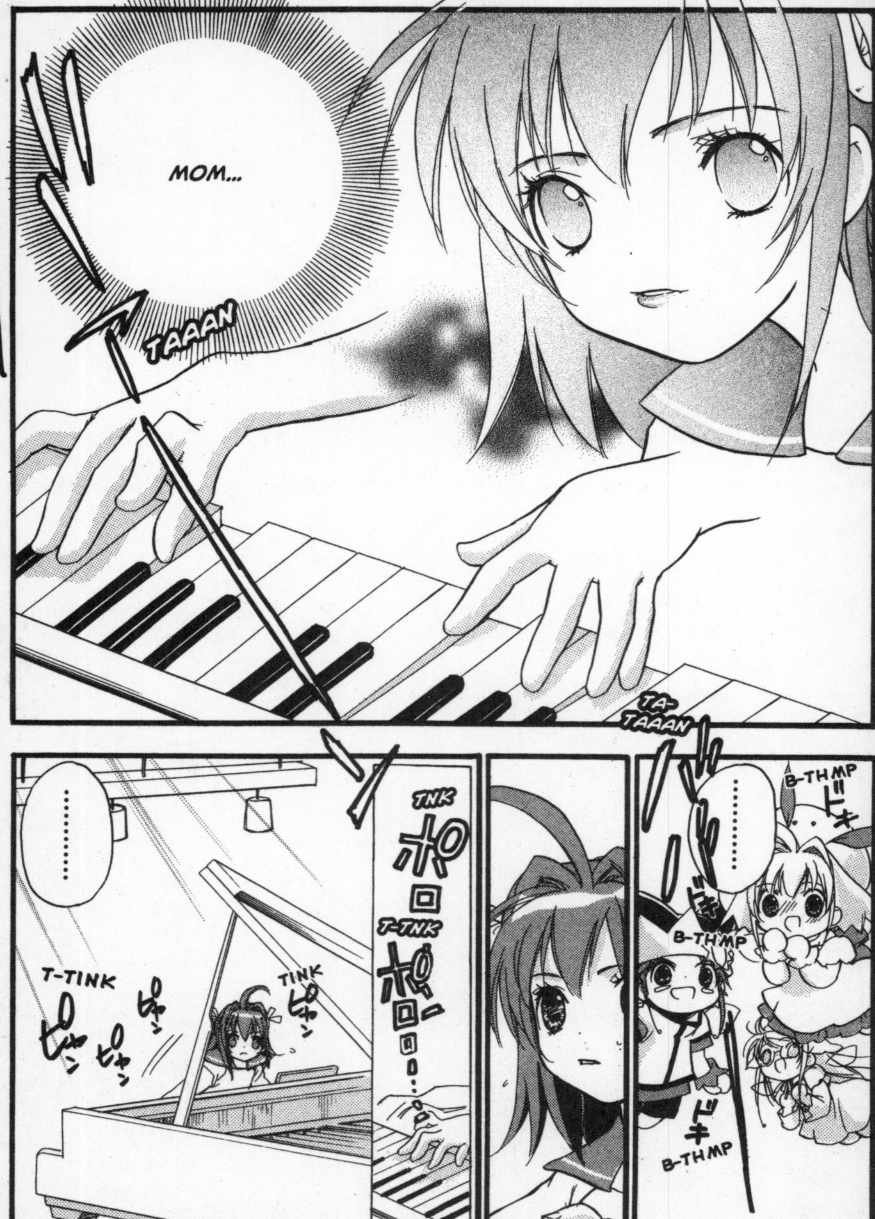

MOM...
TAAAN
TA-TAAAN
......
B-THMP ドキ
B-THMP
B-THMP ドキ
...!
TNK ポロ
T-TNK
......
TINK
T-TINK

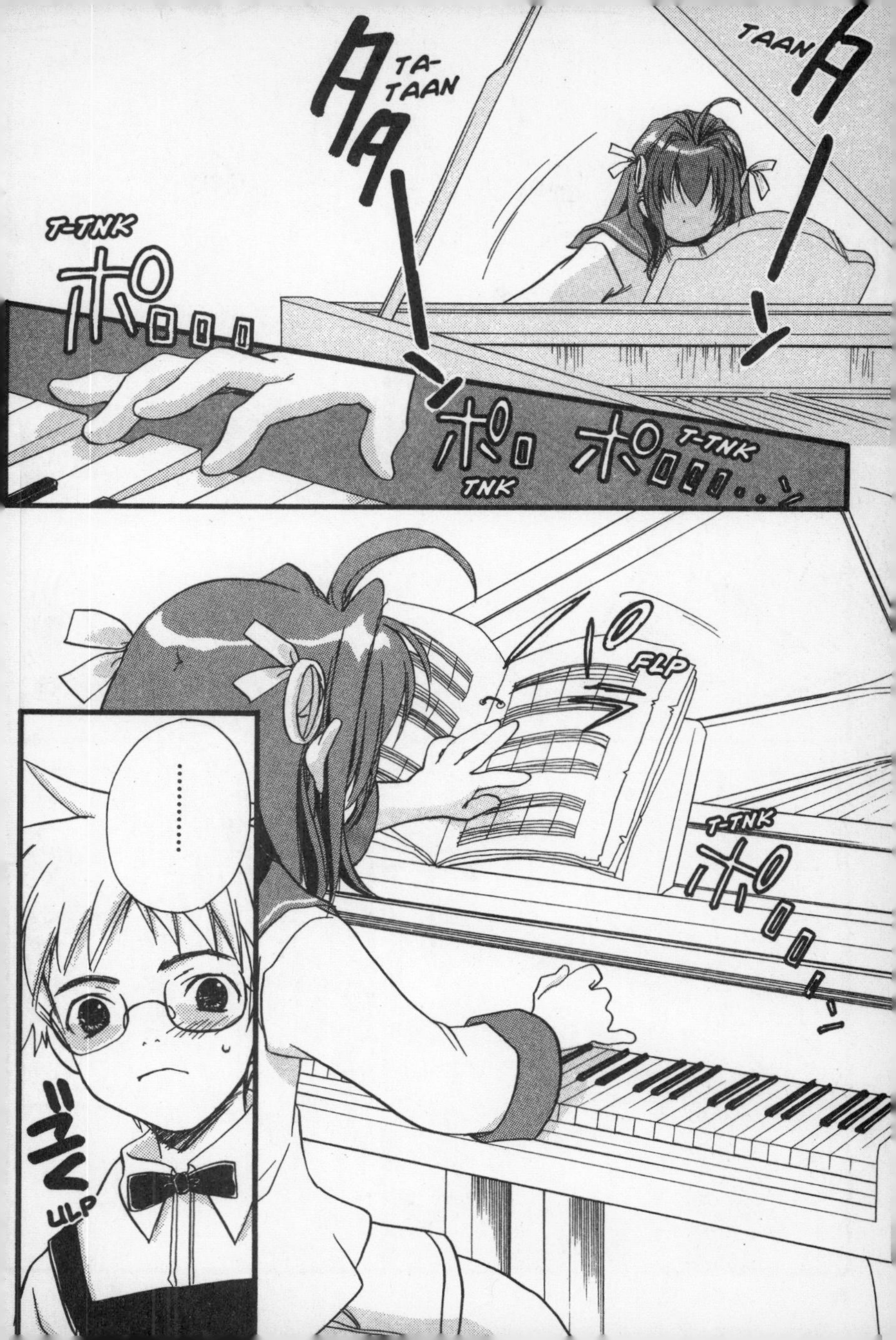
TAAN
TA-
TAAN
T-TNK
T-TNK
TNK
FLP
T-TNK
……
ULP

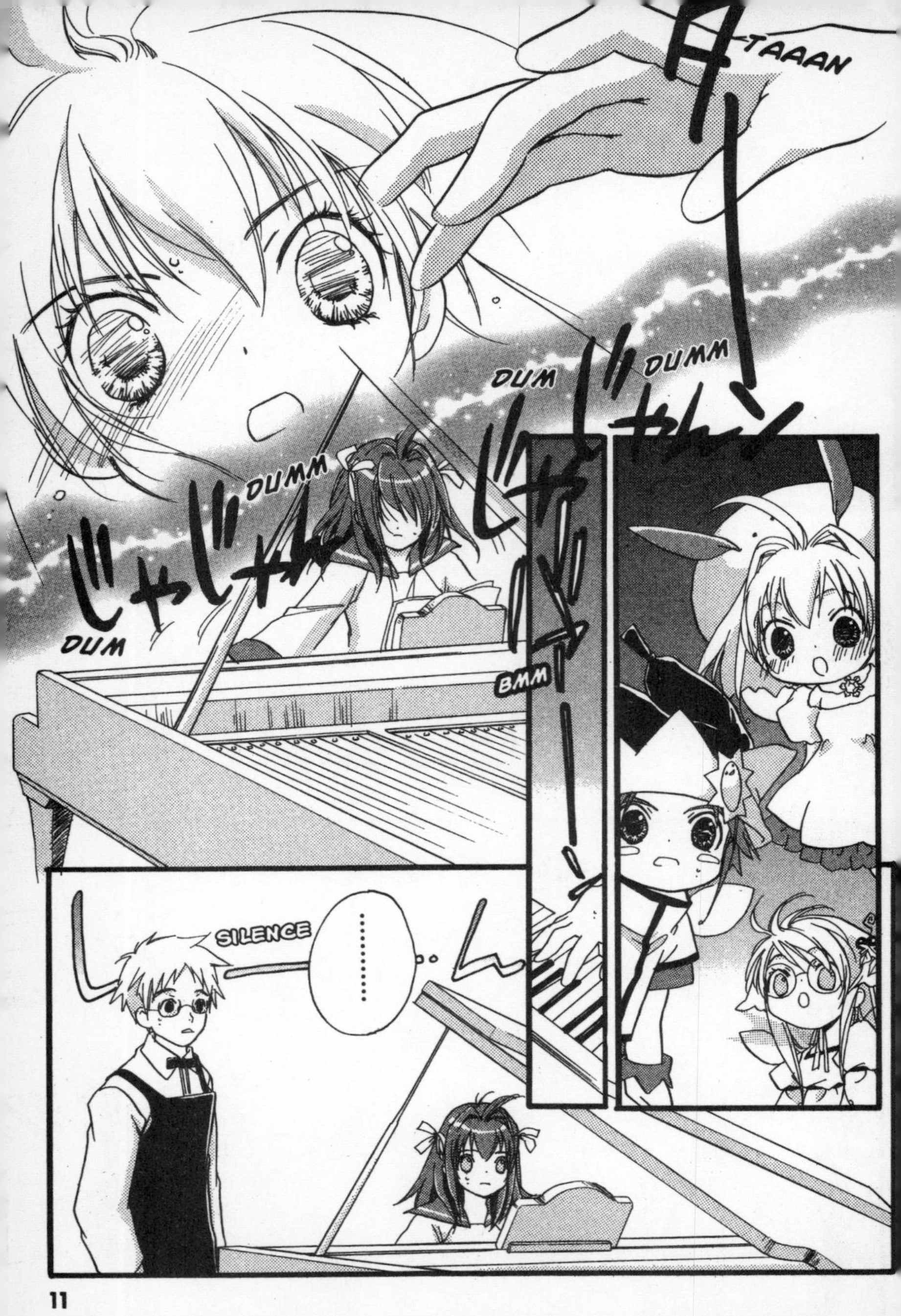
TAAAN
DUMM
DUM
DUMM
DUM
BMM
SILENCE
....

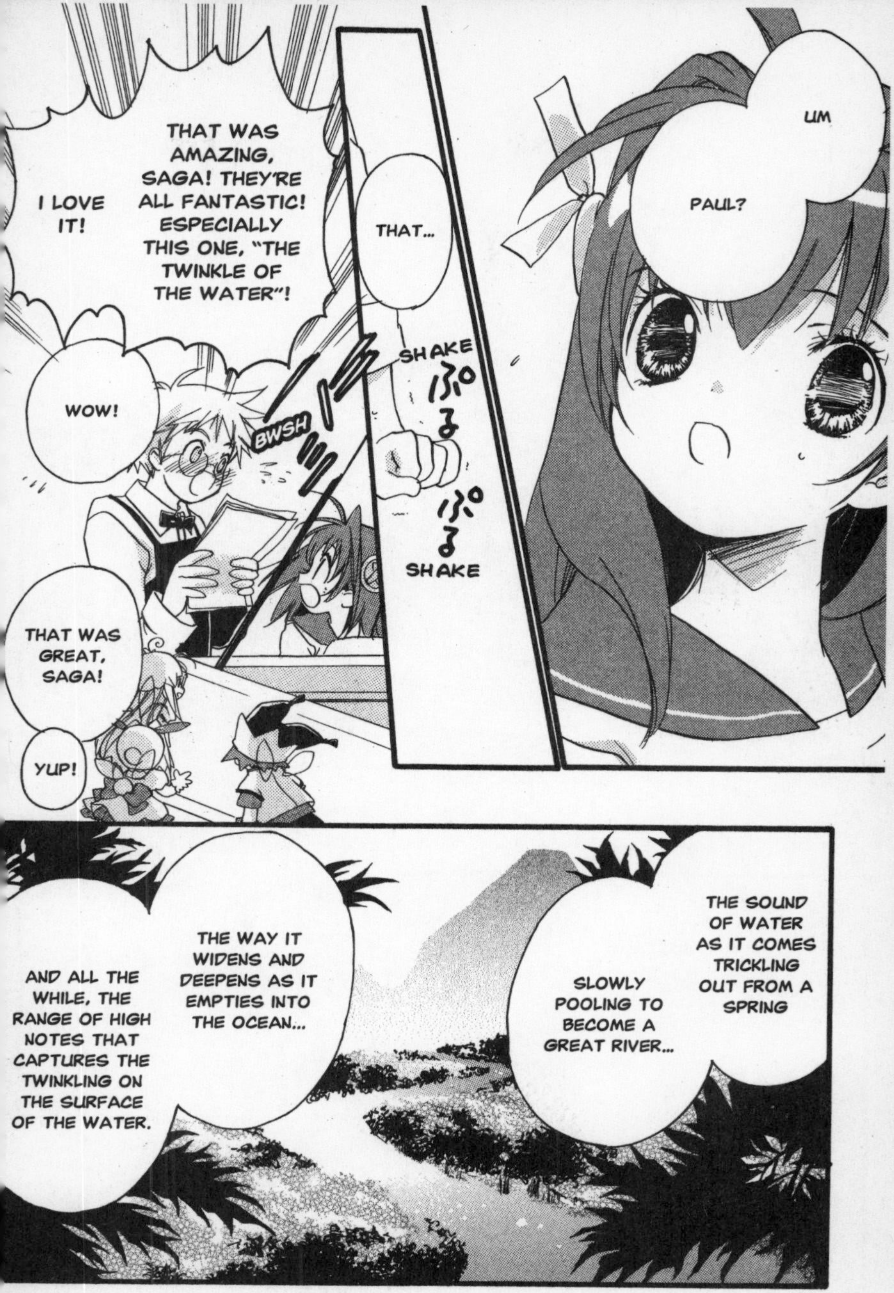
UM
PAUL?
THAT...
SHAKE ぷる
ぷる SHAKE
THAT WAS AMAZING, SAGA! THEY'RE ALL FANTASTIC! ESPECIALLY THIS ONE, "THE TWINKLE OF THE WATER"!
I LOVE IT!
BWSH
WOW!
THAT WAS GREAT, SAGA!
YUP!
THE SOUND OF WATER AS IT COMES TRICKLING OUT FROM A SPRING
SLOWLY POOLING TO BECOME A GREAT RIVER...
THE WAY IT WIDENS AND DEEPENS AS IT EMPTIES INTO THE OCEAN...
AND ALL THE WHILE, THE RANGE OF HIGH NOTES THAT CAPTURES THE TWINKLING ON THE SURFACE OF THE WATER.

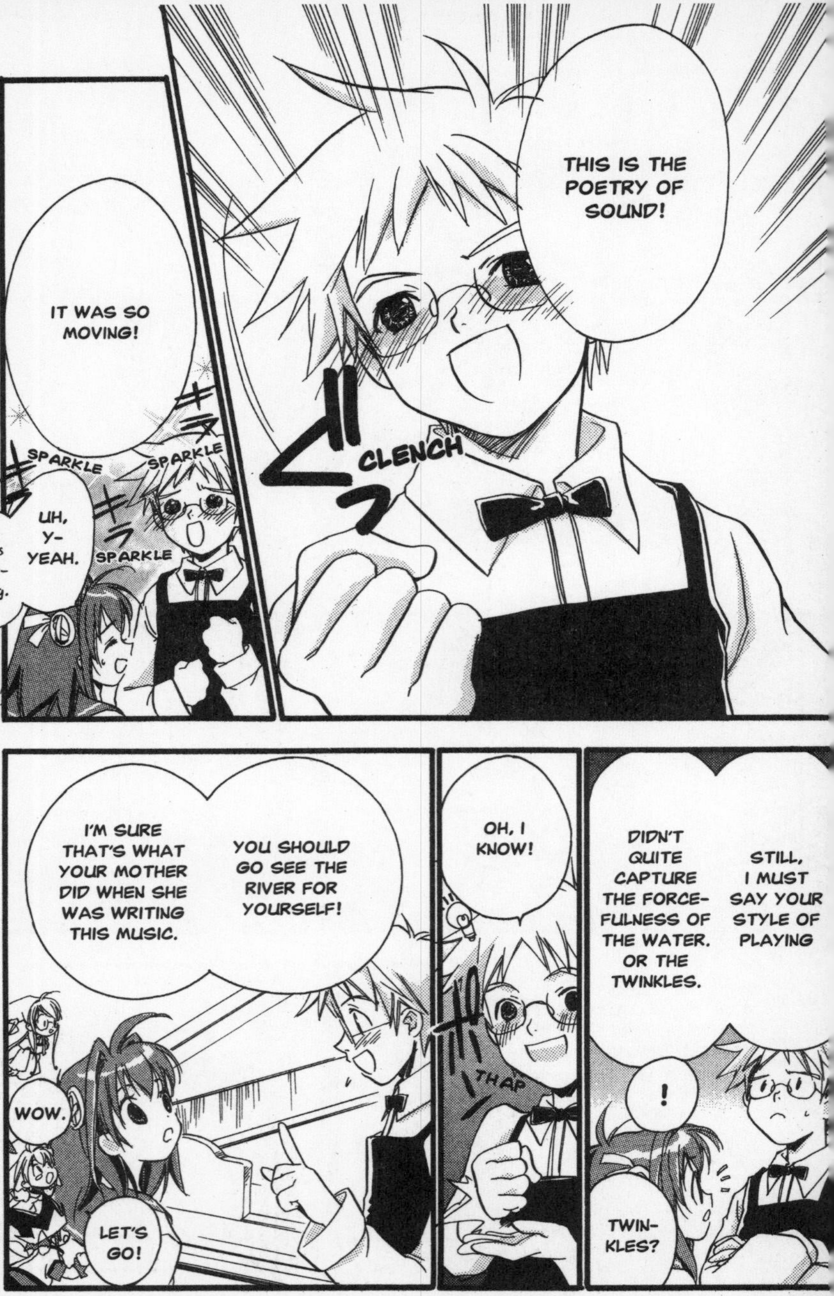
THIS IS THE POETRY OF SOUND!
CLENCH
IT WAS SO MOVING!
SPARKLE
SPARKLE
SPARKLE
UH, Y-YEAH.
He's sparkling.
STILL, I MUST SAY YOUR STYLE OF PLAYING
DIDN'T QUITE CAPTURE THE FORCEFULNESS OF THE WATER. OR THE TWINKLES.
!
TWINKLES?
OH, I KNOW!
THAP
YOU SHOULD GO SEE THE RIVER FOR YOURSELF!
I'M SURE THAT'S WHAT YOUR MOTHER DID WHEN SHE WAS WRITING THIS MUSIC.
WOW.
LET'S GO!

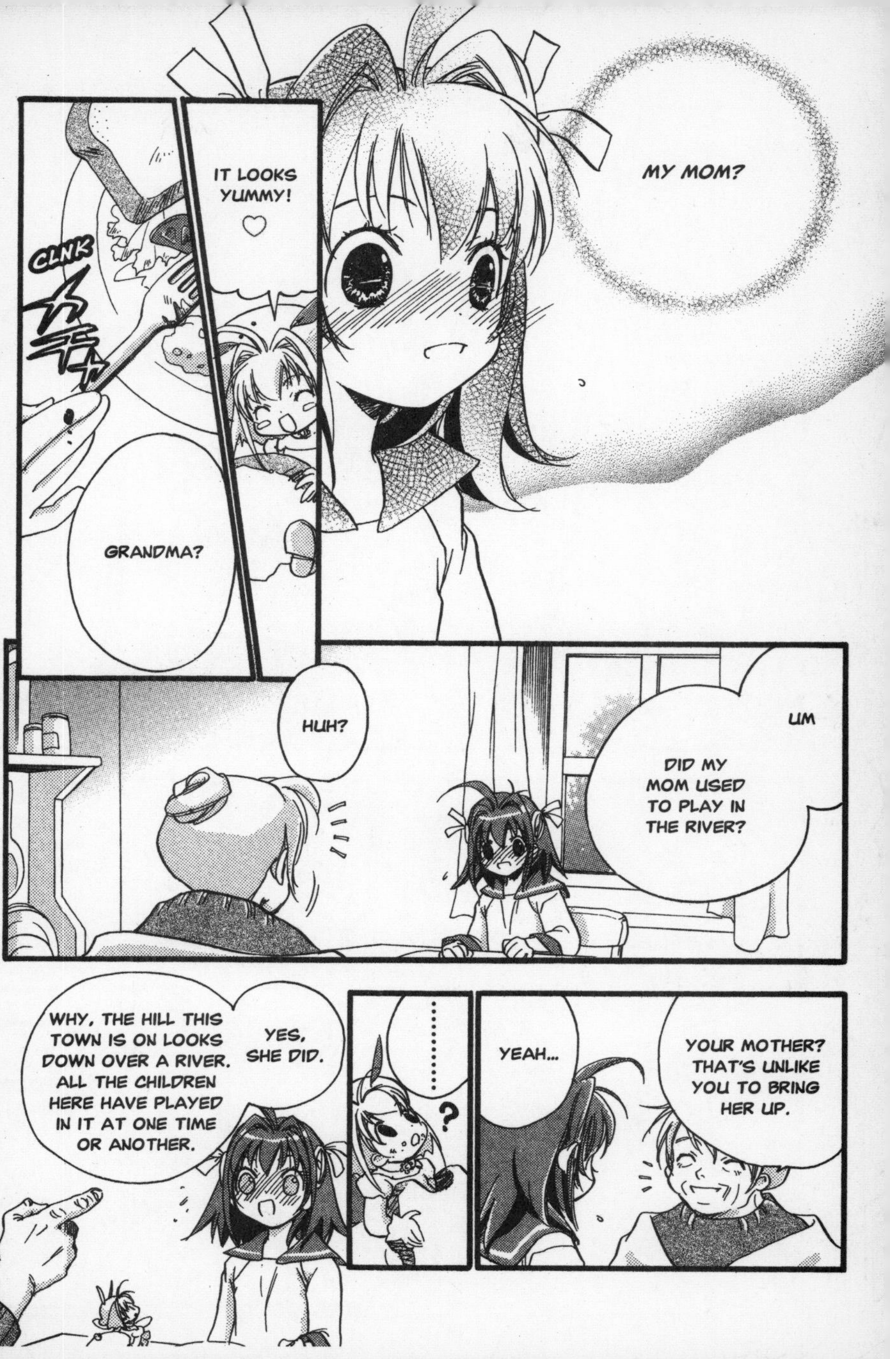
MY MOM?
IT LOOKS YUMMY! ♡
CLNK
GRANDMA?
UM
DID MY MOM USED TO PLAY IN THE RIVER?
HUH?
YOUR MOTHER? THAT'S UNLIKE YOU TO BRING HER UP.
YEAH...
......
?
YES, SHE DID.
WHY, THE HILL THIS TOWN IS ON LOOKS DOWN OVER A RIVER. ALL THE CHILDREN HERE HAVE PLAYED IN IT AT ONE TIME OR ANOTHER.

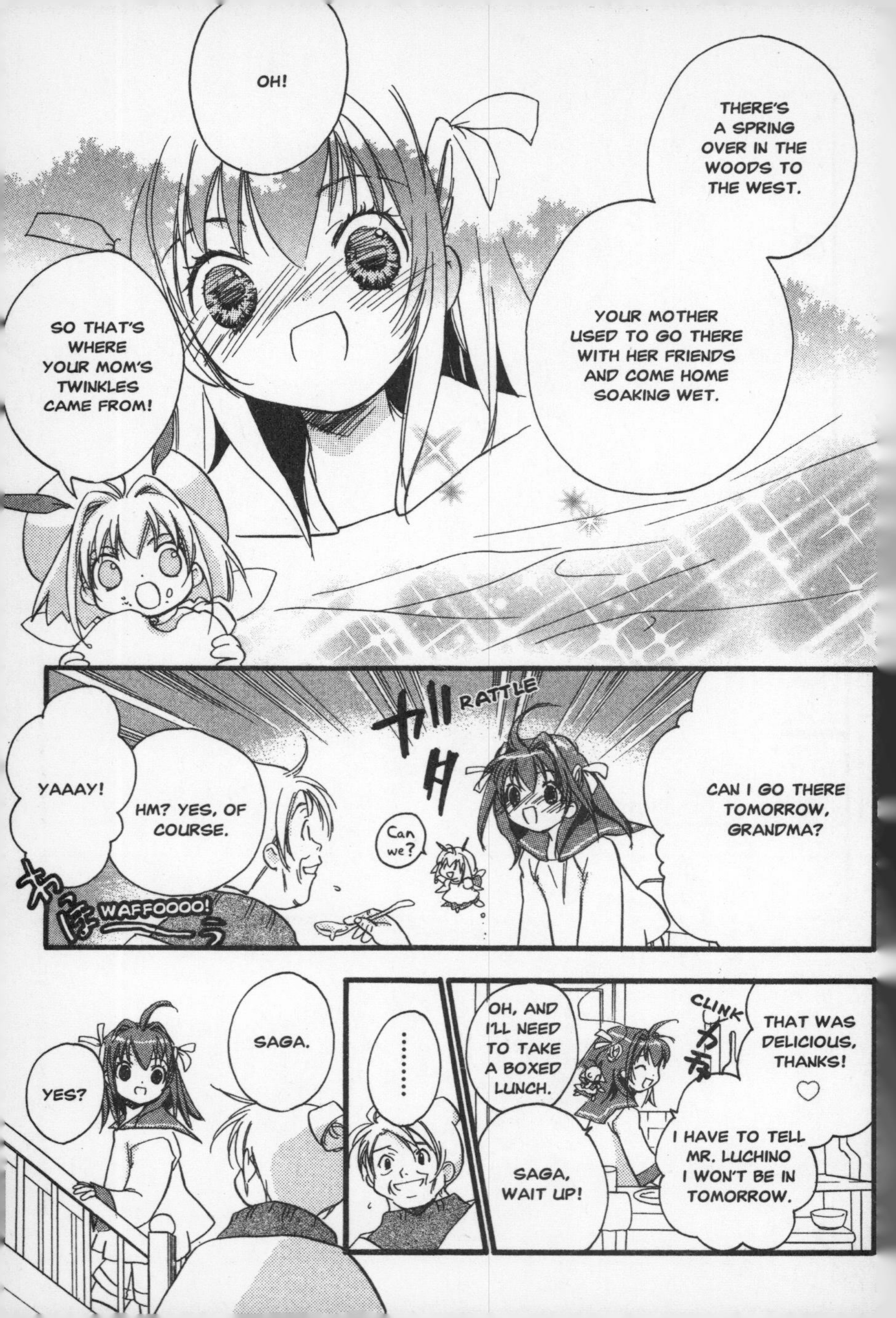
THERE'S A SPRING OVER IN THE WOODS TO THE WEST.
YOUR MOTHER USED TO GO THERE WITH HER FRIENDS AND COME HOME SOAKING WET.
OH!
SO THAT'S WHERE YOUR MOM'S TWINKLES CAME FROM!
CAN I GO THERE TOMORROW, GRANDMA?
RATTLE
Can we?
HM? YES, OF COURSE.
YAAAY!
WAFFOOOO!
THAT WAS DELICIOUS, THANKS!
CLINK
I HAVE TO TELL MR. LUCHINO I WON'T BE IN TOMORROW.
OH, AND I'LL NEED TO TAKE A BOXED LUNCH.
SAGA, WAIT UP!
......
SAGA.
YES?

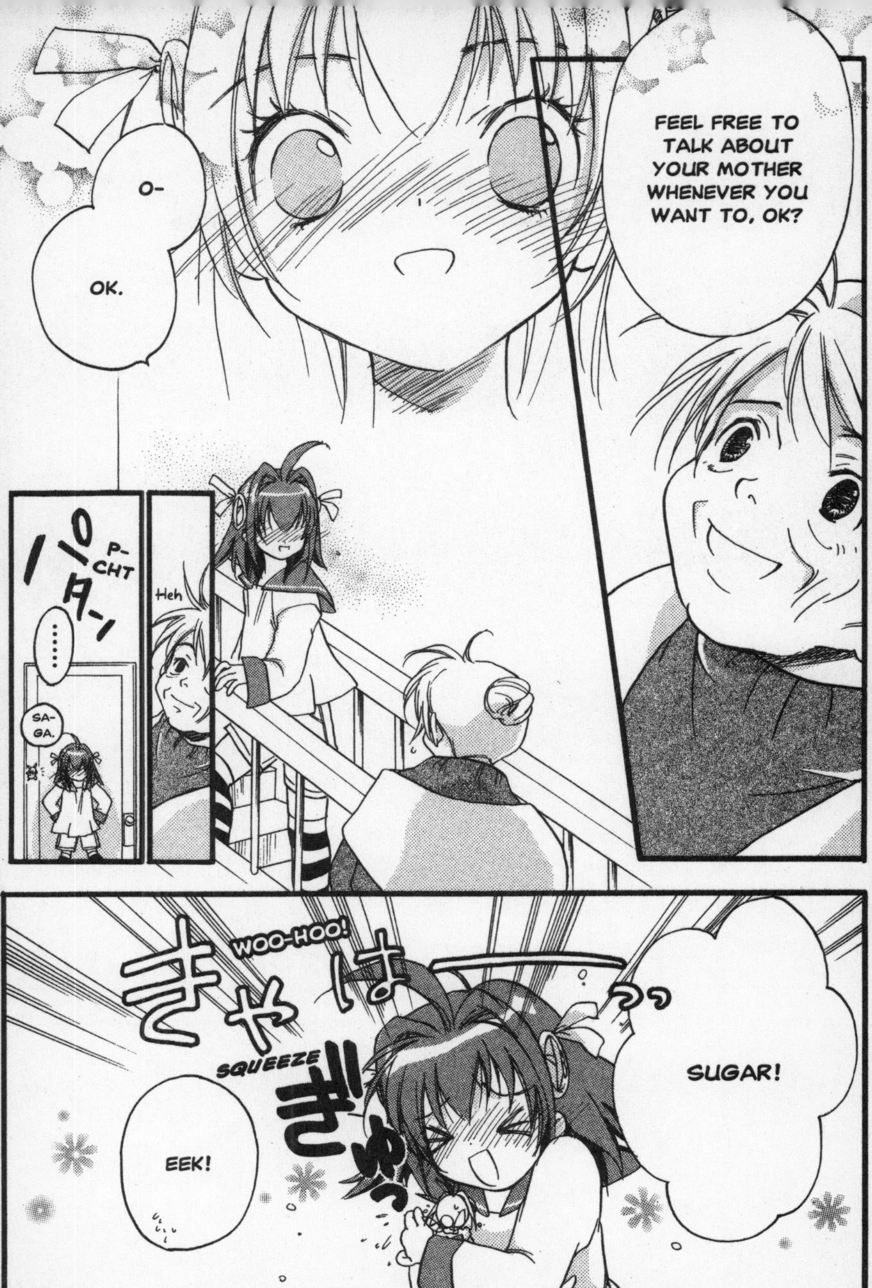
FEEL FREE TO TALK ABOUT YOUR MOTHER WHENEVER YOU WANT TO, OK?
O-
OK.
Heh
P-CHT
......
SA-GA.
SUGAR!
WOO-HOO!
SQUEEZE
EEK!

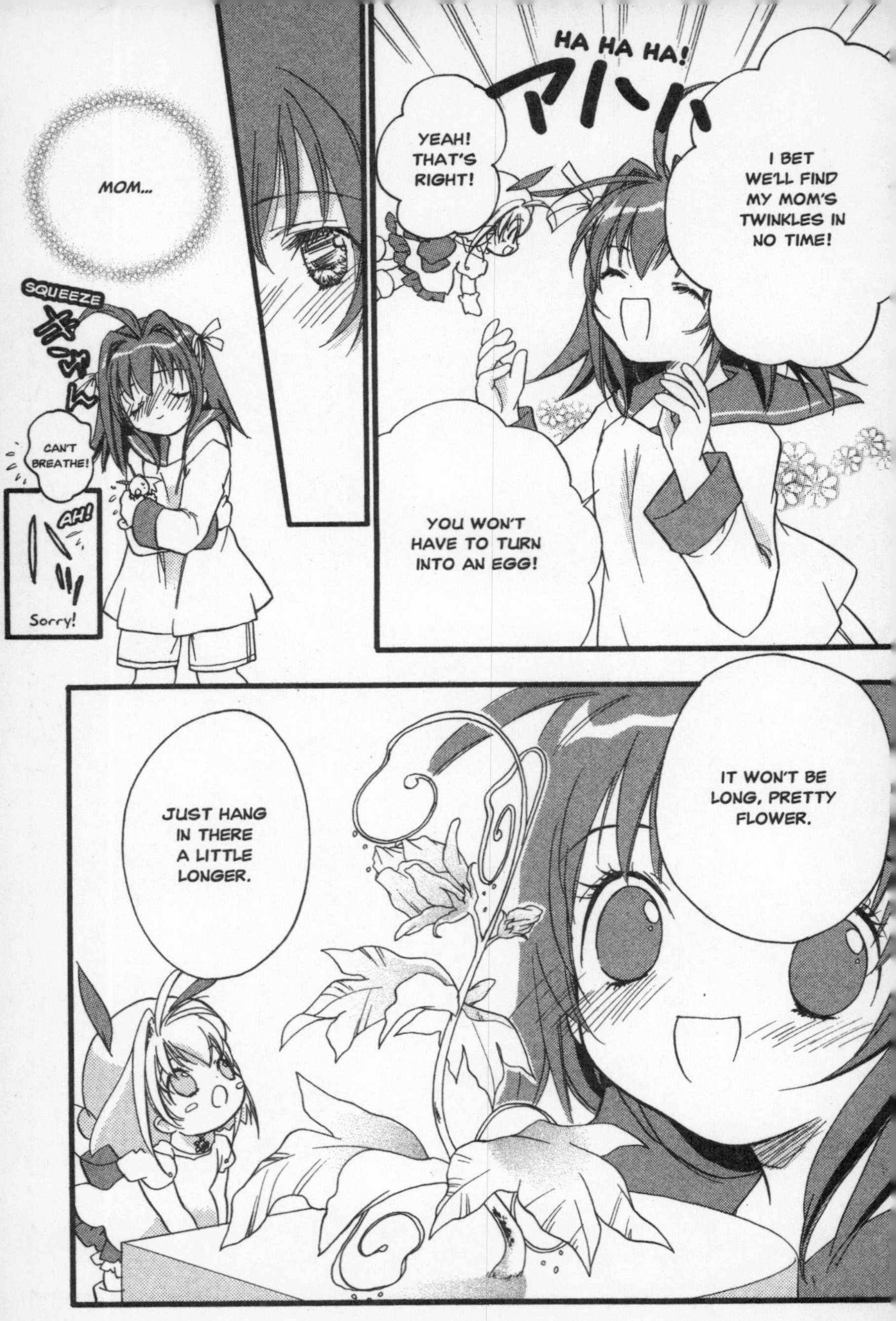
HA HA HA!
アハハ
I BET WE'LL FIND MY MOM'S TWINKLES IN NO TIME!
YEAH! THAT'S RIGHT!
YOU WON'T HAVE TO TURN INTO AN EGG!
MOM...
SQUEEZE
CAN'T BREATHE!
AH!
Sorry!
IT WON'T BE LONG, PRETTY FLOWER.
JUST HANG IN THERE A LITTLE LONGER.

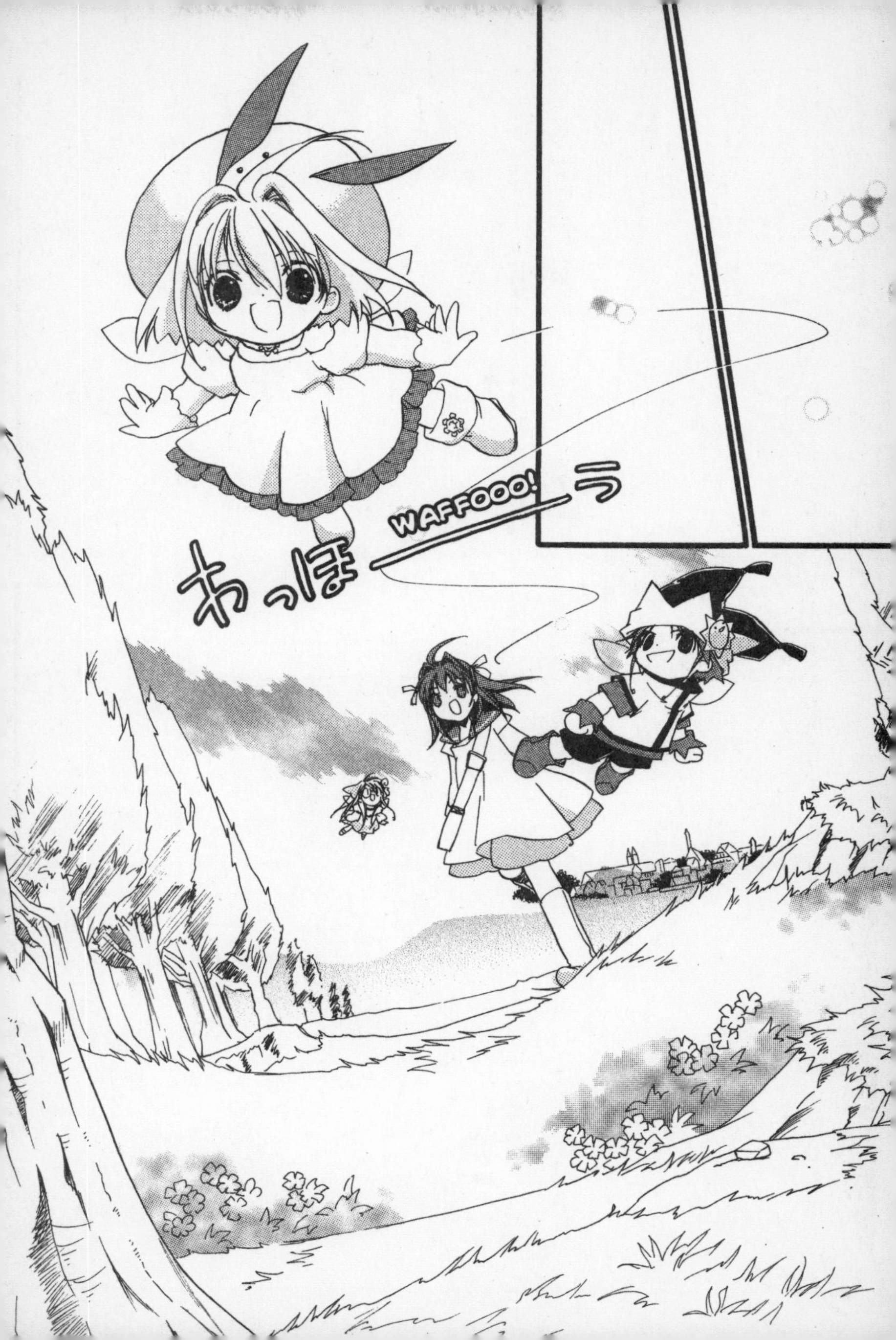
わっほーう
WAFFOOO!

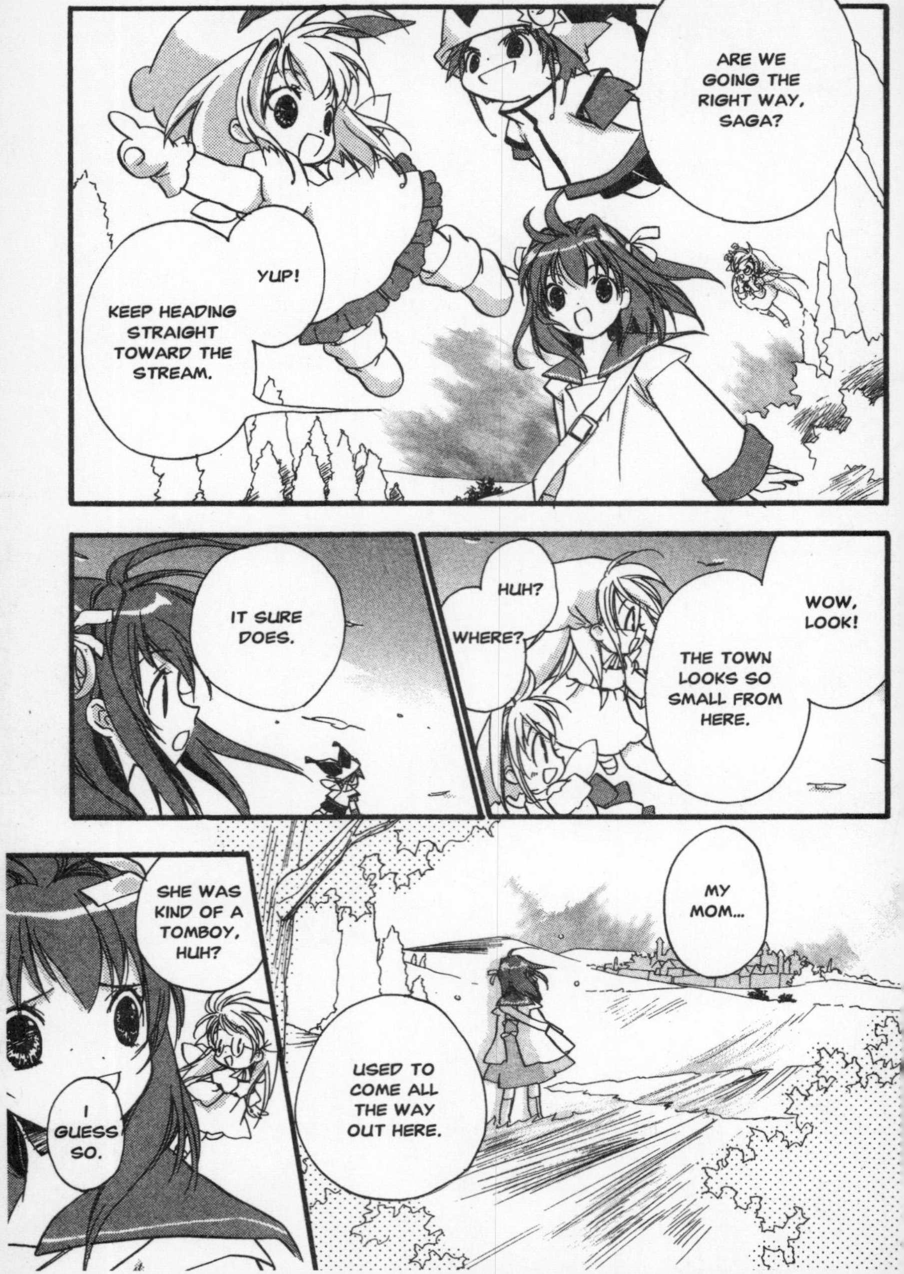
ARE WE GOING THE RIGHT WAY, SAGA?
YUP!
KEEP HEADING STRAIGHT TOWARD THE STREAM.
WOW, LOOK!
THE TOWN LOOKS SO SMALL FROM HERE.
HUH?
WHERE?
IT SURE DOES.
MY MOM...
USED TO COME ALL THE WAY OUT HERE.
SHE WAS KIND OF A TOMBOY, HUH?
I GUESS SO.

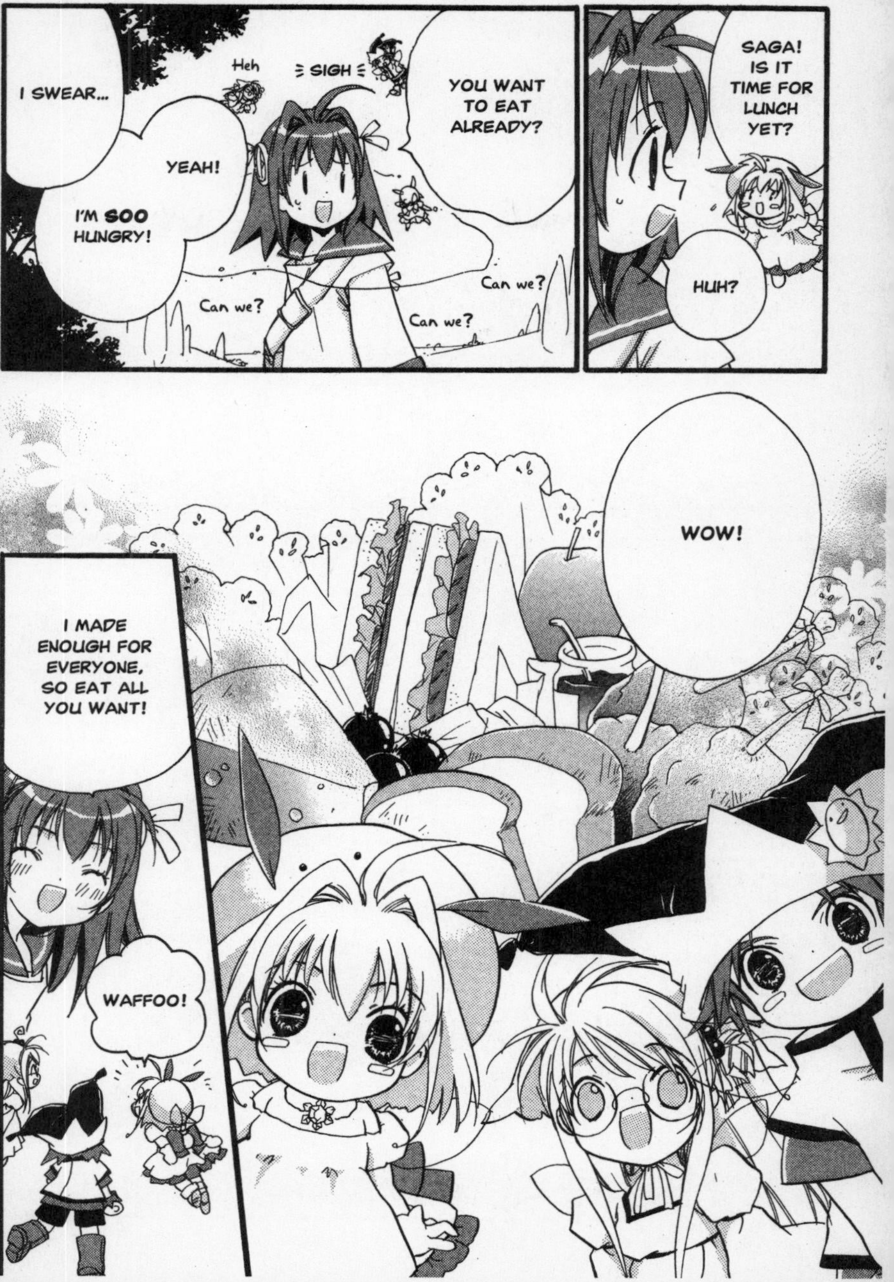
SAGA! IS IT TIME FOR LUNCH YET?
HUH?
YOU WANT TO EAT ALREADY?
SIGH
Heh
I SWEAR...
YEAH!
I'M SOO HUNGRY!
Can we?
Can we?
Can we?
WOW!
I MADE ENOUGH FOR EVERYONE, SO EAT ALL YOU WANT!
WAFFOO!

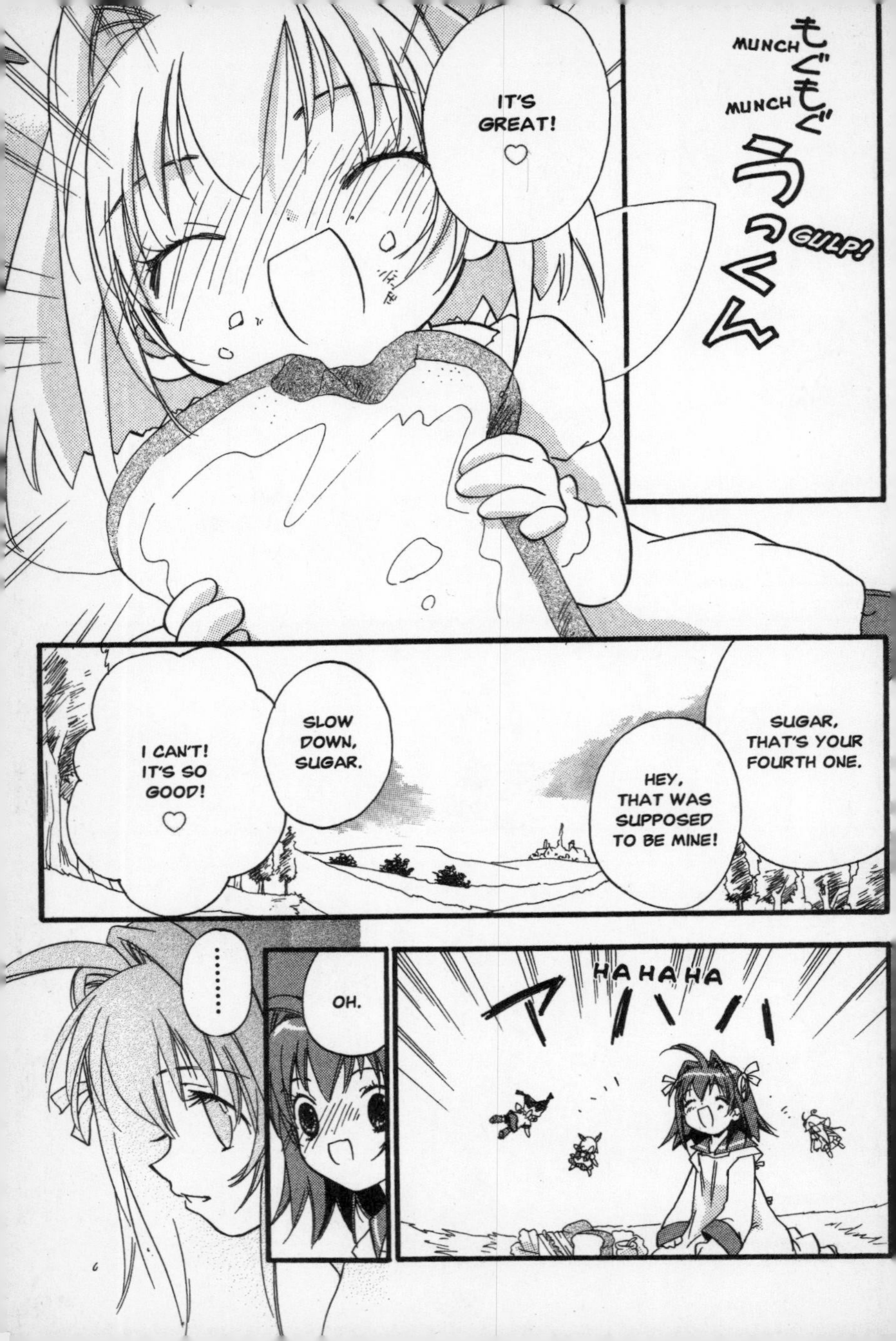

MUNCH もぐ
MUNCH もぐ
うっくん
GULP!
IT'S GREAT! ♡
SUGAR, THAT'S YOUR FOURTH ONE.
HEY, THAT WAS SUPPOSED TO BE MINE!
SLOW DOWN, SUGAR.
I CAN'T! IT'S SO GOOD! ♡
HAHAHA
アハハハ
OH.
....

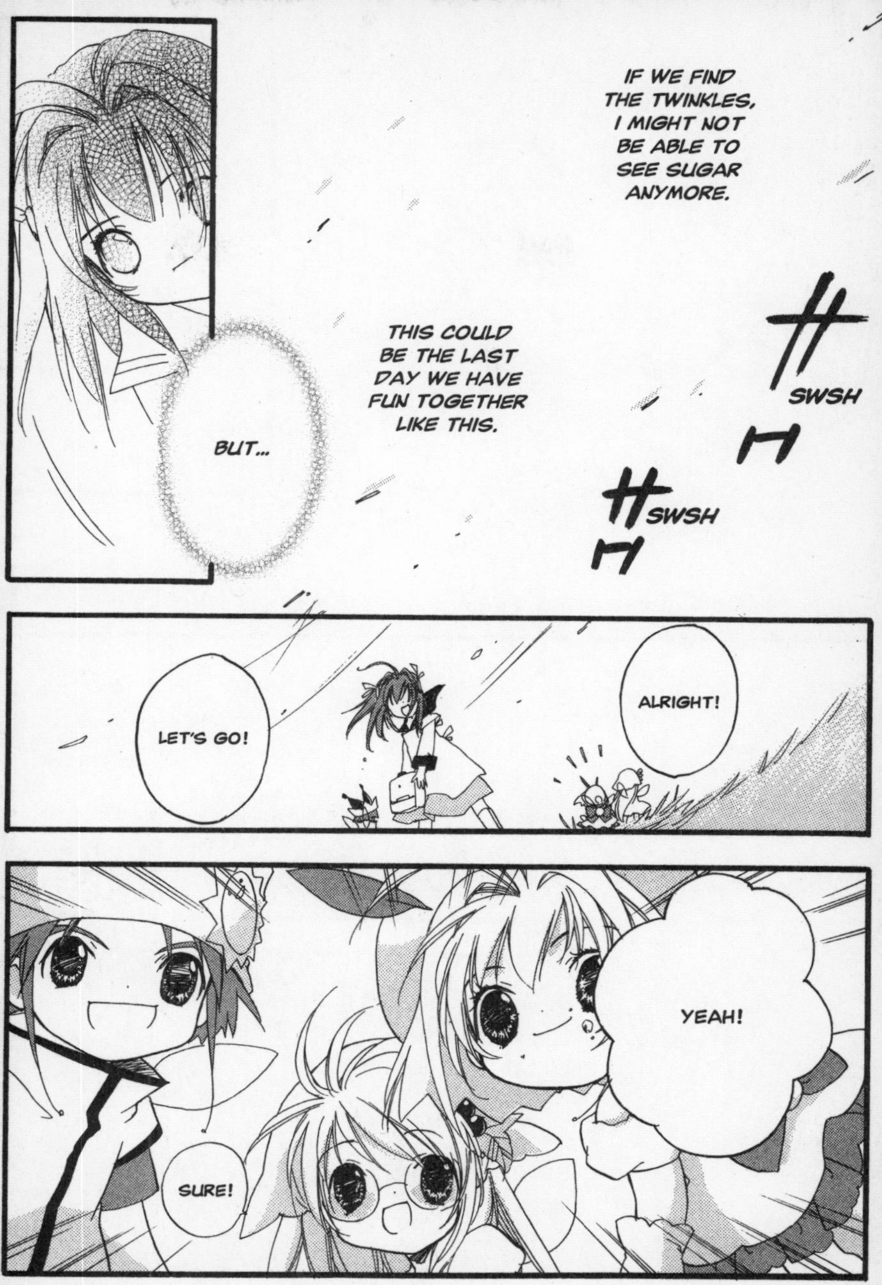

IF WE FIND THE TWINKLES, I MIGHT NOT BE ABLE TO SEE SUGAR ANYMORE.
SWSH
THIS COULD BE THE LAST DAY WE HAVE FUN TOGETHER LIKE THIS.
SWSH
BUT...
ALRIGHT!
LET'S GO!
YEAH!
SURE!

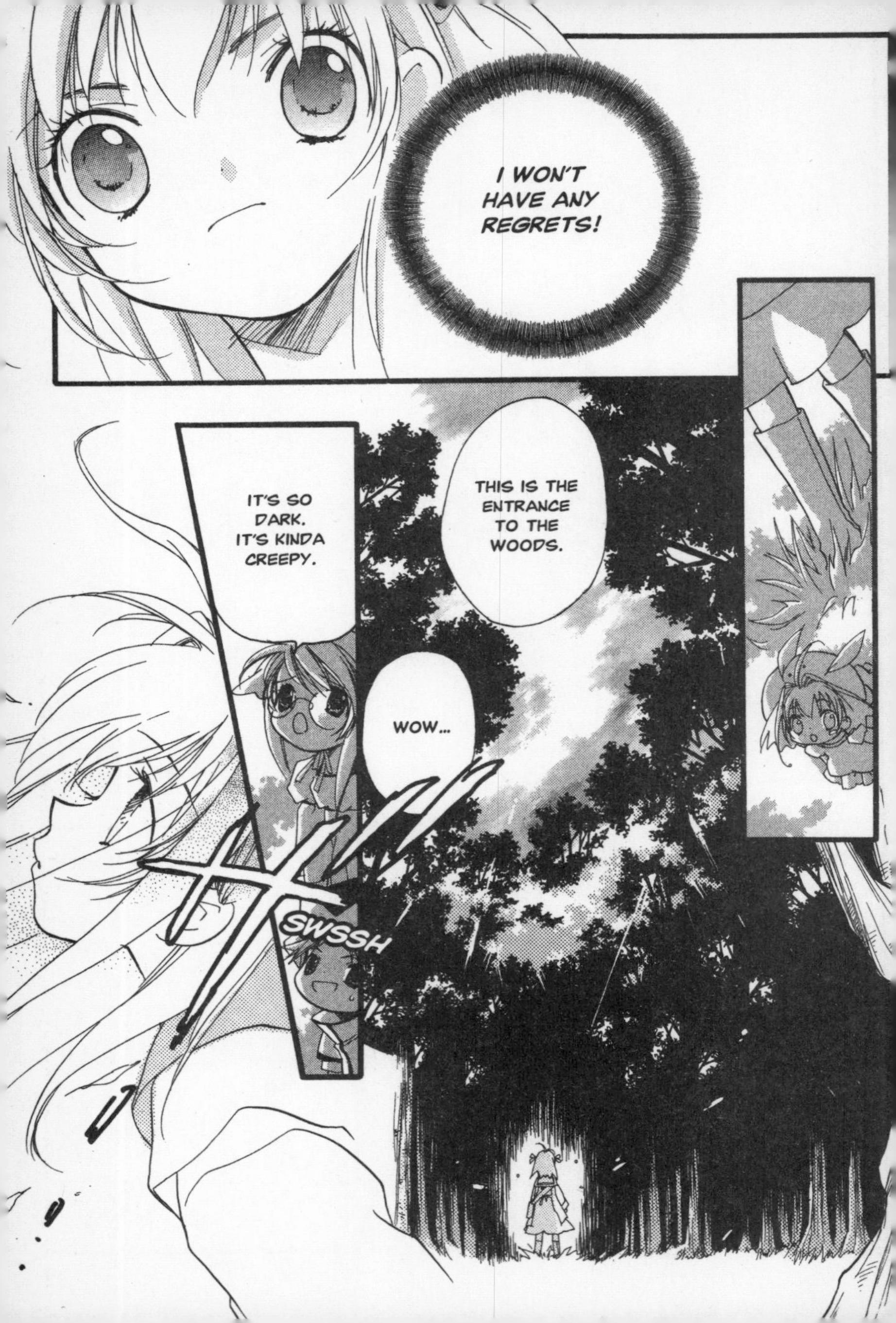
I WON'T HAVE ANY REGRETS!
THIS IS THE ENTRANCE TO THE WOODS.
IT'S SO DARK. IT'S KINDA CREEPY.
WOW...
SWSSH

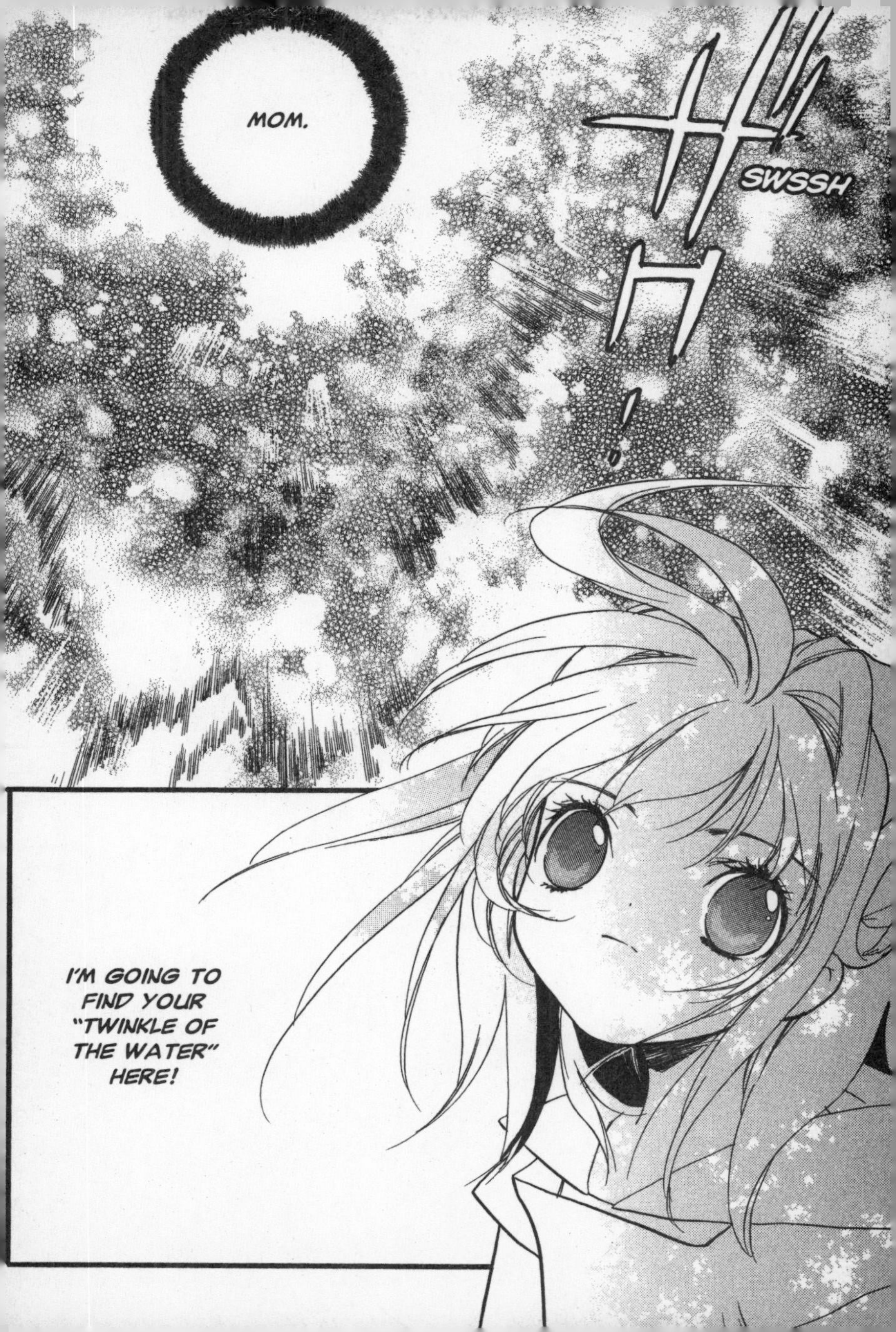
SWSSH
MOM.
I'M GOING TO FIND YOUR "TWINKLE OF THE WATER" HERE!

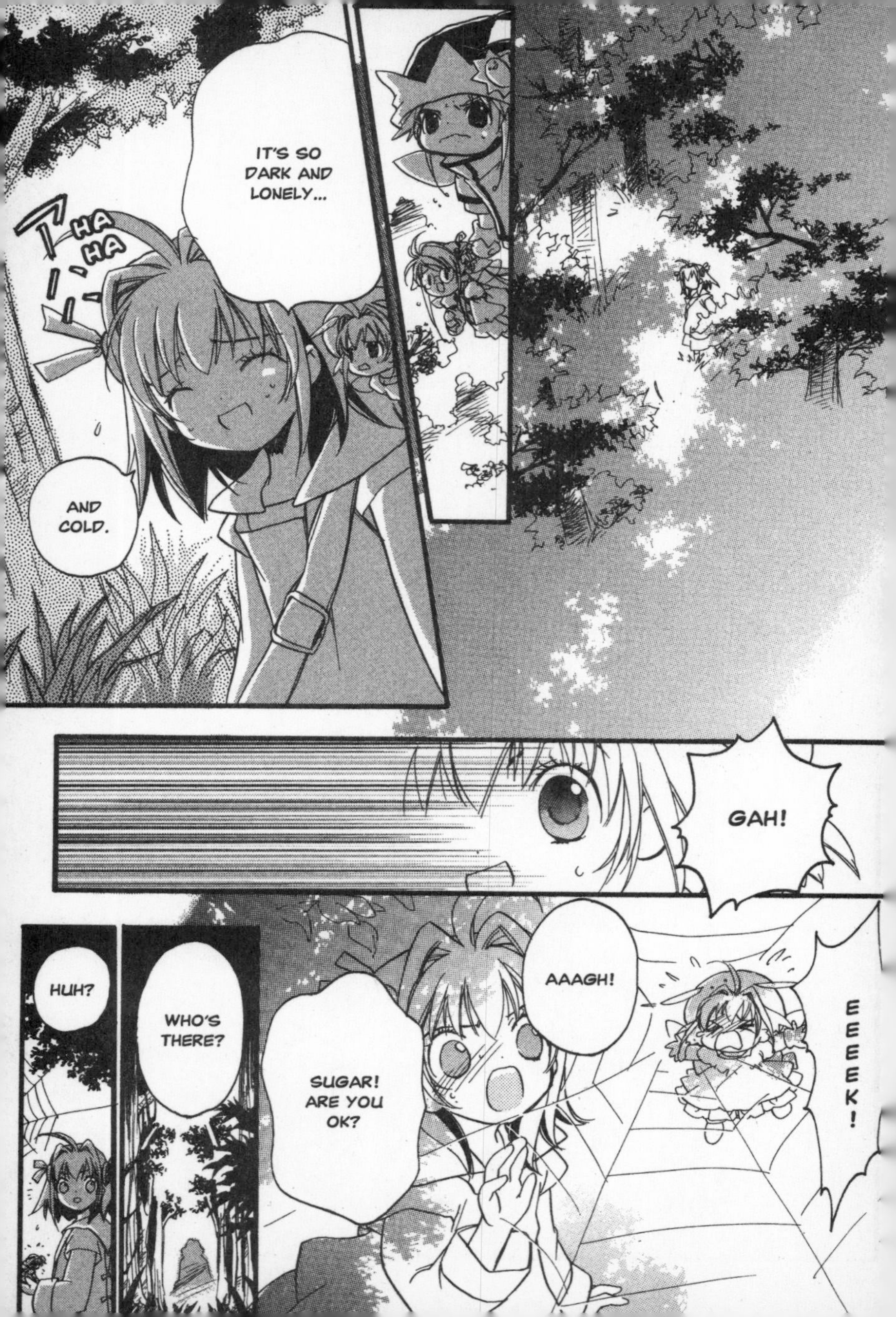
IT'S SO DARK AND LONELY...
HA HA
AND COLD.
GAH!
AAAGH!
EEEEEK!
SUGAR! ARE YOU OK?
WHO'S THERE?
HUH?

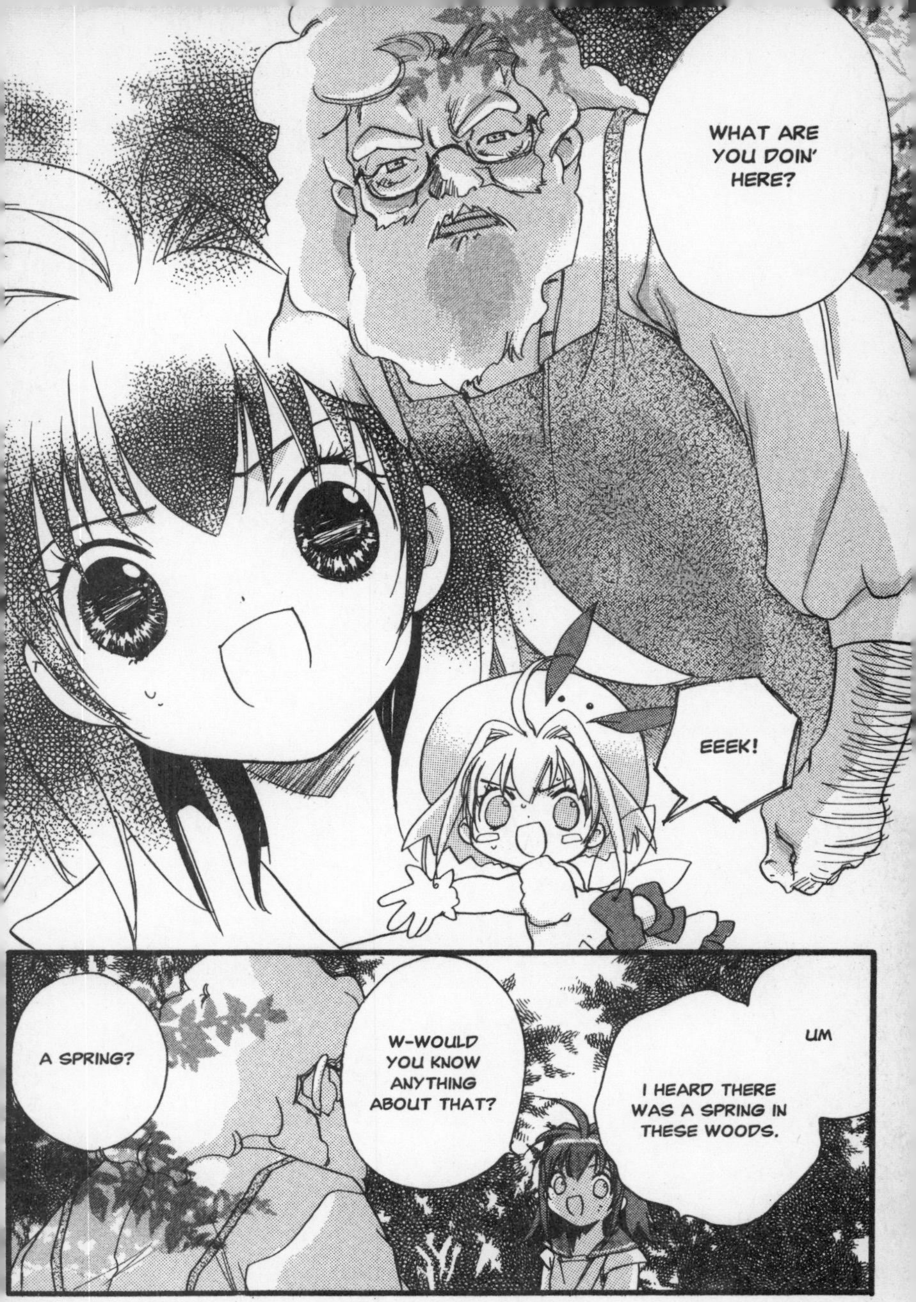
WHAT ARE YOU DOIN' HERE?
EEEK!
UM I HEARD THERE WAS A SPRING IN THESE WOODS.
W-WOULD YOU KNOW ANYTHING ABOUT THAT?
A SPRING?

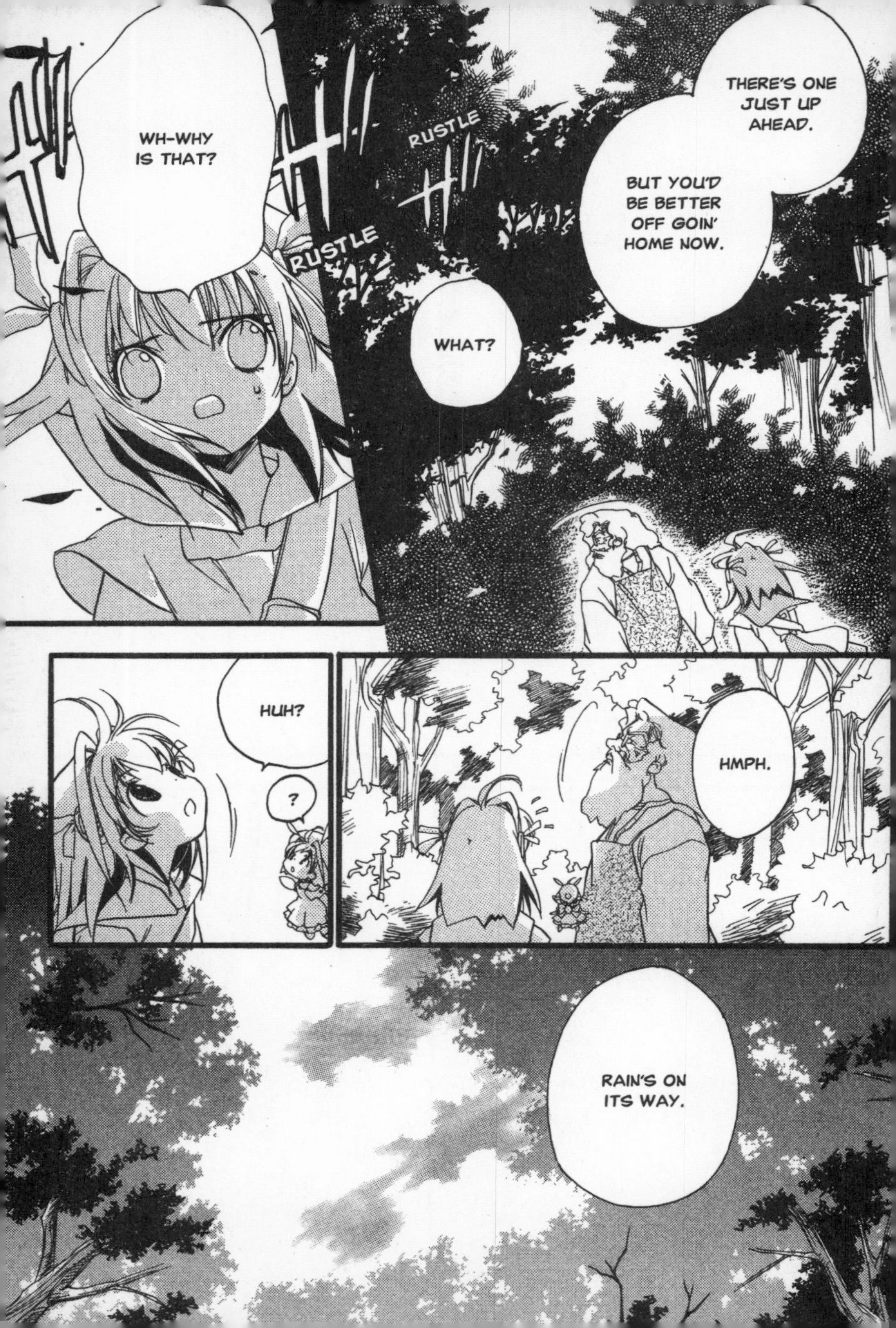
THERE'S ONE JUST UP AHEAD.
BUT YOU'D BE BETTER OFF GOIN' HOME NOW.
WHAT?
RUSTLE
RUSTLE
WH-WHY IS THAT?
HMPH.
HUH?
?
RAIN'S ON ITS WAY.

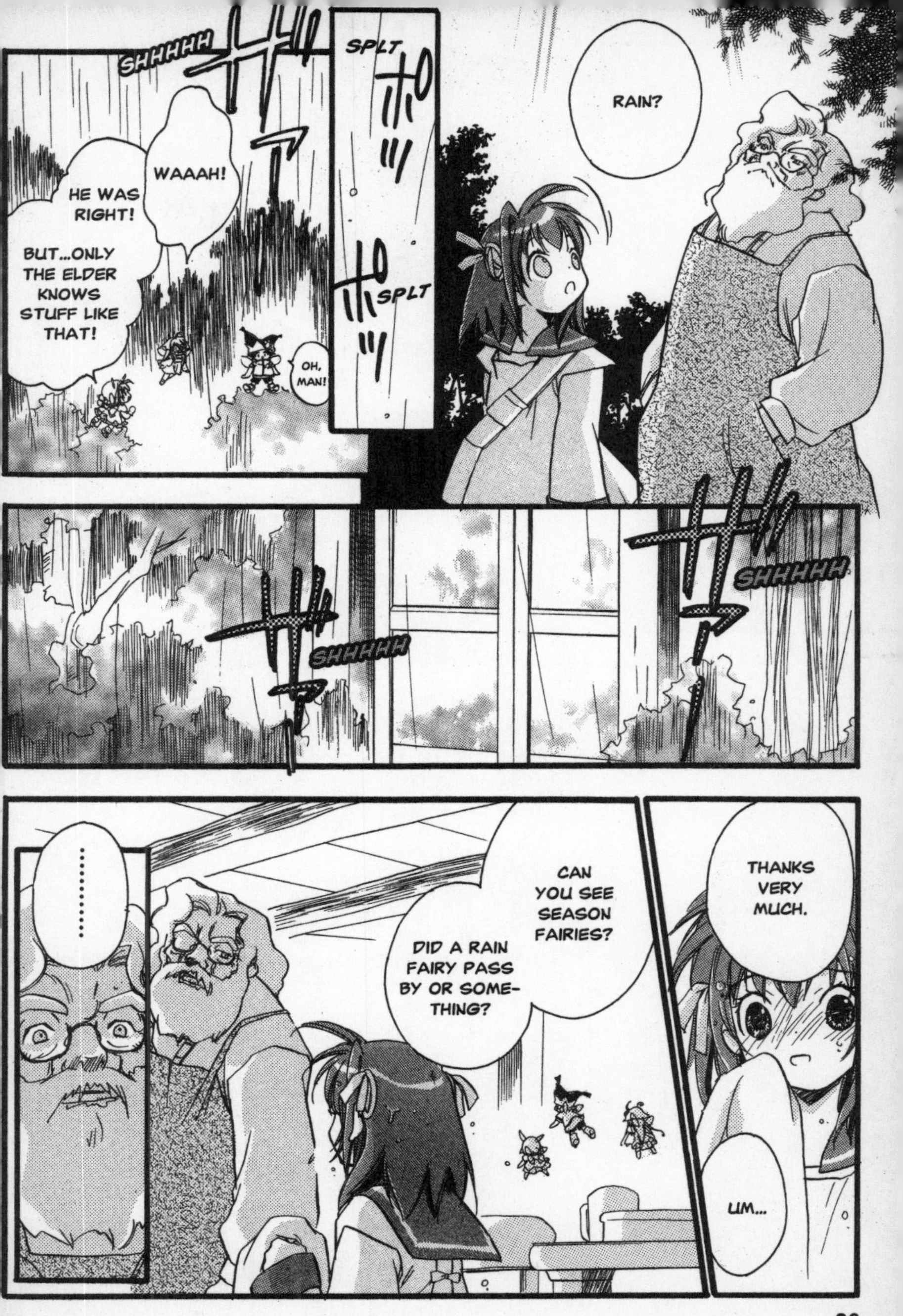
RAIN?
SPLT
SPLT
SHHHHH
WAAAH!
HE WAS RIGHT!
BUT...ONLY THE ELDER KNOWS STUFF LIKE THAT!
OH, MAN!
SHHHHH
SHHHHH
THANKS VERY MUCH.
UM...
CAN YOU SEE SEASON FAIRIES?
DID A RAIN FAIRY PASS BY OR SOME-THING?
....

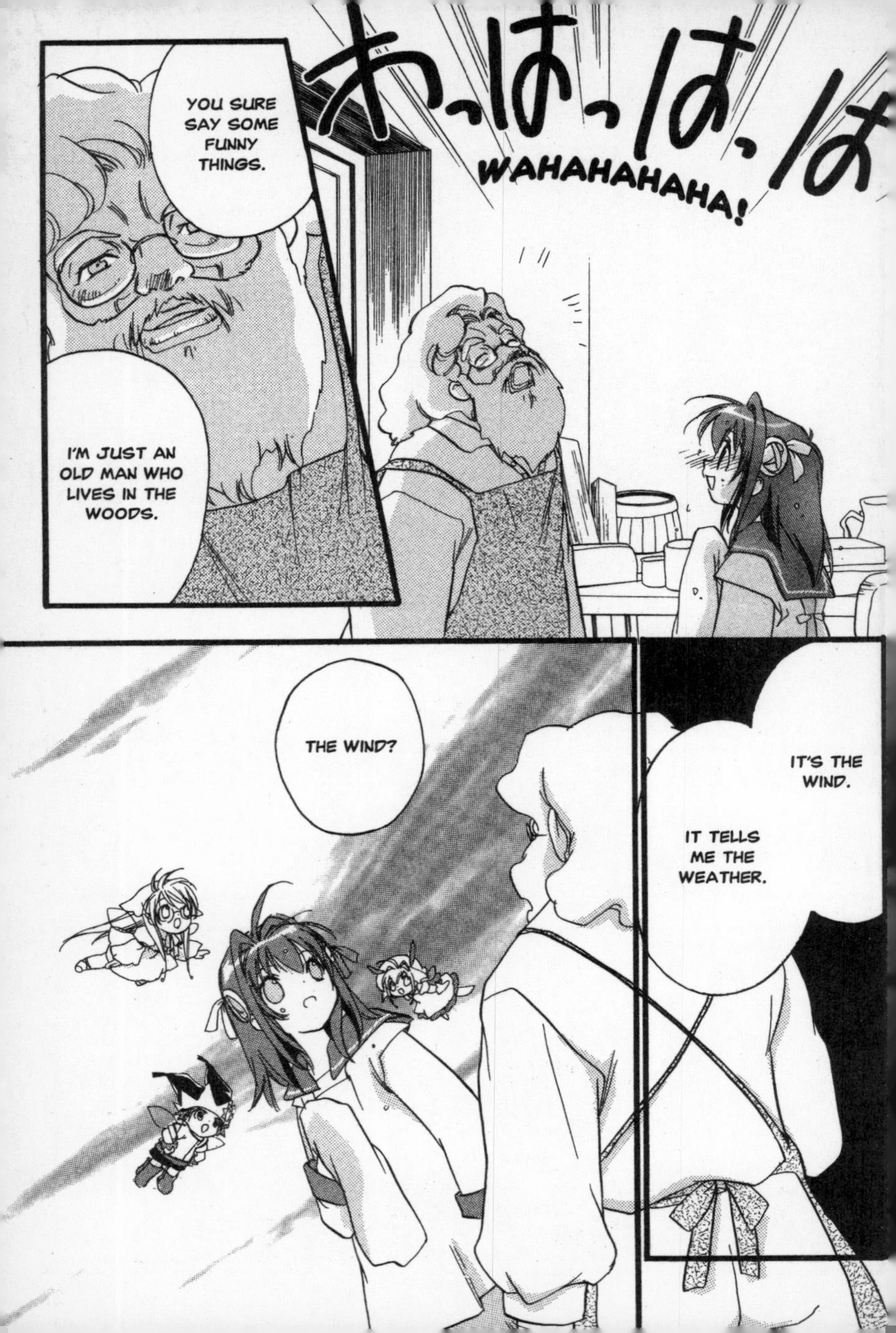
わっはっはっは
WAHAHAHAHAHA!
YOU SURE SAY SOME FUNNY THINGS.
I'M JUST AN OLD MAN WHO LIVES IN THE WOODS.
IT'S THE WIND.
IT TELLS ME THE WEATHER.
THE WIND?

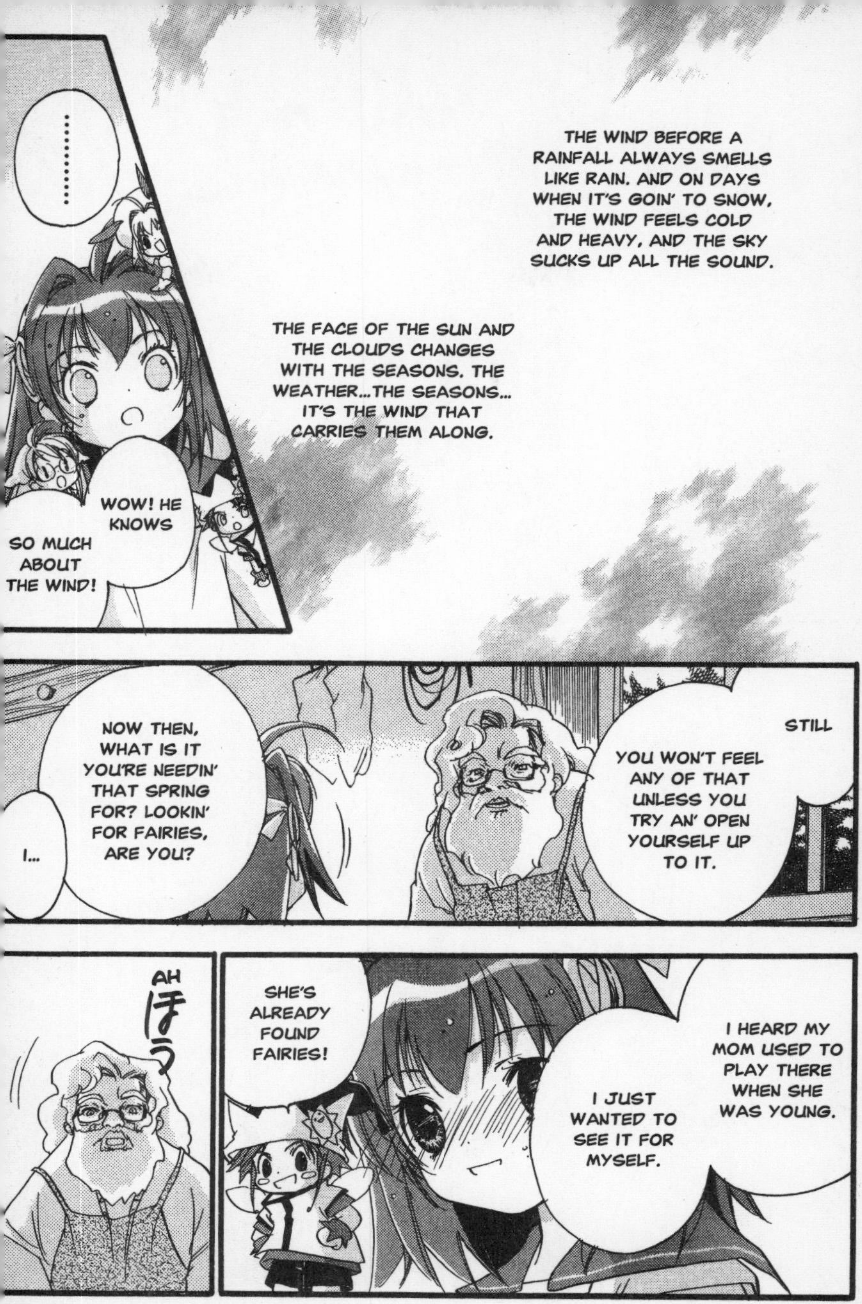
THE WIND BEFORE A RAINFALL ALWAYS SMELLS LIKE RAIN. AND ON DAYS WHEN IT'S GOIN' TO SNOW, THE WIND FEELS COLD AND HEAVY, AND THE SKY SUCKS UP ALL THE SOUND.
THE FACE OF THE SUN AND THE CLOUDS CHANGES WITH THE SEASONS. THE WEATHER...THE SEASONS... IT'S THE WIND THAT CARRIES THEM ALONG.
......
WOW! HE KNOWS
SO MUCH ABOUT THE WIND!
STILL
YOU WON'T FEEL ANY OF THAT UNLESS YOU TRY AN' OPEN YOURSELF UP TO IT.
NOW THEN, WHAT IS IT YOU'RE NEEDIN' THAT SPRING FOR? LOOKIN' FOR FAIRIES, ARE YOU?
I...
I HEARD MY MOM USED TO PLAY THERE WHEN SHE WAS YOUNG.
I JUST WANTED TO SEE IT FOR MYSELF.
SHE'S ALREADY FOUND FAIRIES!
AH
ほう

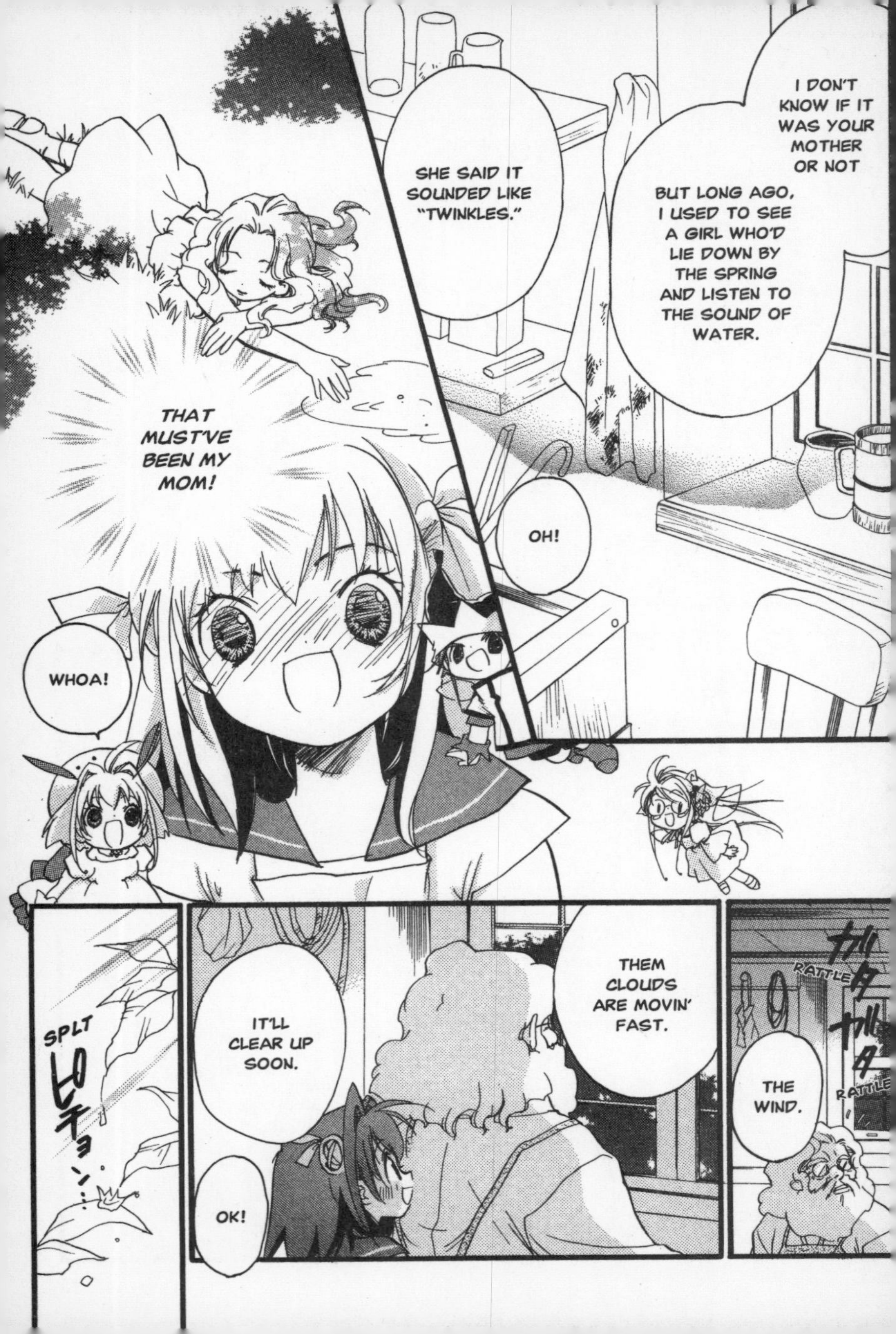
I DON'T KNOW IF IT WAS YOUR MOTHER OR NOT
BUT LONG AGO, I USED TO SEE A GIRL WHO'D LIE DOWN BY THE SPRING AND LISTEN TO THE SOUND OF WATER.
SHE SAID IT SOUNDED LIKE "TWINKLES."
OH!
THAT MUST'VE BEEN MY MOM!
WHOA!
RATTLE
RATTLE
THE WIND.
THEM CLOUDS ARE MOVIN' FAST.
IT'LL CLEAR UP SOON.
OK!
SPLT
ピチョン…

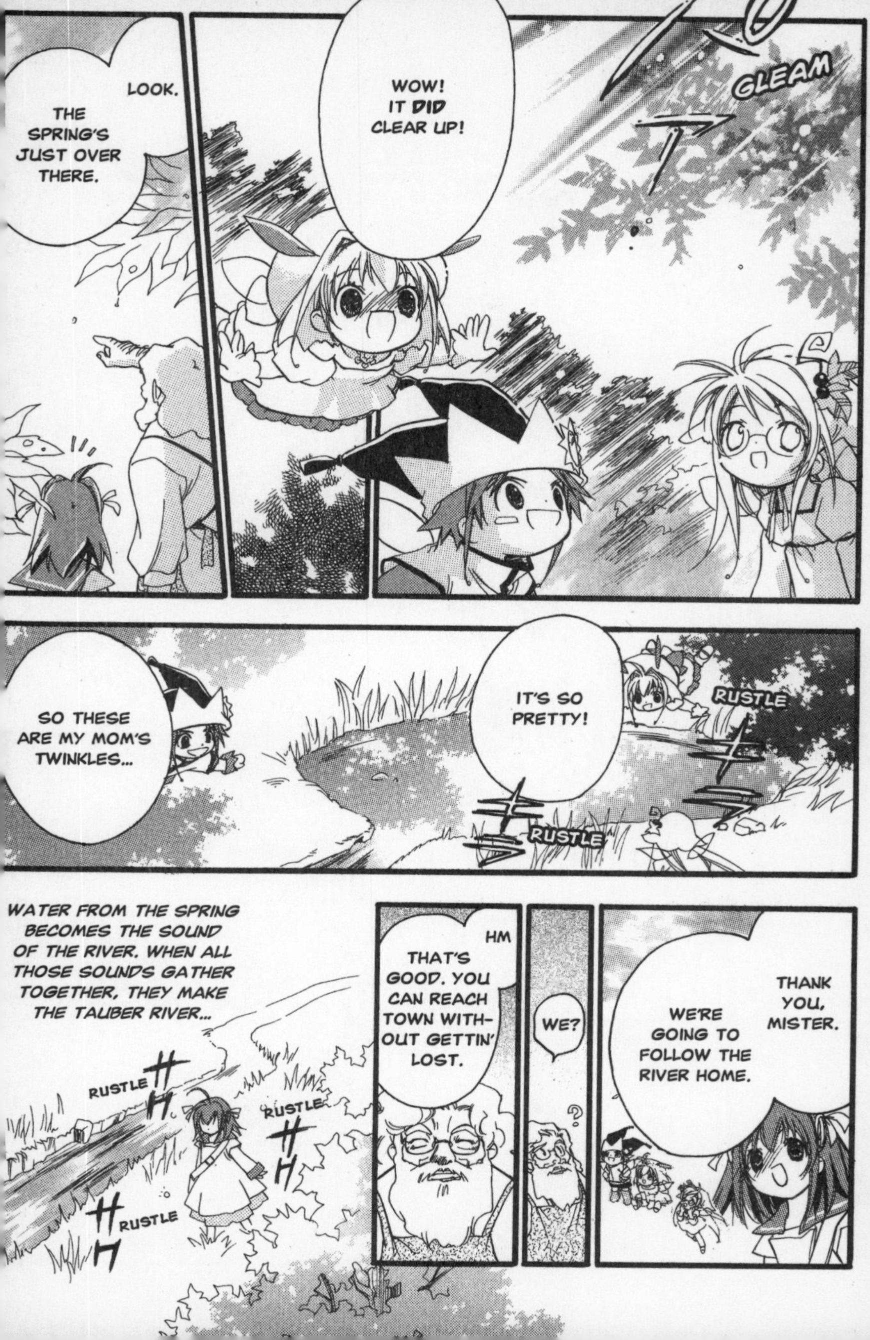
GLEAM
WOW! IT DID CLEAR UP!
LOOK.
THE SPRING'S JUST OVER THERE.
RUSTLE
IT'S SO PRETTY!
RUSTLE
SO THESE ARE MY MOM'S TWINKLES...
THANK YOU, MISTER.
WE'RE GOING TO FOLLOW THE RIVER HOME.
WE?
HM
THAT'S GOOD. YOU CAN REACH TOWN WITH-OUT GETTIN' LOST.
WATER FROM THE SPRING BECOMES THE SOUND OF THE RIVER. WHEN ALL THOSE SOUNDS GATHER TOGETHER, THEY MAKE THE TAUBER RIVER...
RUSTLE
RUSTLE
RUSTLE

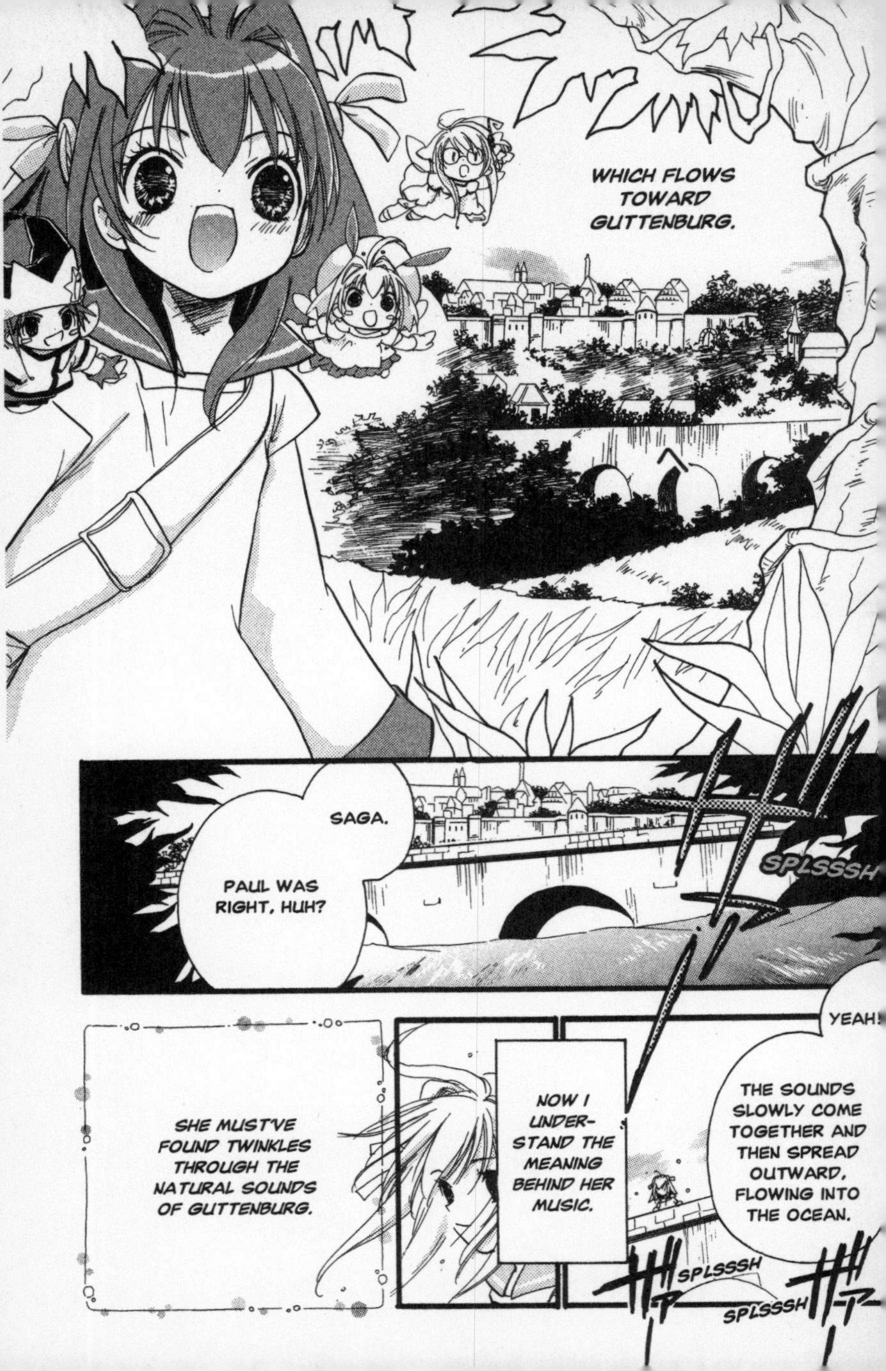
WHICH FLOWS TOWARD GUTTENBURG.
SPLSSSH
SAGA.
PAUL WAS RIGHT, HUH?
YEAH!
THE SOUNDS SLOWLY COME TOGETHER AND THEN SPREAD OUTWARD, FLOWING INTO THE OCEAN.
SPLSSSH
SPLSSSH
NOW I UNDER-STAND THE MEANING BEHIND HER MUSIC.
SHE MUST'VE FOUND TWINKLES THROUGH THE NATURAL SOUNDS OF GUTTENBURG.

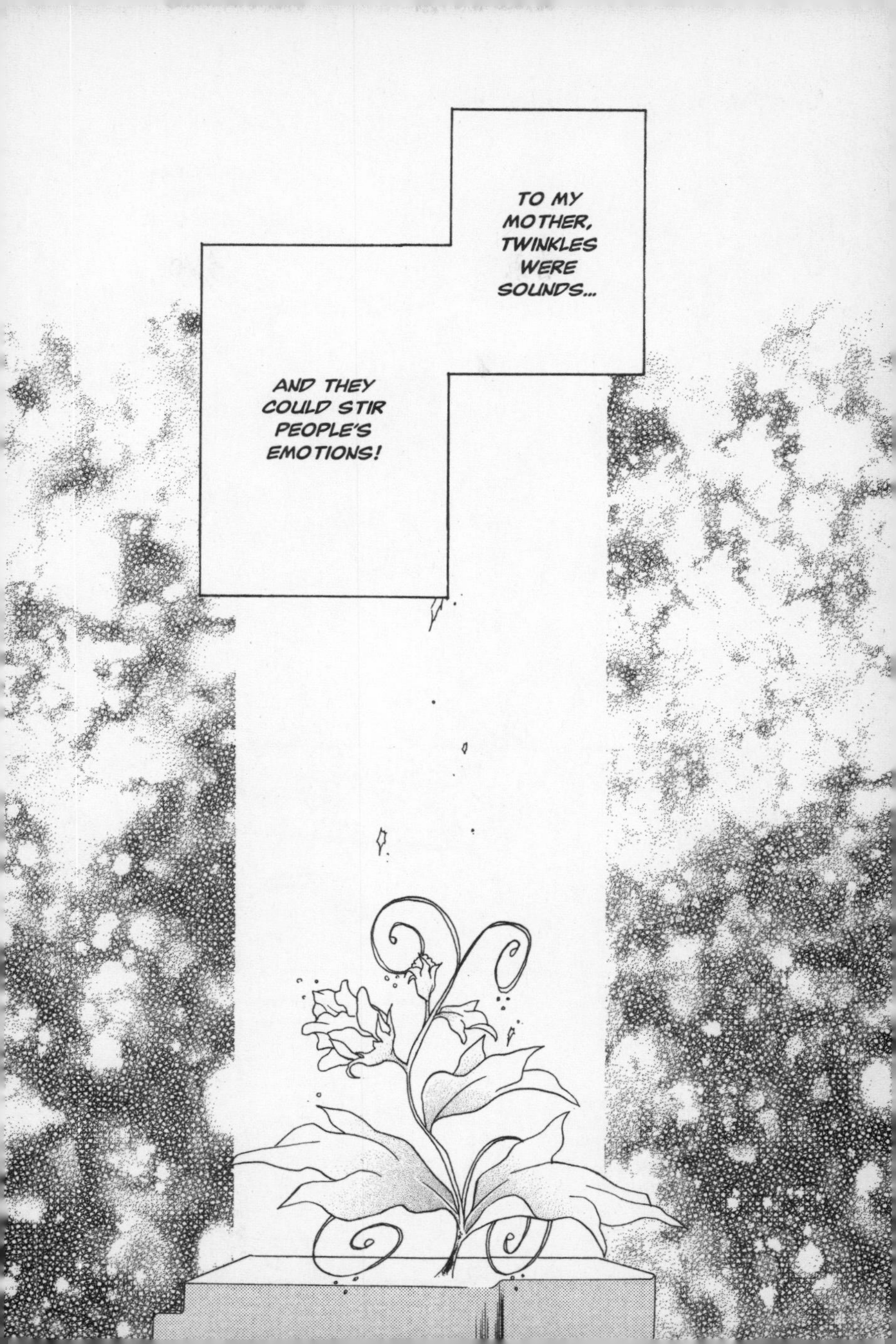
TO MY MOTHER, TWINKLES WERE SOUNDS...
AND THEY COULD STIR PEOPLE'S EMOTIONS!

CHAPTER 11 Be Myself

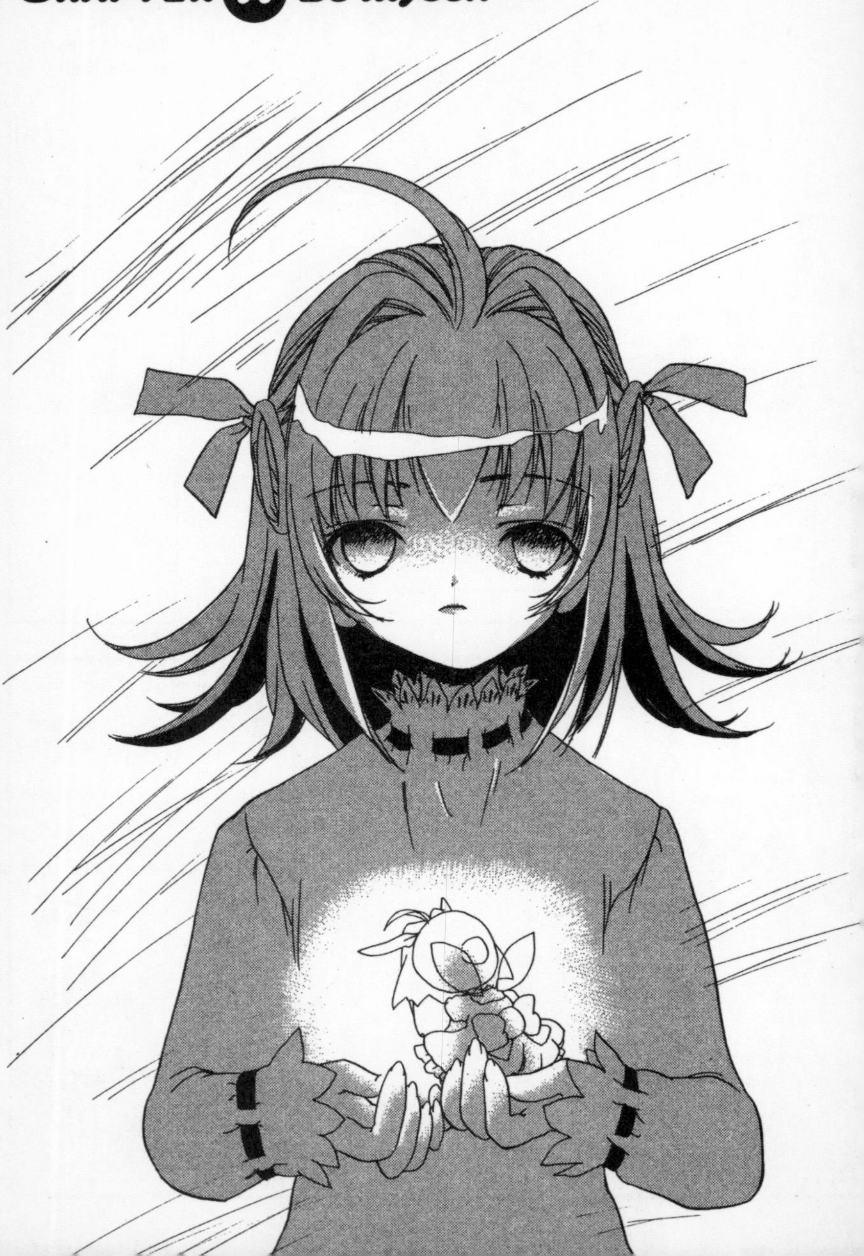

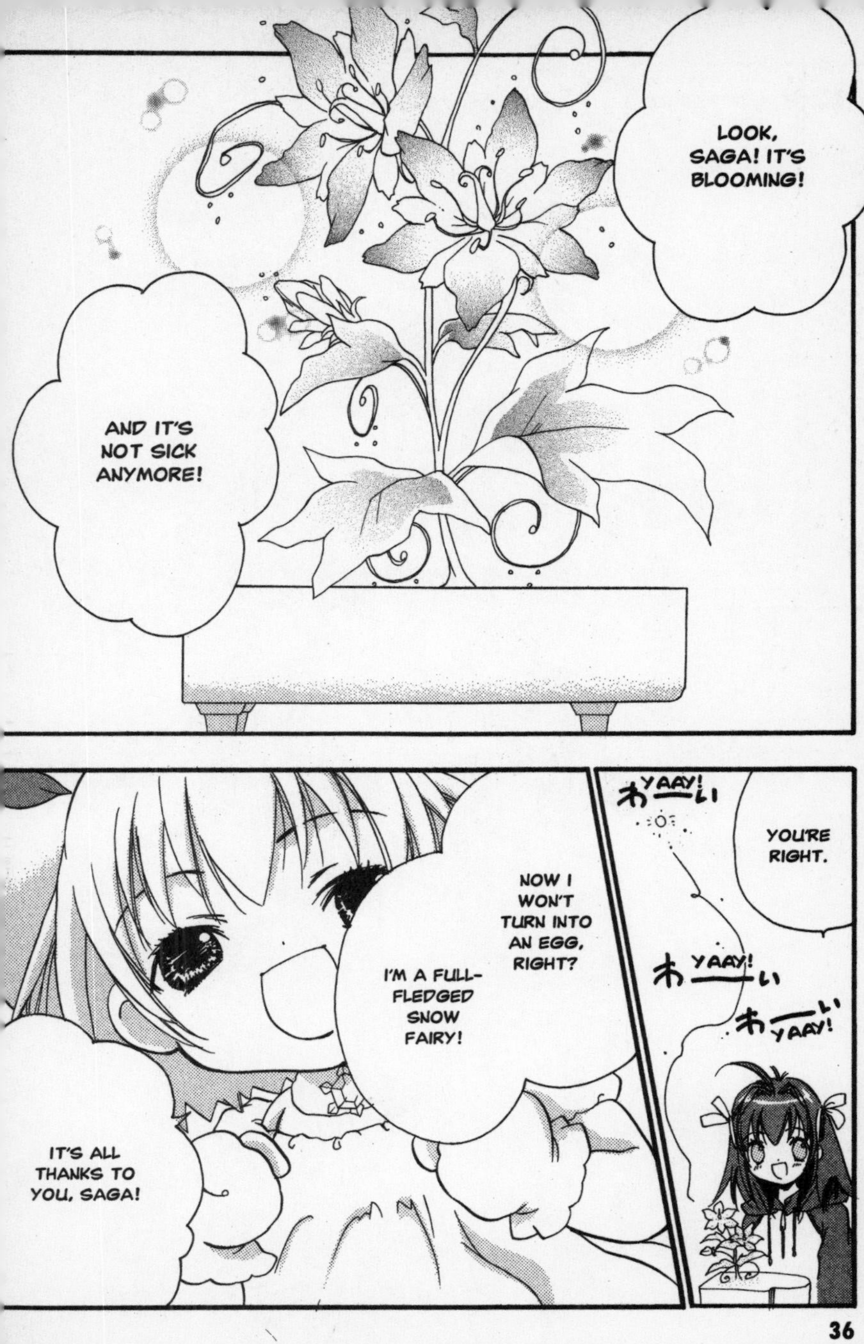

LOOK, SAGA! IT'S BLOOMING!
AND IT'S NOT SICK ANYMORE!
YOU'RE RIGHT.
おーい YAAY!
おーい YAAY!
おーい YAAY!
NOW I WON'T TURN INTO AN EGG, RIGHT?
I'M A FULL-FLEDGED SNOW FAIRY!
IT'S ALL THANKS TO YOU, SAGA!

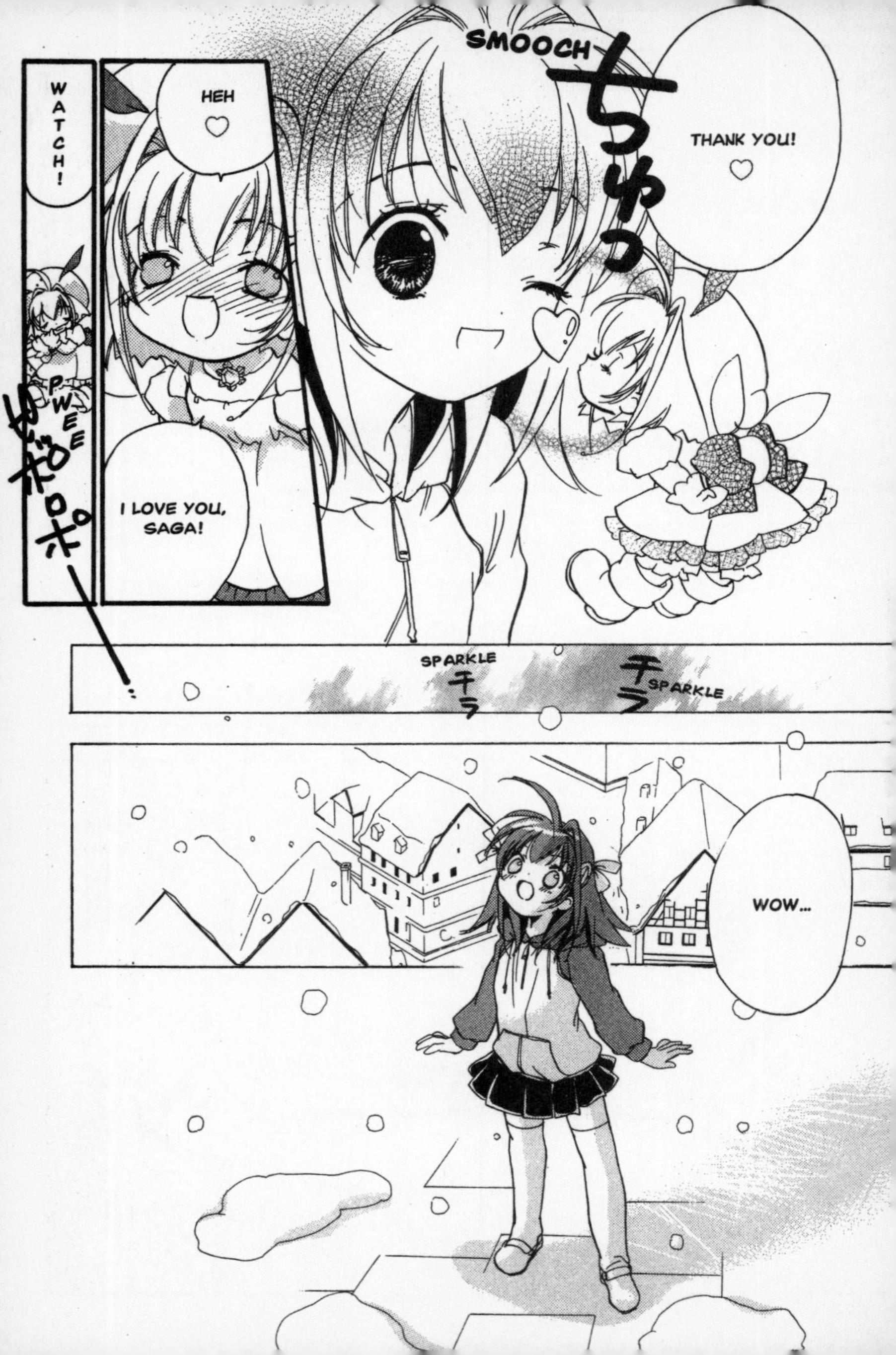
SMOOCH
ちゅっ
THANK YOU! ♡
HEH ♡
I LOVE YOU, SAGA!
WATCH!
PWEE
SPARKLE
チラ
チラ
SPARKLE
WOW...

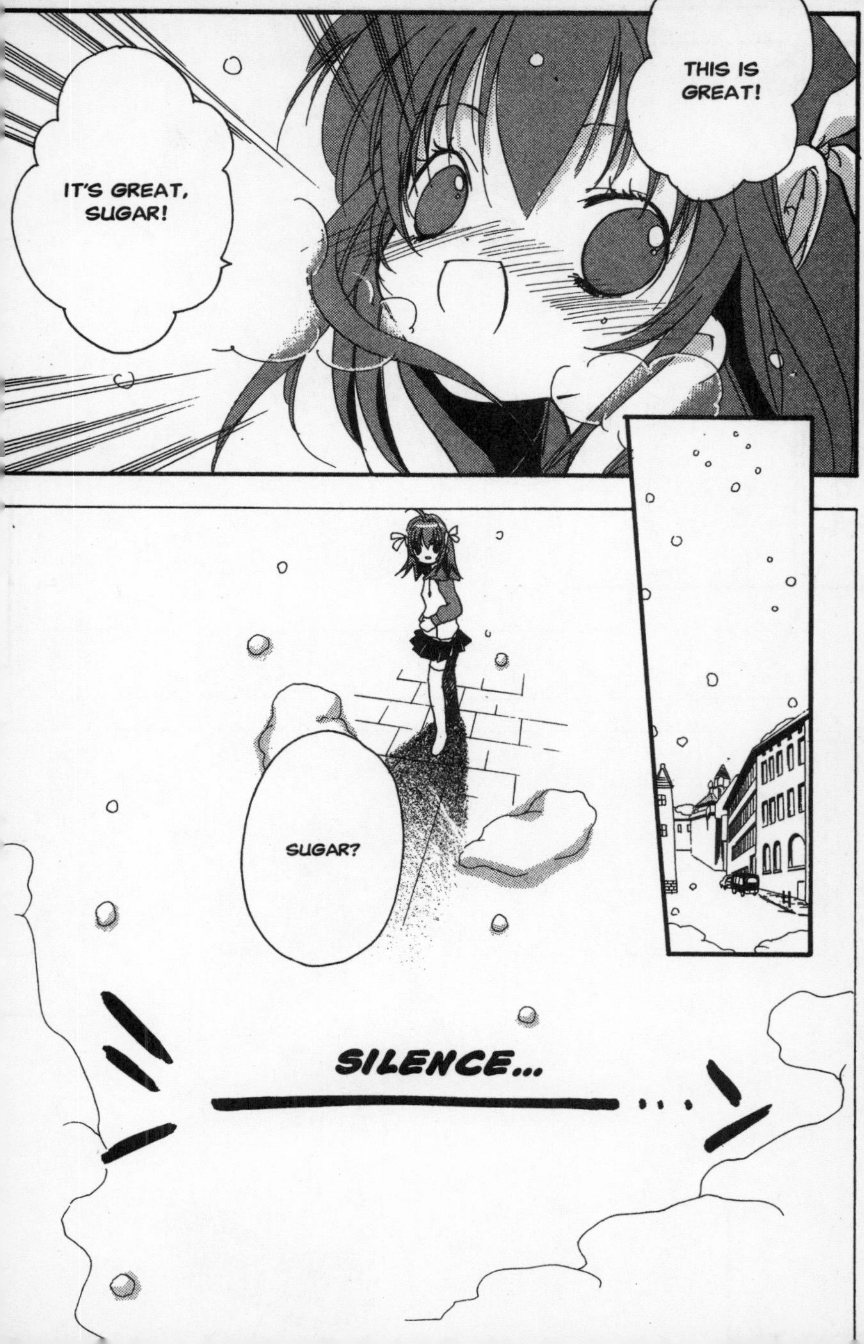
THIS IS GREAT!
IT'S GREAT, SUGAR!
SUGAR?
SILENCE...
———...

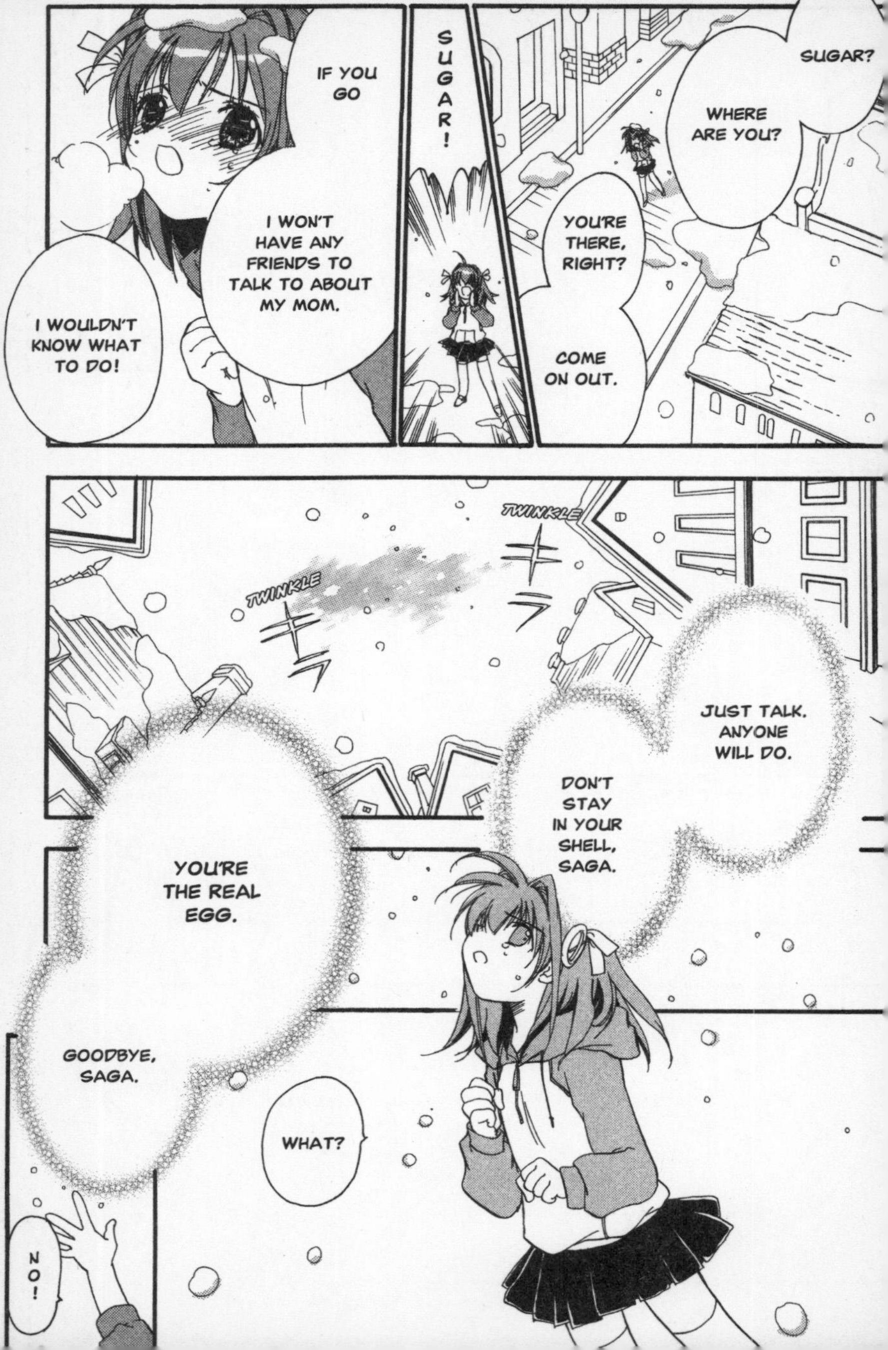
SUGAR?
WHERE ARE YOU?
YOU'RE THERE, RIGHT?
COME ON OUT.
SUGAR!
IF YOU GO
I WON'T HAVE ANY FRIENDS TO TALK TO ABOUT MY MOM.
I WOULDN'T KNOW WHAT TO DO!
TWINKLE
TWINKLE
JUST TALK. ANYONE WILL DO.
DON'T STAY IN YOUR SHELL, SAGA.
YOU'RE THE REAL EGG.
GOODBYE, SAGA.
WHAT?
NO!

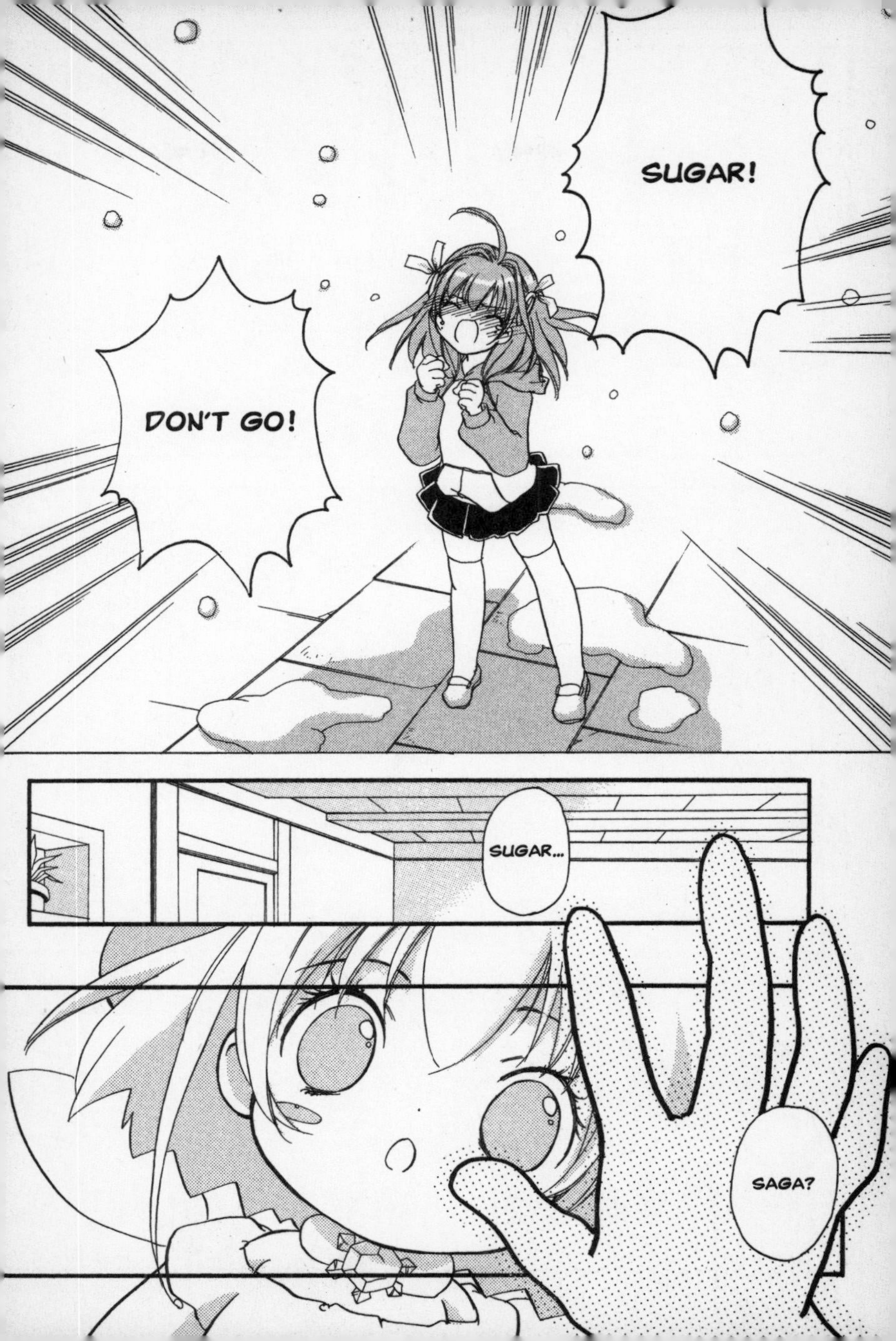
SUGAR!
DON'T GO!
SUGAR...
SAGA?

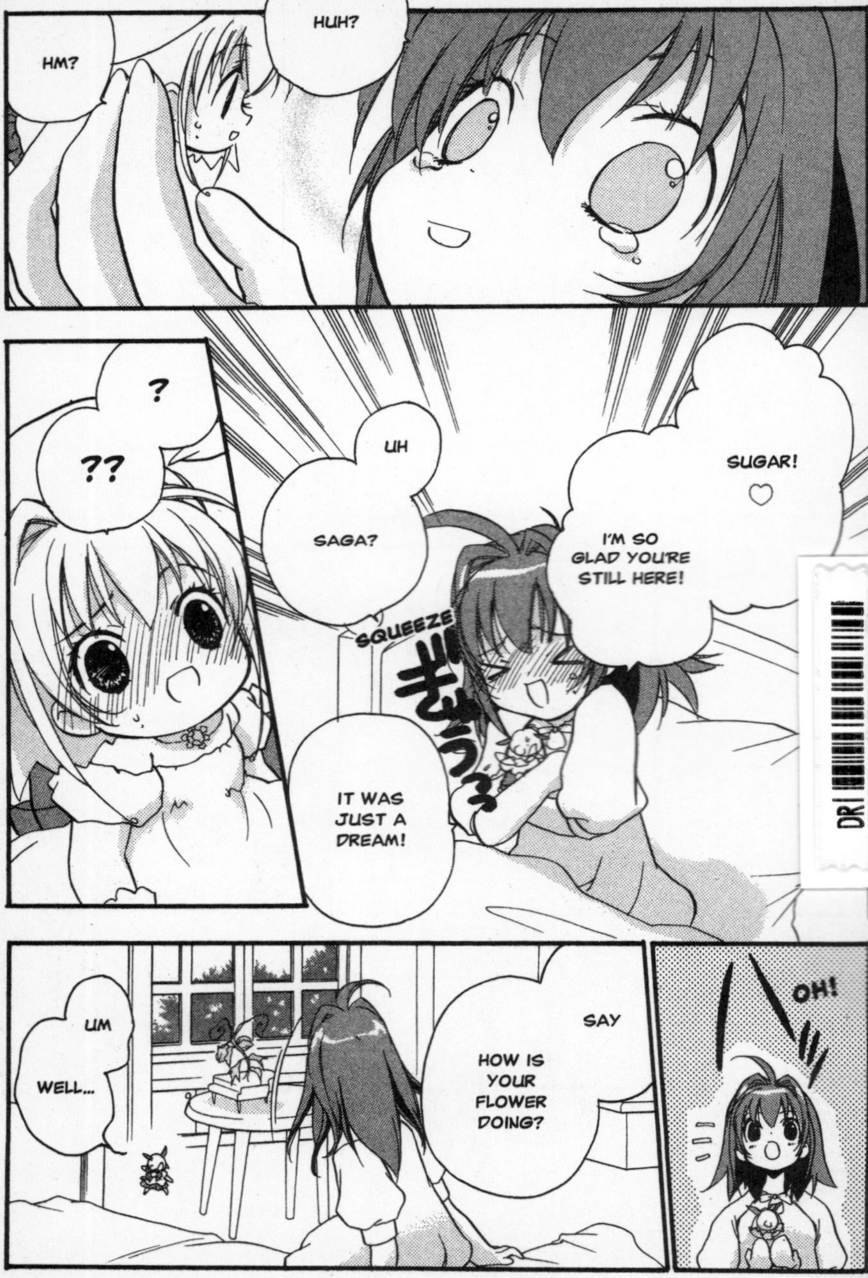
HUH?
HM?
SUGAR! ♡
I'M SO GLAD YOU'RE STILL HERE!
SQUEEZE
IT WAS JUST A DREAM!
UH SAGA?
?
??
OH!
SAY
HOW IS YOUR FLOWER DOING?
UM
WELL...

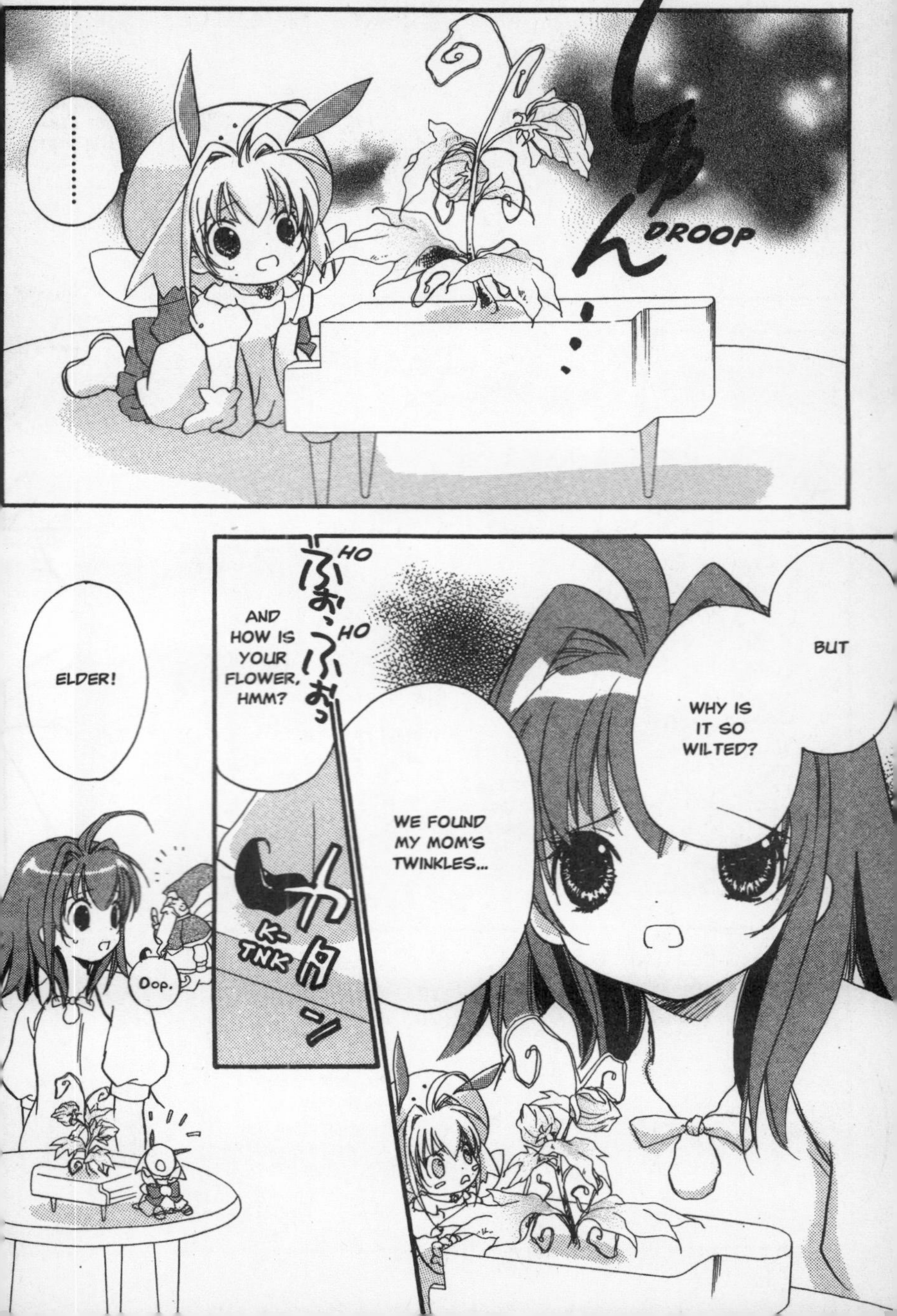
DROOP
......
BUT
WHY IS IT SO WILTED?
WE FOUND MY MOM'S TWINKLES...
HO HO
AND HOW IS YOUR FLOWER, HMM?
K-TNK
ELDER!
Oop.

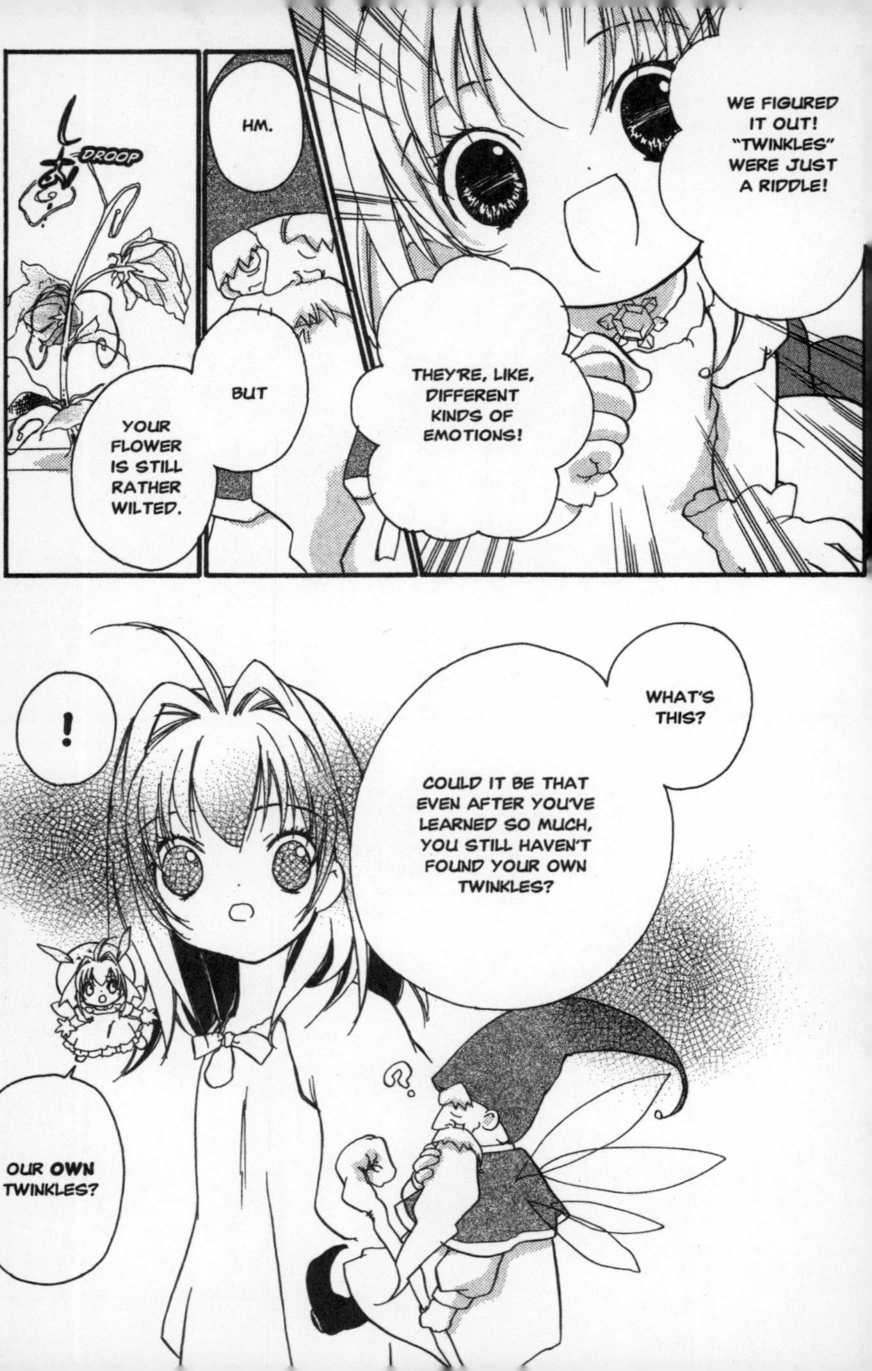
WE FIGURED IT OUT! "TWINKLES" WERE JUST A RIDDLE!
THEY'RE, LIKE, DIFFERENT KINDS OF EMOTIONS!
HM.
BUT
YOUR FLOWER IS STILL RATHER WILTED.
DROOP
WHAT'S THIS?
COULD IT BE THAT EVEN AFTER YOU'VE LEARNED SO MUCH, YOU STILL HAVEN'T FOUND YOUR OWN TWINKLES?
!
OUR OWN TWINKLES?

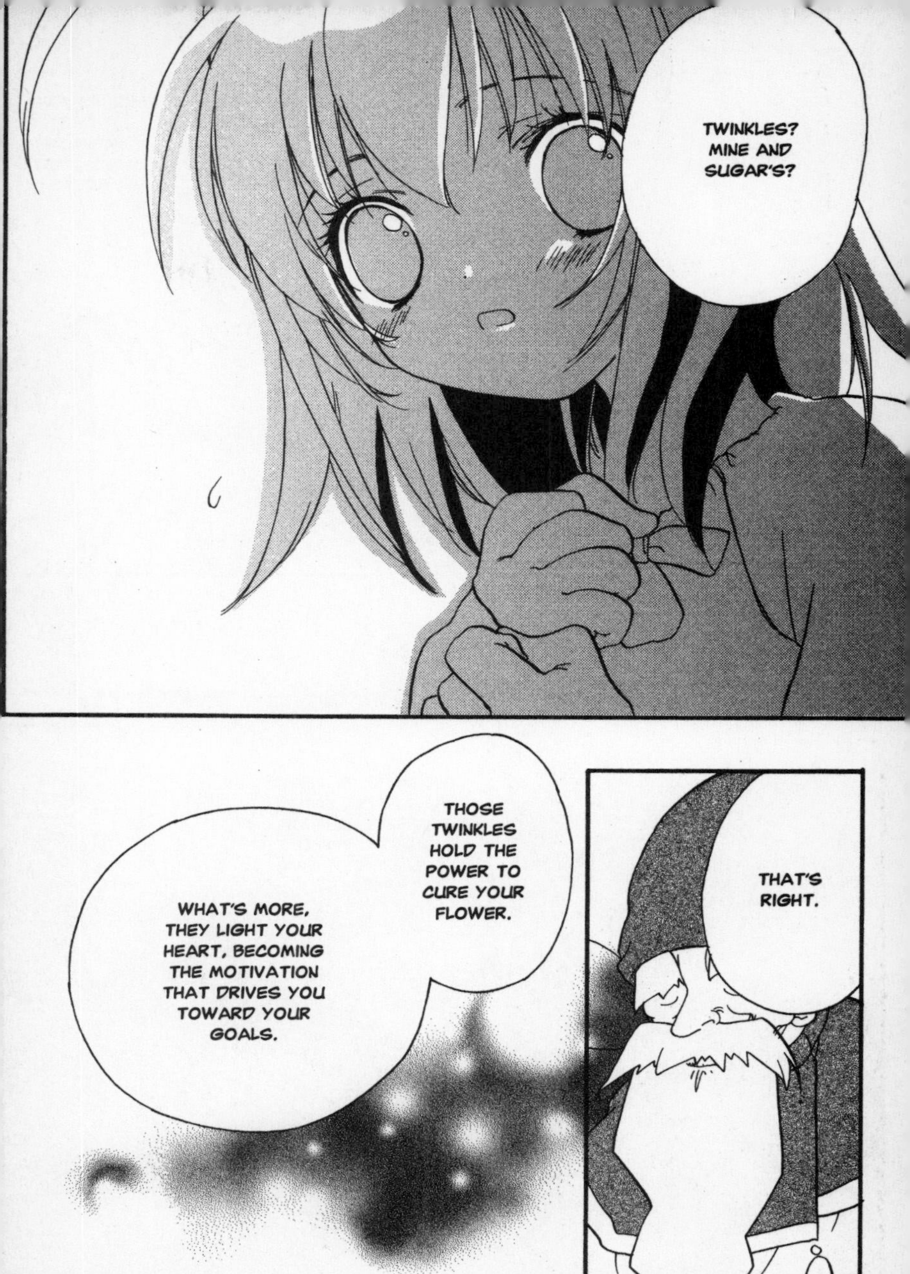
TWINKLES? MINE AND SUGAR'S?
THAT'S RIGHT.
THOSE TWINKLES HOLD THE POWER TO CURE YOUR FLOWER.
WHAT'S MORE, THEY LIGHT YOUR HEART, BECOMING THE MOTIVATION THAT DRIVES YOU TOWARD YOUR GOALS.

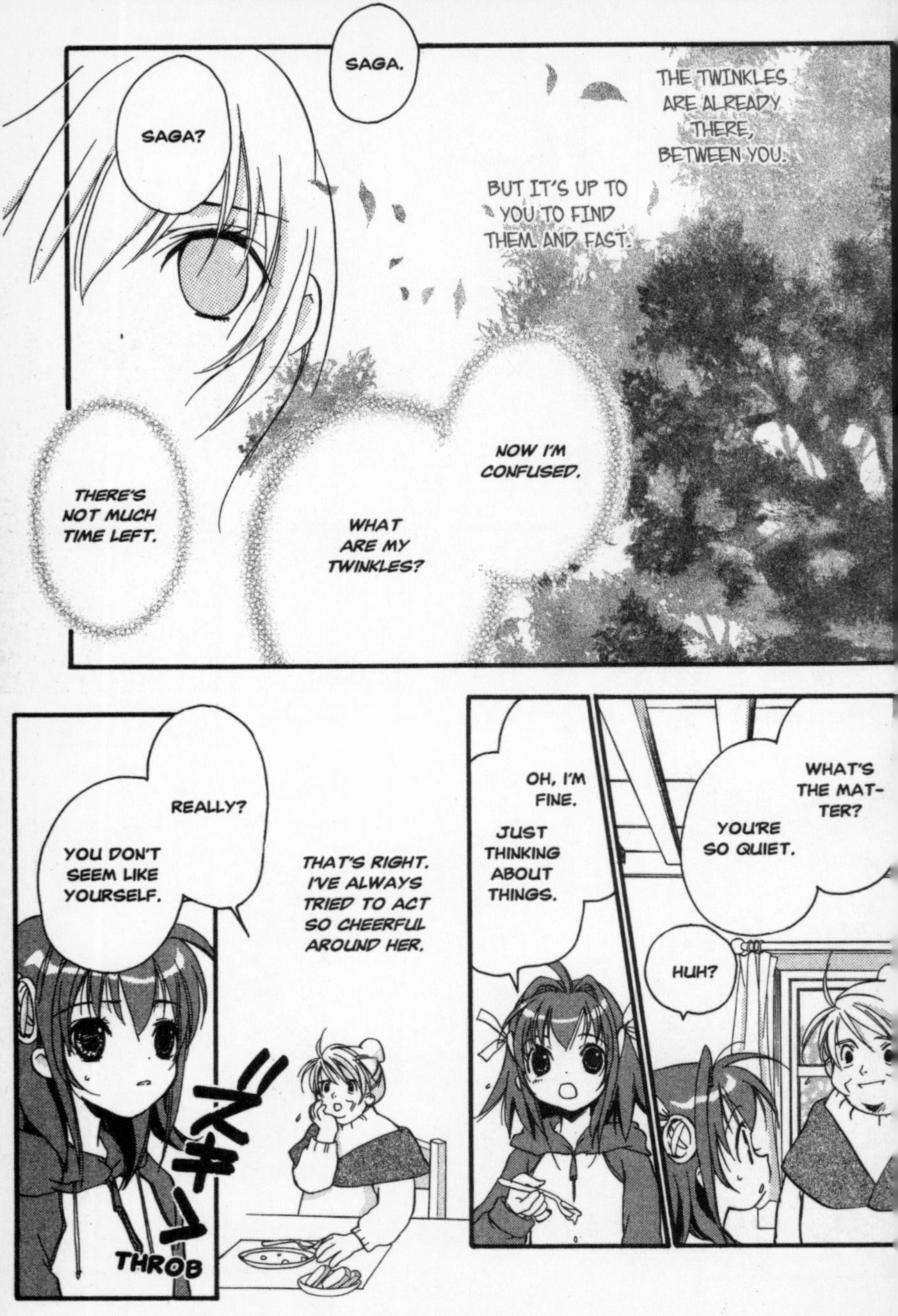
THE TWINKLES ARE ALREADY THERE, BETWEEN YOU.
BUT IT'S UP TO YOU TO FIND THEM AND FAST.
SAGA.
SAGA?
NOW I'M CONFUSED.
WHAT ARE MY TWINKLES?
THERE'S NOT MUCH TIME LEFT.
WHAT'S THE MAT-TER?
YOU'RE SO QUIET.
HUH?
OH, I'M FINE.
JUST THINKING ABOUT THINGS.
REALLY?
YOU DON'T SEEM LIKE YOURSELF.
THAT'S RIGHT. I'VE ALWAYS TRIED TO ACT SO CHEERFUL AROUND HER.
THROB

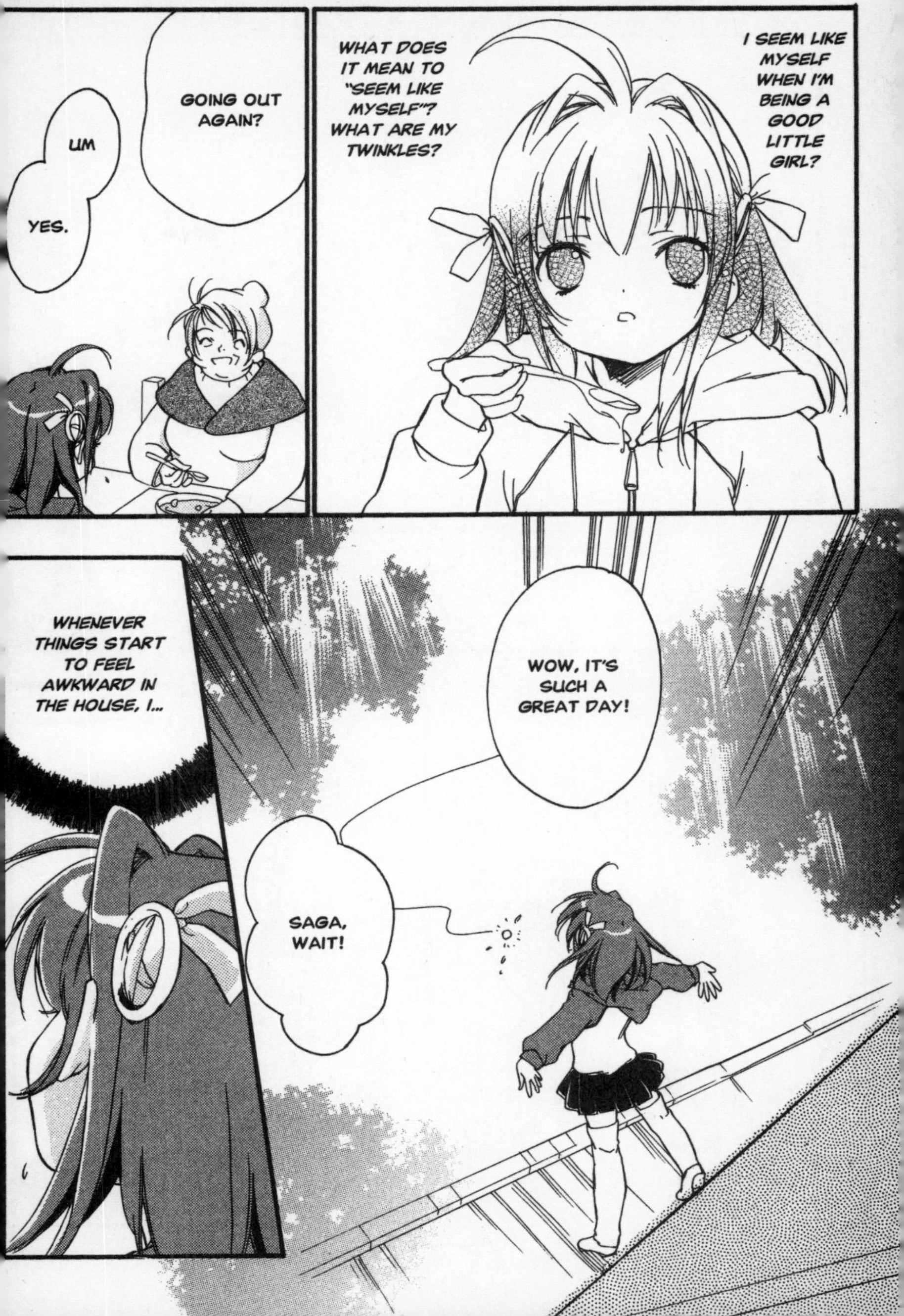
I SEEM LIKE MYSELF WHEN I'M BEING A GOOD LITTLE GIRL?
WHAT DOES IT MEAN TO "SEEM LIKE MYSELF"? WHAT ARE MY TWINKLES?
GOING OUT AGAIN?
UM
YES.
WOW, IT'S SUCH A GREAT DAY!
SAGA, WAIT!
WHENEVER THINGS START TO FEEL AWKWARD IN THE HOUSE, I...

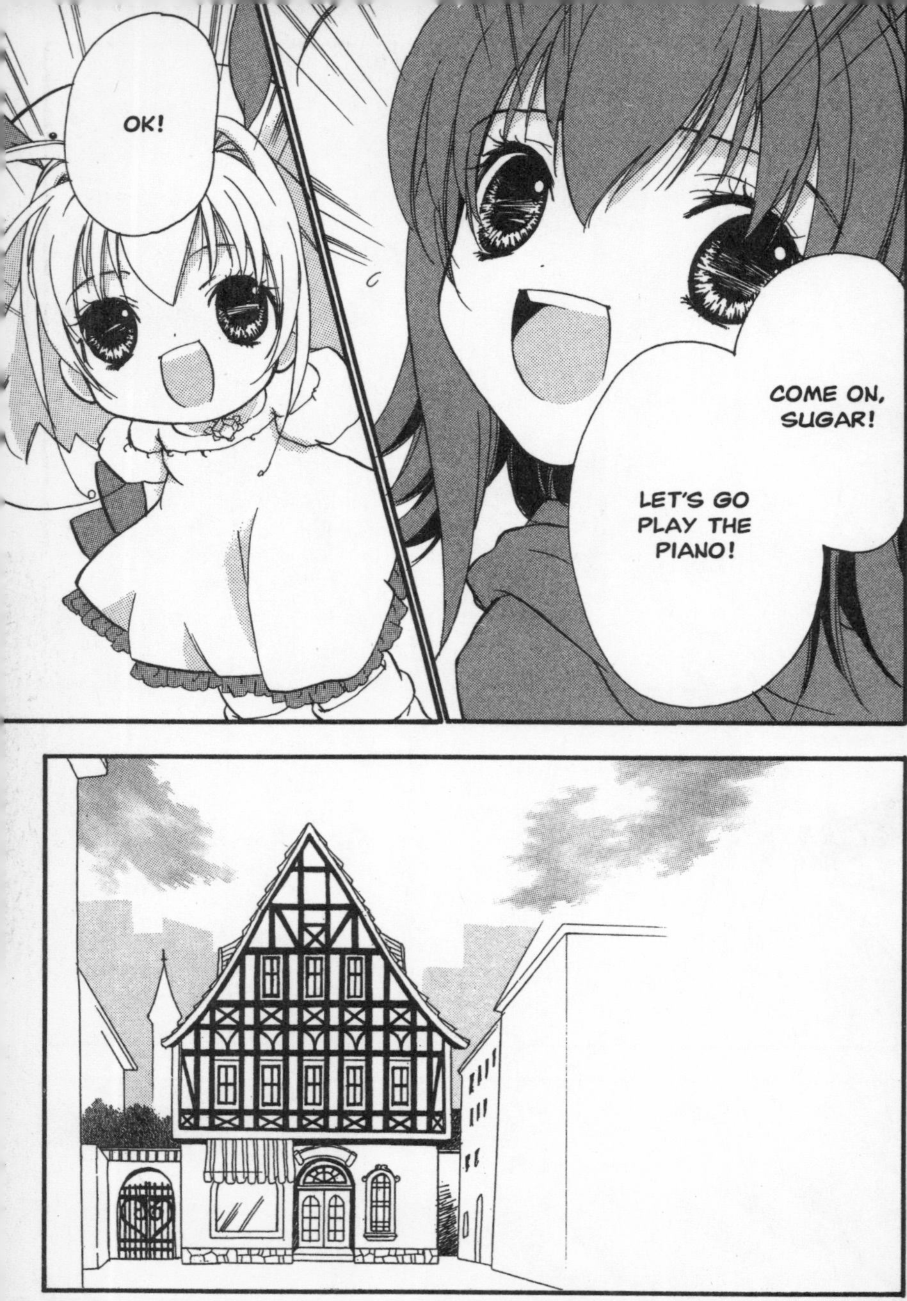
COME ON, SUGAR!
LET'S GO PLAY THE PIANO!
OK!

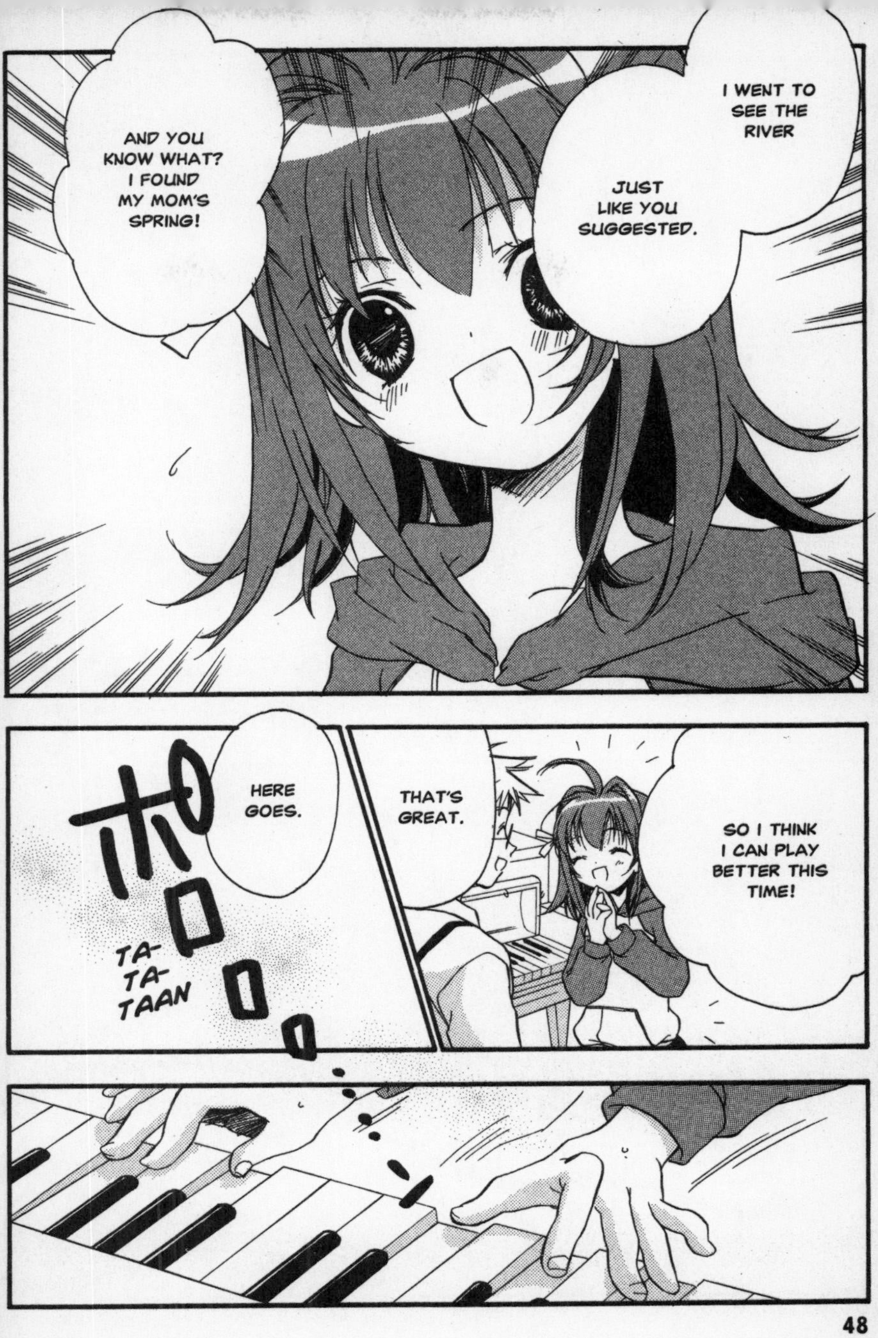
I WENT TO SEE THE RIVER
JUST LIKE YOU SUGGESTED.
AND YOU KNOW WHAT? I FOUND MY MOM'S SPRING!
SO I THINK I CAN PLAY BETTER THIS TIME!
THAT'S GREAT.
HERE GOES.
ポロロロ
TA-TA-TAAN

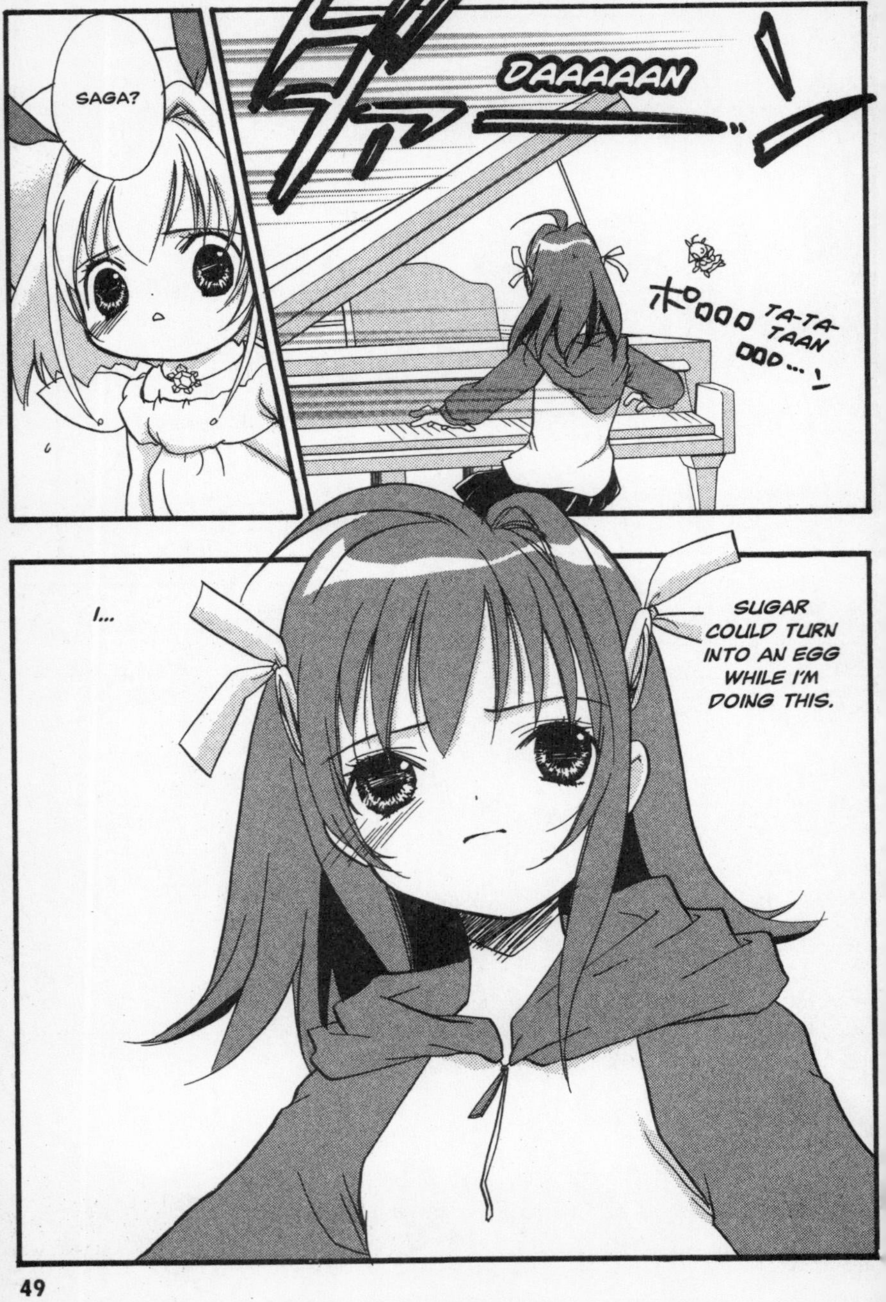
DAAAAAN
TA-TA-TAAN ...!
SAGA?
SUGAR COULD TURN INTO AN EGG WHILE I'M DOING THIS.
I...

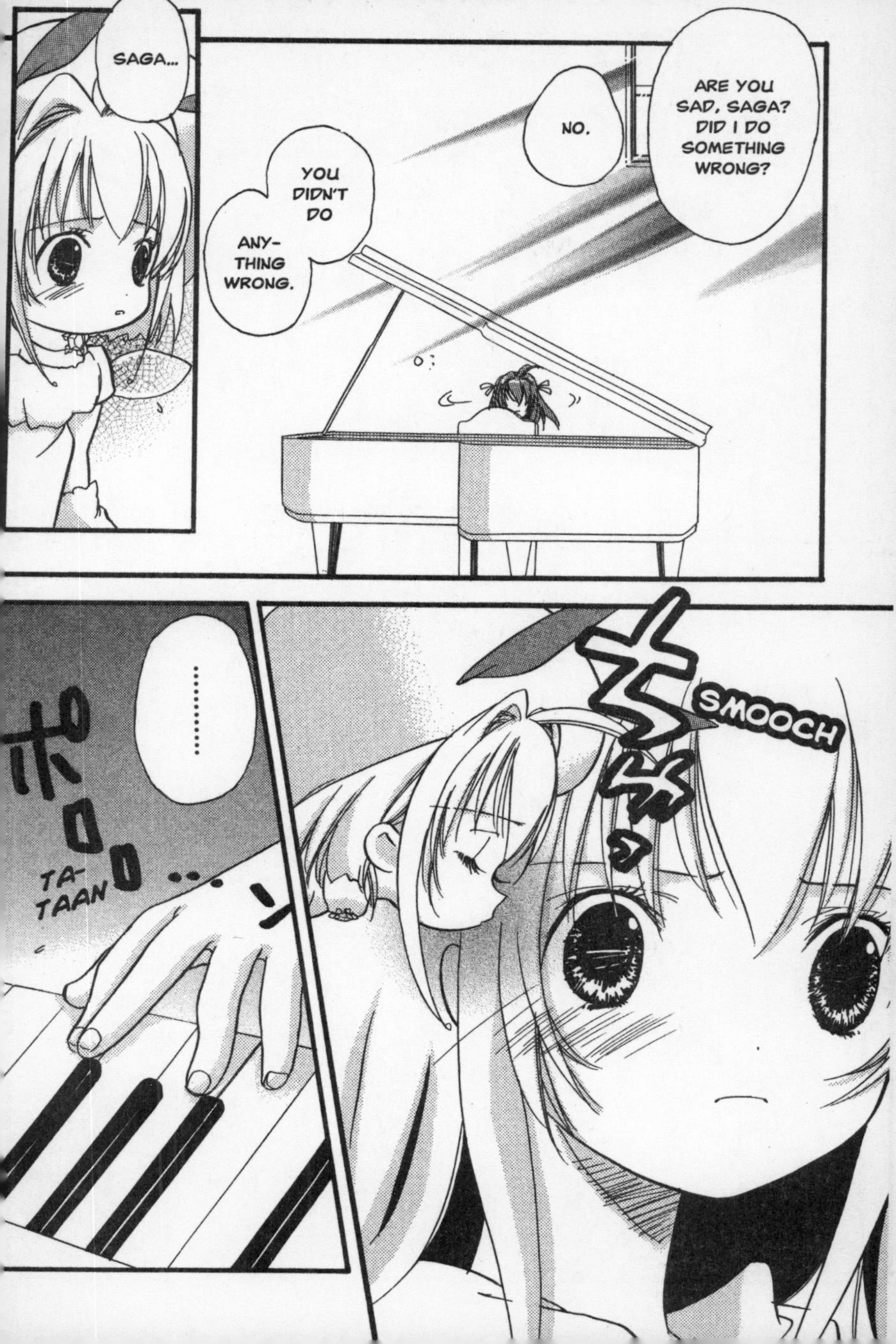
ARE YOU SAD, SAGA? DID I DO SOMETHING WRONG?
NO.
YOU DIDN'T DO ANYTHING WRONG.
SAGA...
SMOOCH
....
TA-TAAN

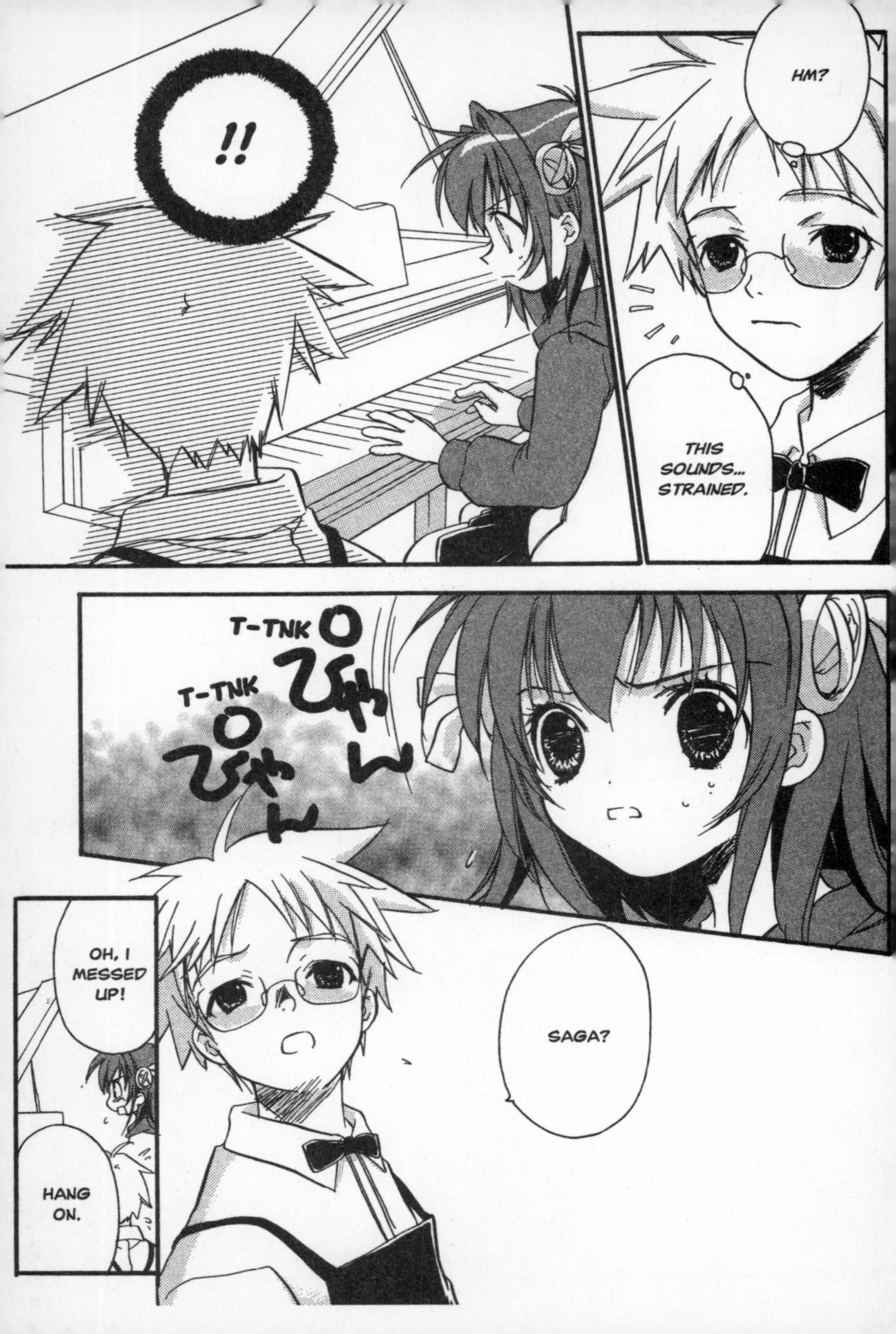
HM?
THIS SOUNDS... STRAINED.
!!
T-TNK
ぴゃん
T-TNK
ぴゃん
SAGA?
OH, I MESSED UP!
HANG ON.

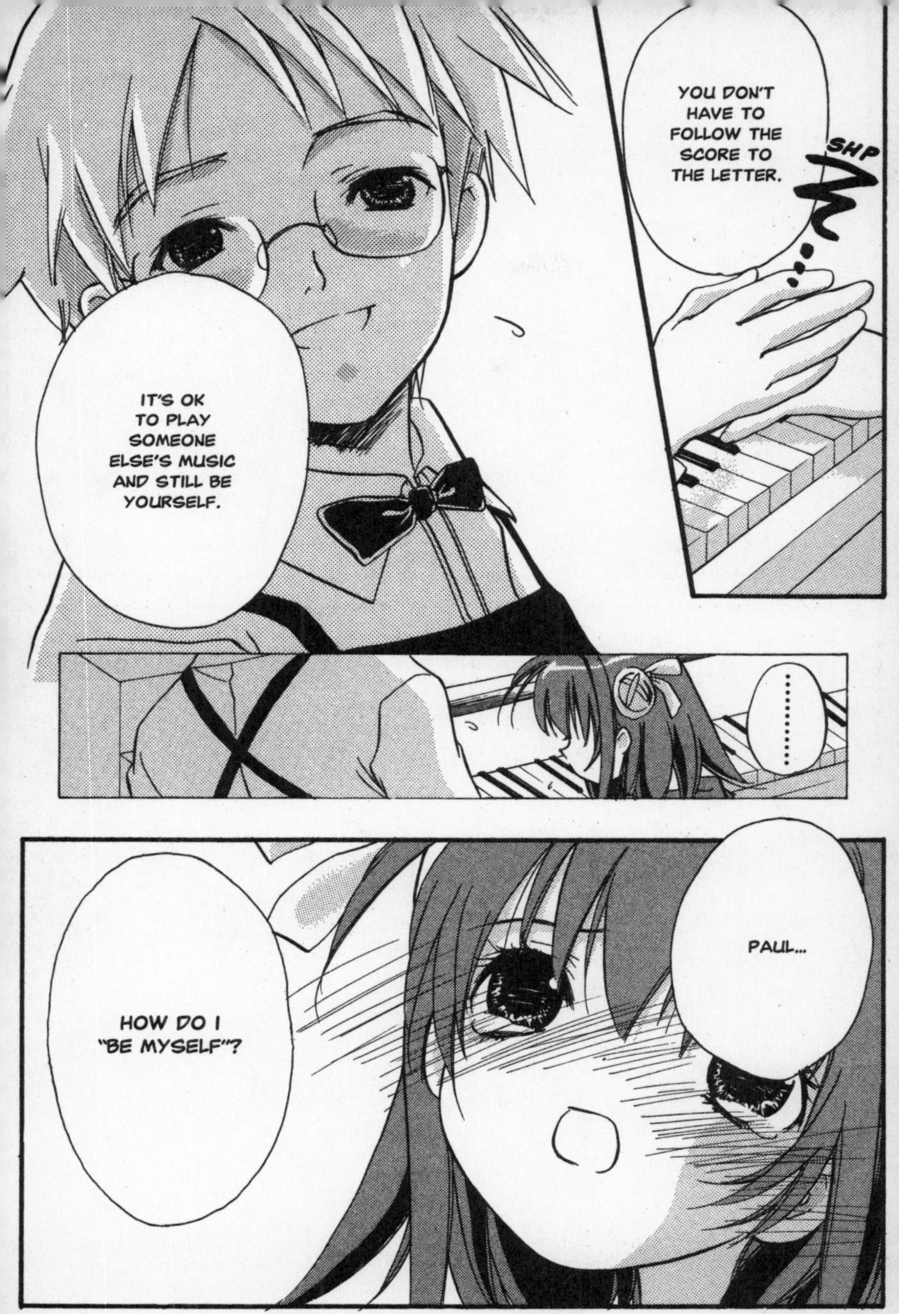
YOU DON'T HAVE TO FOLLOW THE SCORE TO THE LETTER.
SHP
IT'S OK TO PLAY SOMEONE ELSE'S MUSIC AND STILL BE YOURSELF.
......
PAUL...
HOW DO I "BE MYSELF"?

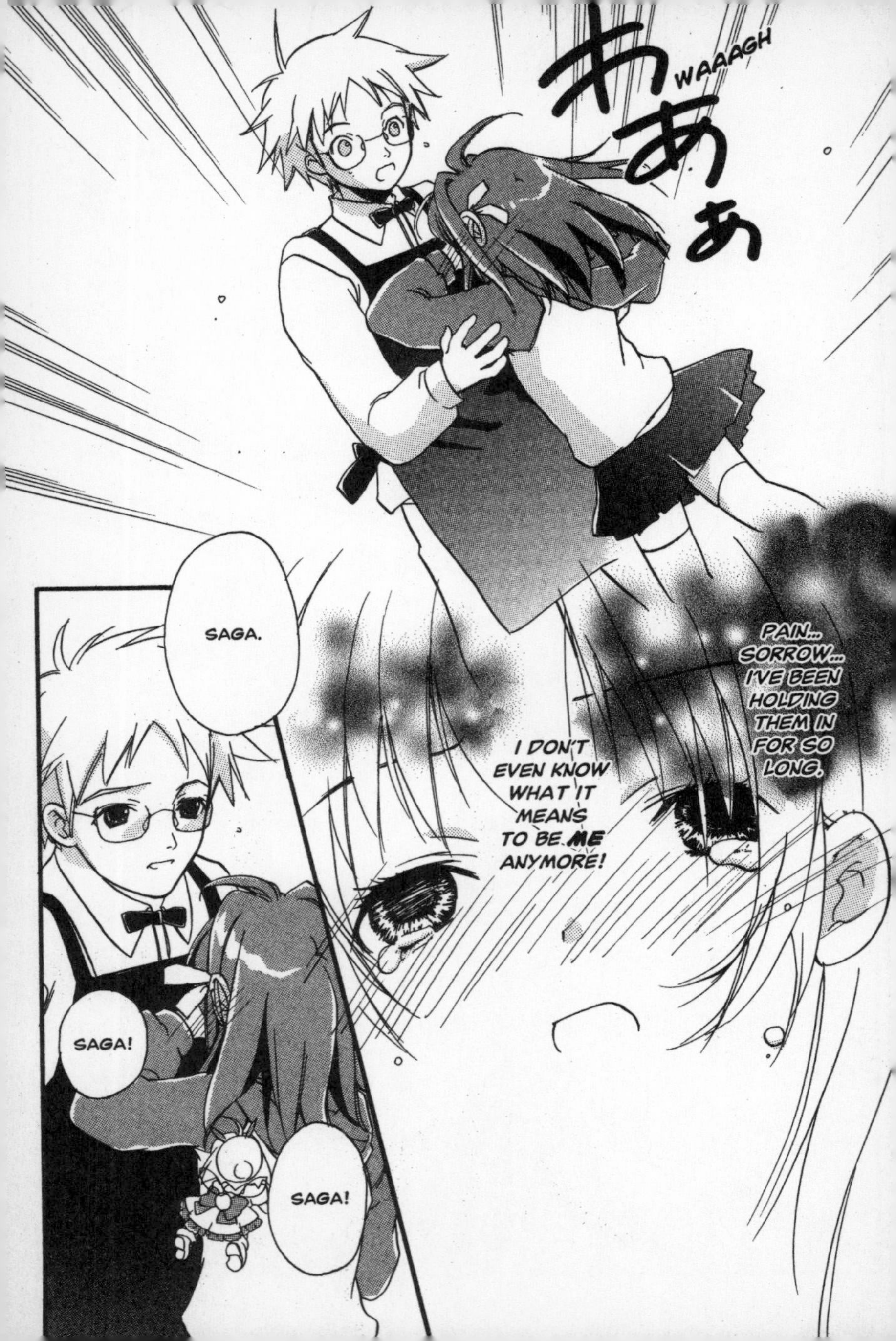
ああぁ
WAAAGH
PAIN... SORROW... I'VE BEEN HOLDING THEM IN FOR SO LONG.
I DON'T EVEN KNOW WHAT IT MEANS TO BE ME ANYMORE!
SAGA.
SAGA!
SAGA!

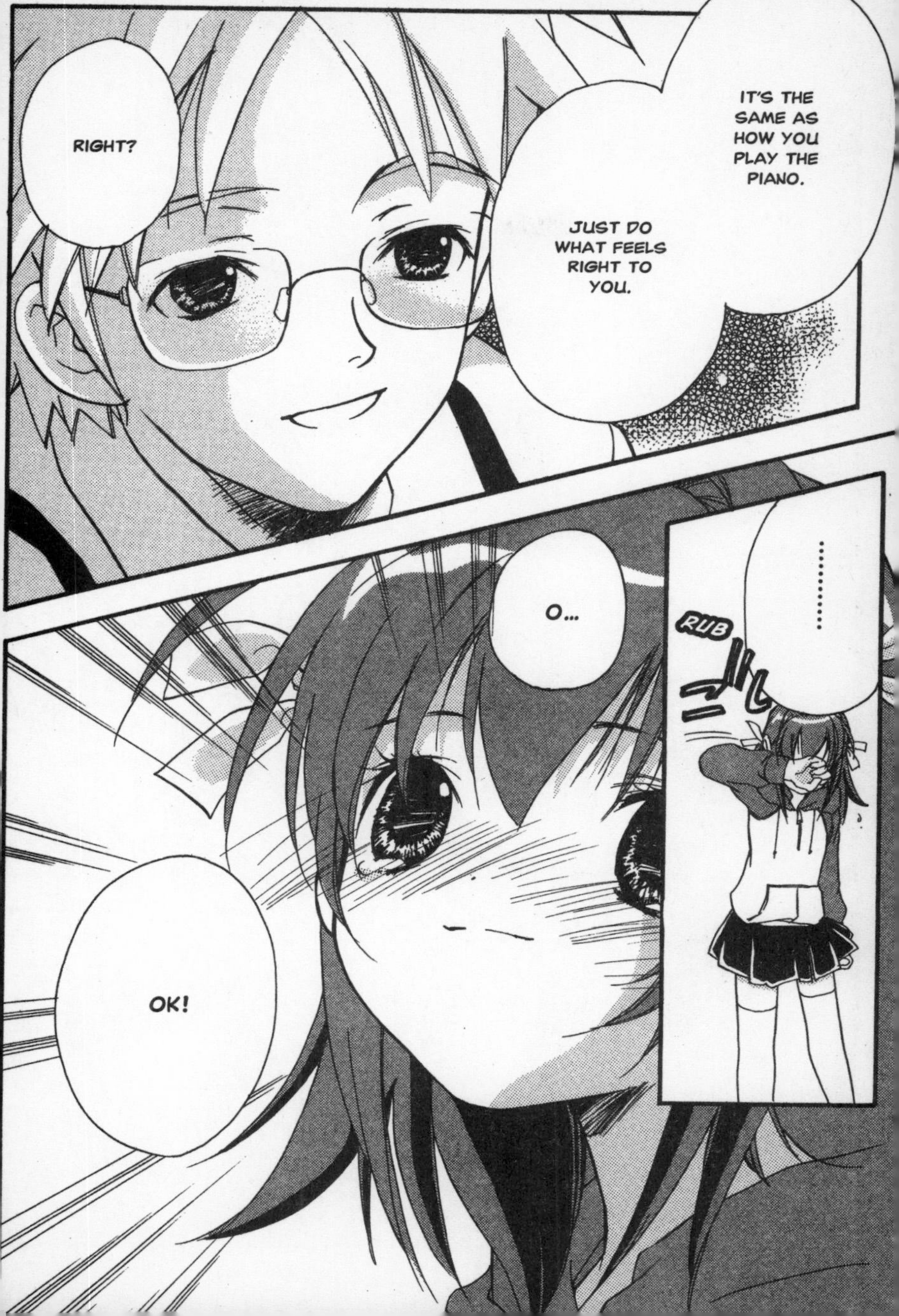
IT'S THE SAME AS HOW YOU PLAY THE PIANO.
JUST DO WHAT FEELS RIGHT TO YOU.
RIGHT?
……
RUB
O...
OK!

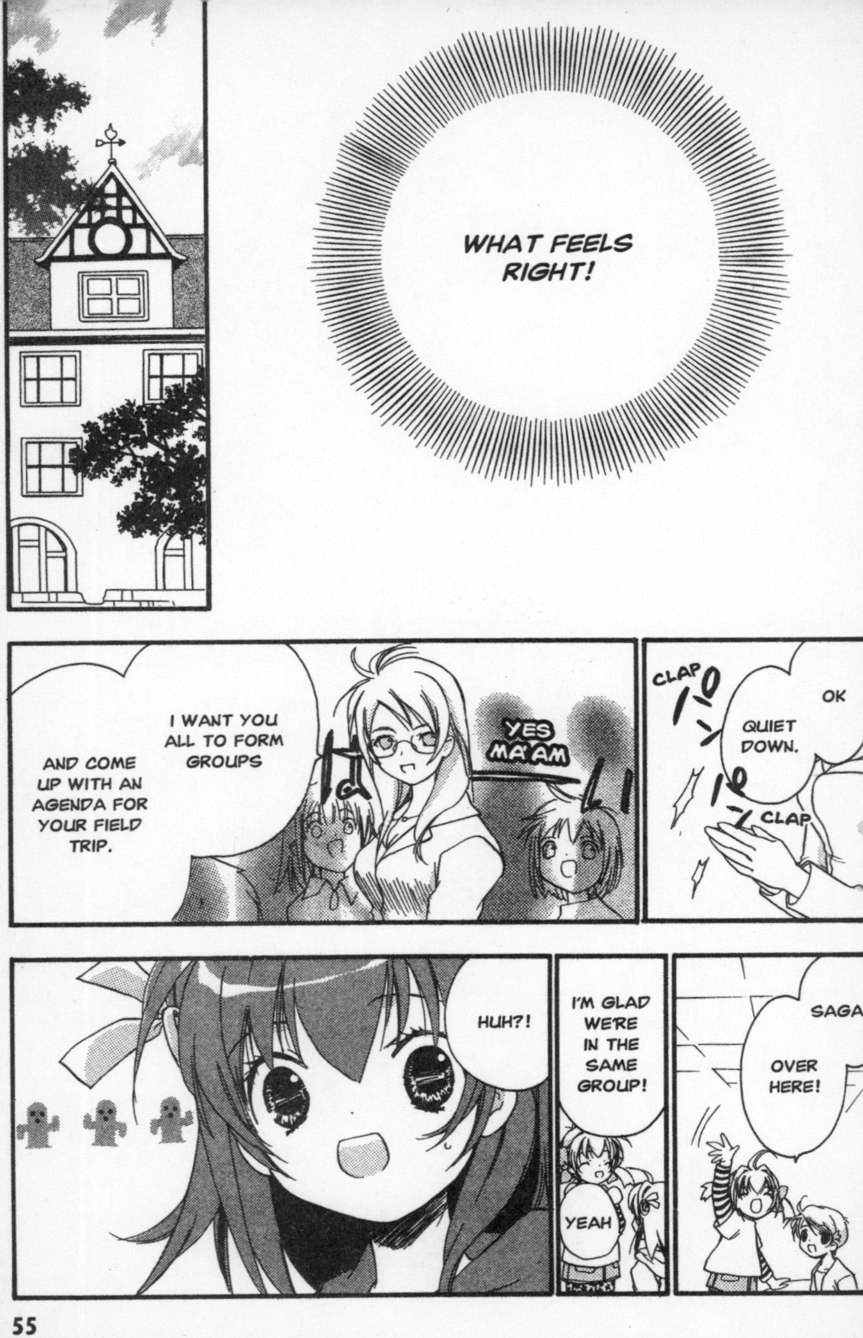
WHAT FEELS RIGHT!
CLAP
OK QUIET DOWN.
CLAP
I WANT YOU ALL TO FORM GROUPS
AND COME UP WITH AN AGENDA FOR YOUR FIELD TRIP.
YES MA'AM
SAGA OVER HERE!
I'M GLAD WE'RE IN THE SAME GROUP!
YEAH
HUH?!

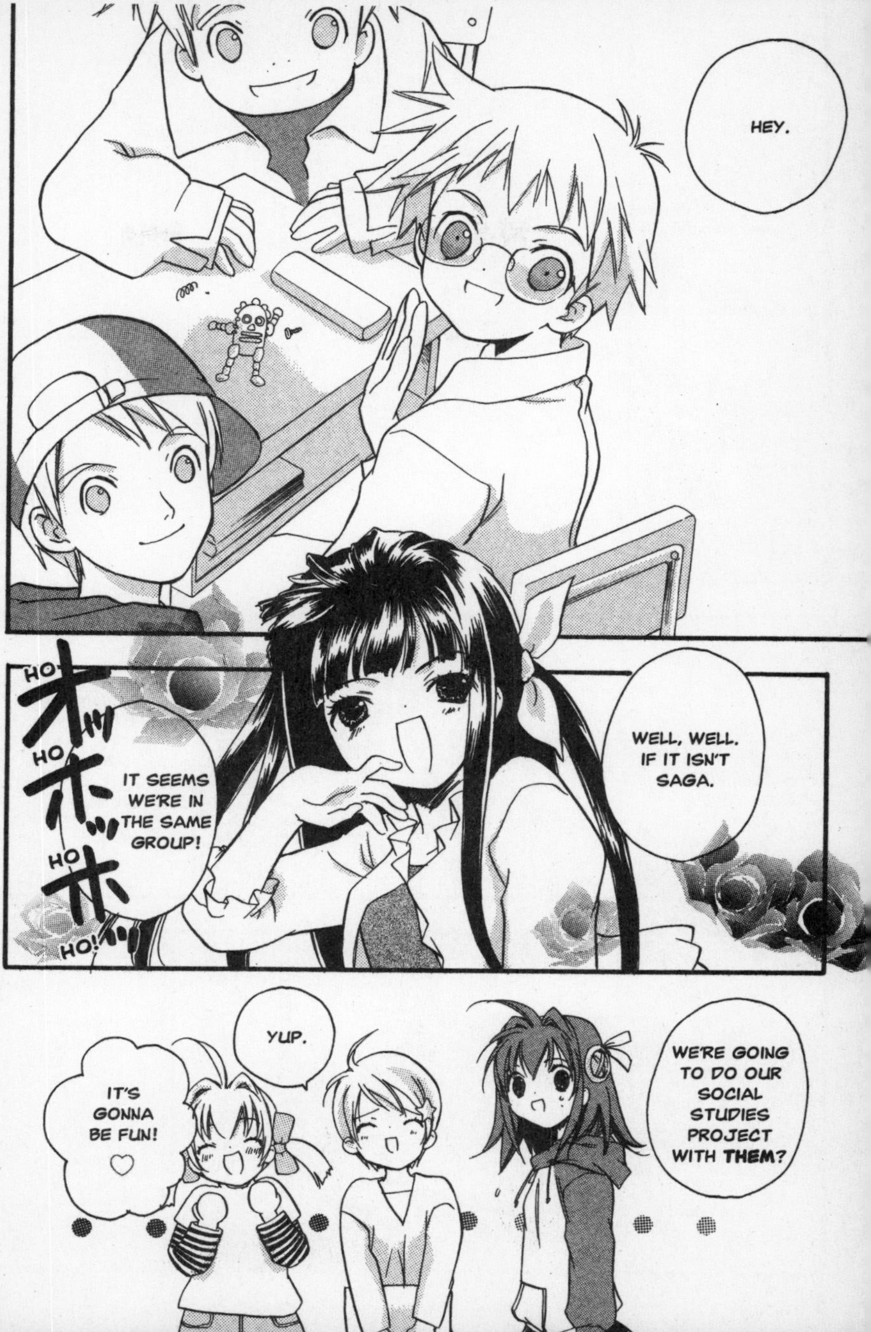
HEY.
WELL, WELL. IF IT ISN'T SAGA.
IT SEEMS WE'RE IN THE SAME GROUP!
HO- HO HO HO!
WE'RE GOING TO DO OUR SOCIAL STUDIES PROJECT WITH **THEM**?
YUP.
IT'S GONNA BE FUN! ♡

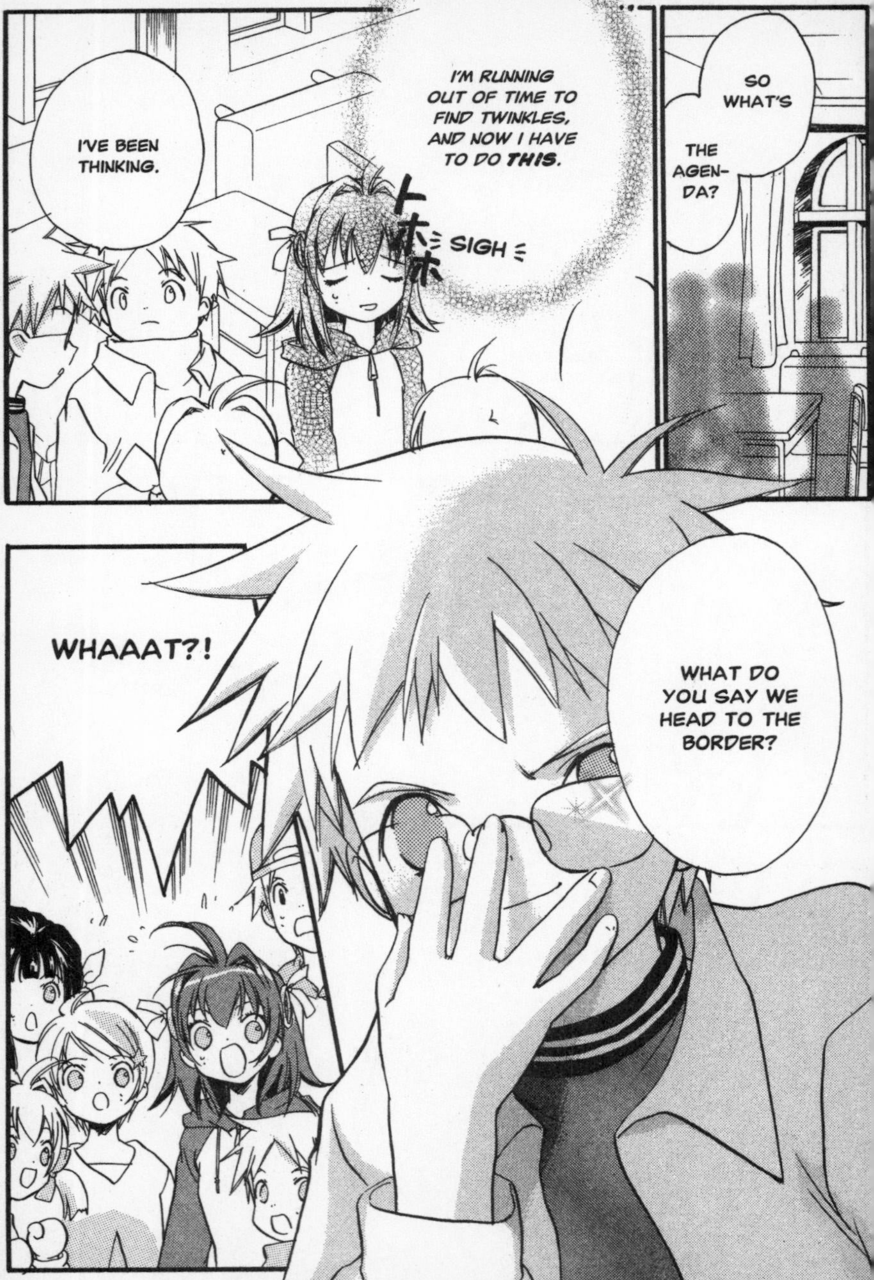
SO WHAT'S THE AGENDA?
I'M RUNNING OUT OF TIME TO FIND TWINKLES, AND NOW I HAVE TO DO **THIS**.
トホホ
SIGH
I'VE BEEN THINKING.
WHAT DO YOU SAY WE HEAD TO THE BORDER?
WHAAAT?!

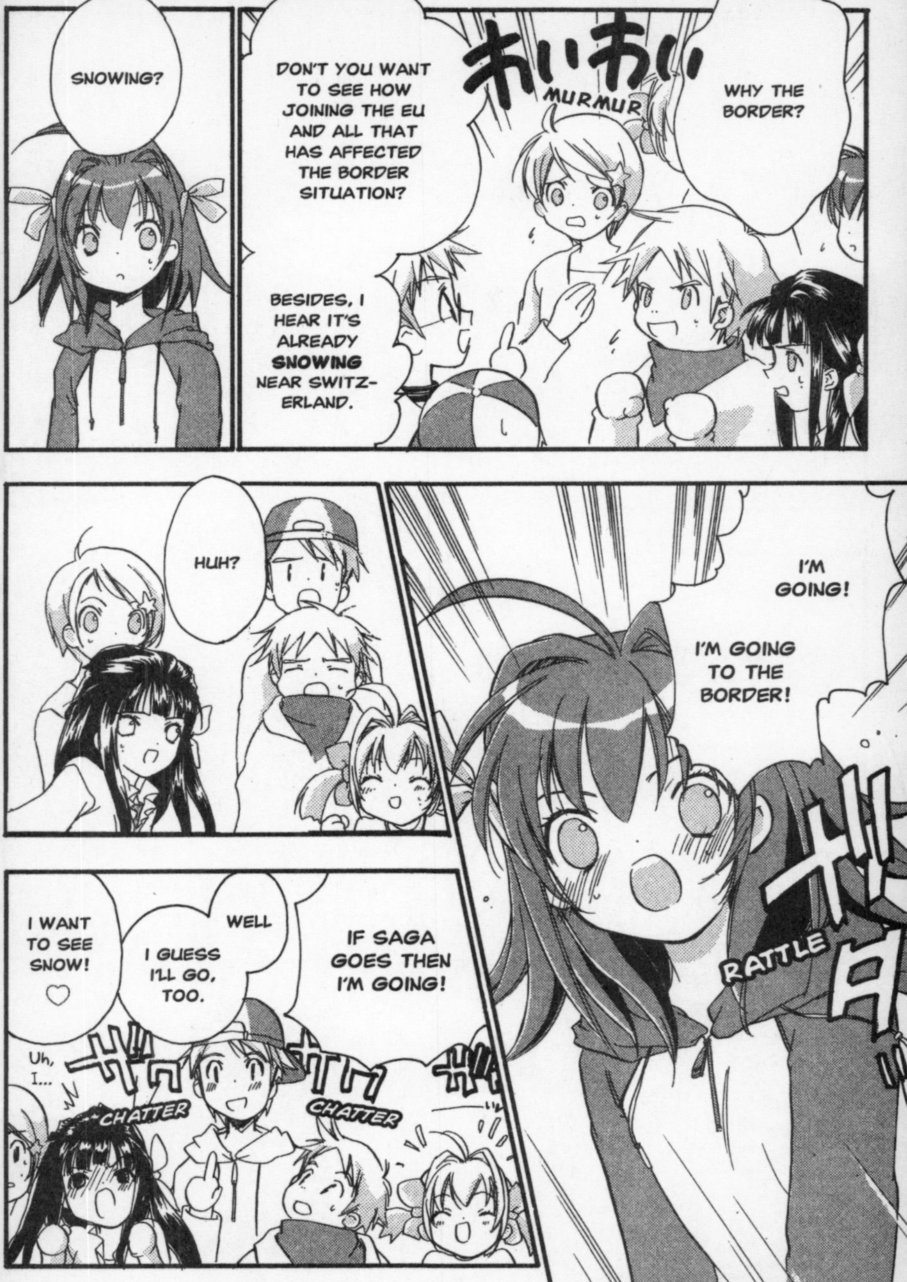
WHY THE BORDER?
わいわい
MURMUR
DON'T YOU WANT TO SEE HOW JOINING THE EU AND ALL THAT HAS AFFECTED THE BORDER SITUATION?
BESIDES, I HEAR IT'S ALREADY **SNOWING** NEAR SWITZ-ERLAND.
SNOWING?
I'M GOING!
I'M GOING TO THE BORDER!
RATTLE
HUH?
IF SAGA GOES THEN I'M GOING!
WELL
I GUESS I'LL GO, TOO.
I WANT TO SEE SNOW! ♡
CHATTER
CHATTER
Uh, I...

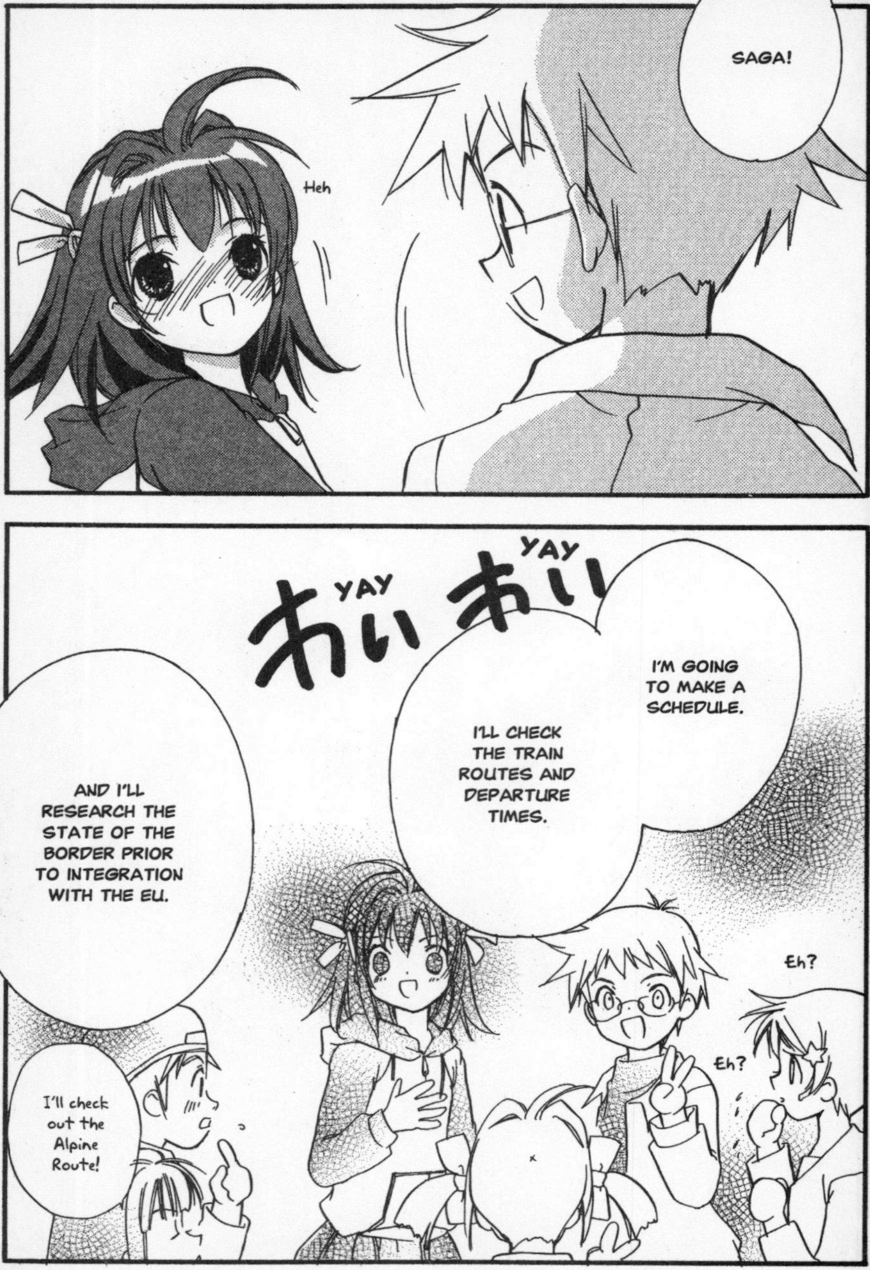
SAGA!
Heh
YAY YAY
わい わい
I'M GOING TO MAKE A SCHEDULE.
I'LL CHECK THE TRAIN ROUTES AND DEPARTURE TIMES.
AND I'LL RESEARCH THE STATE OF THE BORDER PRIOR TO INTEGRATION WITH THE EU.
Eh?
Eh?
I'll check out the Alpine Route!

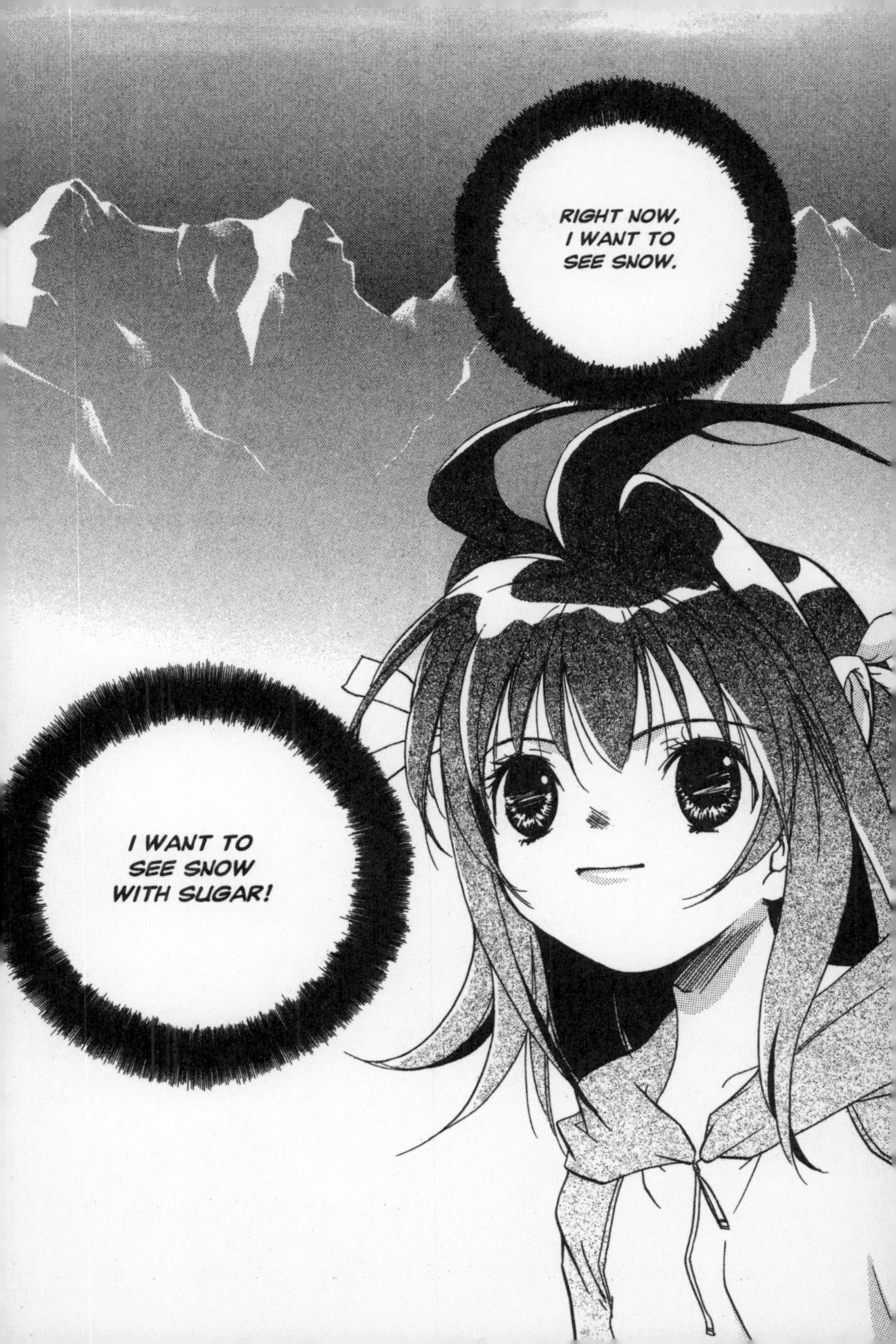
RIGHT NOW, I WANT TO SEE SNOW.
I WANT TO SEE SNOW WITH SUGAR!

CHAPTER 12 Tragedy in the Alps

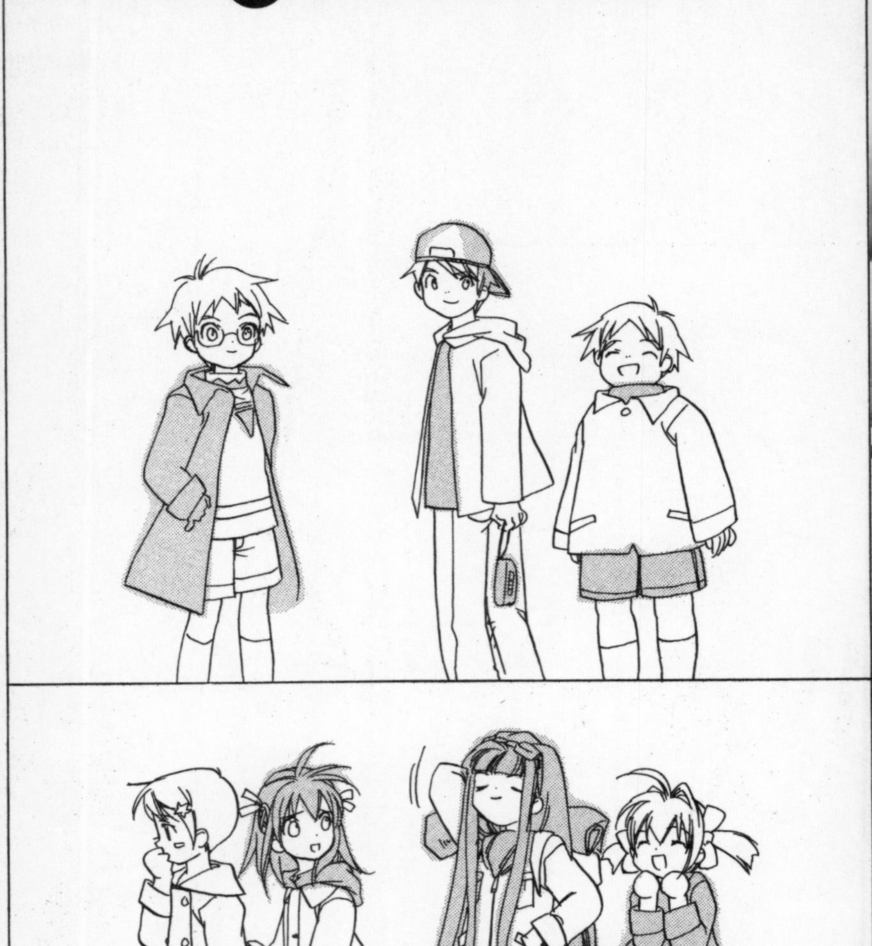

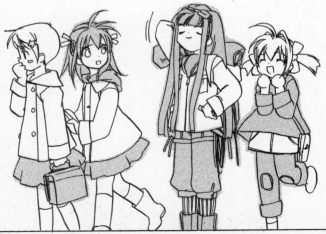

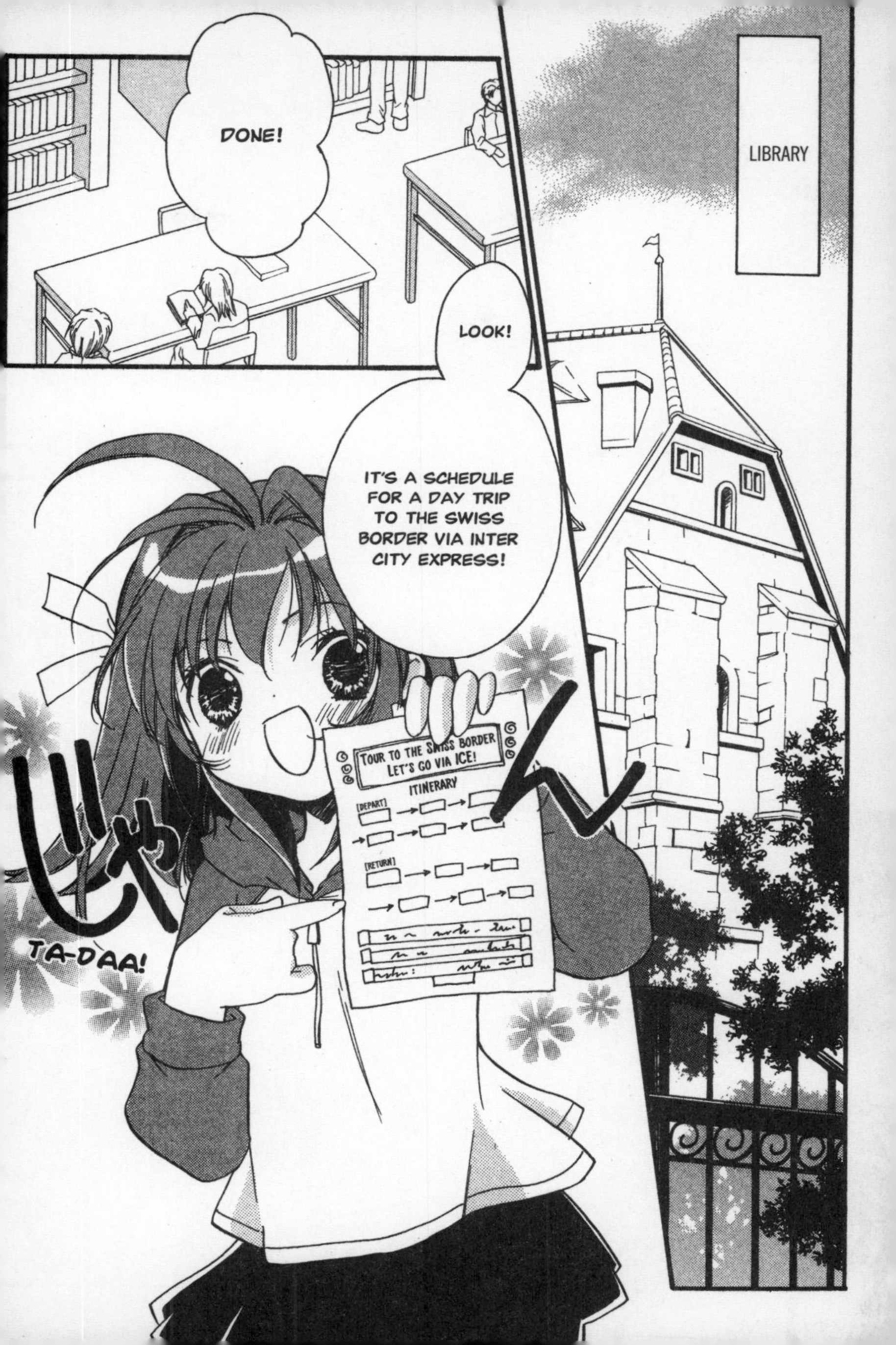
LIBRARY
DONE!
LOOK!
IT'S A SCHEDULE FOR A DAY TRIP TO THE SWISS BORDER VIA INTER CITY EXPRESS!
TOUR TO THE SWISS BORDER LET'S GO VIA ICE!
ITINERARY
[DEPART]
[RETURN]
TA-DAA!

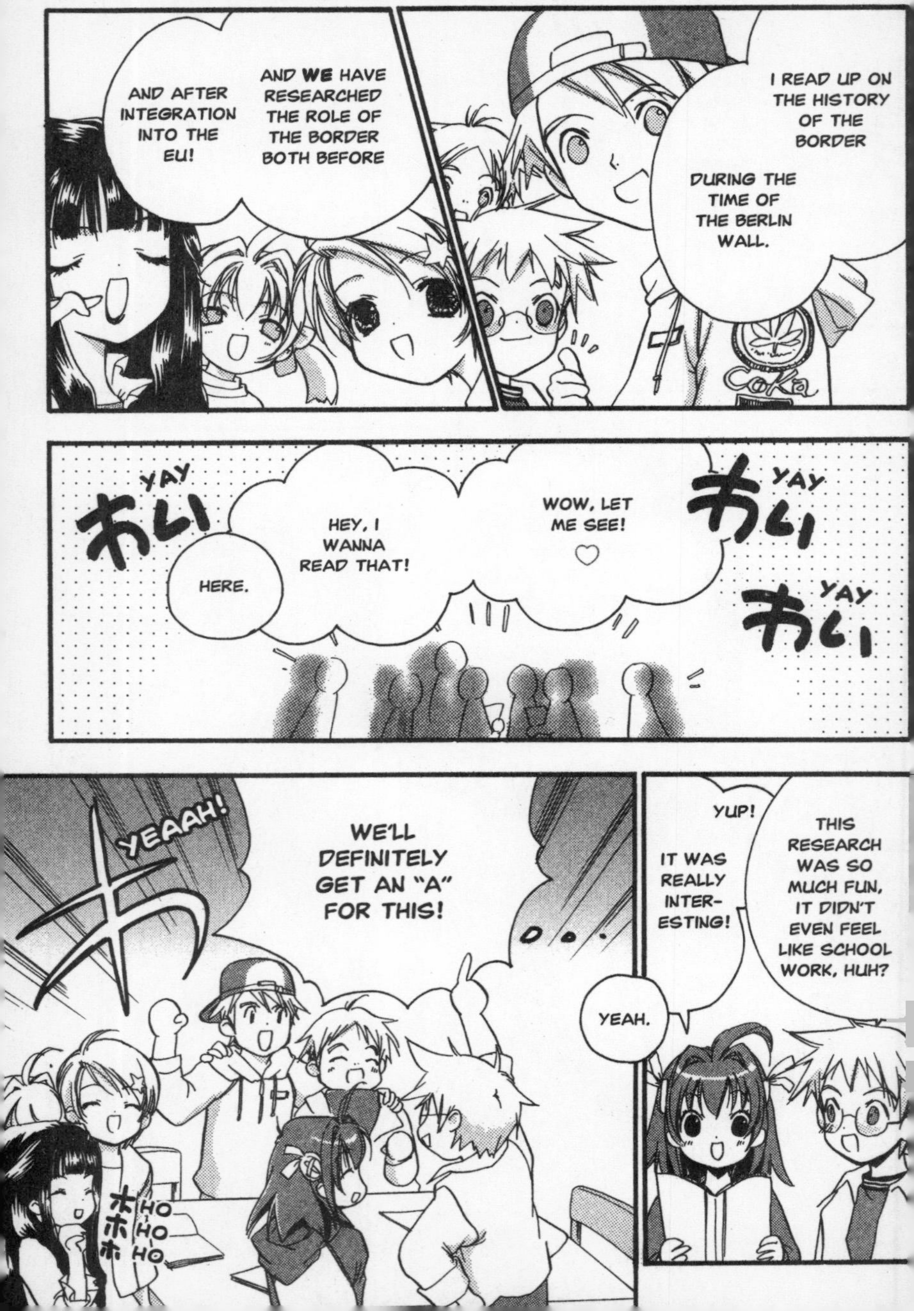
I READ UP ON THE HISTORY OF THE BORDER
DURING THE TIME OF THE BERLIN WALL.
AND **WE** HAVE RESEARCHED THE ROLE OF THE BORDER BOTH BEFORE
AND AFTER INTEGRATION INTO THE EU!
わい YAY
わい YAY
WOW, LET ME SEE! ♡
HEY, I WANNA READ THAT!
HERE.
わい YAY
THIS RESEARCH WAS SO MUCH FUN, IT DIDN'T EVEN FEEL LIKE SCHOOL WORK, HUH?
YUP!
IT WAS REALLY INTER-ESTING!
YEAH.
WE'LL DEFINITELY GET AN "A" FOR THIS!
YEAAAH!
ホホホ HO HO HO

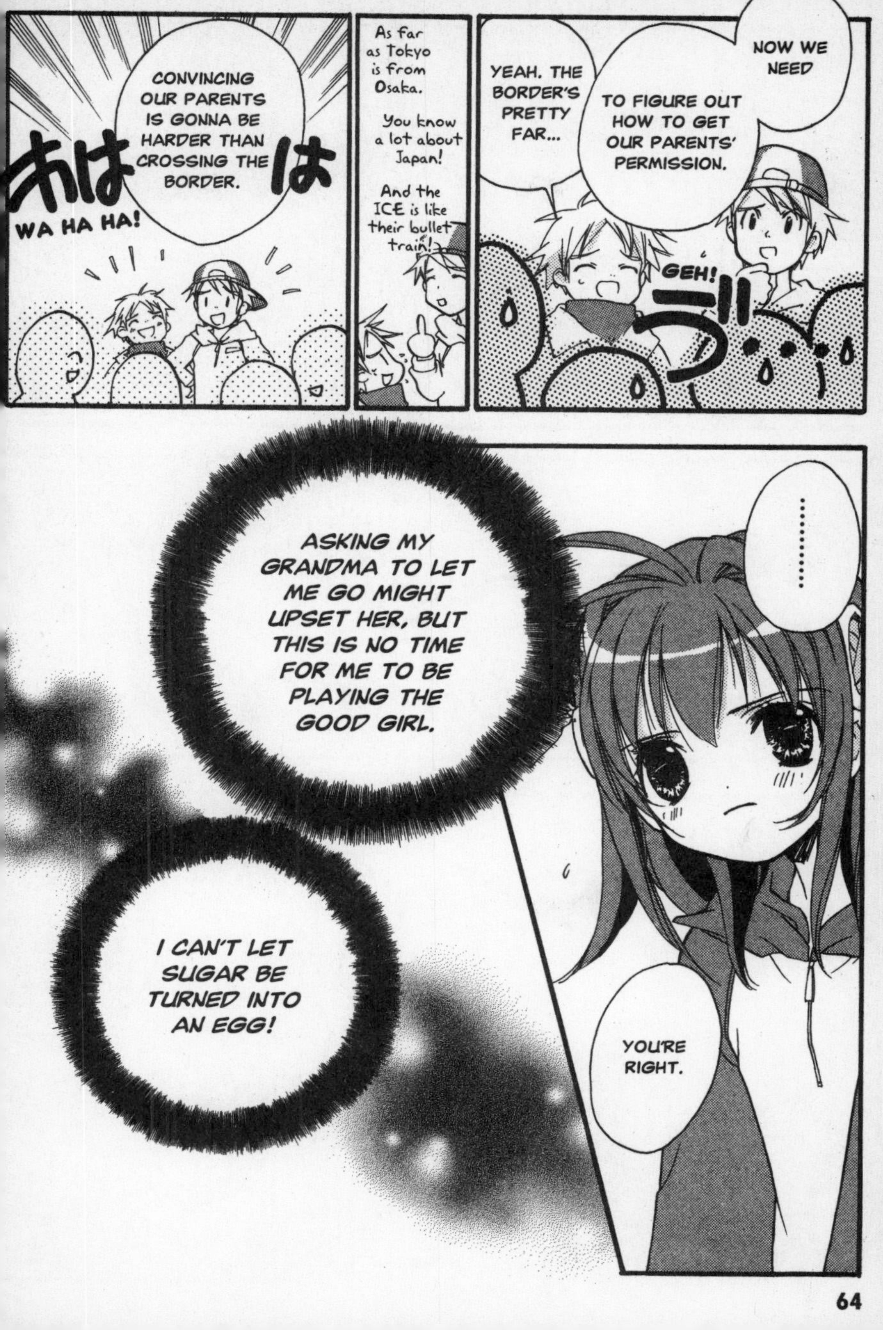

NOW WE NEED
TO FIGURE OUT HOW TO GET OUR PARENTS' PERMISSION.
YEAH. THE BORDER'S PRETTY FAR...
GEH!
う
As far as Tokyo is from Osaka.
You know a lot about Japan!
And the ICE is like their bullet train!
CONVINCING OUR PARENTS IS GONNA BE HARDER THAN CROSSING THE BORDER.
あはは
WA HA HA!
......
ASKING MY GRANDMA TO LET ME GO MIGHT UPSET HER, BUT THIS IS NO TIME FOR ME TO BE PLAYING THE GOOD GIRL.
YOU'RE RIGHT.
I CAN'T LET SUGAR BE TURNED INTO AN EGG!

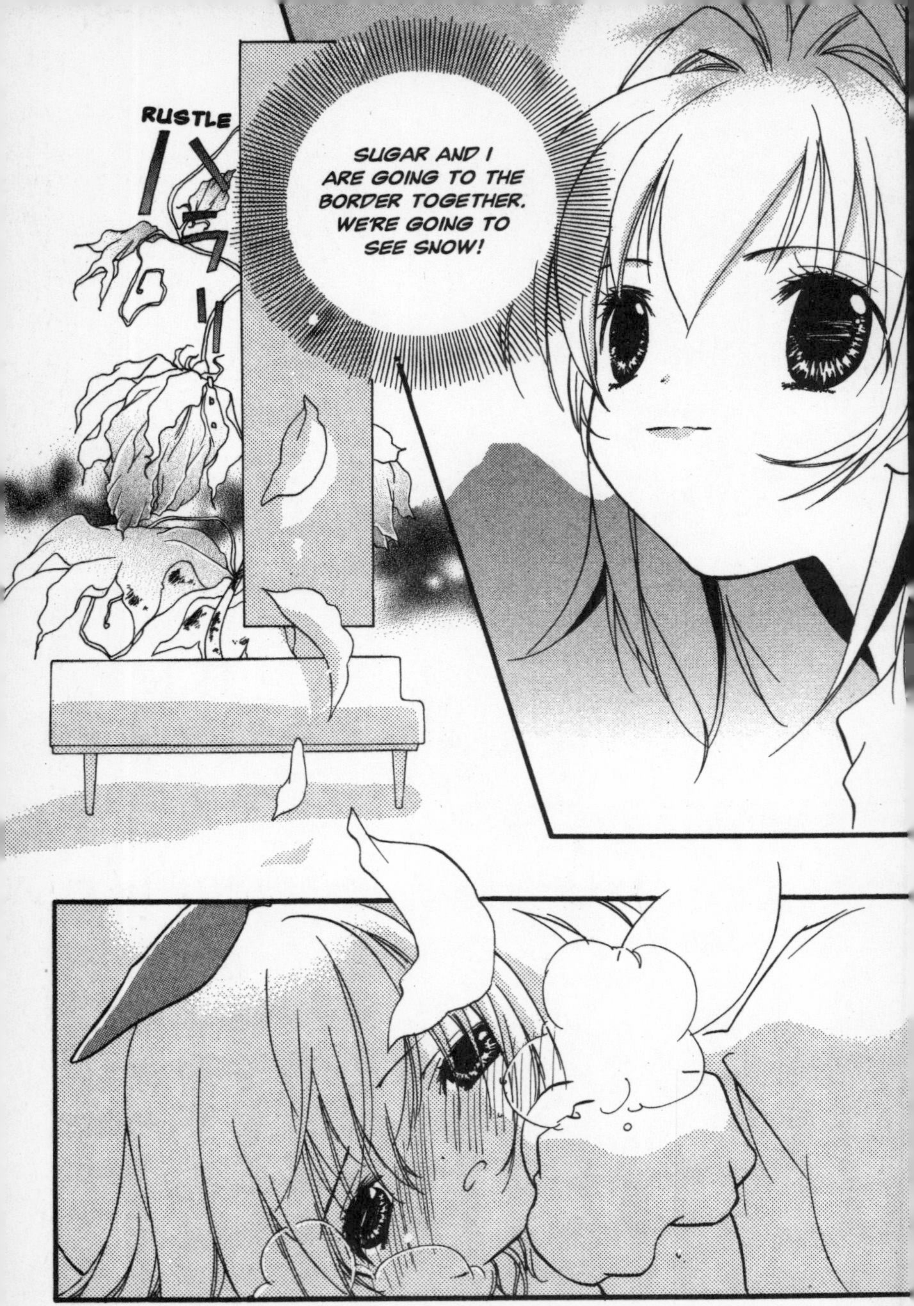
SUGAR AND I ARE GOING TO THE BORDER TOGETHER. WE'RE GOING TO SEE SNOW!
RUSTLE

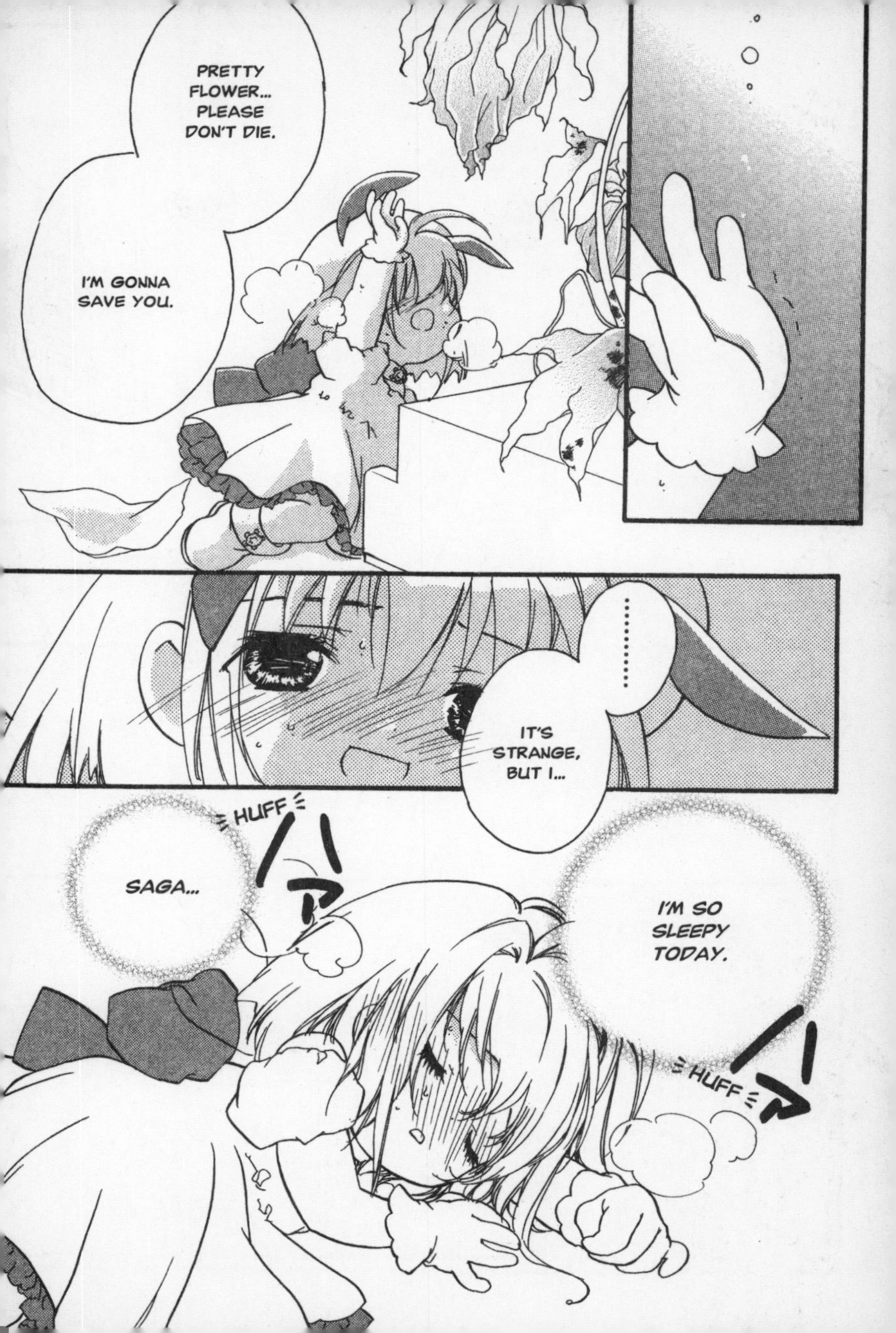
PRETTY FLOWER... PLEASE DON'T DIE.
I'M GONNA SAVE YOU.
......
IT'S STRANGE, BUT I...
I'M SO SLEEPY TODAY.
HUFF
HUFF
SAGA...

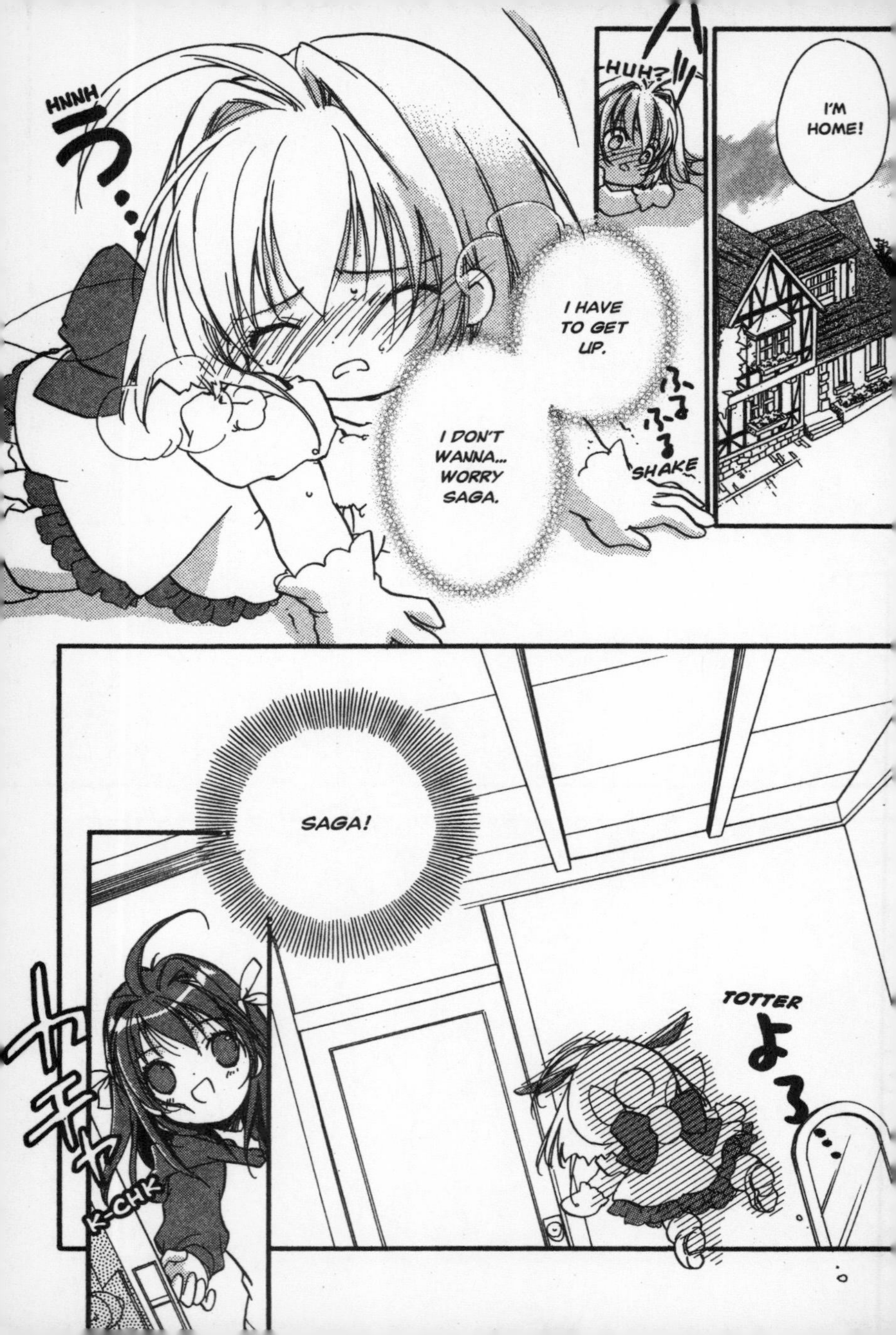
I'M HOME!
HUH?
I HAVE TO GET UP.
ふるふる
SHAKE
I DON'T WANNA... WORRY SAGA.
HNNH
う...
SAGA!
TOTTER
よろ...
カチャ
K-CHK

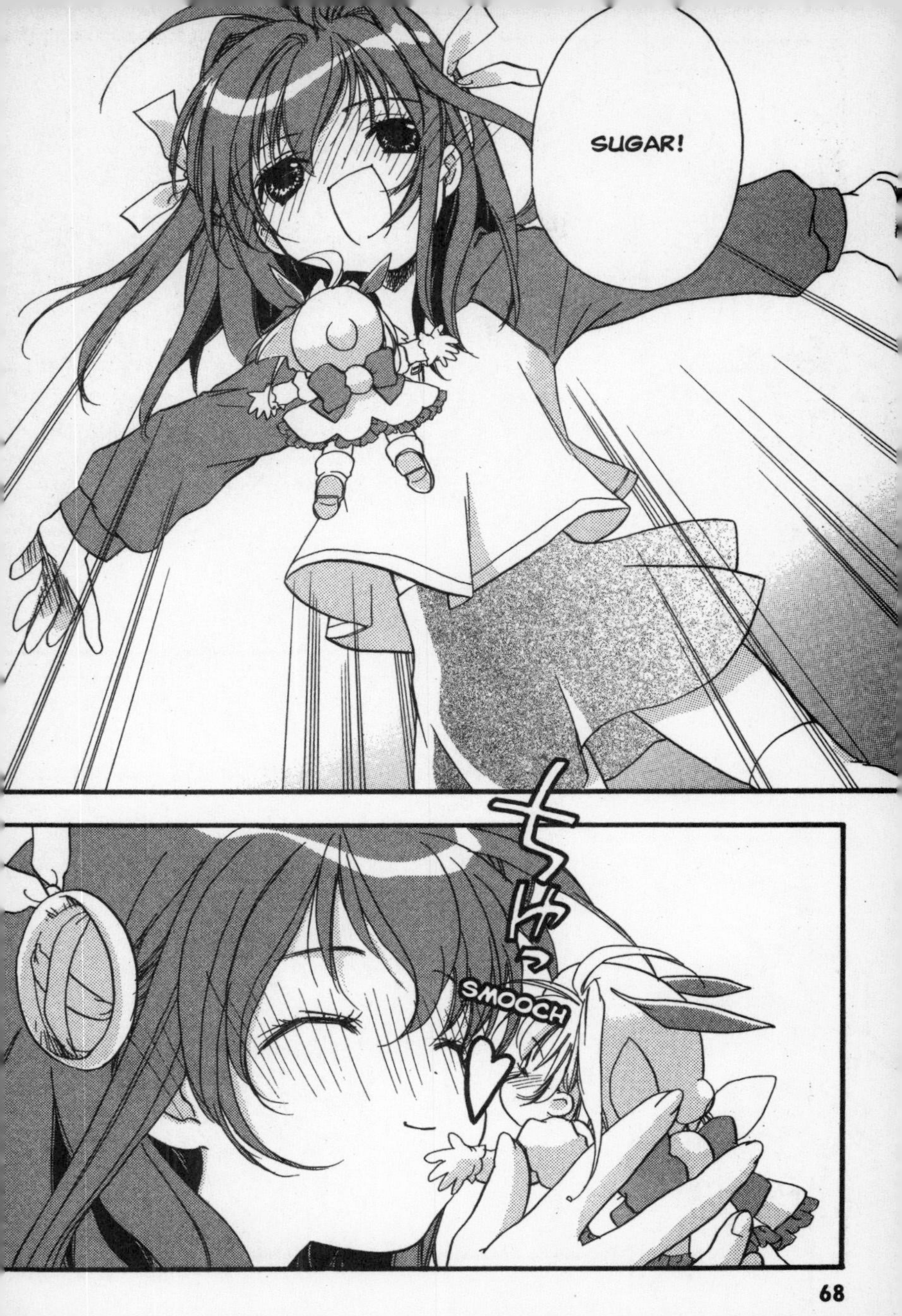
SUGAR!
ちゅっ
SMOOCH

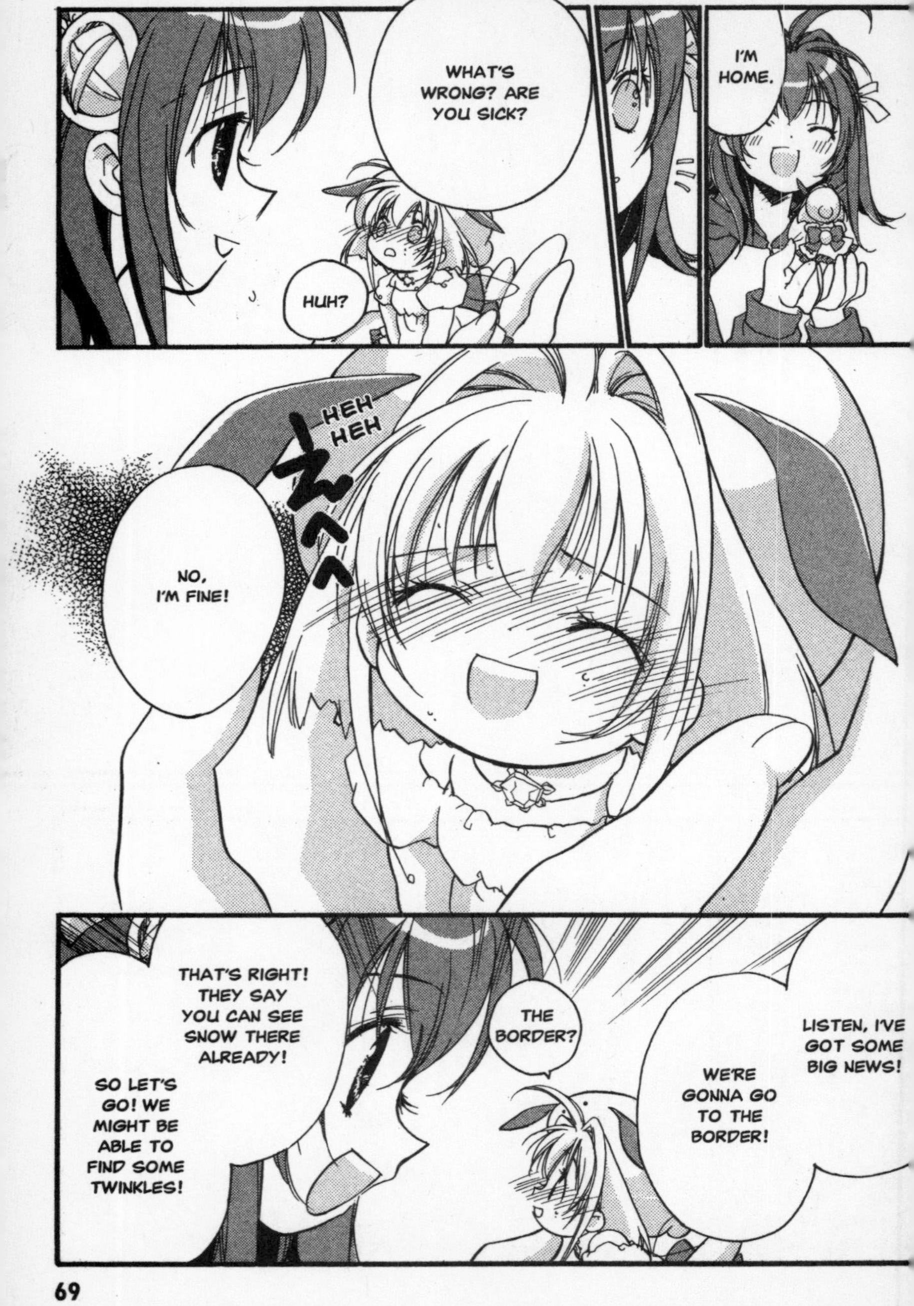
I'M HOME.
WHAT'S WRONG? ARE YOU SICK?
HUH?
HEH HEH
NO, I'M FINE!
LISTEN, I'VE GOT SOME BIG NEWS!
WE'RE GONNA GO TO THE BORDER!
THE BORDER?
THAT'S RIGHT! THEY SAY YOU CAN SEE SNOW THERE ALREADY!
SO LET'S GO! WE MIGHT BE ABLE TO FIND SOME TWINKLES!

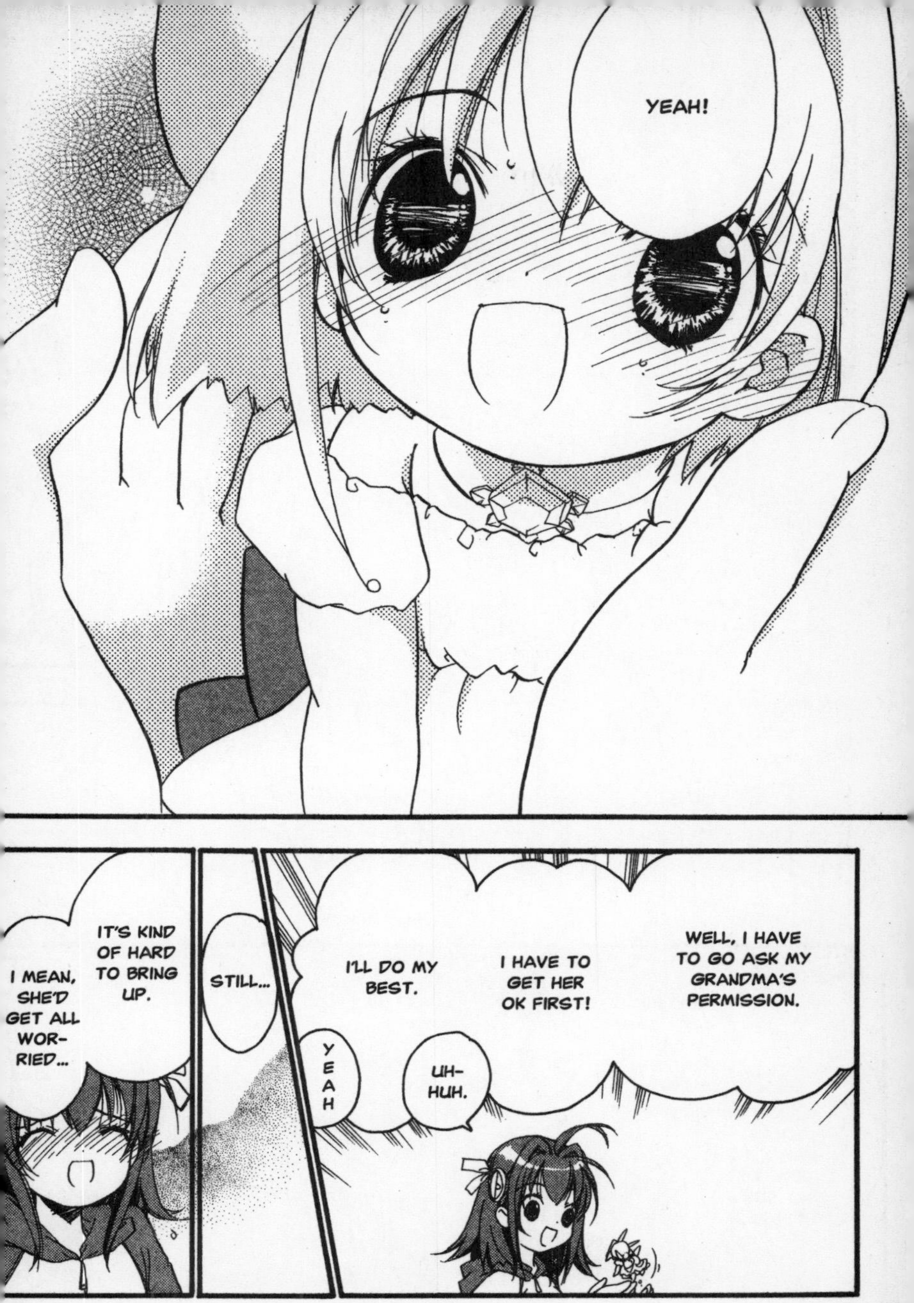
YEAH!
WELL, I HAVE TO GO ASK MY GRANDMA'S PERMISSION.
I HAVE TO GET HER OK FIRST!
I'LL DO MY BEST.
UH-HUH.
YEAH
STILL...
IT'S KIND OF HARD TO BRING UP.
I MEAN, SHE'D GET ALL WOR-RIED...

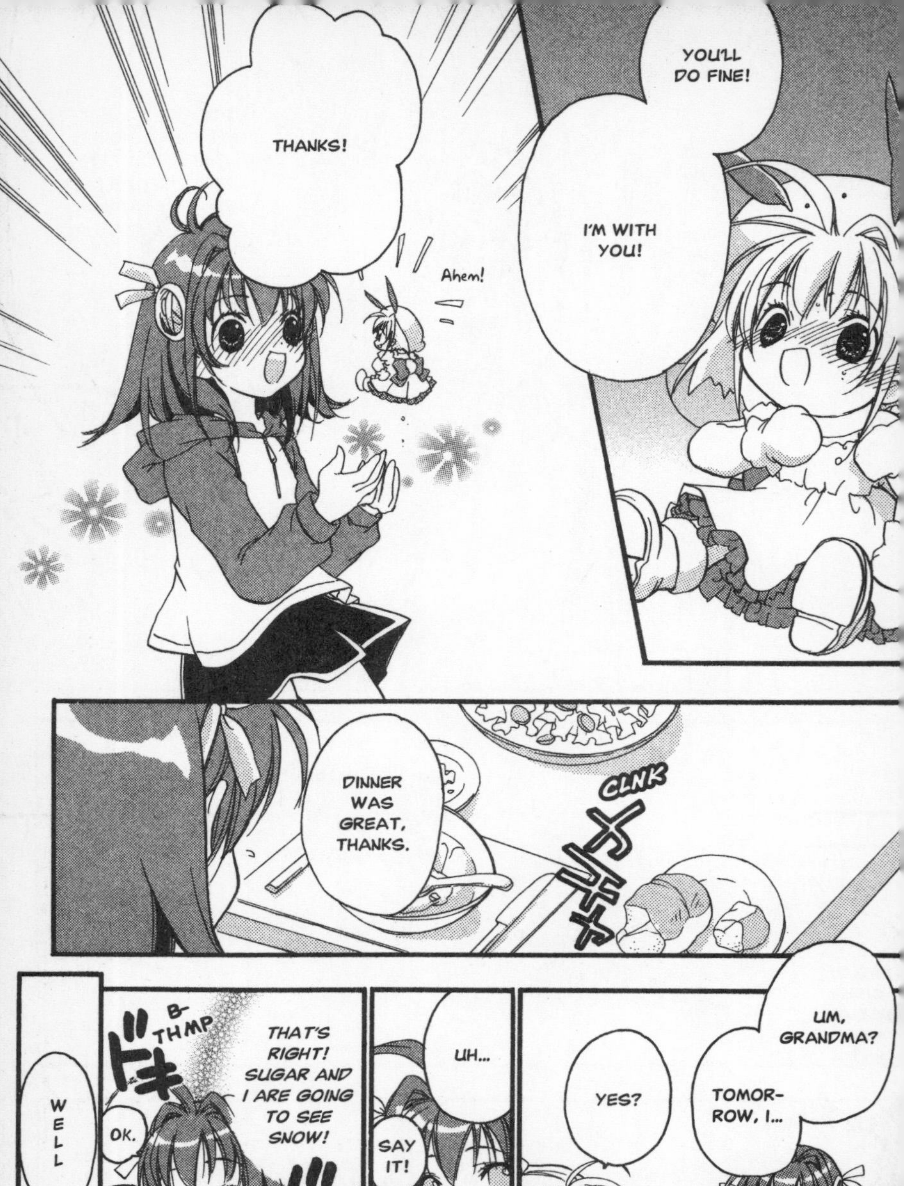
YOU'LL DO FINE!
I'M WITH YOU!
THANKS!
Ahem!
DINNER WAS GREAT, THANKS.
CLNK
UM, GRANDMA?
YES?
TOMOR-ROW, I...
UH...
SAY IT!
THAT'S RIGHT! SUGAR AND I ARE GOING TO SEE SNOW!
B-THMP
OK.
Ha!
B-THMP
WELL

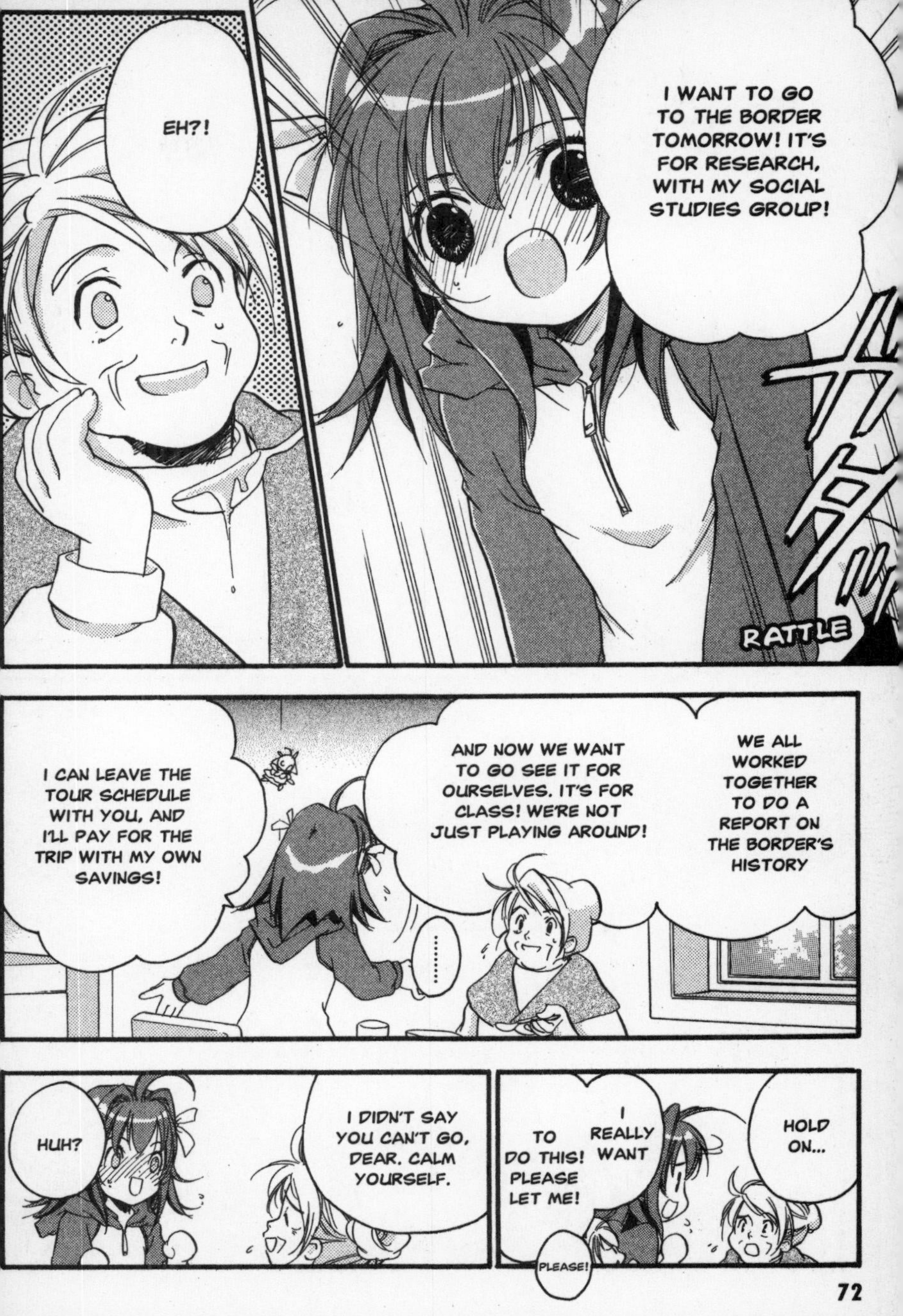

I WANT TO GO TO THE BORDER TOMORROW! IT'S FOR RESEARCH, WITH MY SOCIAL STUDIES GROUP!
RATTLE
EH?!
WE ALL WORKED TOGETHER TO DO A REPORT ON THE BORDER'S HISTORY
AND NOW WE WANT TO GO SEE IT FOR OURSELVES. IT'S FOR CLASS! WE'RE NOT JUST PLAYING AROUND!
I CAN LEAVE THE TOUR SCHEDULE WITH YOU, AND I'LL PAY FOR THE TRIP WITH MY OWN SAVINGS!
....
HOLD ON...
I REALLY WANT TO DO THIS! PLEASE LET ME!
PLEASE!
I DIDN'T SAY YOU CAN'T GO, DEAR. CALM YOURSELF.
HUH?

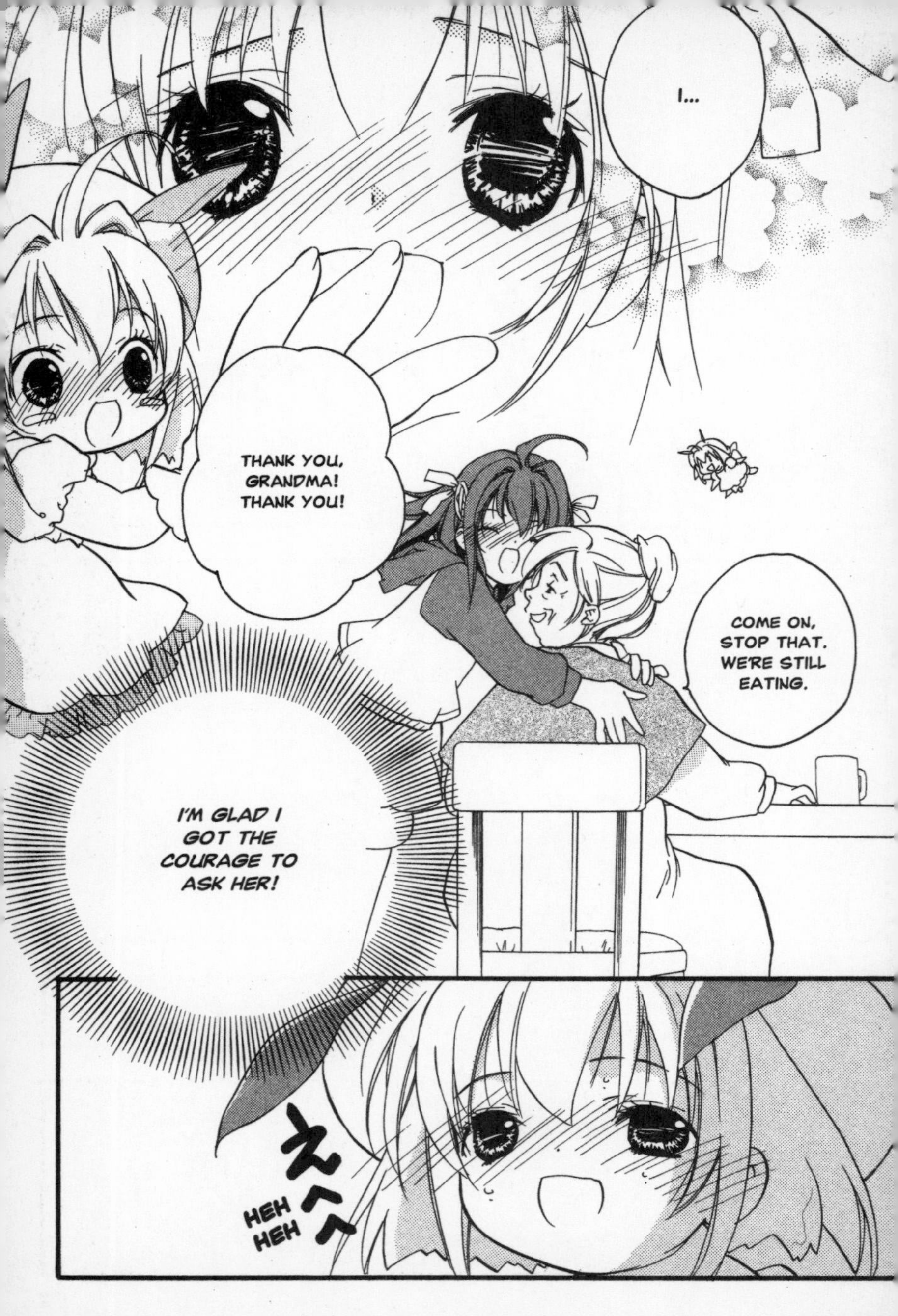
I...
THANK YOU, GRANDMA! THANK YOU!
COME ON, STOP THAT. WE'RE STILL EATING.
I'M GLAD I GOT THE COURAGE TO ASK HER!
えへへ
HEH HEH

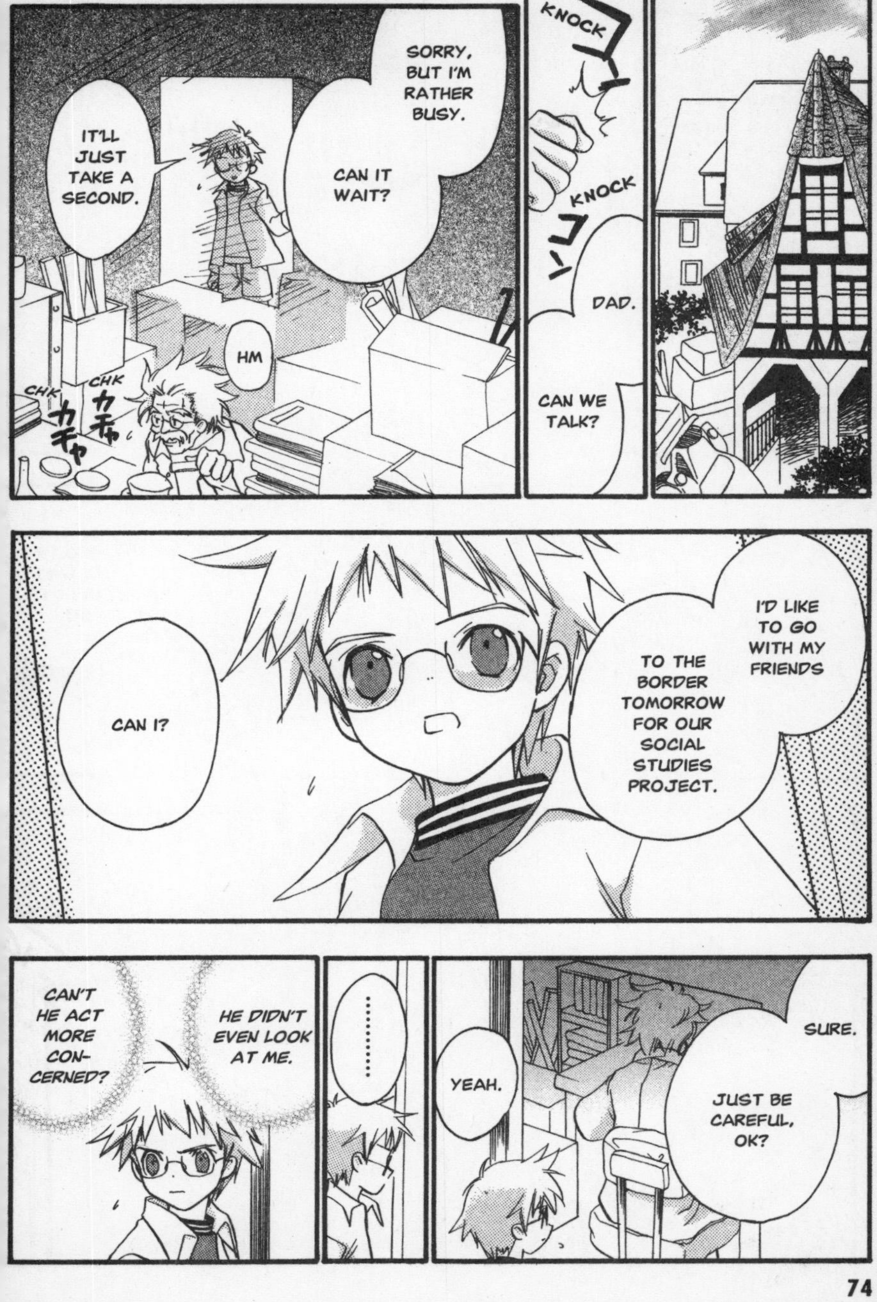
KNOCK
KNOCK
コンコン
DAD.
CAN WE TALK?
SORRY, BUT I'M RATHER BUSY.
CAN IT WAIT?
IT'LL JUST TAKE A SECOND.
HM
CHK カチャ
CHK カチャ
I'D LIKE TO GO WITH MY FRIENDS
TO THE BORDER TOMORROW FOR OUR SOCIAL STUDIES PROJECT.
CAN I?
SURE.
JUST BE CAREFUL, OK?
YEAH.
....
HE DIDN'T EVEN LOOK AT ME.
CAN'T HE ACT MORE CON-CERNED?

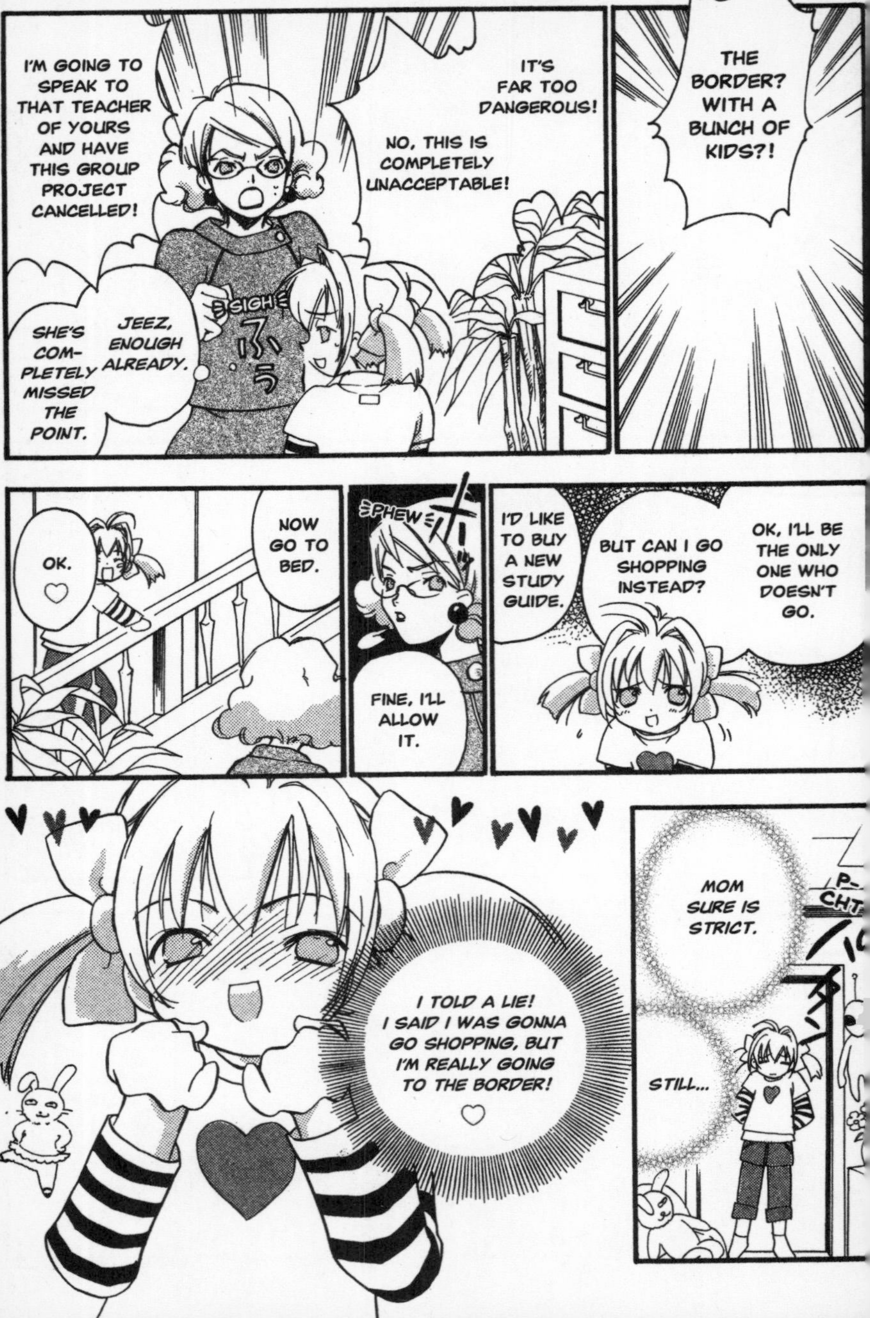
THE BORDER? WITH A BUNCH OF KIDS?!
IT'S FAR TOO DANGEROUS!
NO, THIS IS COMPLETELY UNACCEPTABLE!
I'M GOING TO SPEAK TO THAT TEACHER OF YOURS AND HAVE THIS GROUP PROJECT CANCELLED!
SIGH
JEEZ, ENOUGH ALREADY.
SHE'S COM-PLETELY MISSED THE POINT.
OK, I'LL BE THE ONLY ONE WHO DOESN'T GO.
BUT CAN I GO SHOPPING INSTEAD?
I'D LIKE TO BUY A NEW STUDY GUIDE.
PHEW
FINE, I'LL ALLOW IT.
NOW GO TO BED.
OK. ♡
P-CHT
MOM SURE IS STRICT.
STILL...
I TOLD A LIE! I SAID I WAS GONNA GO SHOPPING, BUT I'M REALLY GOING TO THE BORDER! ♡

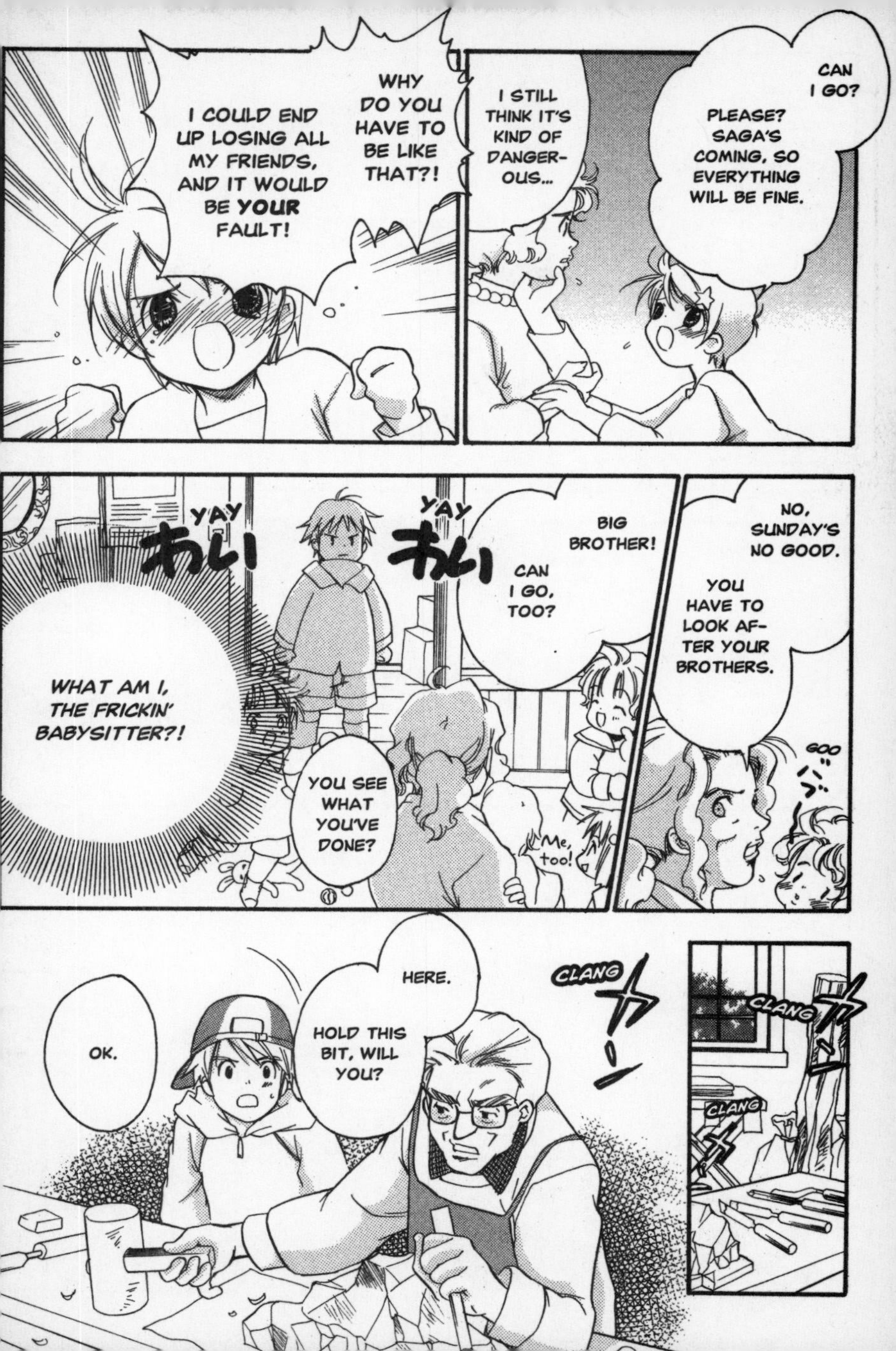
CAN I GO?
PLEASE? SAGA'S COMING, SO EVERYTHING WILL BE FINE.
I STILL THINK IT'S KIND OF DANGER-OUS...
WHY DO YOU HAVE TO BE LIKE THAT?!
I COULD END UP LOSING ALL MY FRIENDS, AND IT WOULD BE **YOUR** FAULT!
NO, SUNDAY'S NO GOOD.
YOU HAVE TO LOOK AF-TER YOUR BROTHERS.
GOO
BIG BROTHER!
CAN I GO, TOO?
YAY
YAY
Me, too!
YOU SEE WHAT YOU'VE DONE?
WHAT AM I, THE FRICKIN' BABYSITTER?!
CLANG
CLANG
CLANG
HERE.
HOLD THIS BIT, WILL YOU?
OK.

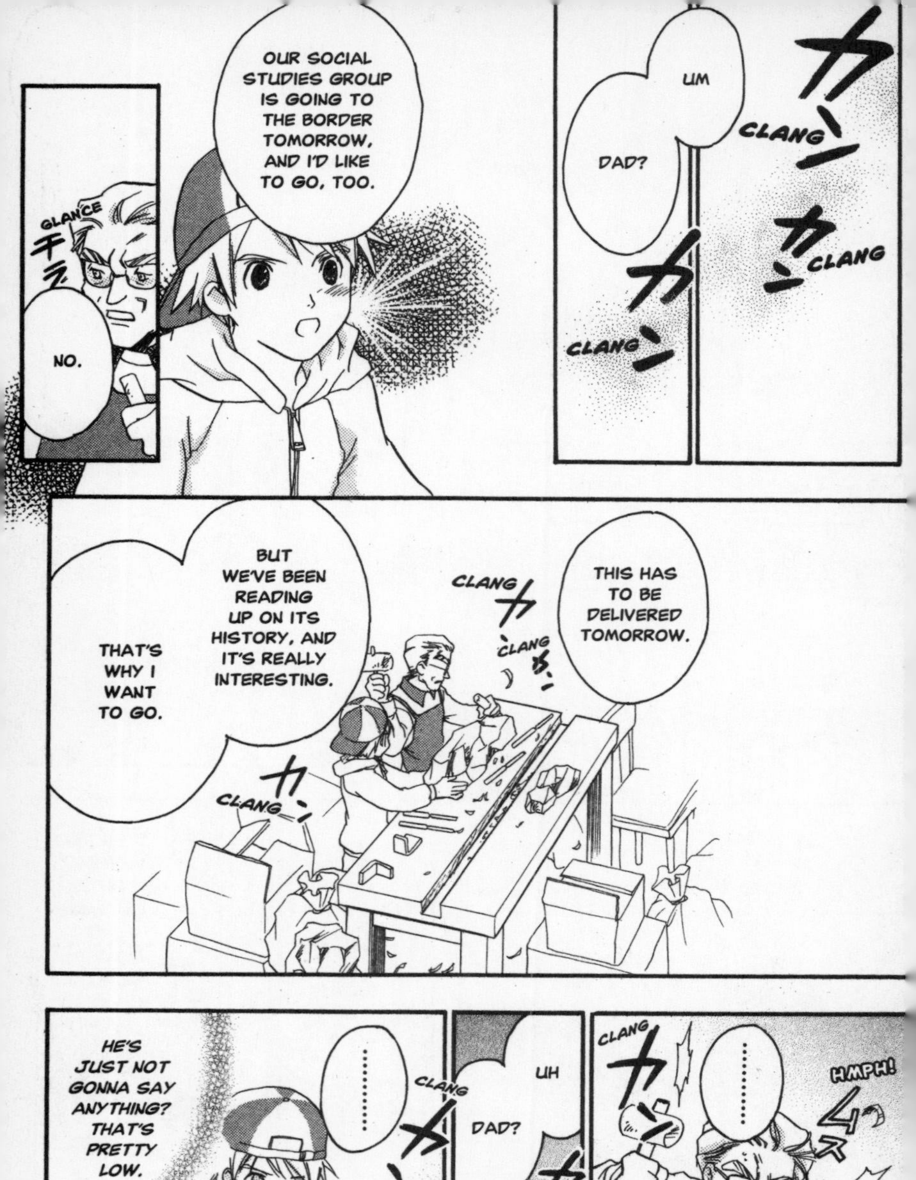
CLANG
CLANG
CLANG
UM
DAD?
OUR SOCIAL STUDIES GROUP IS GOING TO THE BORDER TOMORROW, AND I'D LIKE TO GO, TOO.
GLANCE
NO.
THIS HAS TO BE DELIVERED TOMORROW.
CLANG
CLANG
BUT WE'VE BEEN READING UP ON ITS HISTORY, AND IT'S REALLY INTERESTING.
THAT'S WHY I WANT TO GO.
CLANG
CLANG
......
HMPH!
CLANG
UH
DAD?
CLANG
......
CLANG
HE'S JUST NOT GONNA SAY ANYTHING? THAT'S PRETTY LOW.
CLANG

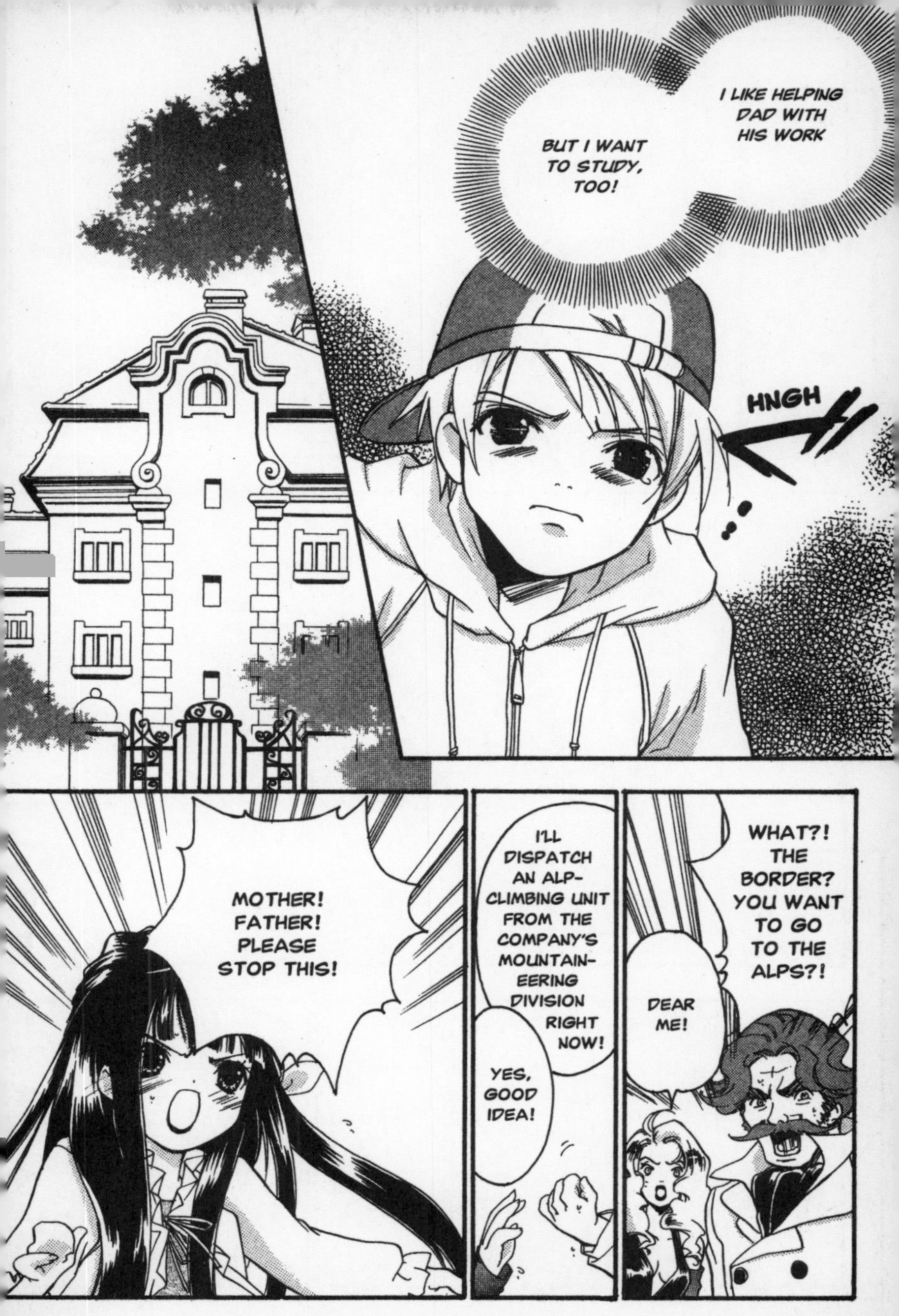
I LIKE HELPING DAD WITH HIS WORK
BUT I WANT TO STUDY, TOO!
HNGH
WHAT?! THE BORDER? YOU WANT TO GO TO THE ALPS?!
DEAR ME!
I'LL DISPATCH AN ALP-CLIMBING UNIT FROM THE COMPANY'S MOUNTAIN-EERING DIVISION RIGHT NOW!
YES, GOOD IDEA!
MOTHER! FATHER! PLEASE STOP THIS!

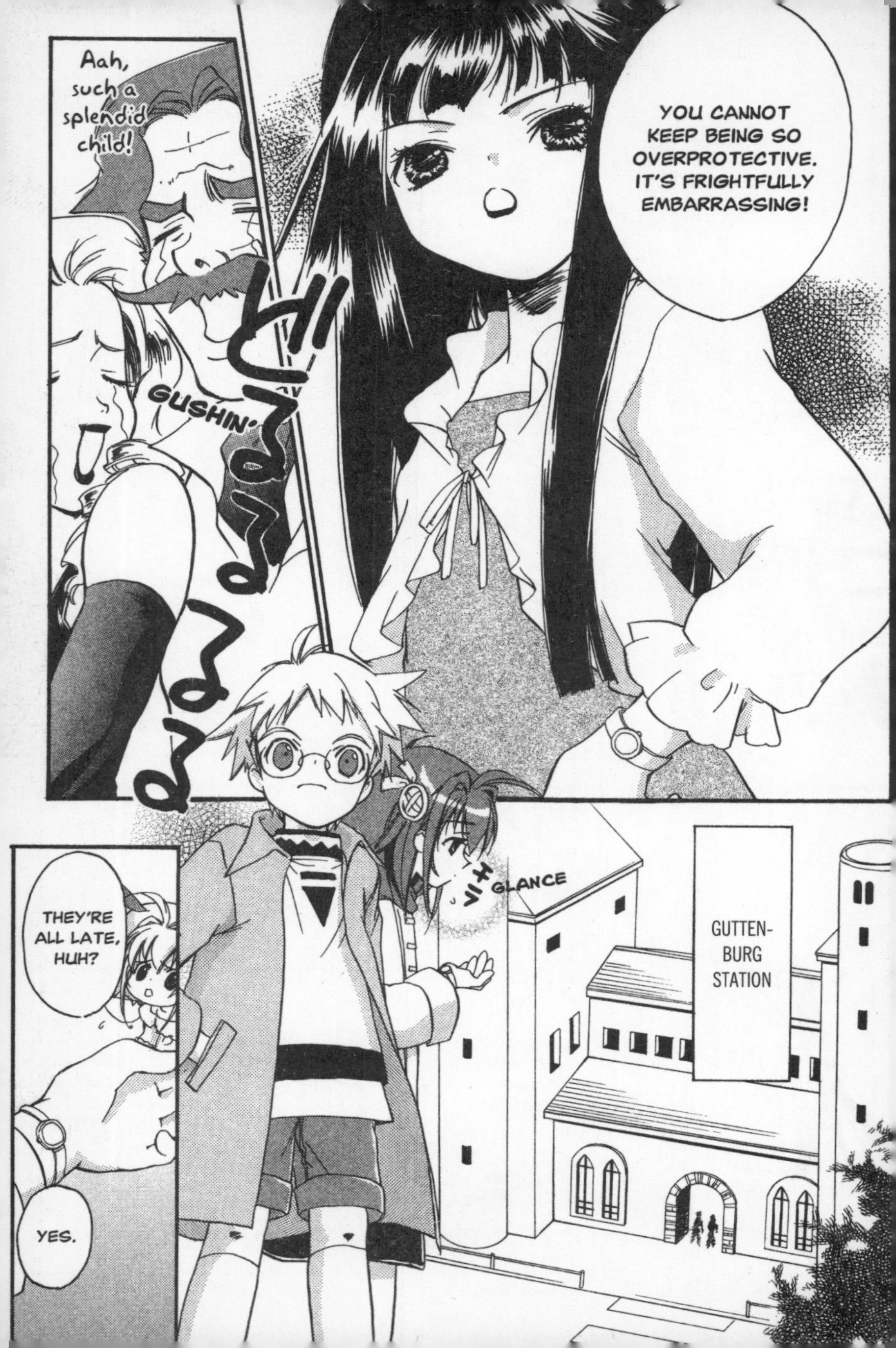
YOU CANNOT KEEP BEING SO OVERPROTECTIVE. IT'S FRIGHTFULLY EMBARRASSING!
Aah, such a splendid child!
GUSHIN
GUTTEN-BURG STATION
GLANCE
THEY'RE ALL LATE, HUH?
YES.

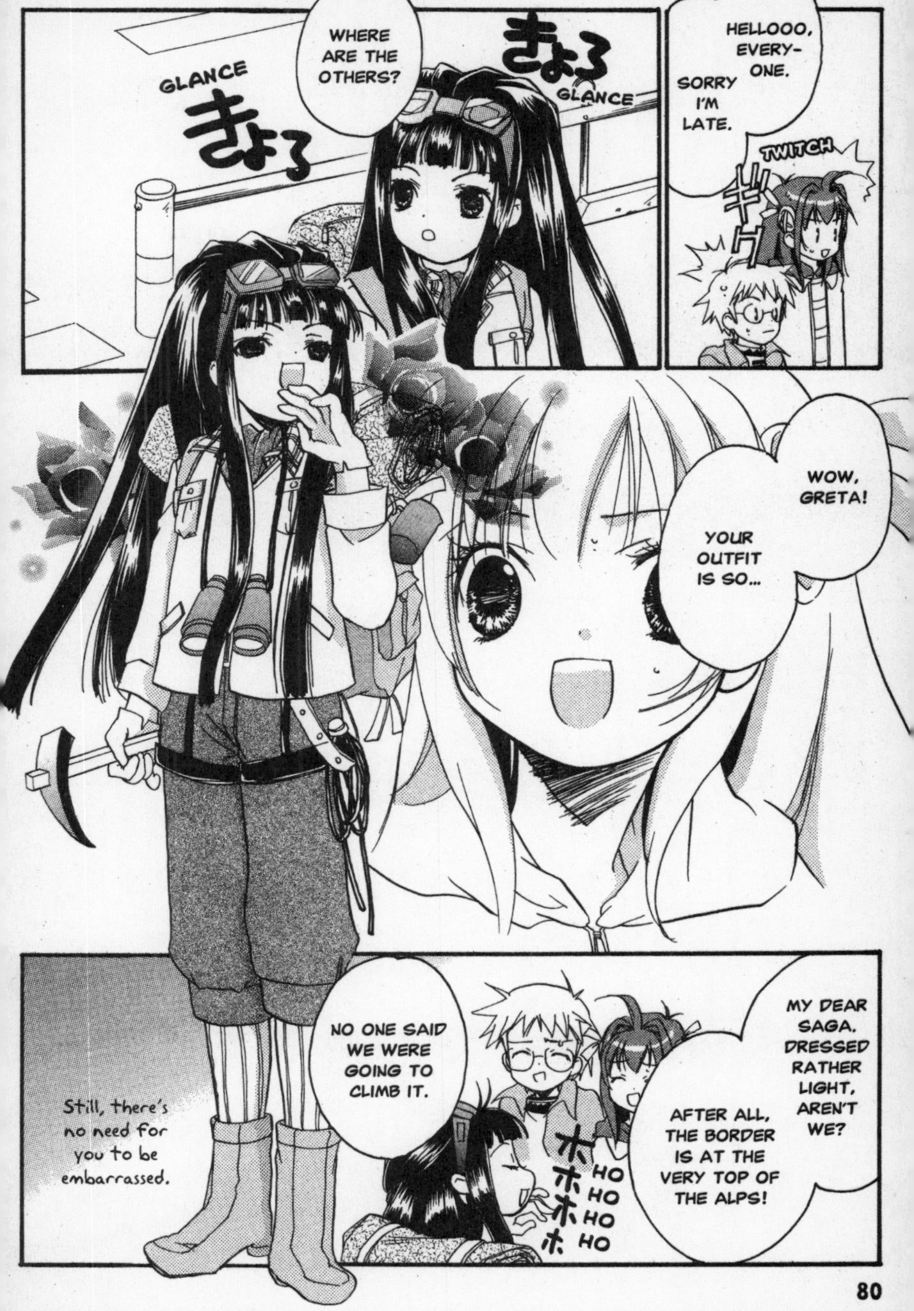
HELLOOO, EVERY-ONE.
SORRY I'M LATE.
TWITCH
ギクッ
WHERE ARE THE OTHERS?
きょろ
GLANCE
きょろ
GLANCE
WOW, GRETA!
YOUR OUTFIT IS SO...
MY DEAR SAGA. DRESSED RATHER LIGHT, AREN'T WE?
AFTER ALL, THE BORDER IS AT THE VERY TOP OF THE ALPS!
NO ONE SAID WE WERE GOING TO CLIMB IT.
ホホホホ
HO HO HO HO
Still, there's no need for you to be embarrassed.

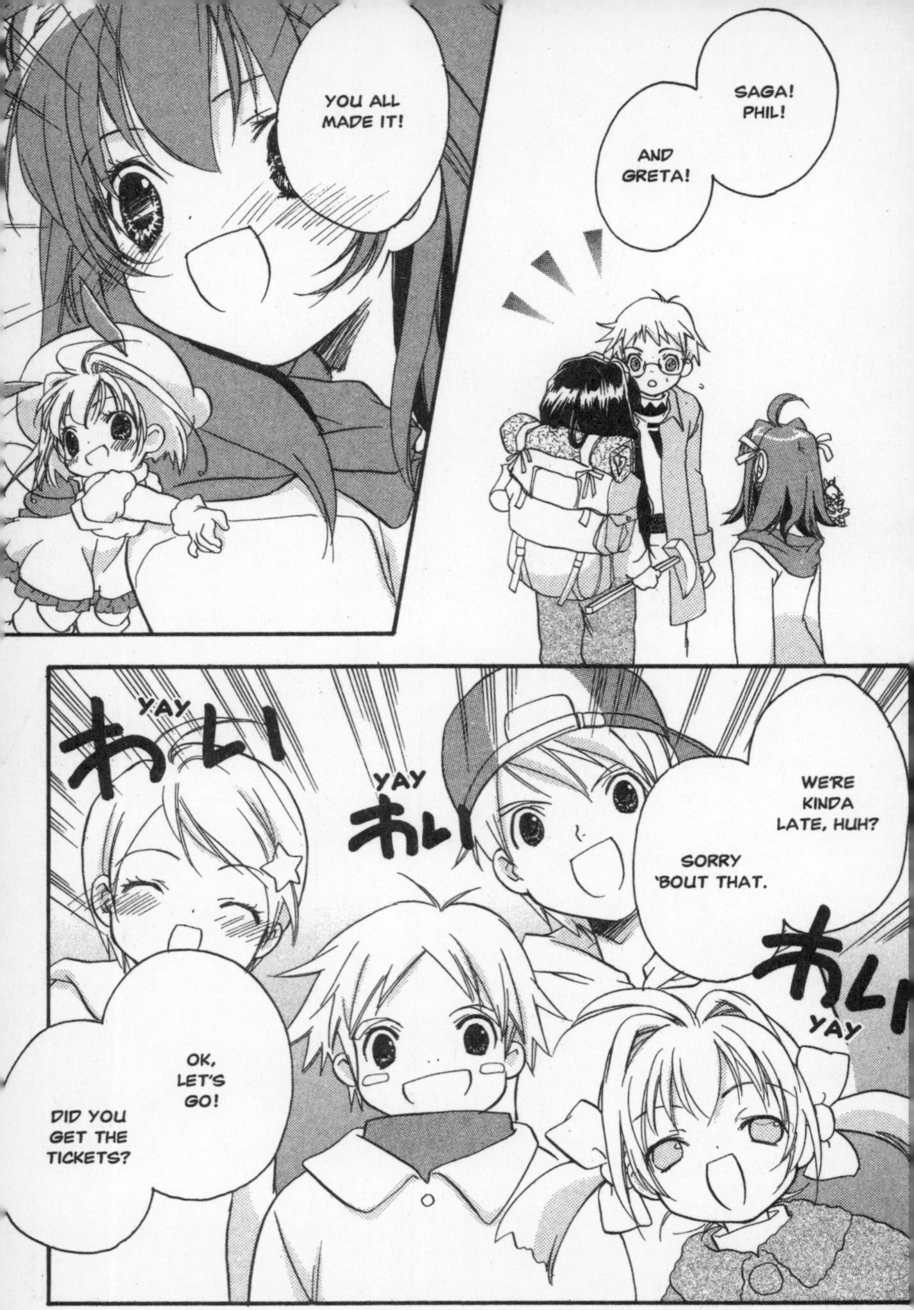
SAGA! PHIL!
AND GRETA!
YOU ALL MADE IT!
WE'RE KINDA LATE, HUH?
SORRY 'BOUT THAT.
YAY
YAY
YAY
OK, LET'S GO!
DID YOU GET THE TICKETS?

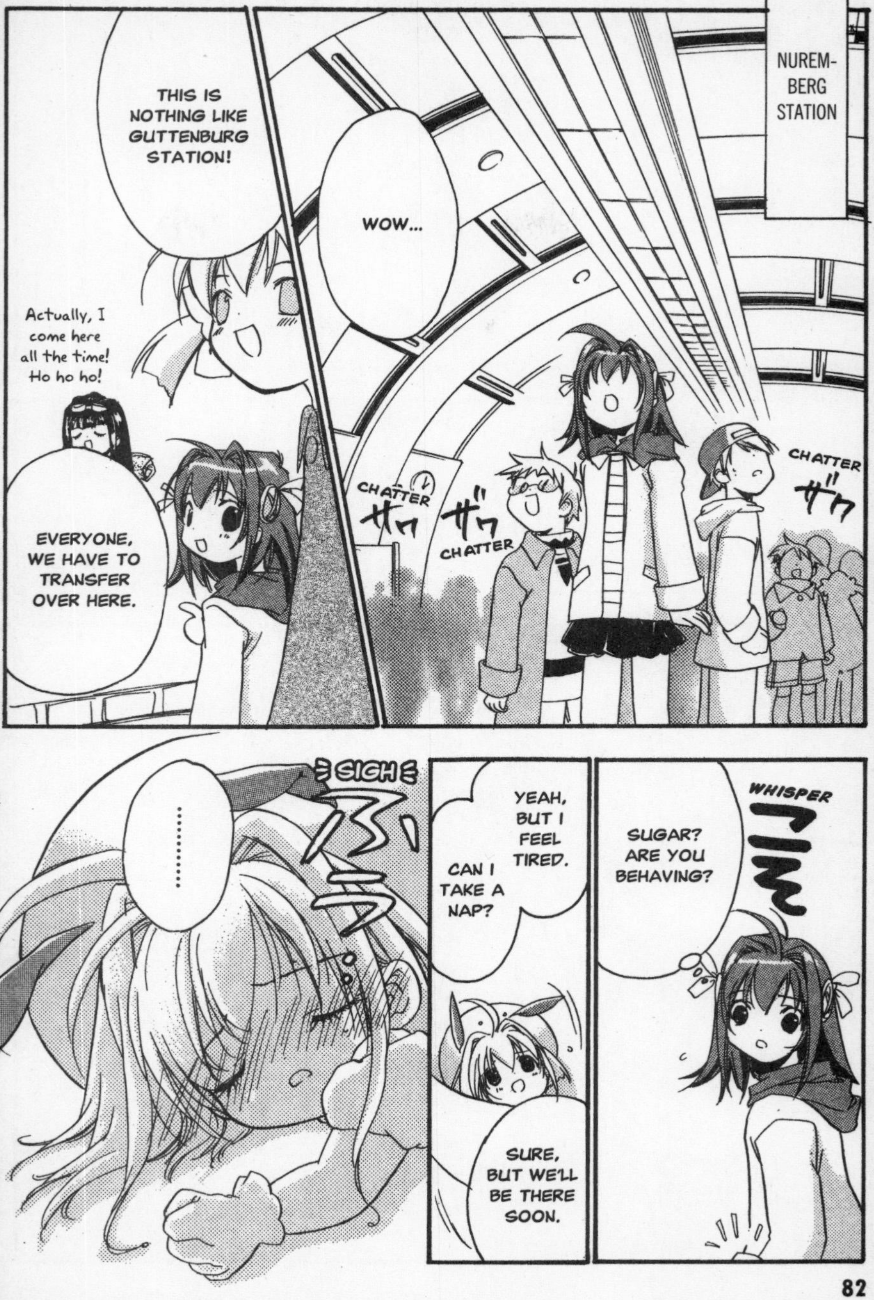
NUREMBERG STATION
WOW...
CHATTER
CHATTER
CHATTER
THIS IS NOTHING LIKE GUTTENBURG STATION!
Actually, I come here all the time! Ho ho ho!
EVERYONE, WE HAVE TO TRANSFER OVER HERE.
WHISPER
SUGAR? ARE YOU BEHAVING?
YEAH, BUT I FEEL TIRED.
CAN I TAKE A NAP?
SURE, BUT WE'LL BE THERE SOON.
SIGH
....

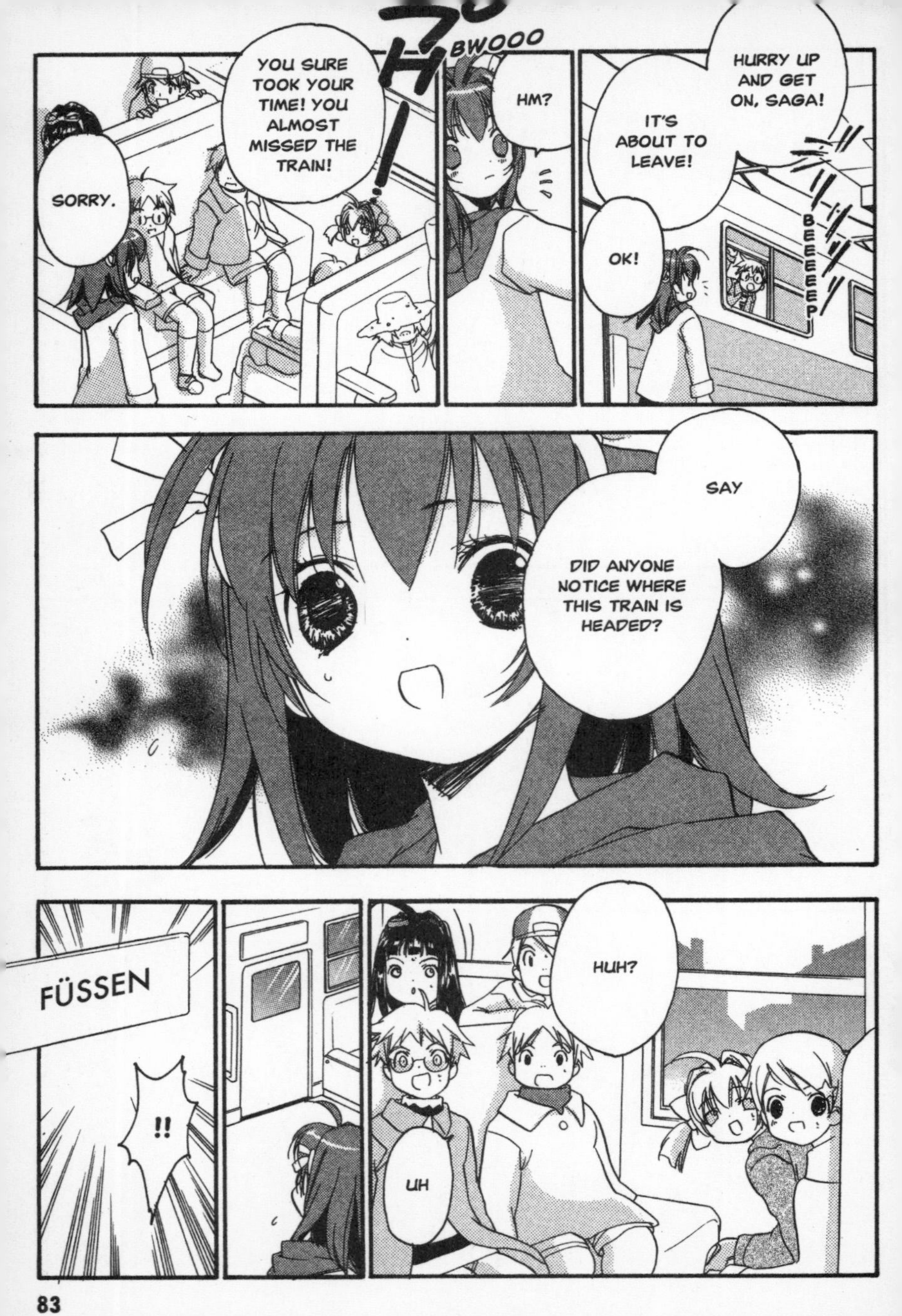
HURRY UP AND GET ON, SAGA!
IT'S ABOUT TO LEAVE!
OK!
BEEEEEEP
BWOOO
HM?
YOU SURE TOOK YOUR TIME! YOU ALMOST MISSED THE TRAIN!
SORRY.
SAY
DID ANYONE NOTICE WHERE THIS TRAIN IS HEADED?
HUH?
UH
FÜSSEN
!!

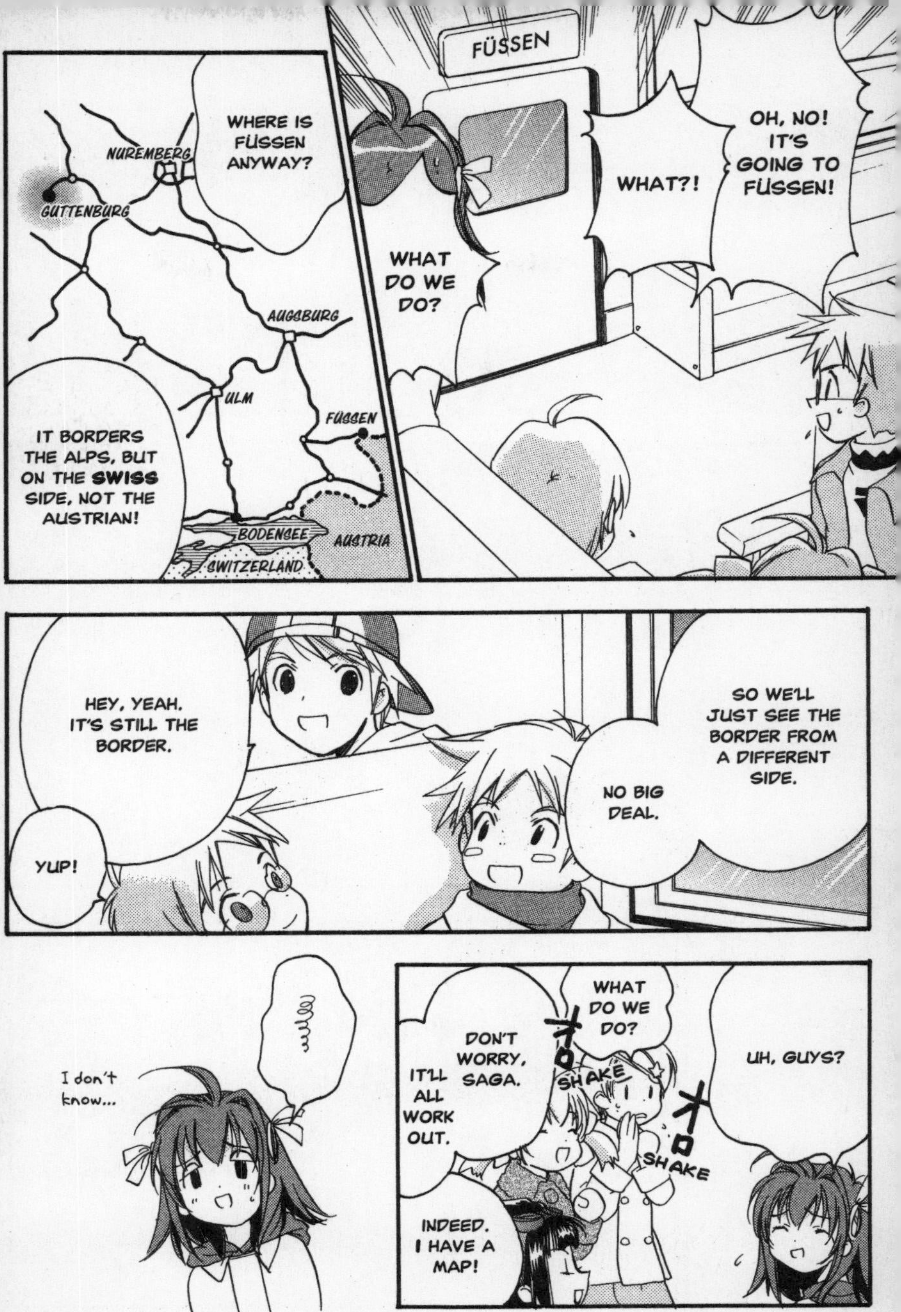
FÜSSEN
OH, NO! IT'S GOING TO FÜSSEN!
WHAT?!
WHAT DO WE DO?
WHERE IS FÜSSEN ANYWAY?
NUREMBERG
GUTTENBURG
AUGSBURG
ULM
FÜSSEN
BODENSEE
AUSTRIA
SWITZERLAND
IT BORDERS THE ALPS, BUT ON THE **SWISS** SIDE, NOT THE AUSTRIAN!
SO WE'LL JUST SEE THE BORDER FROM A DIFFERENT SIDE.
NO BIG DEAL.
HEY, YEAH. IT'S STILL THE BORDER.
YUP!
UH, GUYS?
WHAT DO WE DO?
SHAKE
SHAKE
DON'T WORRY, SAGA.
IT'LL ALL WORK OUT.
INDEED. I HAVE A MAP!
I don't know...

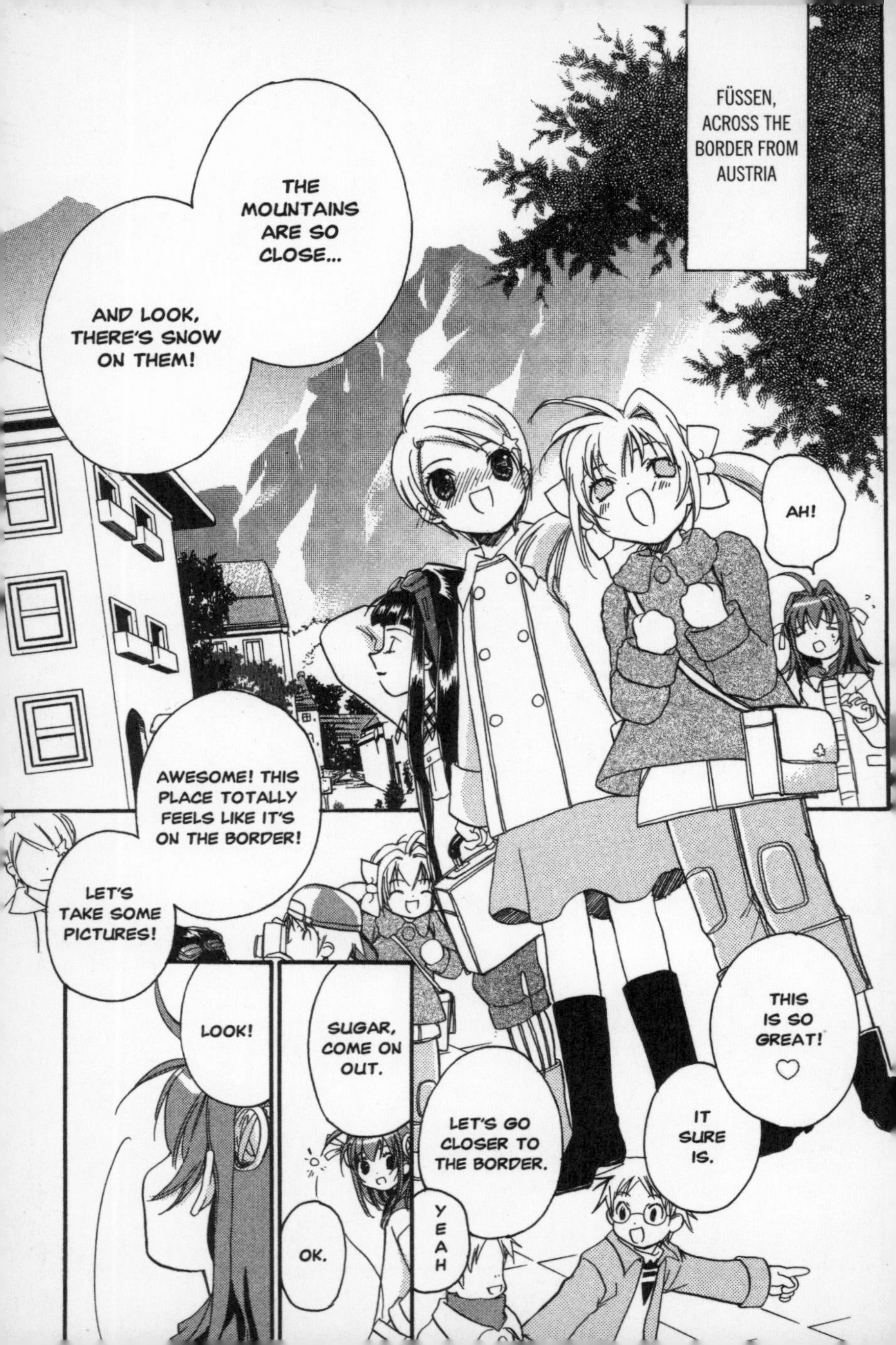
FÜSSEN, ACROSS THE BORDER FROM AUSTRIA
AH!
THE MOUNTAINS ARE SO CLOSE...
AND LOOK, THERE'S SNOW ON THEM!
THIS IS SO GREAT! ♡
IT SURE IS.
LET'S GO CLOSER TO THE BORDER.
YEAH
AWESOME! THIS PLACE TOTALLY FEELS LIKE IT'S ON THE BORDER!
LET'S TAKE SOME PICTURES!
SUGAR, COME ON OUT.
OK.
LOOK!

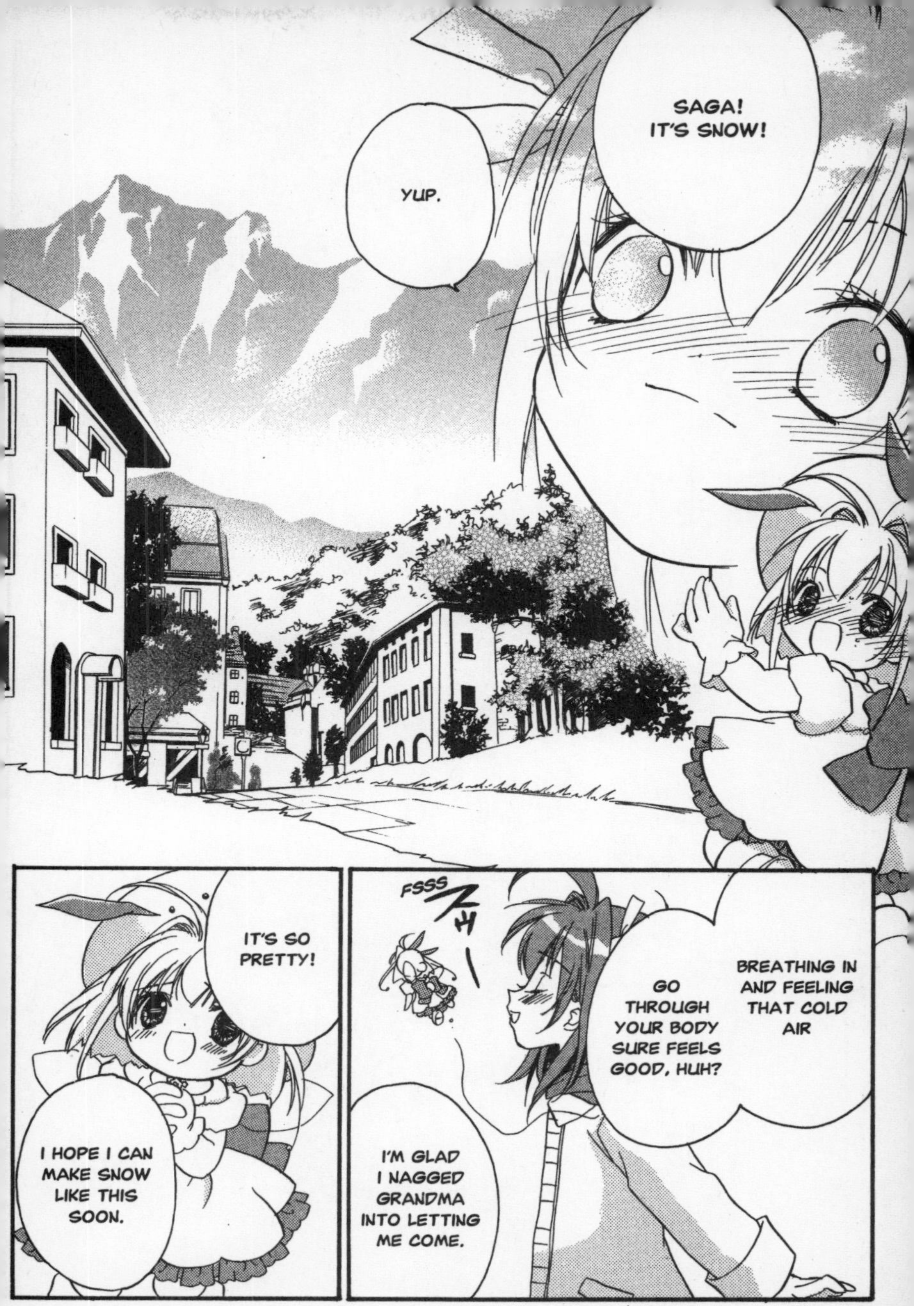
SAGA! IT'S SNOW!
YUP.
BREATHING IN AND FEELING THAT COLD AIR
GO THROUGH YOUR BODY SURE FEELS GOOD, HUH?
FSSS
I'M GLAD I NAGGED GRANDMA INTO LETTING ME COME.
IT'S SO PRETTY!
I HOPE I CAN MAKE SNOW LIKE THIS SOON.

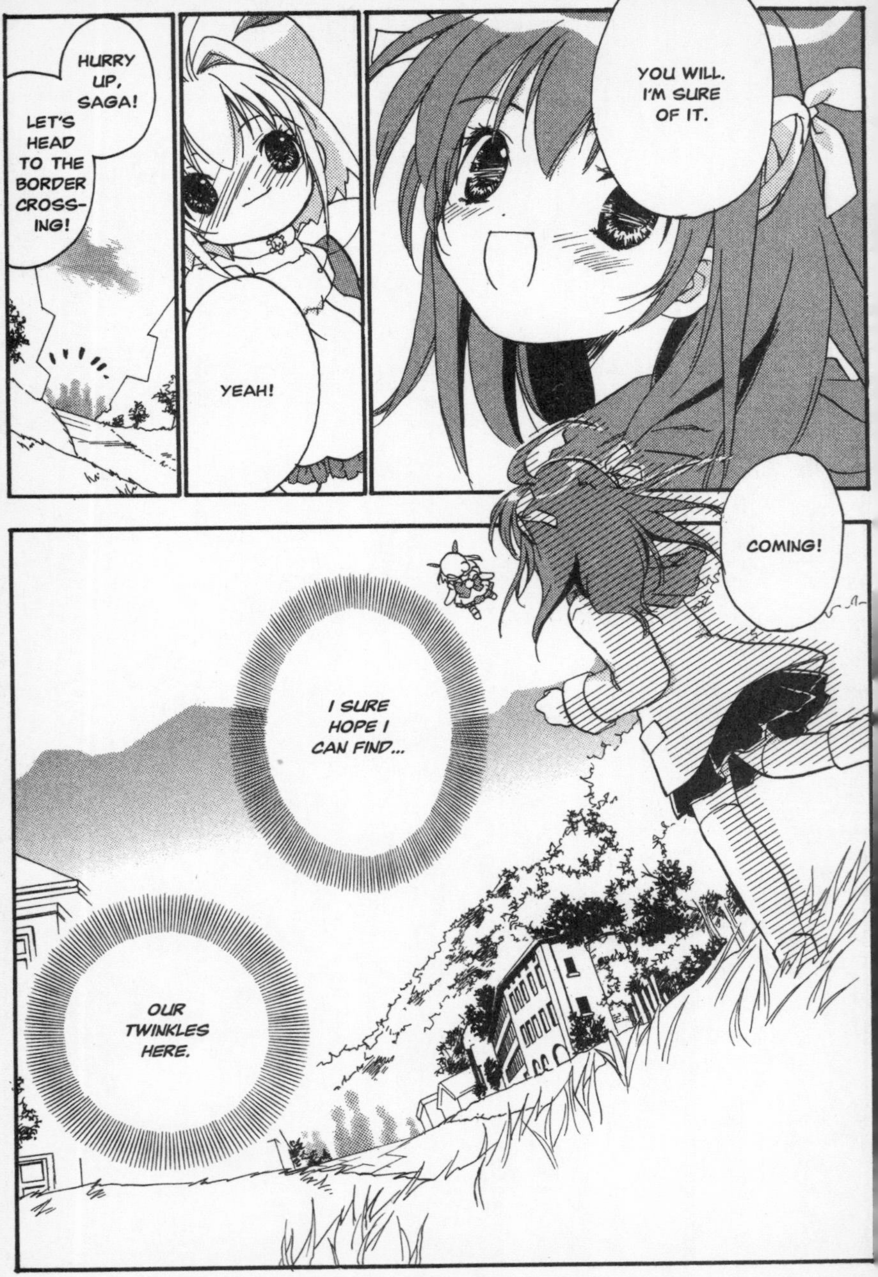
YOU WILL. I'M SURE OF IT.
YEAH!
HURRY UP, SAGA! LET'S HEAD TO THE BORDER CROSSING!
COMING!
I SURE HOPE I CAN FIND...
OUR TWINKLES HERE.

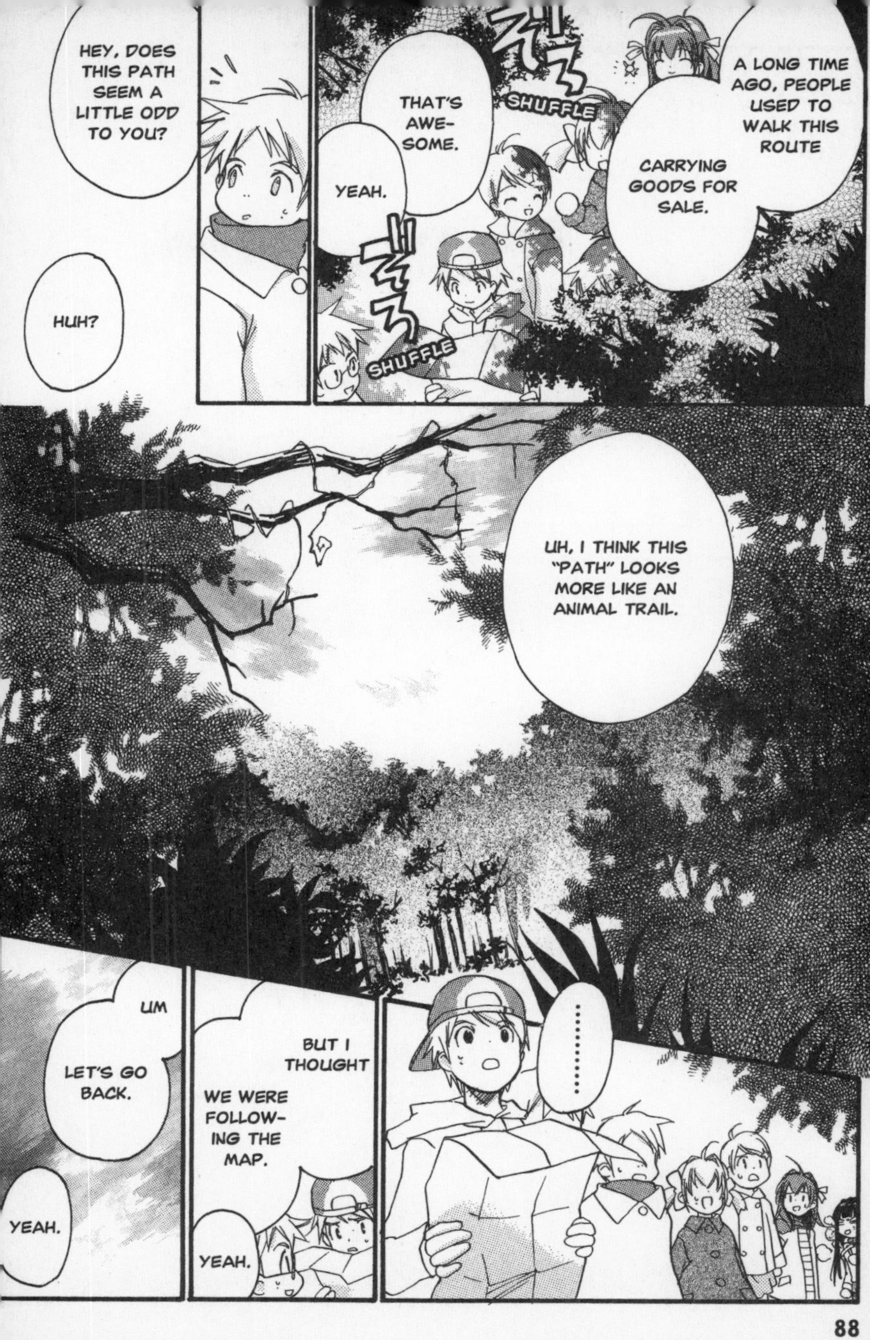
A LONG TIME AGO, PEOPLE USED TO WALK THIS ROUTE
CARRYING GOODS FOR SALE.
SHUFFLE
THAT'S AWE-SOME.
YEAH.
SHUFFLE
HEY, DOES THIS PATH SEEM A LITTLE ODD TO YOU?
HUH?
UH, I THINK THIS "PATH" LOOKS MORE LIKE AN ANIMAL TRAIL.
......
BUT I THOUGHT
WE WERE FOLLOW-ING THE MAP.
YEAH.
UM
LET'S GO BACK.
YEAH.

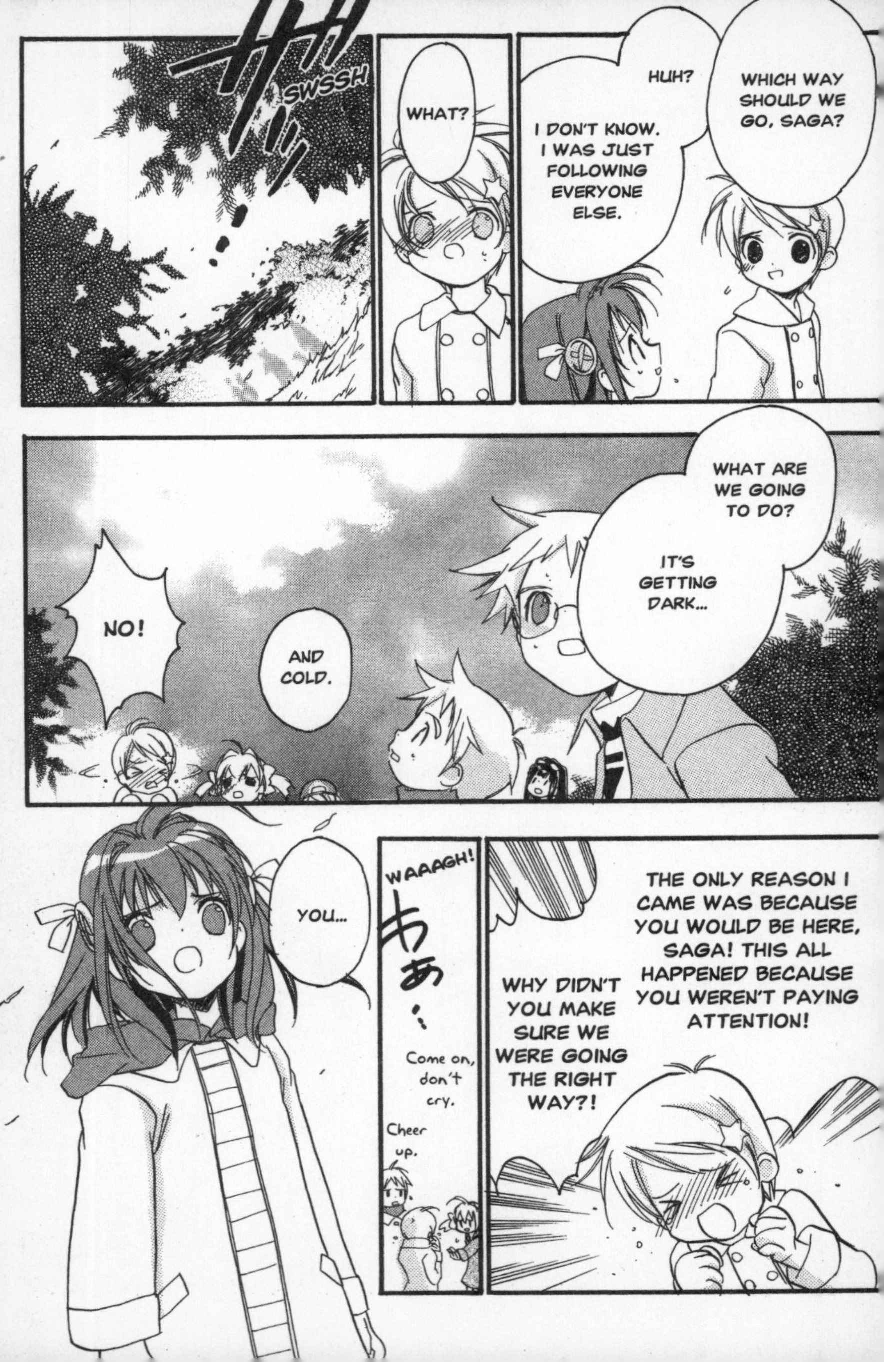
WHICH WAY SHOULD WE GO, SAGA?
HUH?
I DON'T KNOW. I WAS JUST FOLLOWING EVERYONE ELSE.
WHAT?
SWSSH
WHAT ARE WE GOING TO DO?
IT'S GETTING DARK...
AND COLD.
NO!
THE ONLY REASON I CAME WAS BECAUSE YOU WOULD BE HERE, SAGA! THIS ALL HAPPENED BECAUSE YOU WEREN'T PAYING ATTENTION!
WHY DIDN'T YOU MAKE SURE WE WERE GOING THE RIGHT WAY?!
WAAAGH!
やあ
Come on, don't cry.
Cheer up.
YOU...

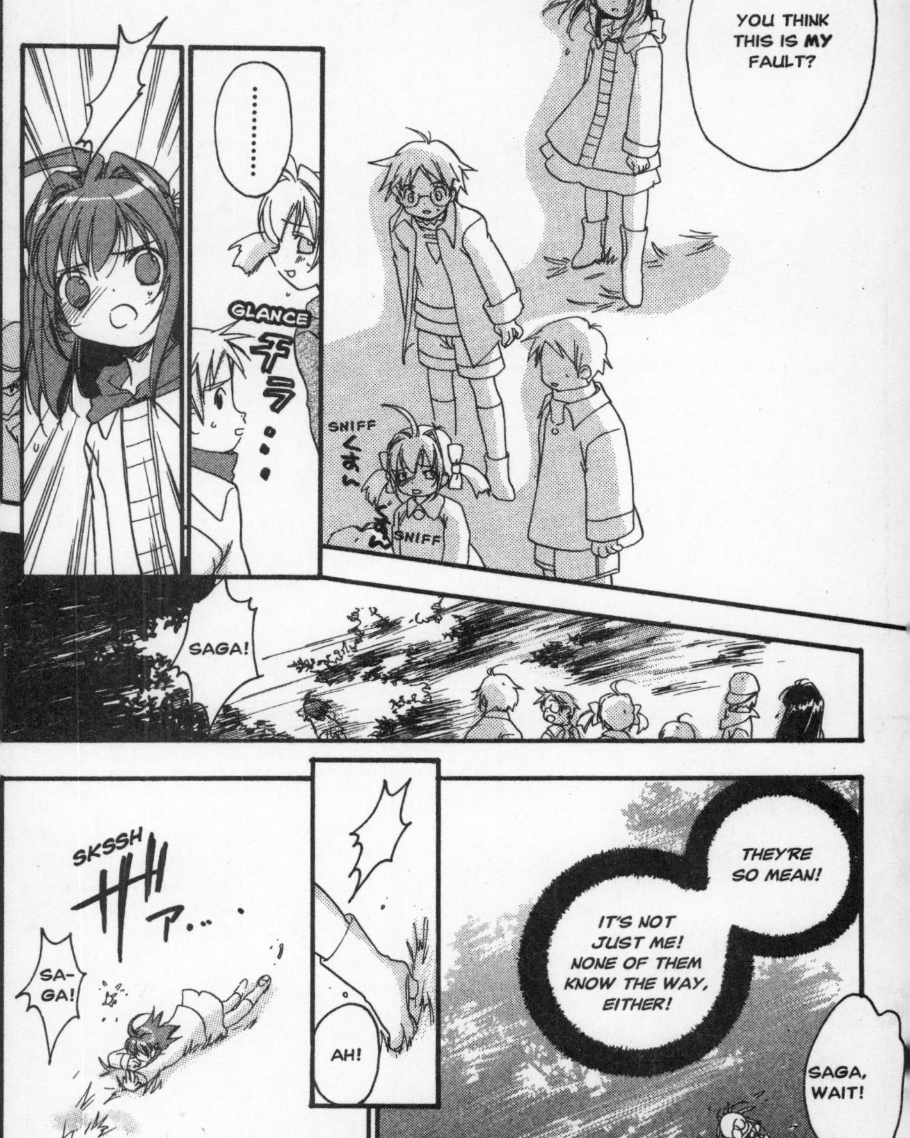
YOU THINK THIS IS MY FAULT?
SNIFF
くすん
SNIFF
......
GLANCE
チラ...
SAGA!
THEY'RE SO MEAN!
IT'S NOT JUST ME! NONE OF THEM KNOW THE WAY, EITHER!
SAGA, WAIT!
AH!
SKSSH
ザア...
SA-GA!

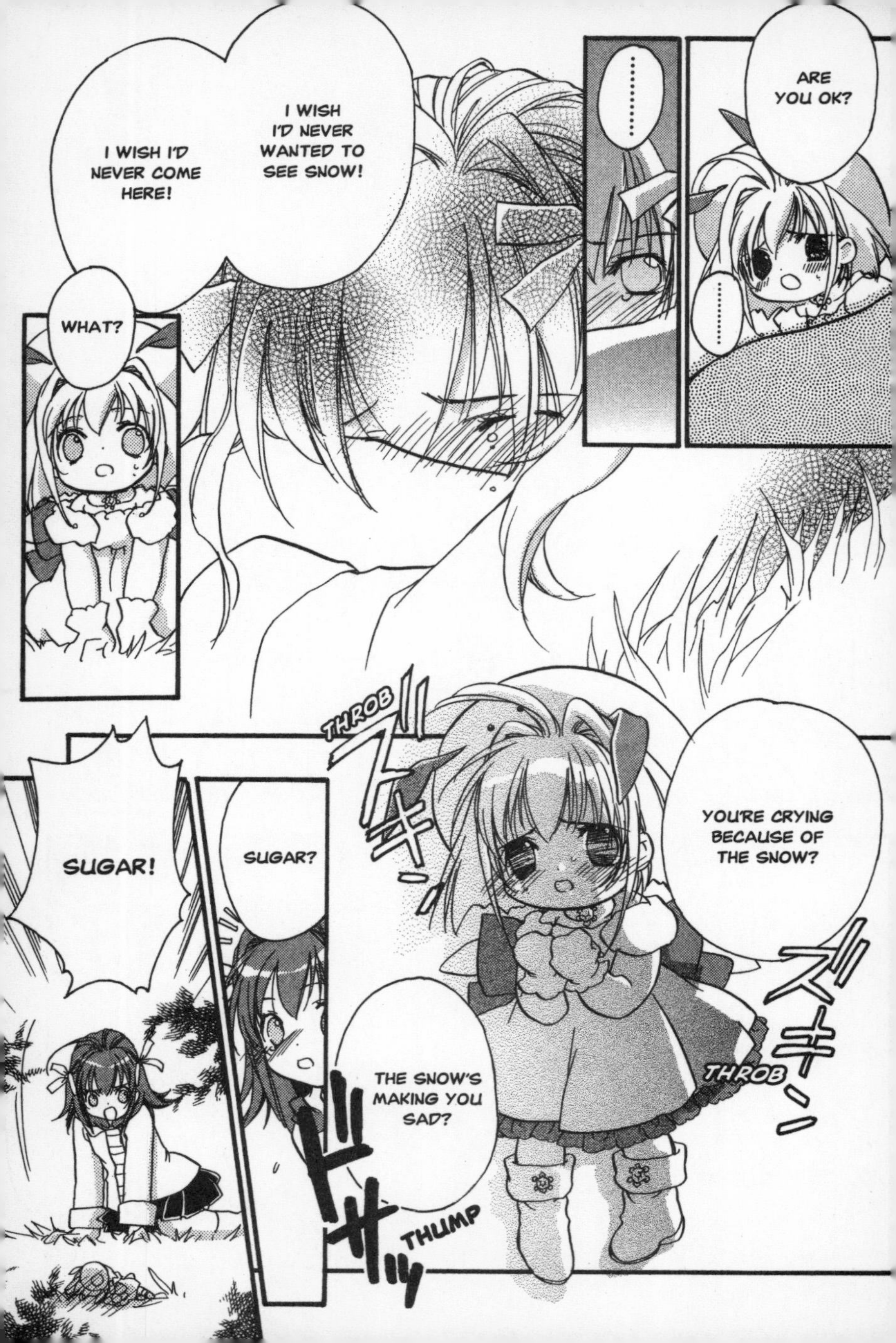
ARE YOU OK?
......
......
I WISH I'D NEVER WANTED TO SEE SNOW!
I WISH I'D NEVER COME HERE!
WHAT?
THROB
YOU'RE CRYING BECAUSE OF THE SNOW?
THROB
THE SNOW'S MAKING YOU SAD?
THUMP
SUGAR?
SUGAR!

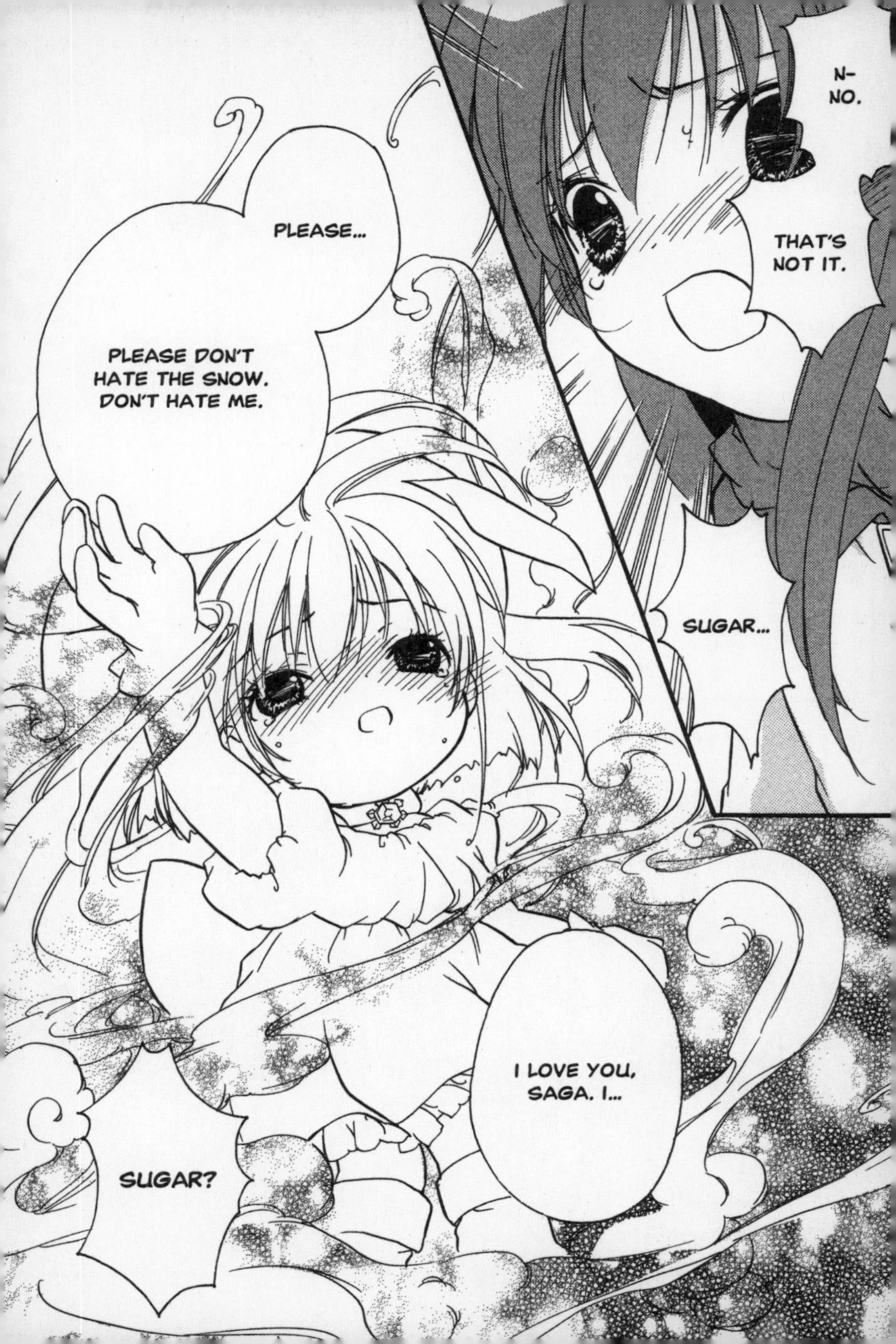
N-
NO.
THAT'S NOT IT.
SUGAR...
PLEASE...
PLEASE DON'T HATE THE SNOW. DON'T HATE ME.
I LOVE YOU, SAGA. I...
SUGAR?

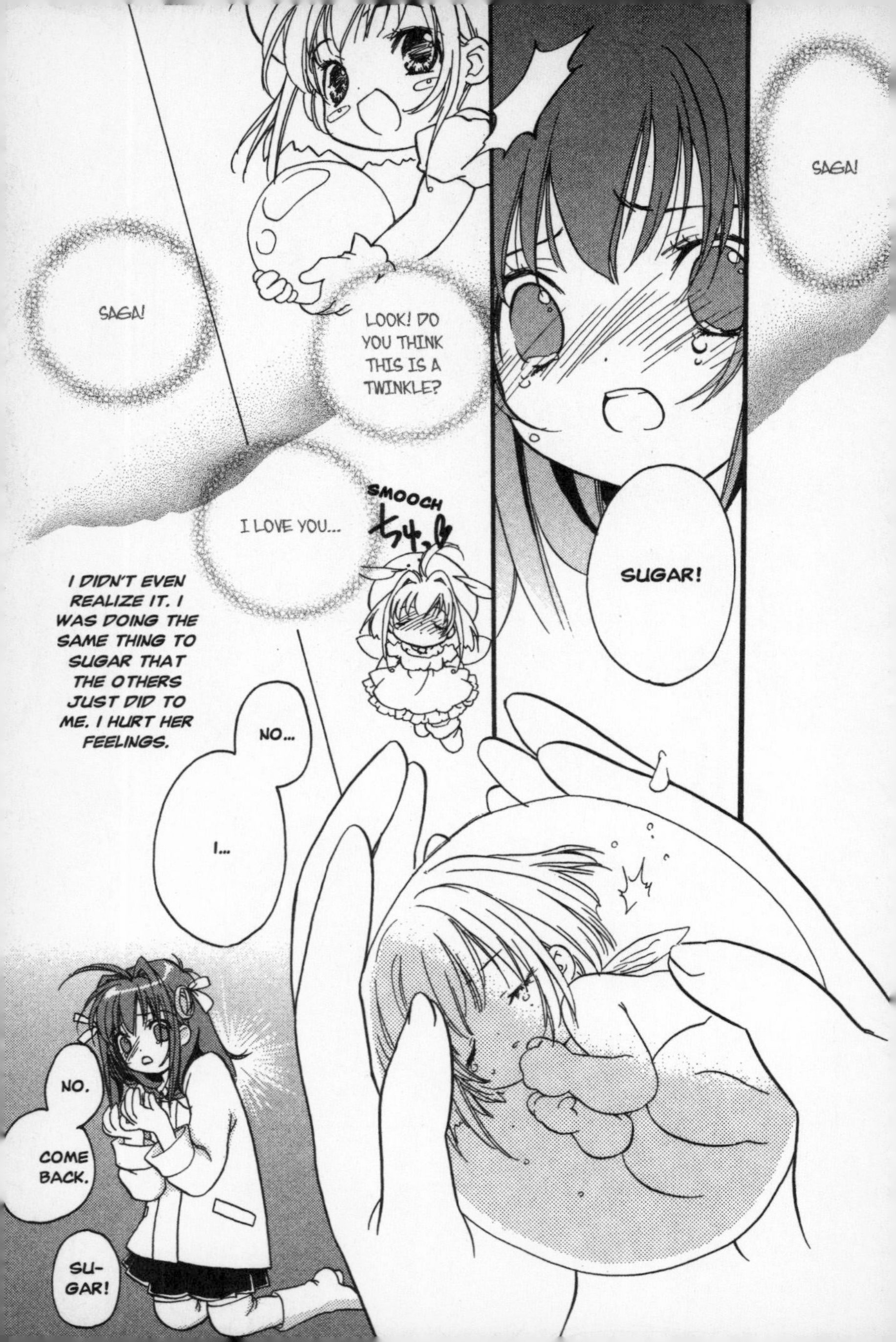
SAGA!
SUGAR!
LOOK! DO YOU THINK THIS IS A TWINKLE?
SAGA!
SMOOCH
I LOVE YOU...
I DIDN'T EVEN REALIZE IT. I WAS DOING THE SAME THING TO SUGAR THAT THE OTHERS JUST DID TO ME. I HURT HER FEELINGS.
NO...
I...
NO.
COME BACK.
SU-GAR!

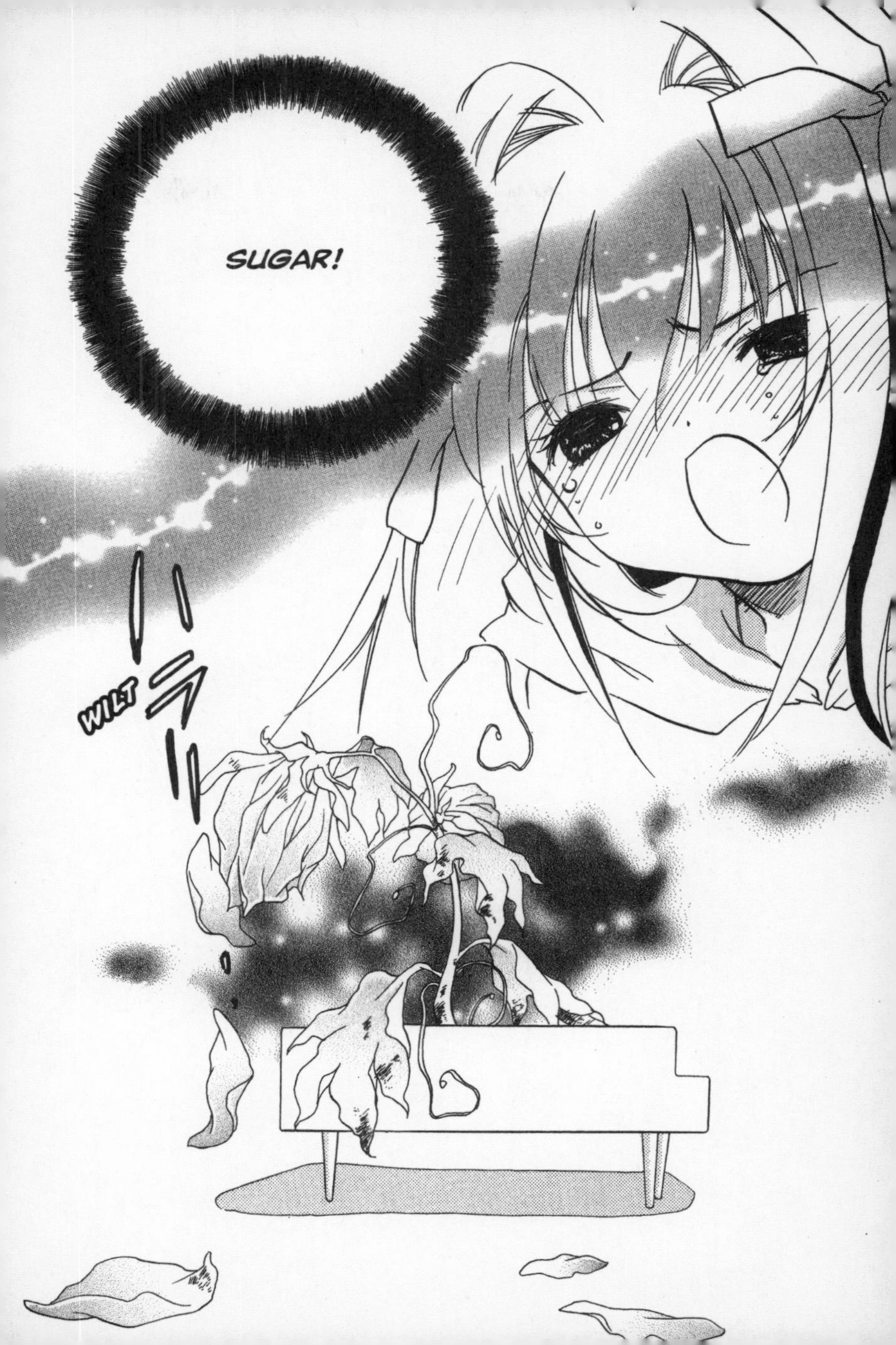
SUGAR!
WILT

Chapter 13

Real Twinkles

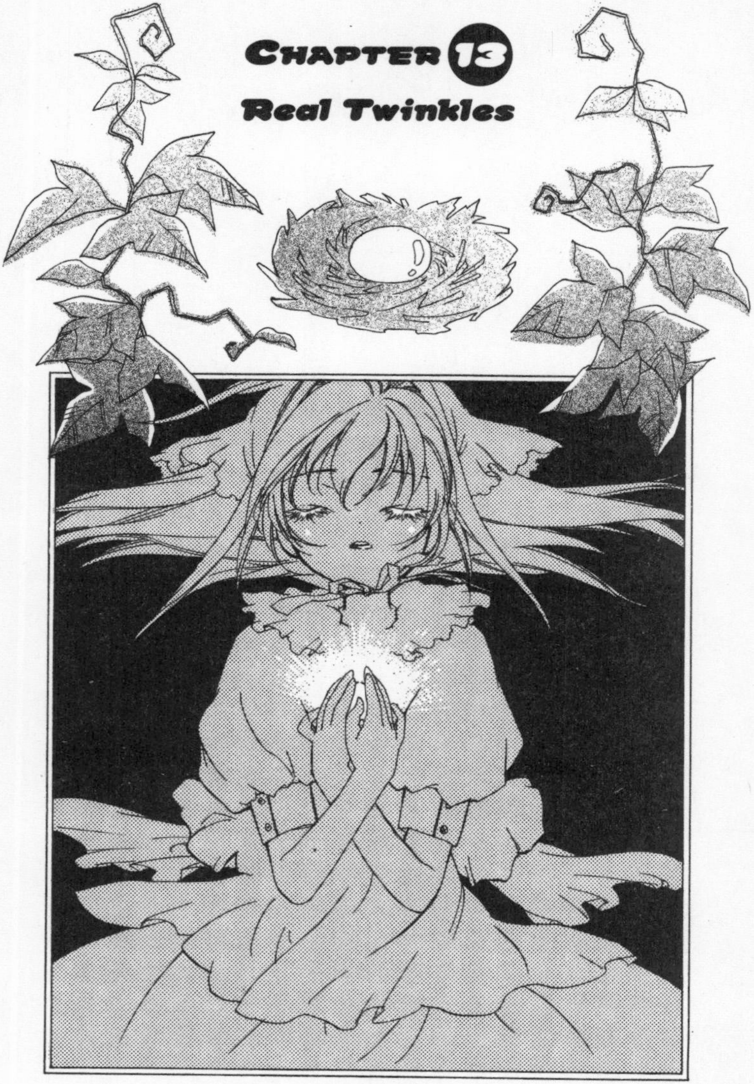

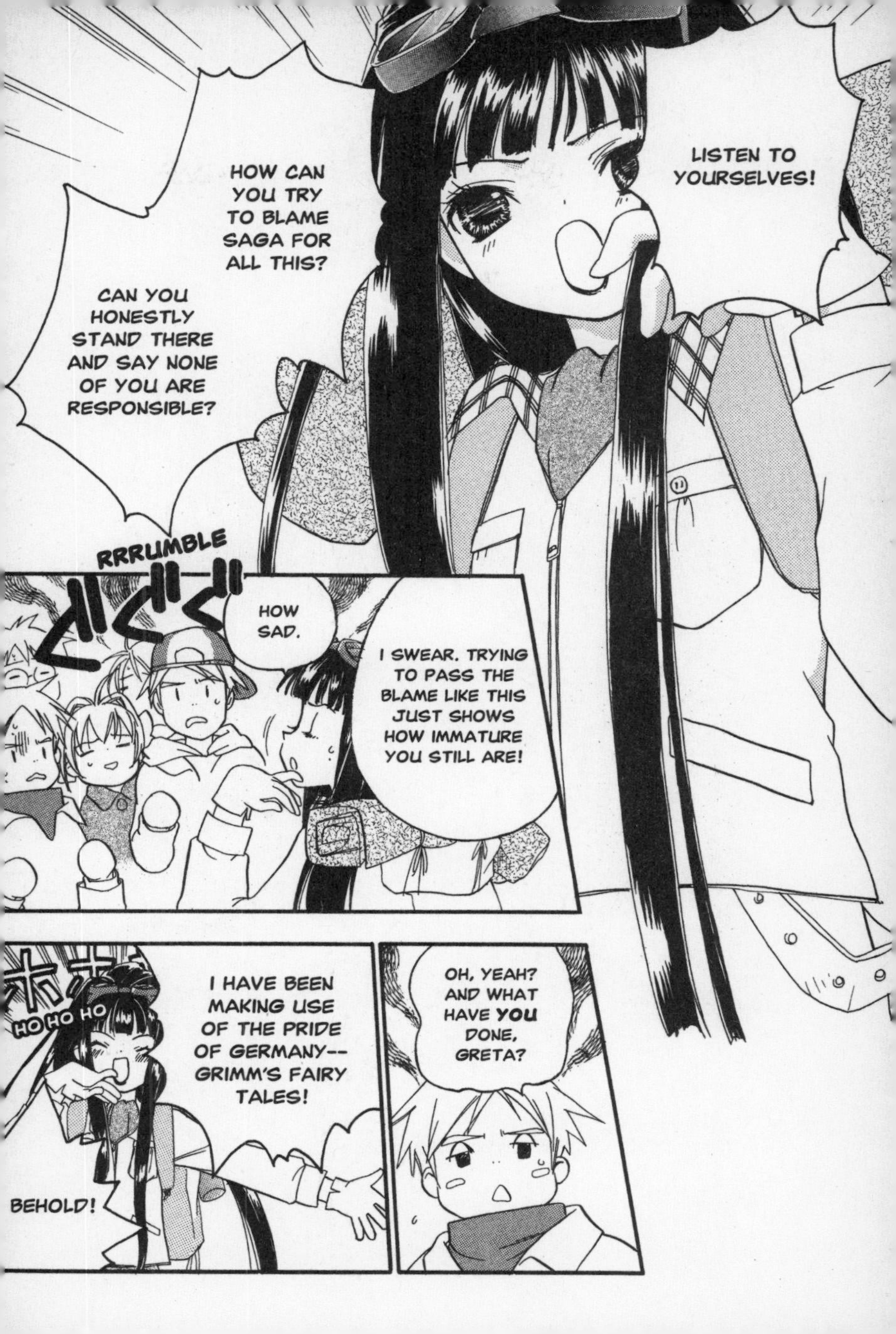
LISTEN TO YOURSELVES!
HOW CAN YOU TRY TO BLAME SAGA FOR ALL THIS?
CAN YOU HONESTLY STAND THERE AND SAY NONE OF YOU ARE RESPONSIBLE?
RRRUMBLE
HOW SAD.
I SWEAR. TRYING TO PASS THE BLAME LIKE THIS JUST SHOWS HOW IMMATURE YOU STILL ARE!
OH, YEAH? AND WHAT HAVE **YOU** DONE, GRETA?
HO HO HO
I HAVE BEEN MAKING USE OF THE PRIDE OF GERMANY-- GRIMM'S FAIRY TALES!
BEHOLD!

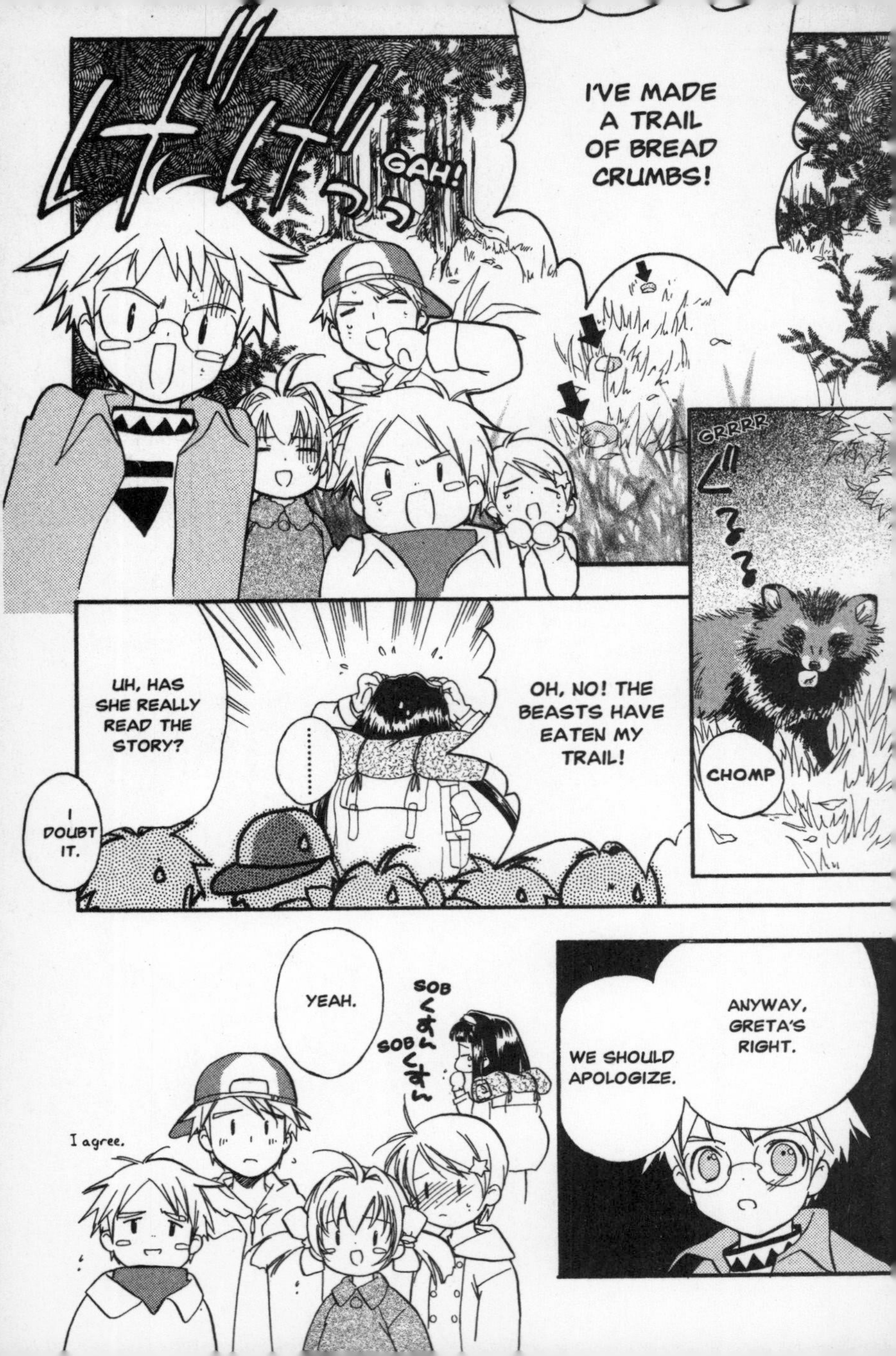
I'VE MADE A TRAIL OF BREAD CRUMBS!
GAH!
GRRRR
CHOMP
OH, NO! THE BEASTS HAVE EATEN MY TRAIL!
......
UH, HAS SHE REALLY READ THE STORY?
I DOUBT IT.
ANYWAY, GRETA'S RIGHT.
WE SHOULD APOLOGIZE.
SOB くすん
SOB くすん
YEAH.
I agree.

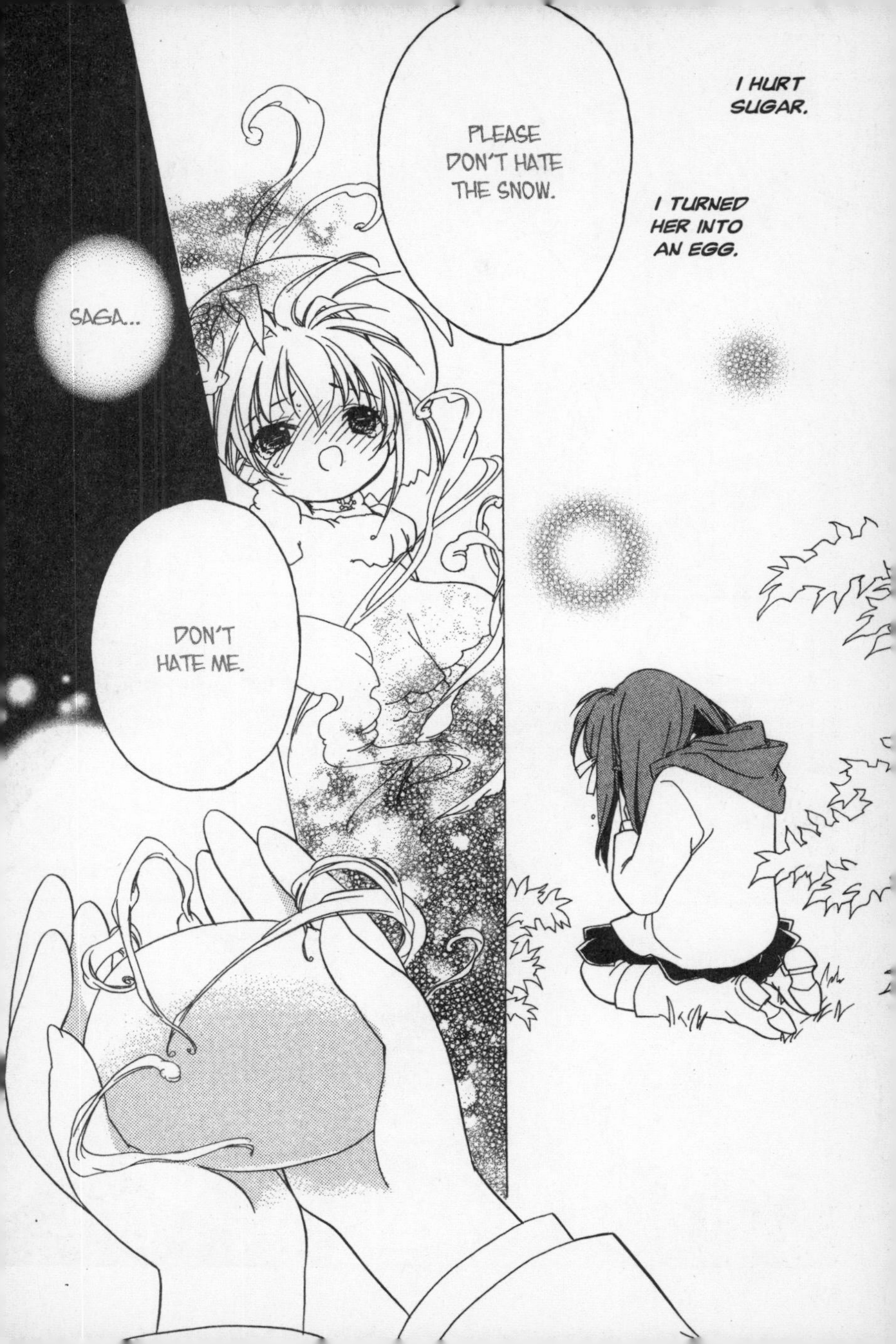
I HURT SUGAR.
I TURNED HER INTO AN EGG.
PLEASE DON'T HATE THE SNOW.
SAGA...
DON'T HATE ME.

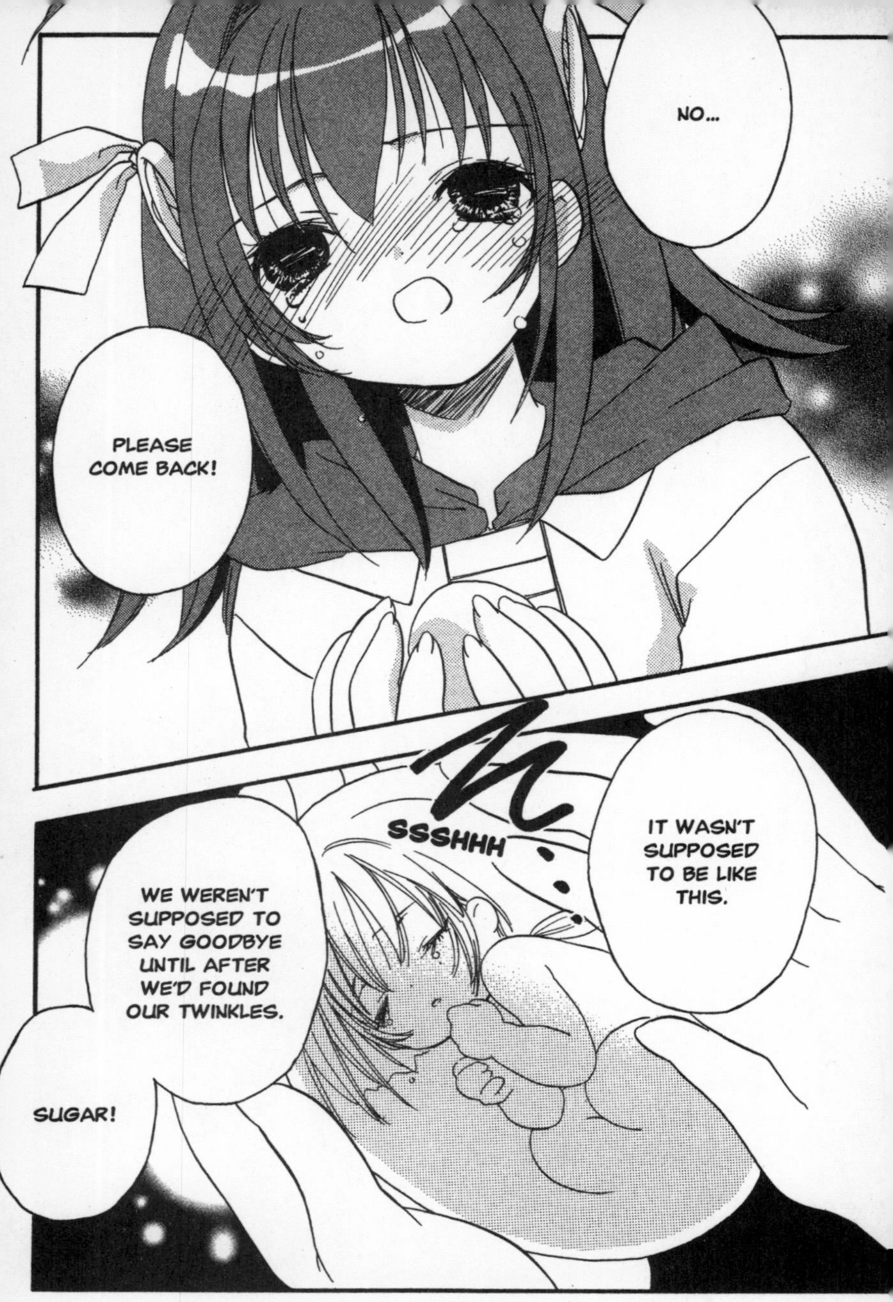
NO...
PLEASE COME BACK!
IT WASN'T SUPPOSED TO BE LIKE THIS.
SSSHHH
WE WEREN'T SUPPOSED TO SAY GOODBYE UNTIL AFTER WE'D FOUND OUR TWINKLES.
SUGAR!

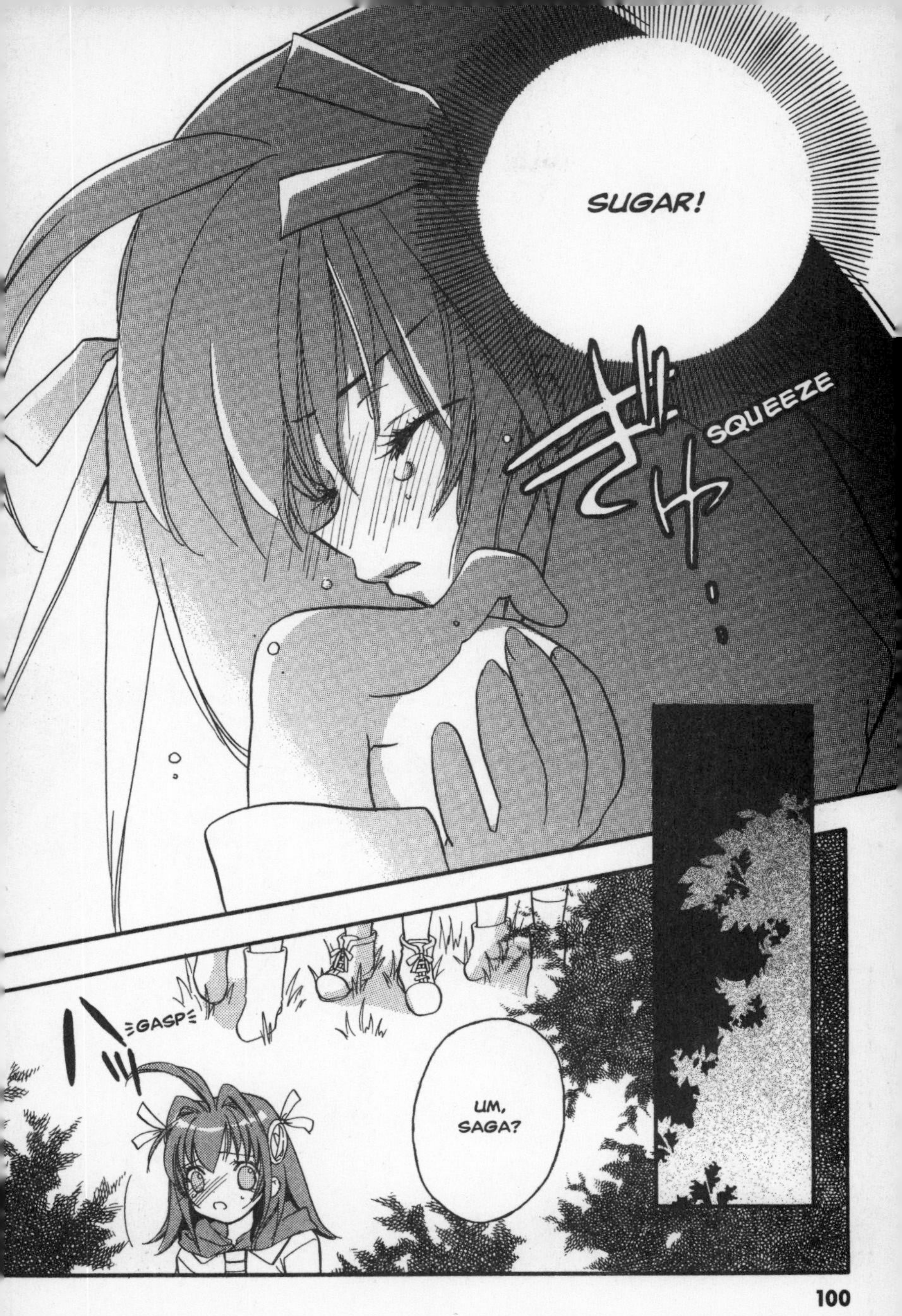

SUGAR!
ぎゅ
SQUEEZE
GASP
UM, SAGA?

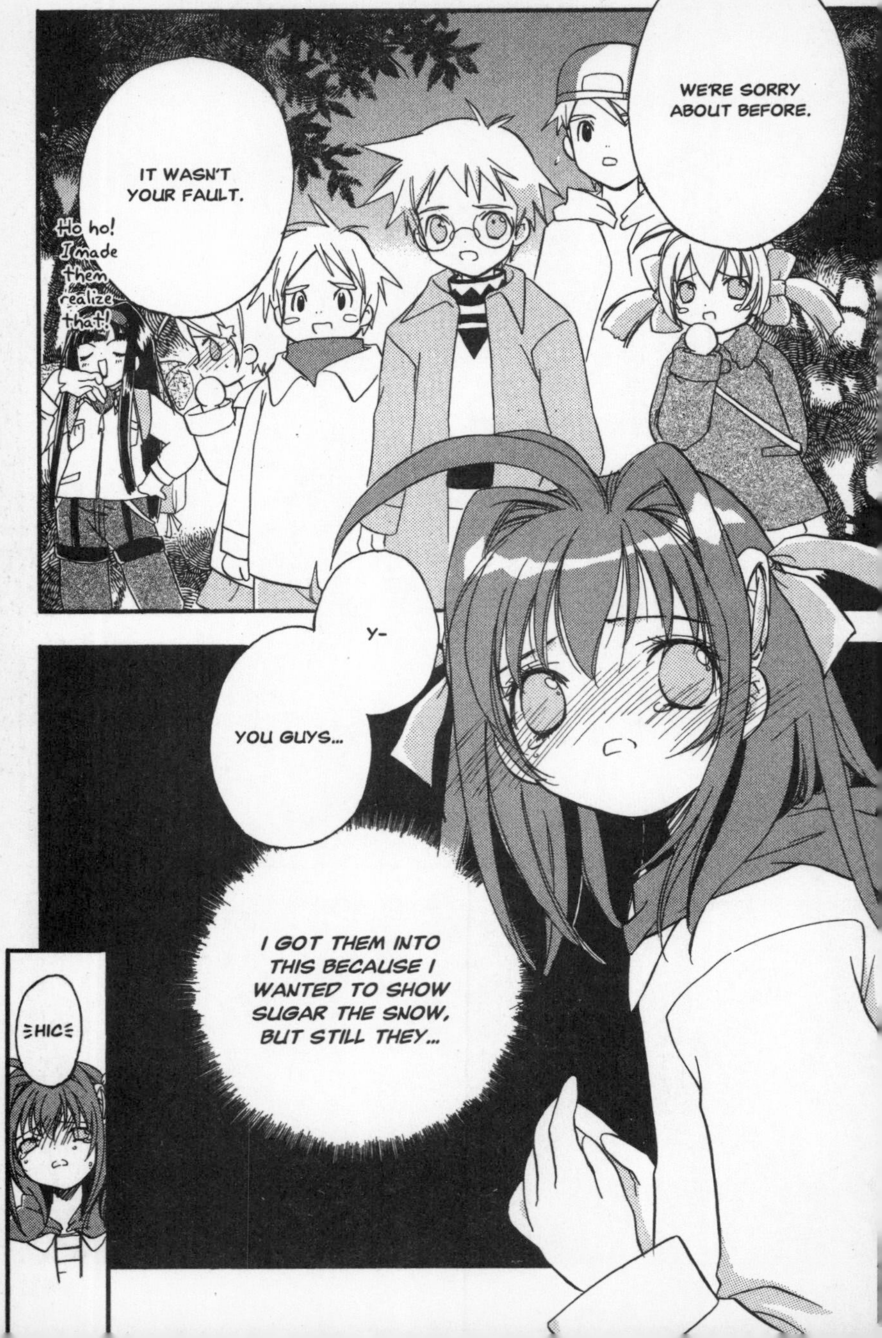
WE'RE SORRY ABOUT BEFORE.
IT WASN'T YOUR FAULT.
Ho ho! I made them realize that!
Y-
YOU GUYS...
I GOT THEM INTO THIS BECAUSE I WANTED TO SHOW SUGAR THE SNOW, BUT STILL THEY...
HIC

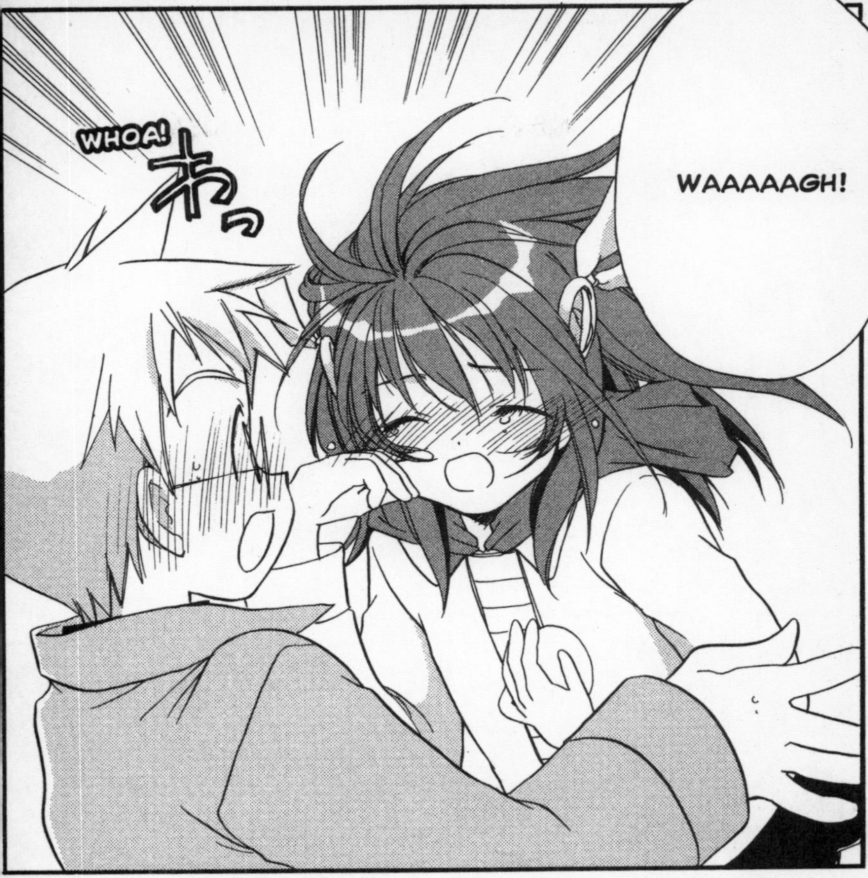
WAAAAAGH!
WHOA!
わっ
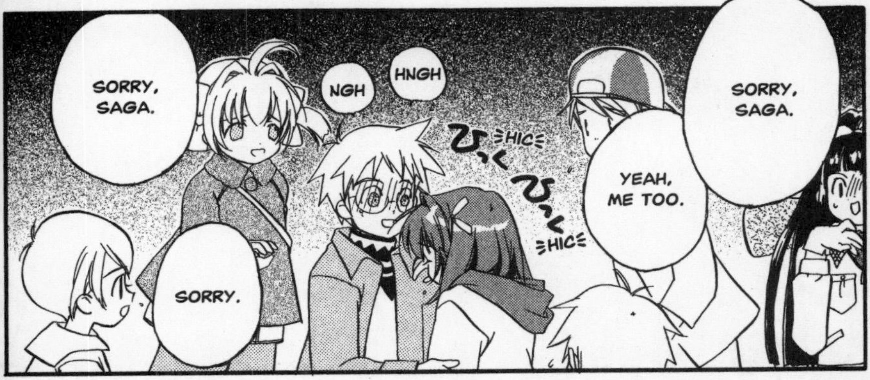
SORRY, SAGA.
YEAH, ME TOO.
ひっく
HIC
ひっく
HIC
HNGH
NGH
SORRY, SAGA.
SORRY.

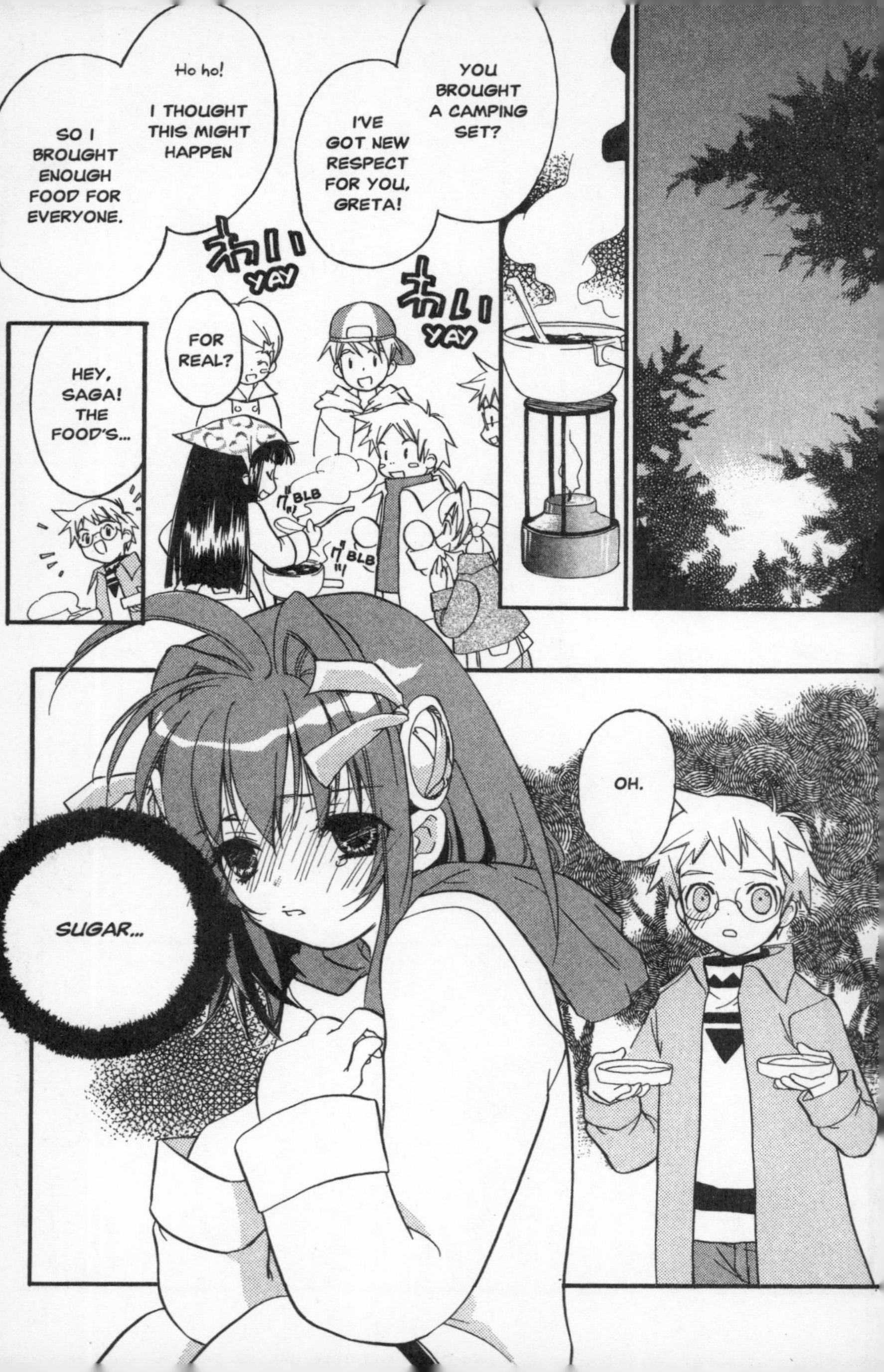
YOU BROUGHT A CAMPING SET?
I'VE GOT NEW RESPECT FOR YOU, GRETA!
Ho ho!
I THOUGHT THIS MIGHT HAPPEN
SO I BROUGHT ENOUGH FOOD FOR EVERYONE.
YAY
YAY
FOR REAL?
BLB
BLB
HEY, SAGA! THE FOOD'S...
OH.
SUGAR...

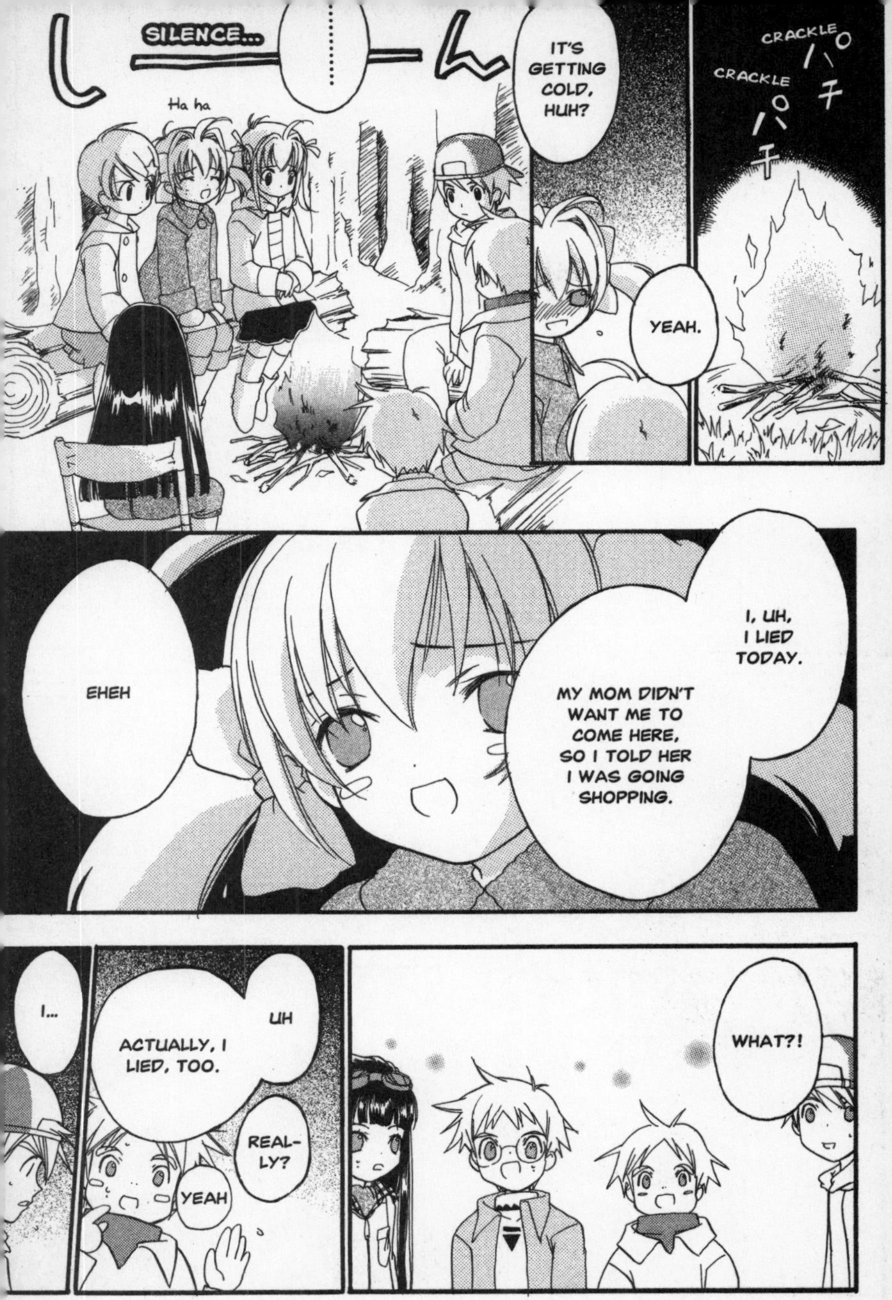

CRACKLE
パチ
CRACKLE
パチ
IT'S GETTING COLD, HUH?
YEAH.
SILENCE...
しーん
......
Ha ha
I, UH, I LIED TODAY.
MY MOM DIDN'T WANT ME TO COME HERE, SO I TOLD HER I WAS GOING SHOPPING.
EHEH
WHAT?!
UH
ACTUALLY, I LIED, TOO.
REAL-LY?
YEAH
I...

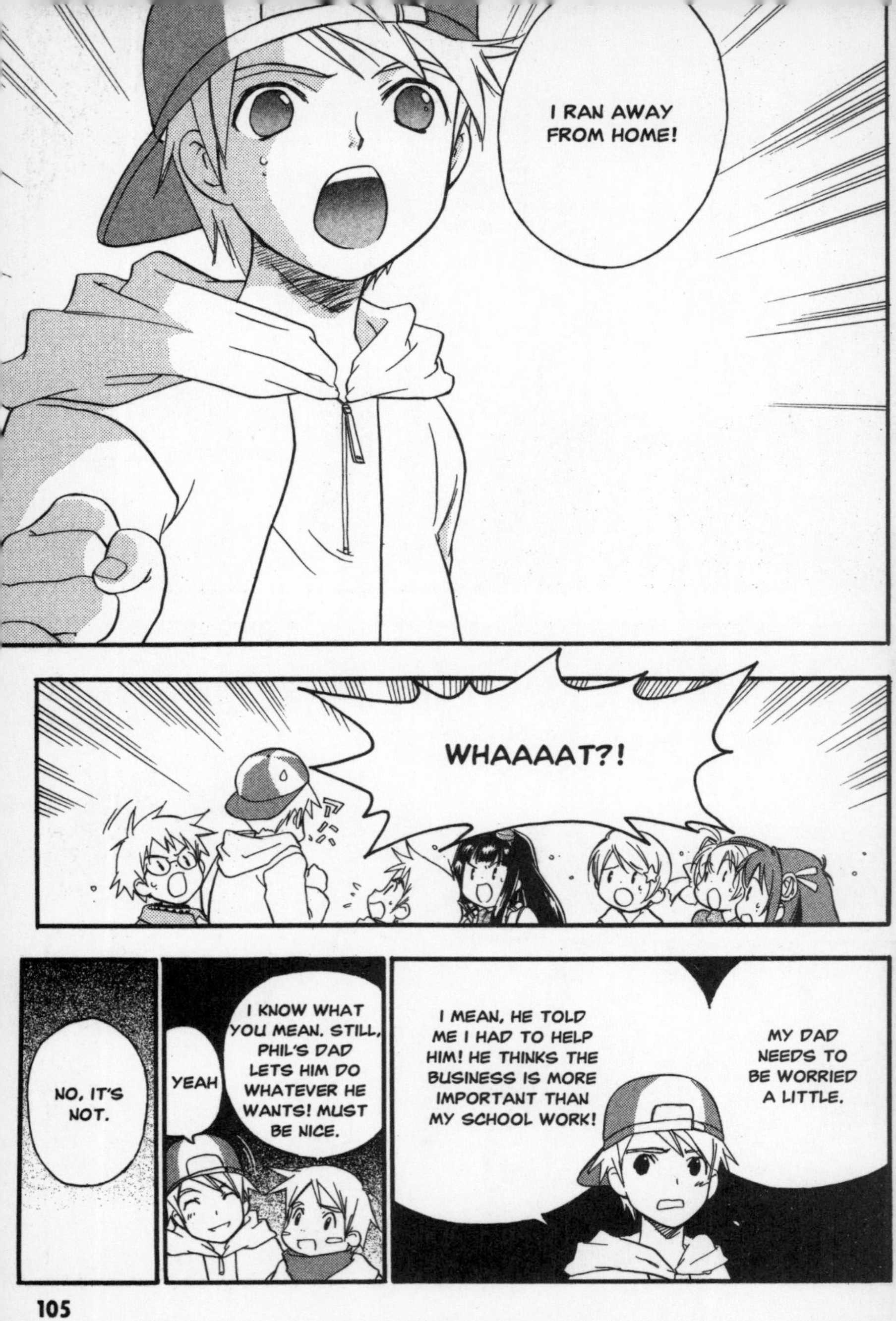
I RAN AWAY FROM HOME!
WHAAAAT?!
MY DAD NEEDS TO BE WORRIED A LITTLE.
I MEAN, HE TOLD ME I HAD TO HELP HIM! HE THINKS THE BUSINESS IS MORE IMPORTANT THAN MY SCHOOL WORK!
I KNOW WHAT YOU MEAN. STILL, PHIL'S DAD LETS HIM DO WHATEVER HE WANTS! MUST BE NICE.
YEAH
NO, IT'S NOT.

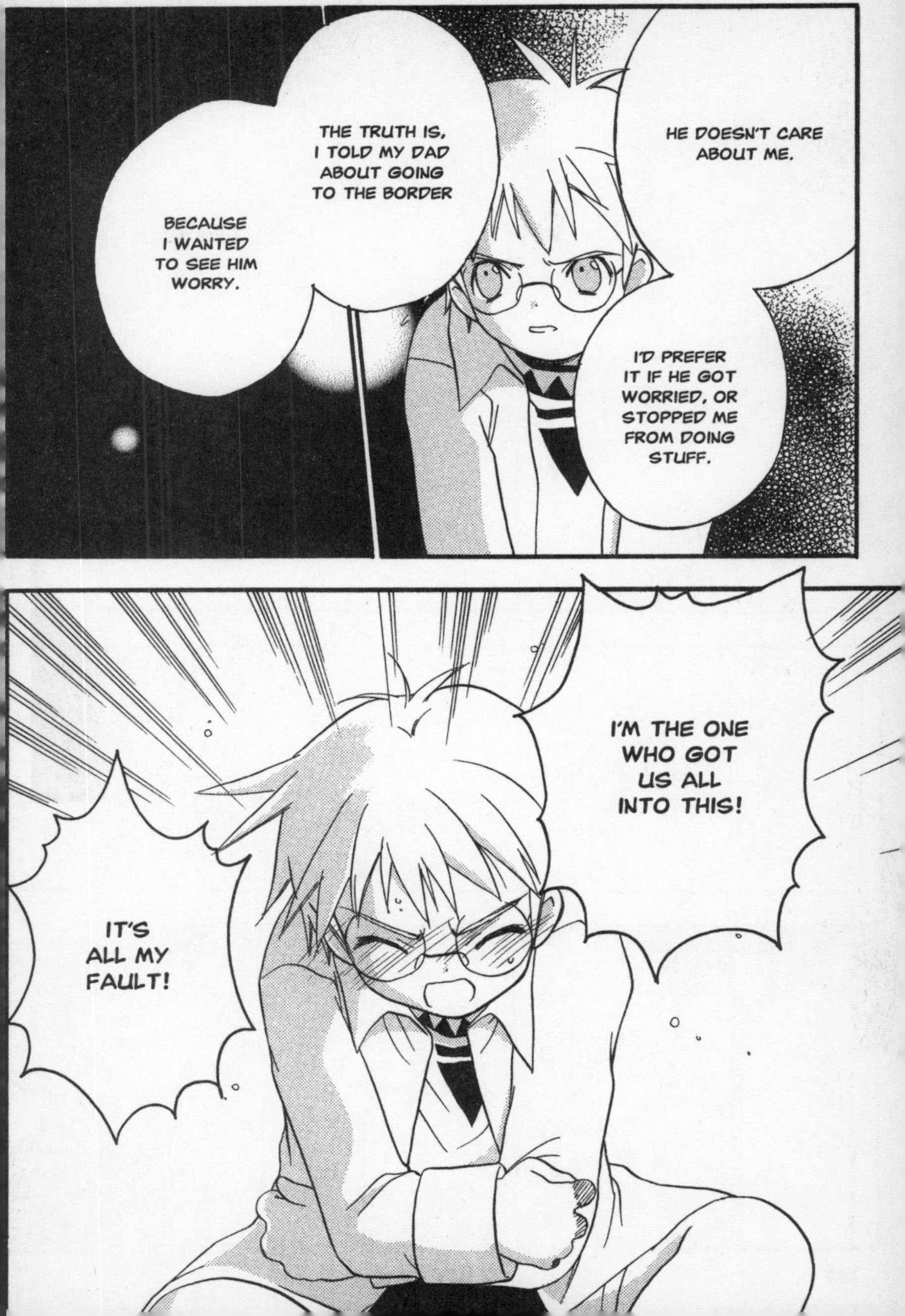
THE TRUTH IS, I TOLD MY DAD ABOUT GOING TO THE BORDER
BECAUSE I WANTED TO SEE HIM WORRY.
HE DOESN'T CARE ABOUT ME.
I'D PREFER IT IF HE GOT WORRIED, OR STOPPED ME FROM DOING STUFF.
I'M THE ONE WHO GOT US ALL INTO THIS!
IT'S ALL MY FAULT!

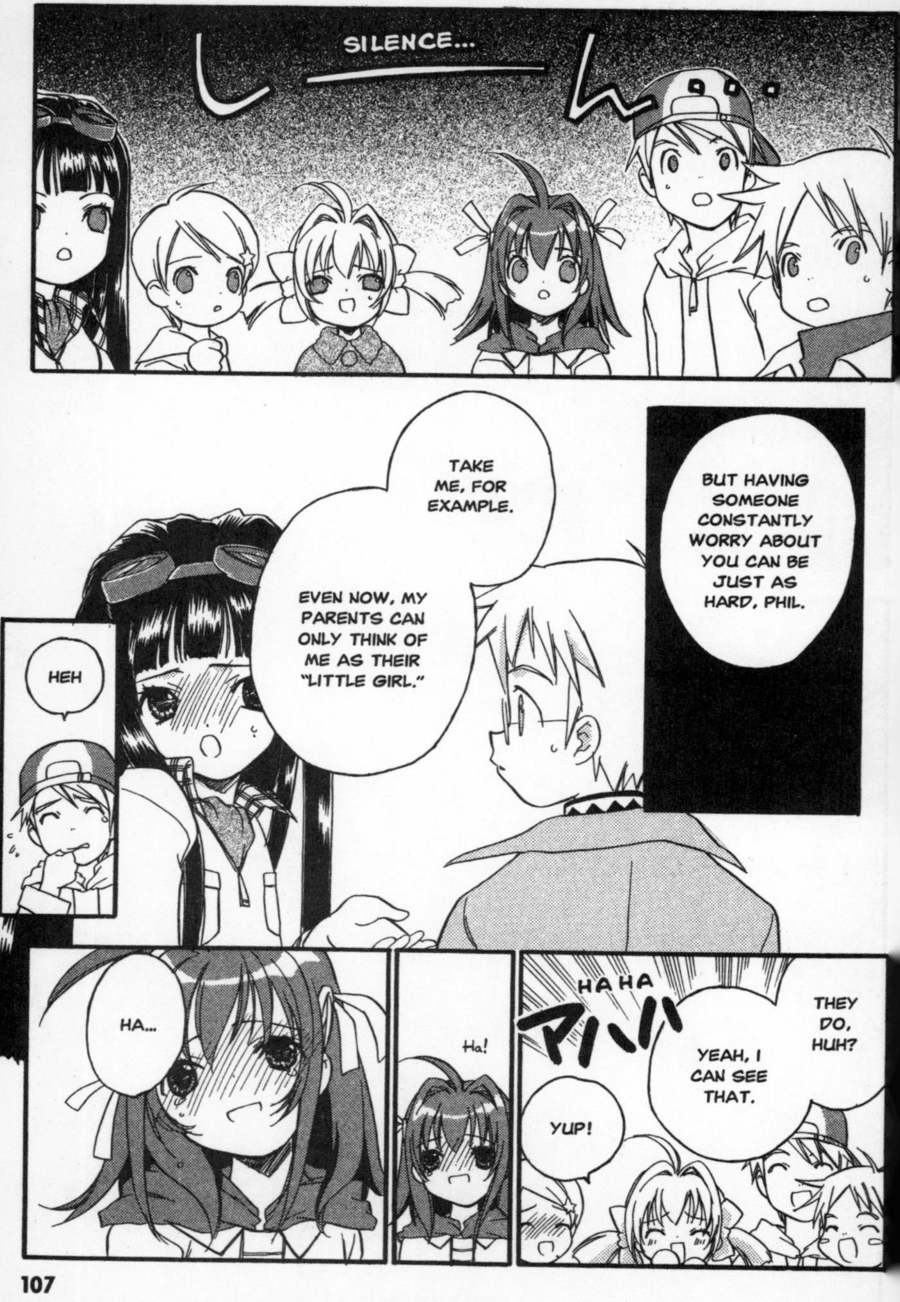
SILENCE...
BUT HAVING SOMEONE CONSTANTLY WORRY ABOUT YOU CAN BE JUST AS HARD, PHIL.
TAKE ME, FOR EXAMPLE.
EVEN NOW, MY PARENTS CAN ONLY THINK OF ME AS THEIR "LITTLE GIRL."
HEH
HAHA
THEY DO, HUH?
YEAH, I CAN SEE THAT.
YUP!
Ha!
HA...

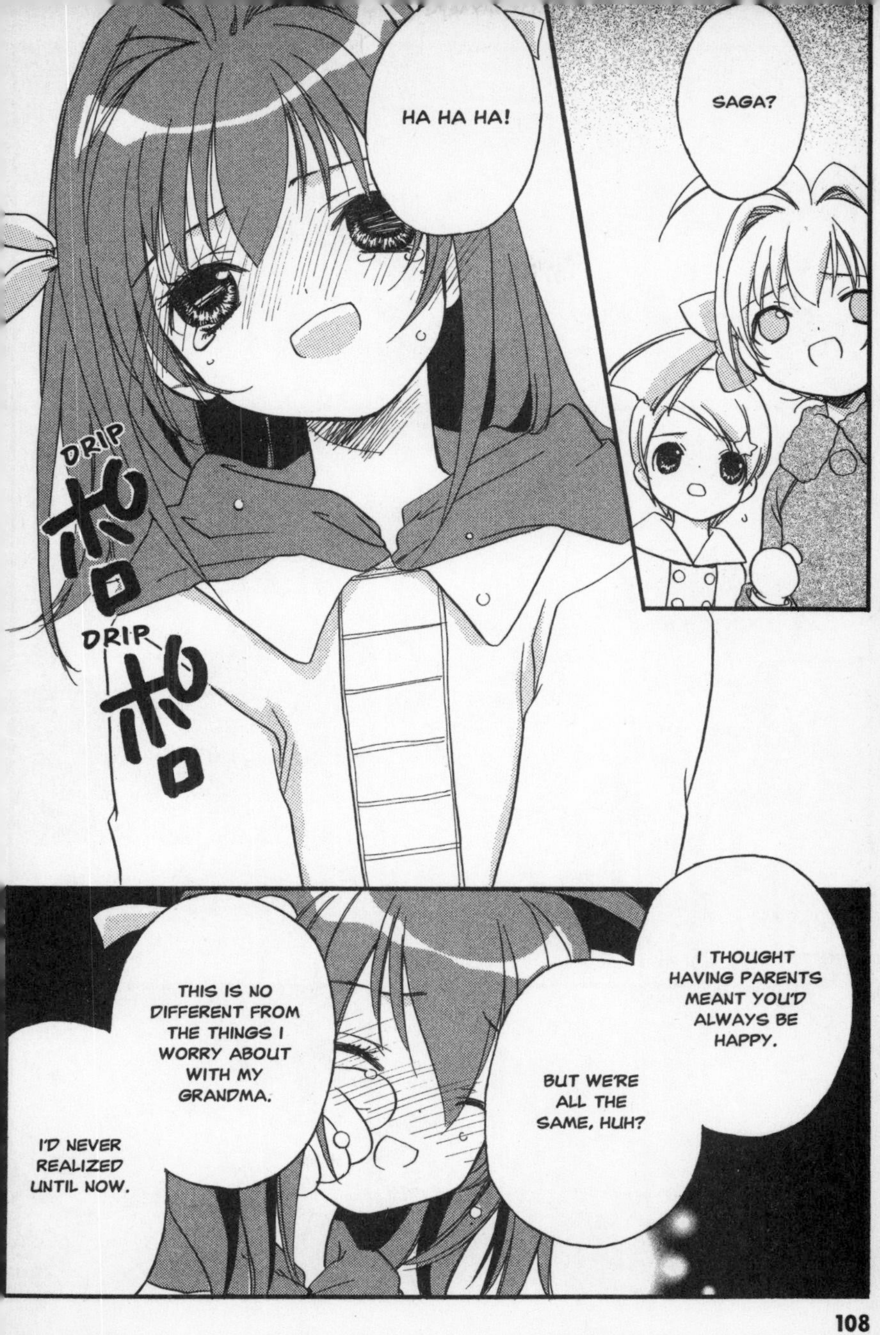
SAGA?
HA HA HA!
DRIP ポロ
DRIP ポロ
I THOUGHT HAVING PARENTS MEANT YOU'D ALWAYS BE HAPPY.
BUT WE'RE ALL THE SAME, HUH?
THIS IS NO DIFFERENT FROM THE THINGS I WORRY ABOUT WITH MY GRANDMA.
I'D NEVER REALIZED UNTIL NOW.

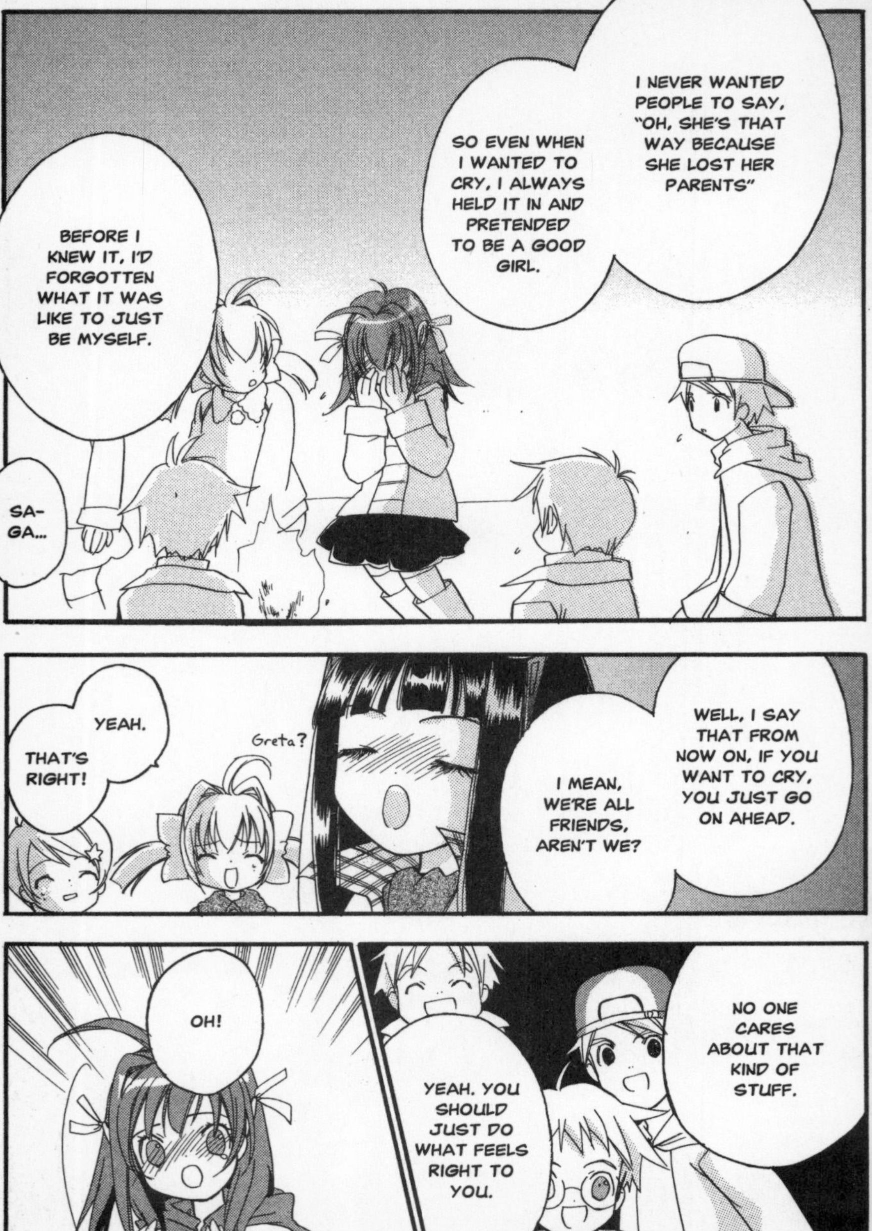
I NEVER WANTED PEOPLE TO SAY, "OH, SHE'S THAT WAY BECAUSE SHE LOST HER PARENTS"
SO EVEN WHEN I WANTED TO CRY, I ALWAYS HELD IT IN AND PRETENDED TO BE A GOOD GIRL.
BEFORE I KNEW IT, I'D FORGOTTEN WHAT IT WAS LIKE TO JUST BE MYSELF.
SA-GA...
WELL, I SAY THAT FROM NOW ON, IF YOU WANT TO CRY, YOU JUST GO ON AHEAD.
I MEAN, WE'RE ALL FRIENDS, AREN'T WE?
Greta?
YEAH. THAT'S RIGHT!
NO ONE CARES ABOUT THAT KIND OF STUFF.
YEAH. YOU SHOULD JUST DO WHAT FEELS RIGHT TO YOU.
OH!

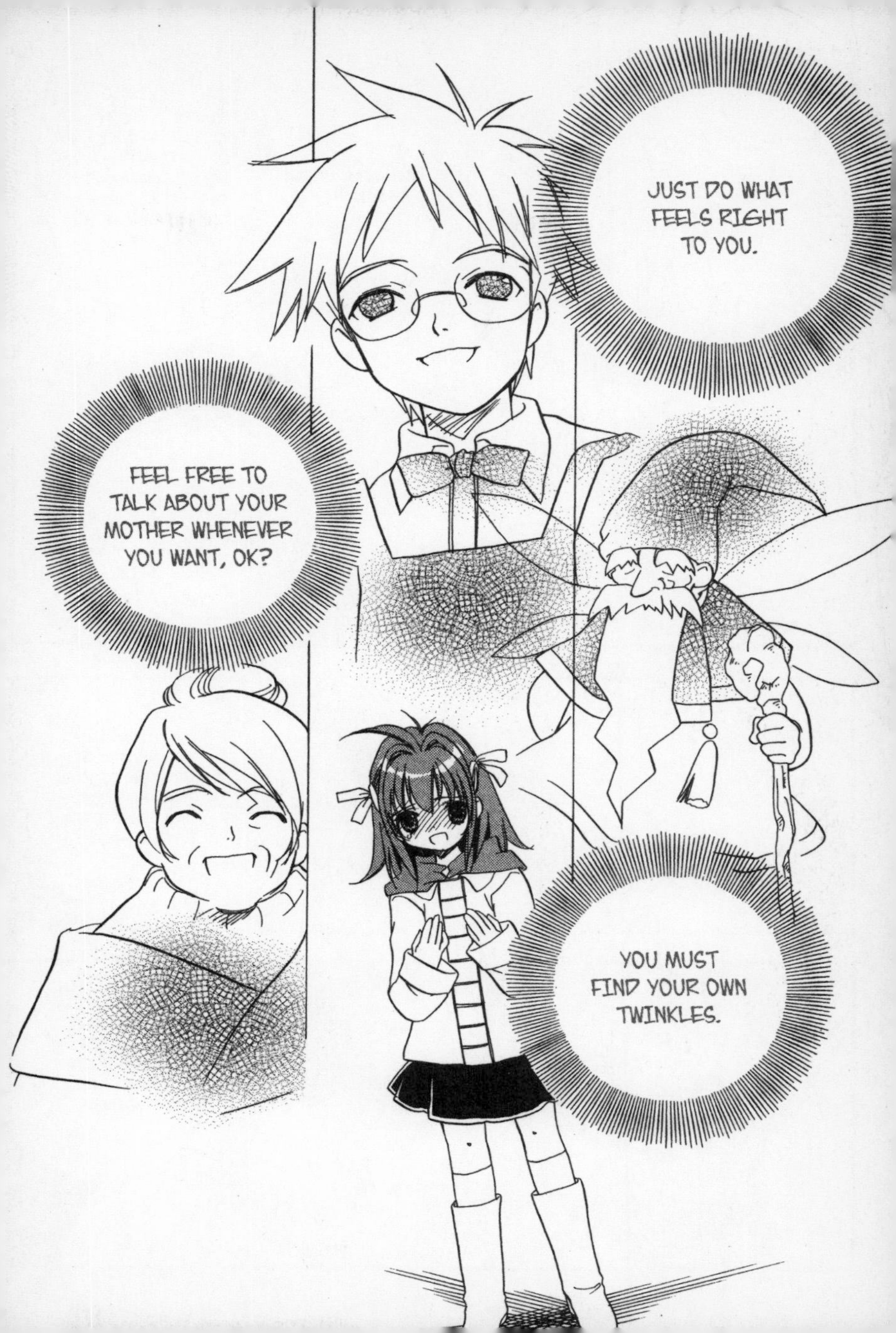
JUST DO WHAT FEELS RIGHT TO YOU.
FEEL FREE TO TALK ABOUT YOUR MOTHER WHENEVER YOU WANT, OK?
YOU MUST FIND YOUR OWN TWINKLES.

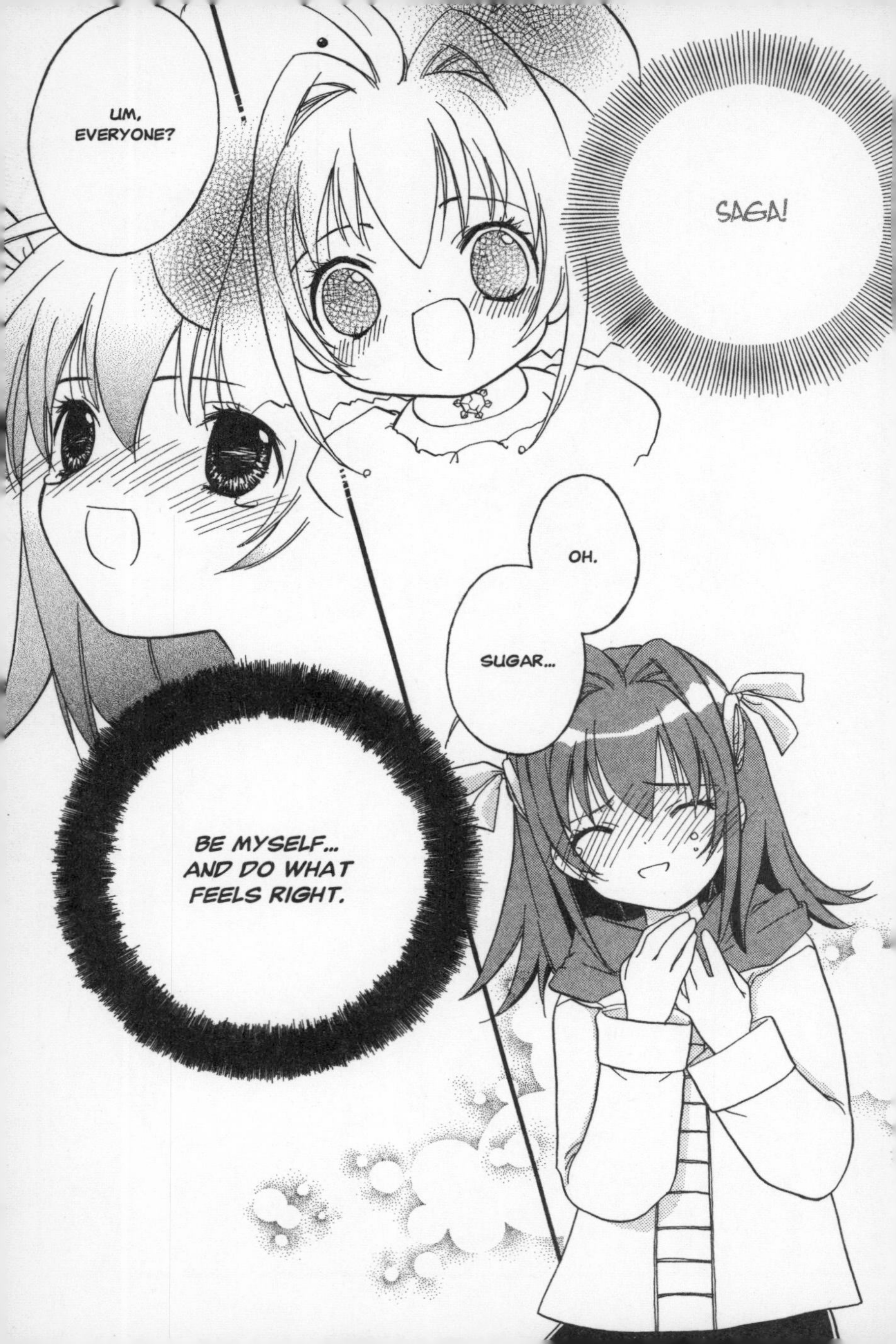
SAGA!
UM, EVERYONE?
OH. SUGAR...
BE MYSELF... AND DO WHAT FEELS RIGHT.

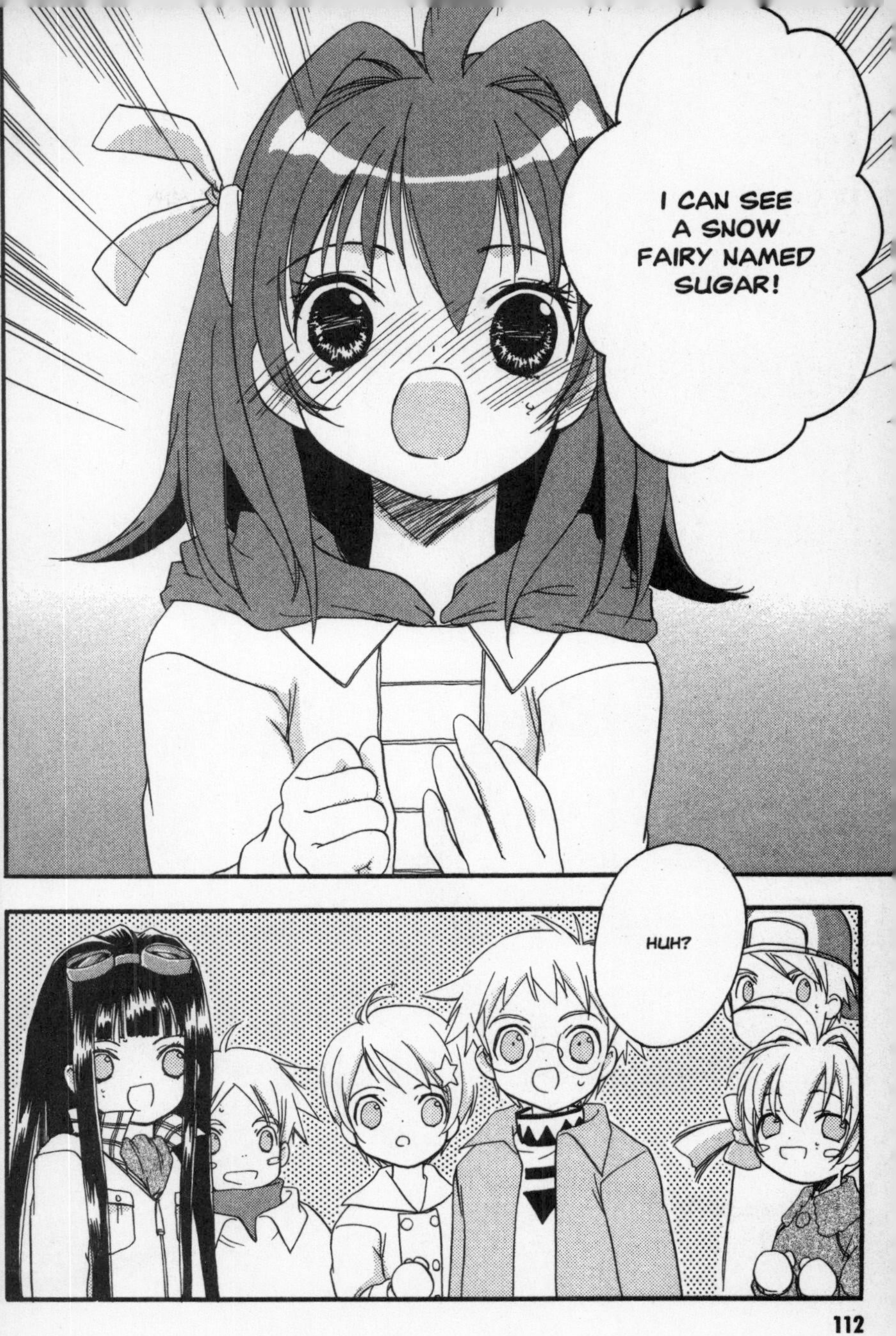
I CAN SEE A SNOW FAIRY NAMED SUGAR!
HUH?

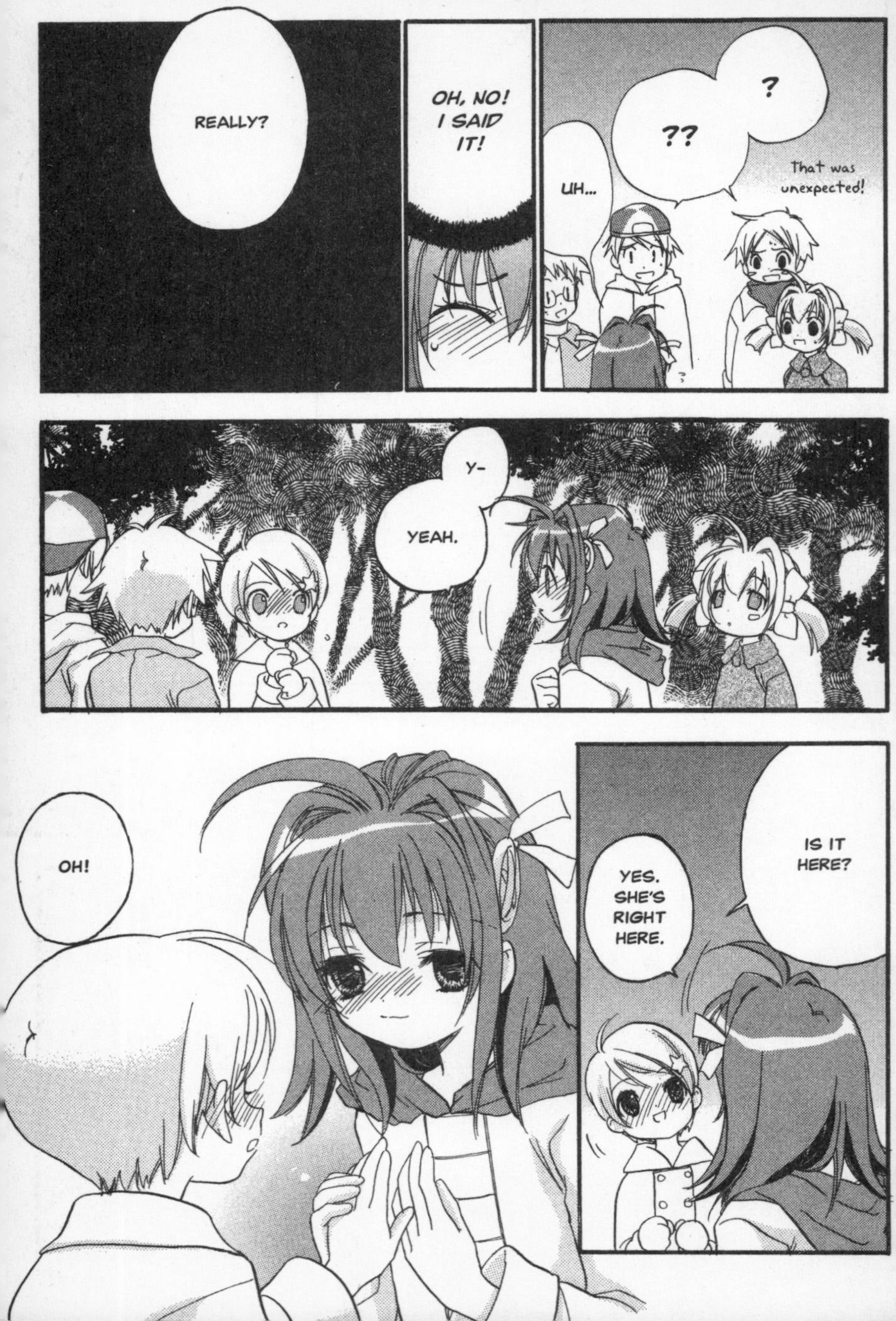
?
??
That was unexpected!
UH...
OH, NO! I SAID IT!
REALLY?
Y-
YEAH.
IS IT HERE?
YES. SHE'S RIGHT HERE.
OH!

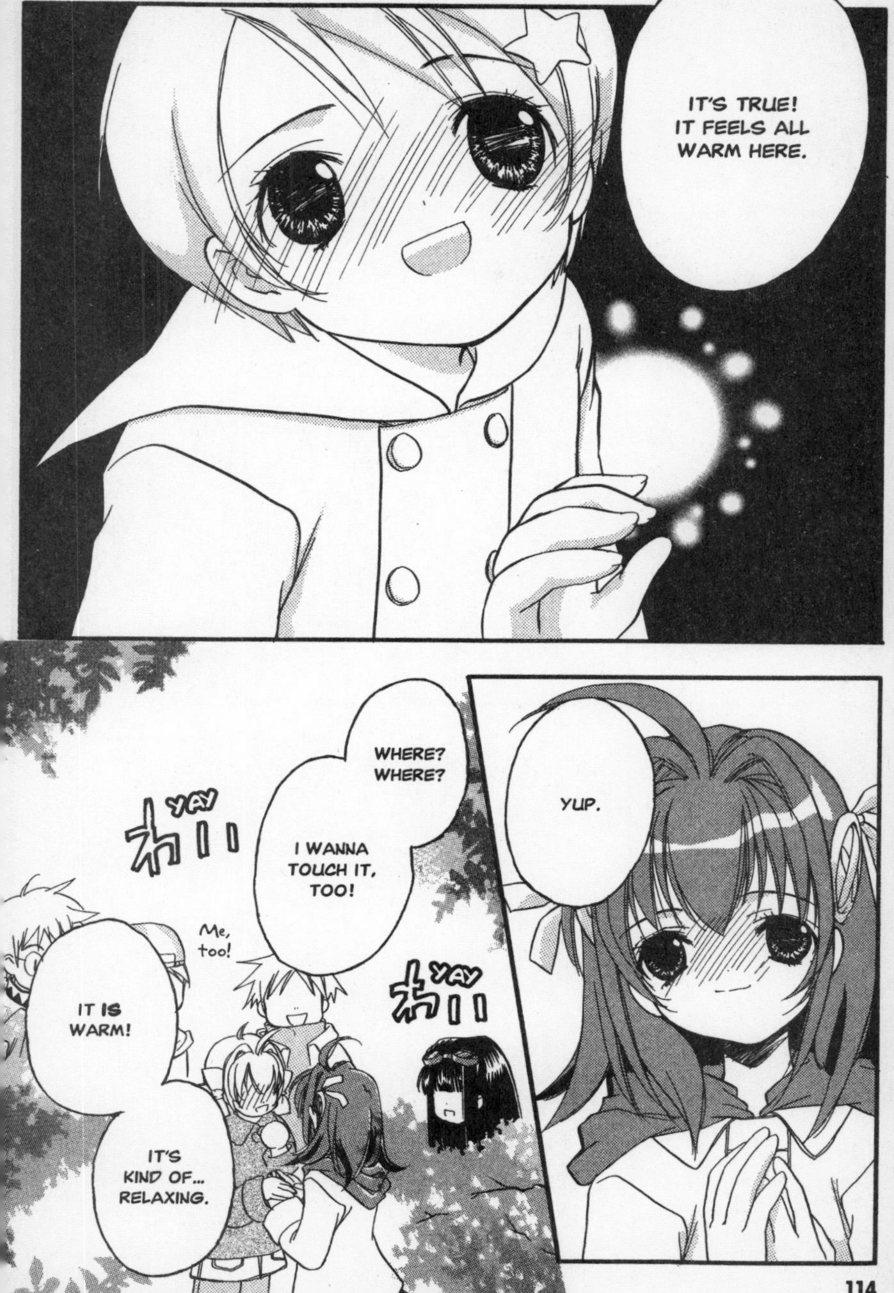

IT'S TRUE! IT FEELS ALL WARM HERE.
YUP.
WHERE? WHERE?
I WANNA TOUCH IT, TOO!
わ YAY
Me, too!
わ YAY
IT IS WARM!
IT'S KIND OF... RELAXING.

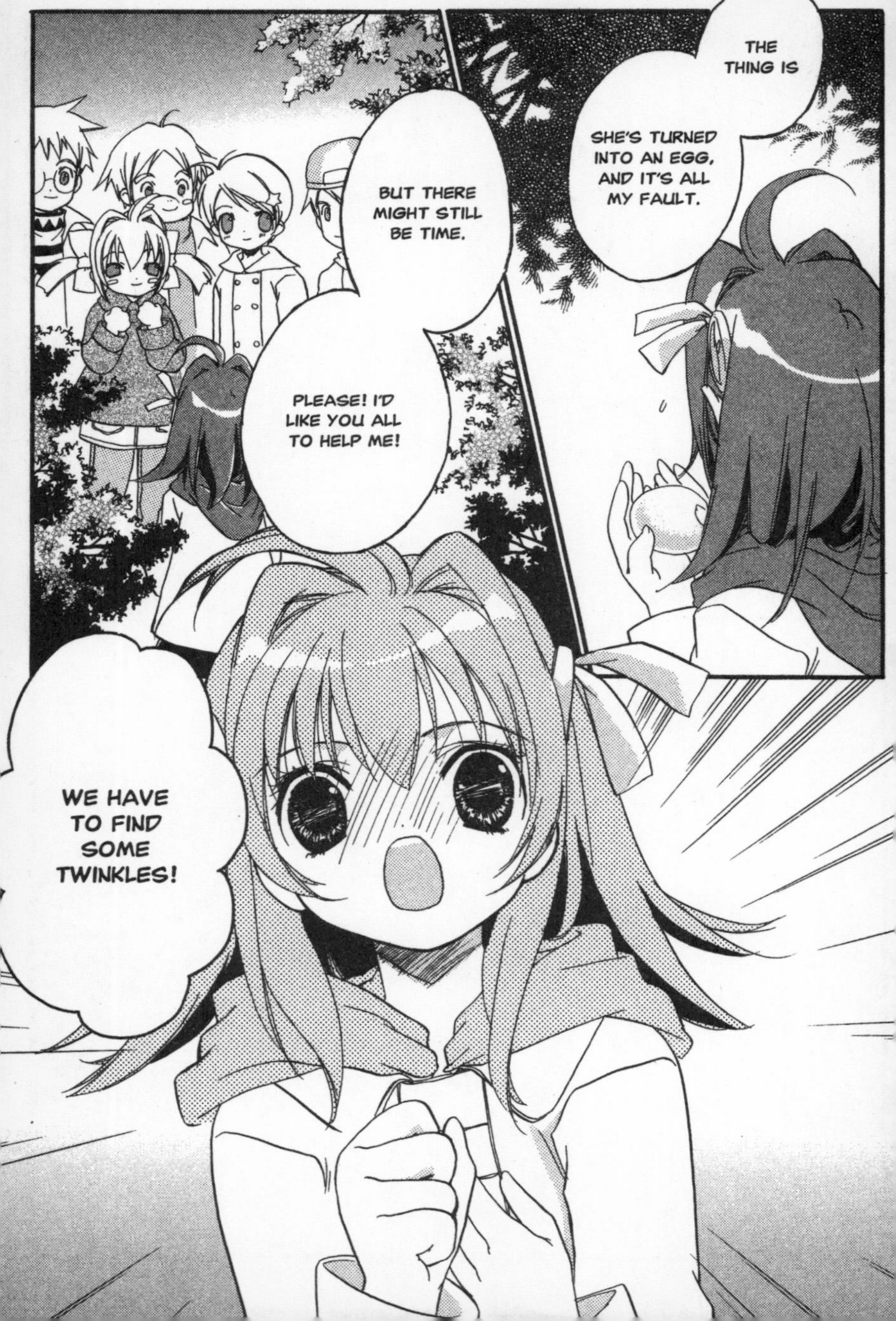
THE THING IS
SHE'S TURNED INTO AN EGG, AND IT'S ALL MY FAULT.
BUT THERE MIGHT STILL BE TIME.
PLEASE! I'D LIKE YOU ALL TO HELP ME!
WE HAVE TO FIND SOME TWINKLES!

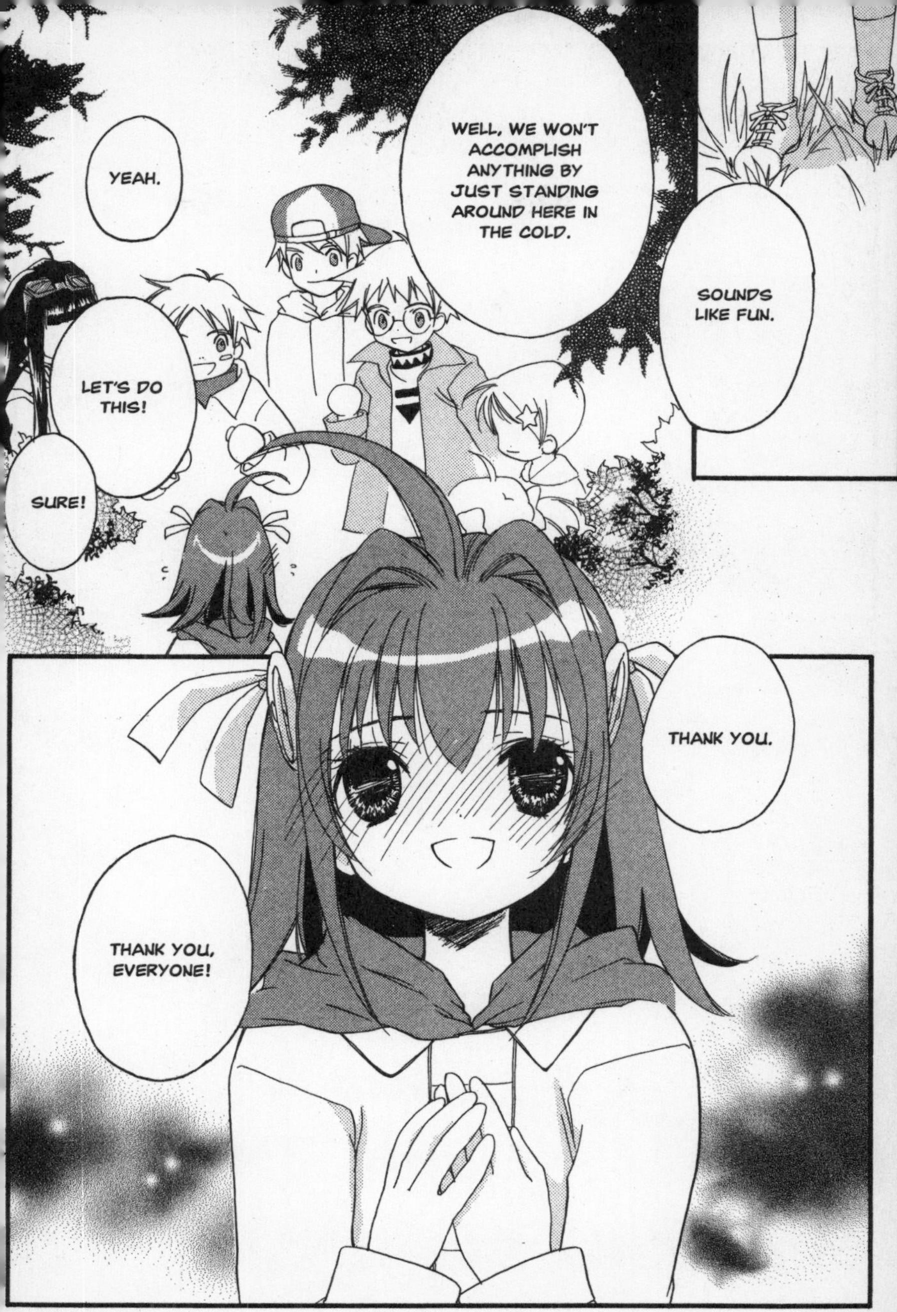
SOUNDS LIKE FUN.
WELL, WE WON'T ACCOMPLISH ANYTHING BY JUST STANDING AROUND HERE IN THE COLD.
YEAH.
LET'S DO THIS!
SURE!
THANK YOU.
THANK YOU, EVERYONE!

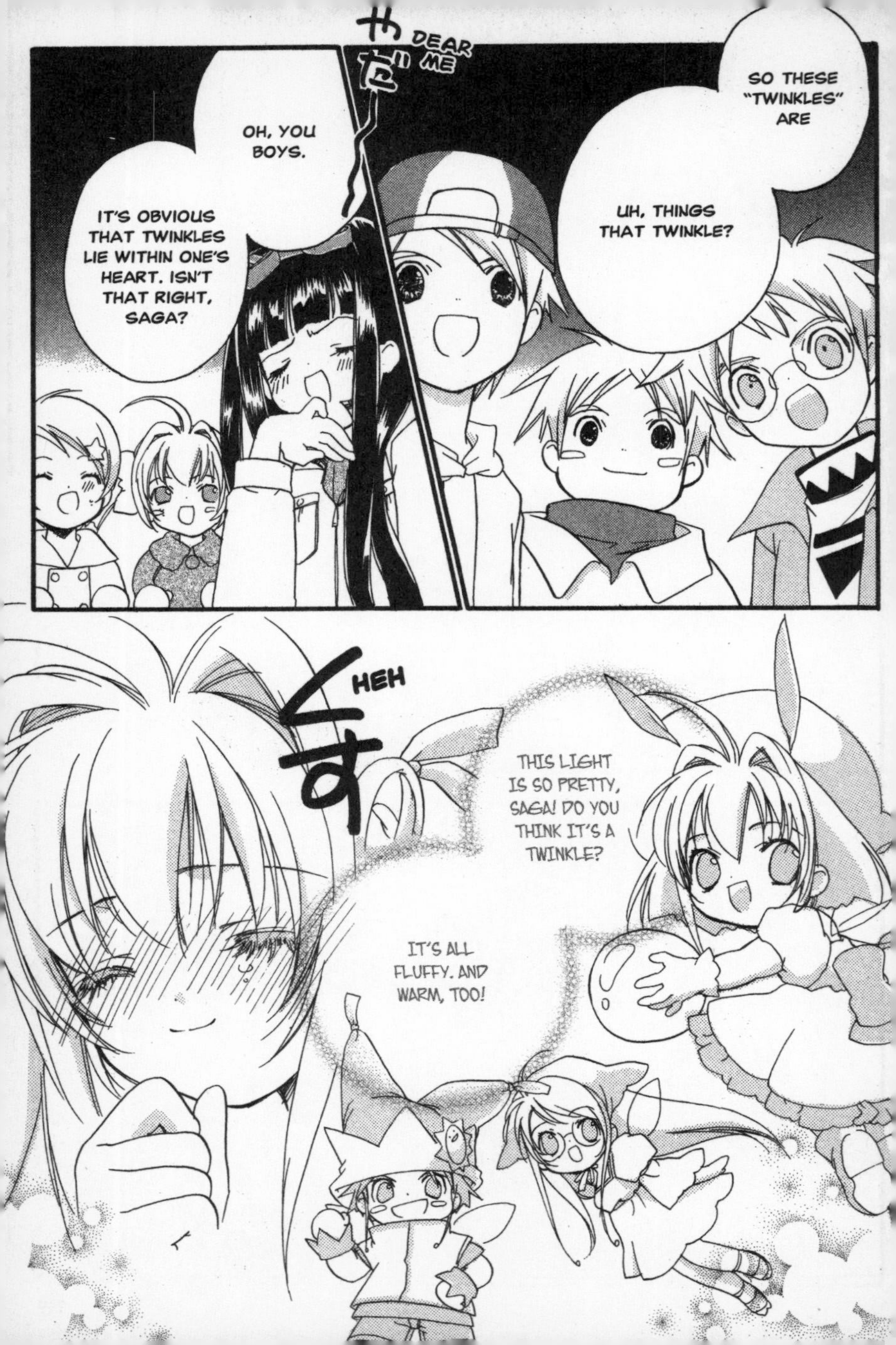

SO THESE "TWINKLES" ARE
UH, THINGS THAT TWINKLE?
やだ
DEAR ME
OH, YOU BOYS.
IT'S OBVIOUS THAT TWINKLES LIE WITHIN ONE'S HEART. ISN'T THAT RIGHT, SAGA?
THIS LIGHT IS SO PRETTY, SAGA! DO YOU THINK IT'S A TWINKLE?
くす
HEH
IT'S ALL FLUFFY. AND WARM, TOO!

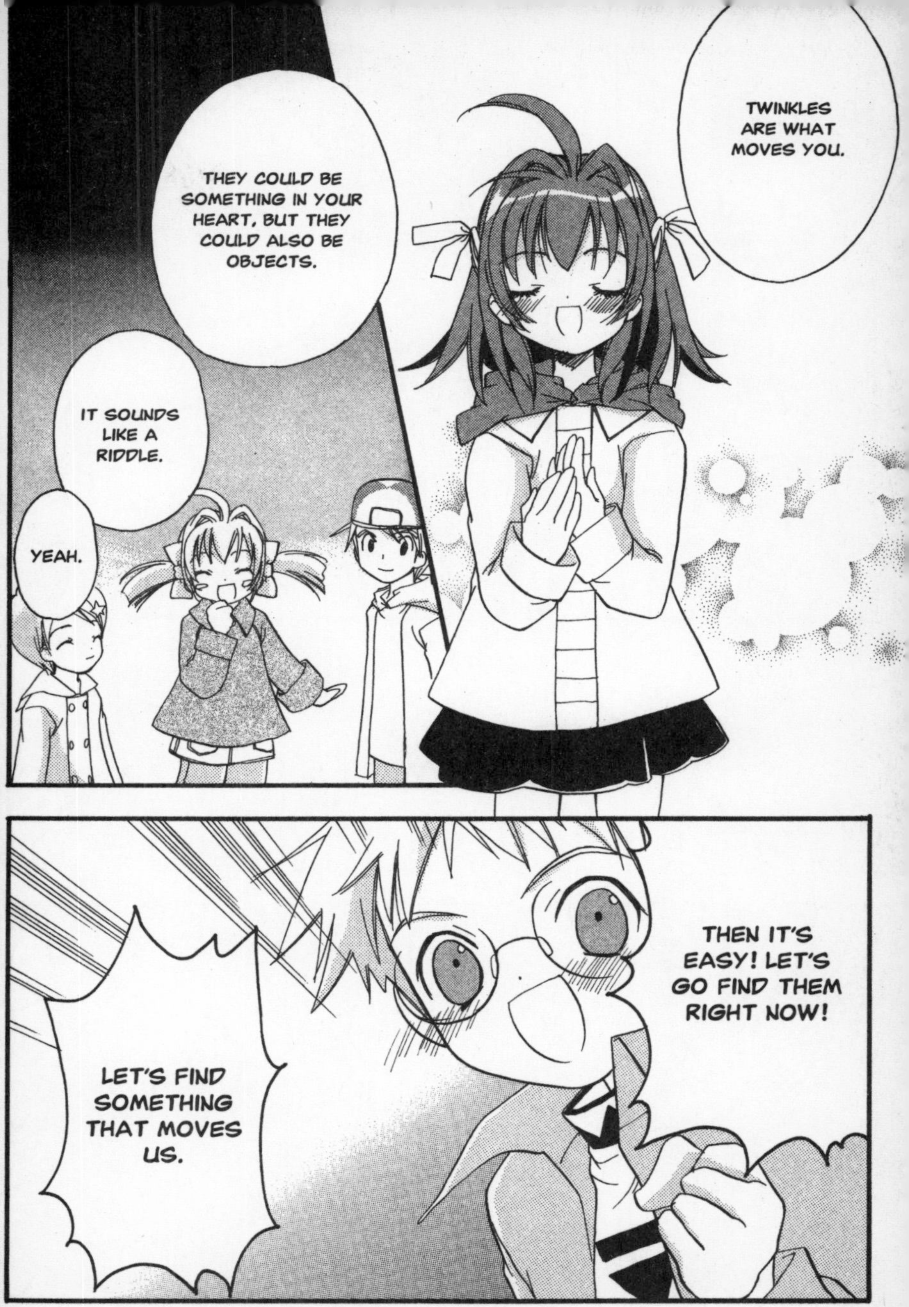
TWINKLES ARE WHAT MOVES YOU.
THEY COULD BE SOMETHING IN YOUR HEART, BUT THEY COULD ALSO BE OBJECTS.
IT SOUNDS LIKE A RIDDLE.
YEAH.
THEN IT'S EASY! LET'S GO FIND THEM RIGHT NOW!
LET'S FIND SOMETHING THAT MOVES US.

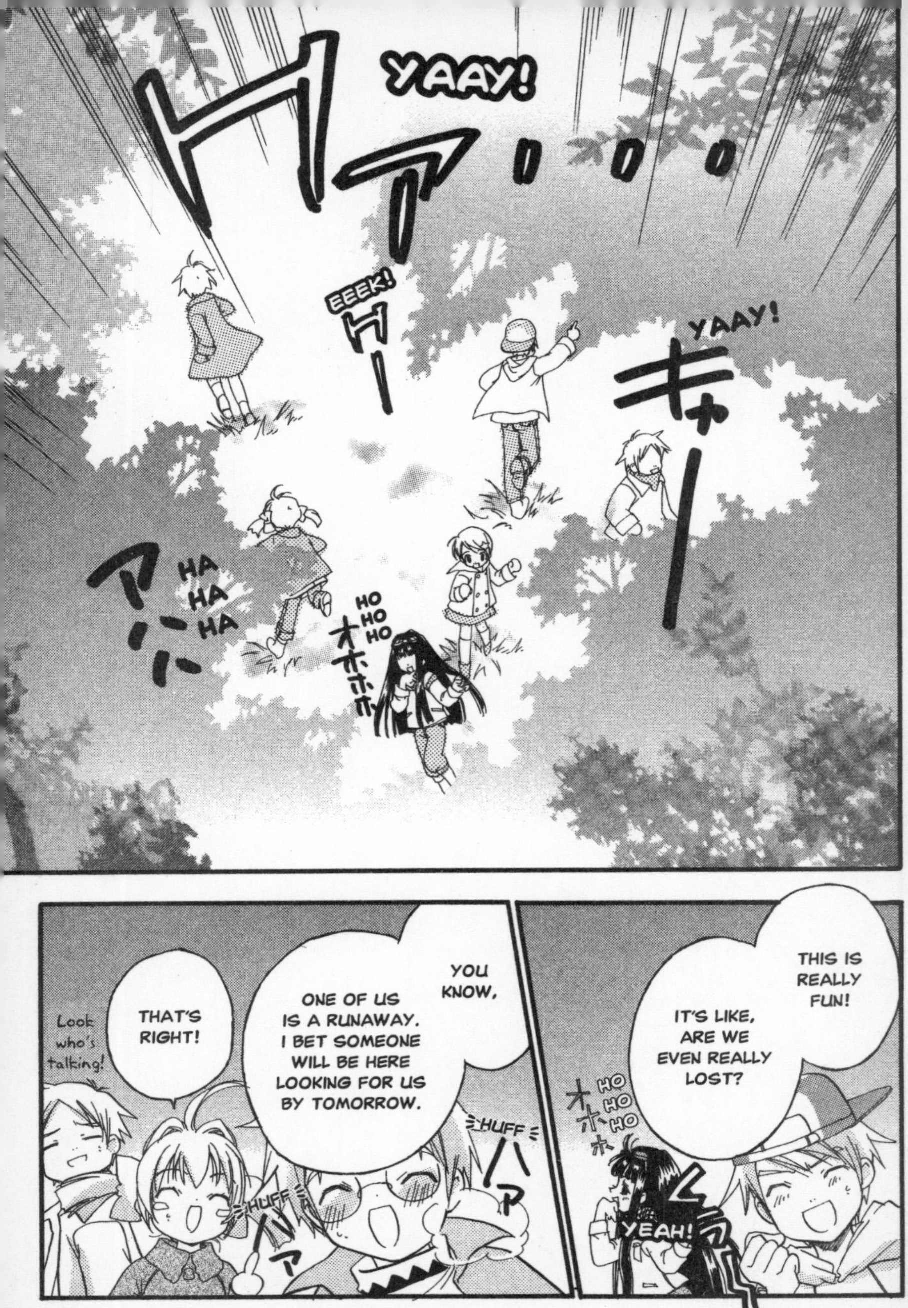
YAAY!
ワァ...
YAAY!
キャー
EEEK!
ヒー
HO HO HO
オホホホ
HA HA HA
アハハ
THIS IS REALLY FUN!
IT'S LIKE, ARE WE EVEN REALLY LOST?
HO HO HO
YEAH!
YOU KNOW,
ONE OF US IS A RUNAWAY. I BET SOMEONE WILL BE HERE LOOKING FOR US BY TOMORROW.
HUFF
HUFF
THAT'S RIGHT!
Look who's talking!

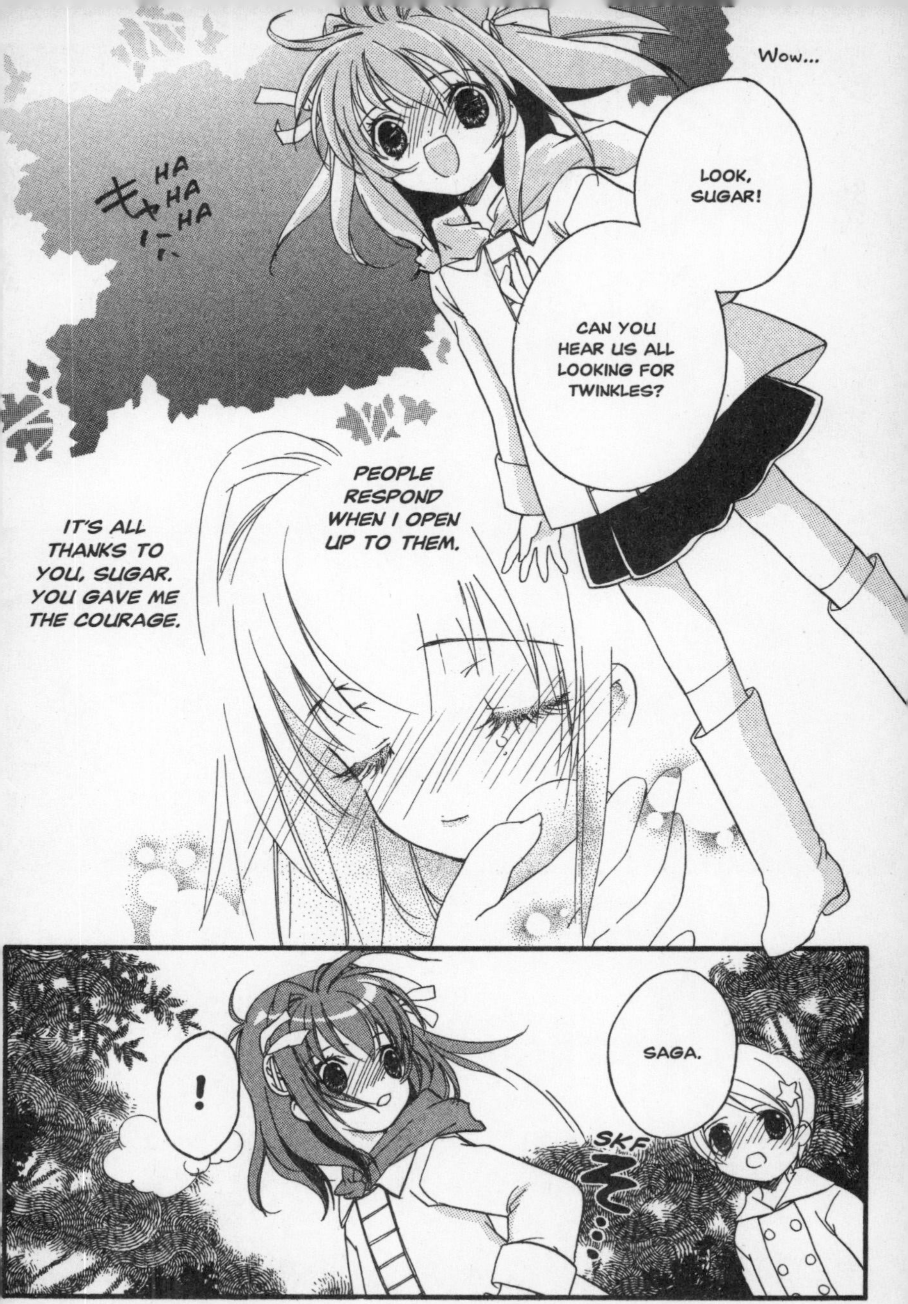
Wow...
LOOK, SUGAR!
CAN YOU HEAR US ALL LOOKING FOR TWINKLES?
HA HA HA
PEOPLE RESPOND WHEN I OPEN UP TO THEM.
IT'S ALL THANKS TO YOU, SUGAR. YOU GAVE ME THE COURAGE.
SAGA.
SKF
!

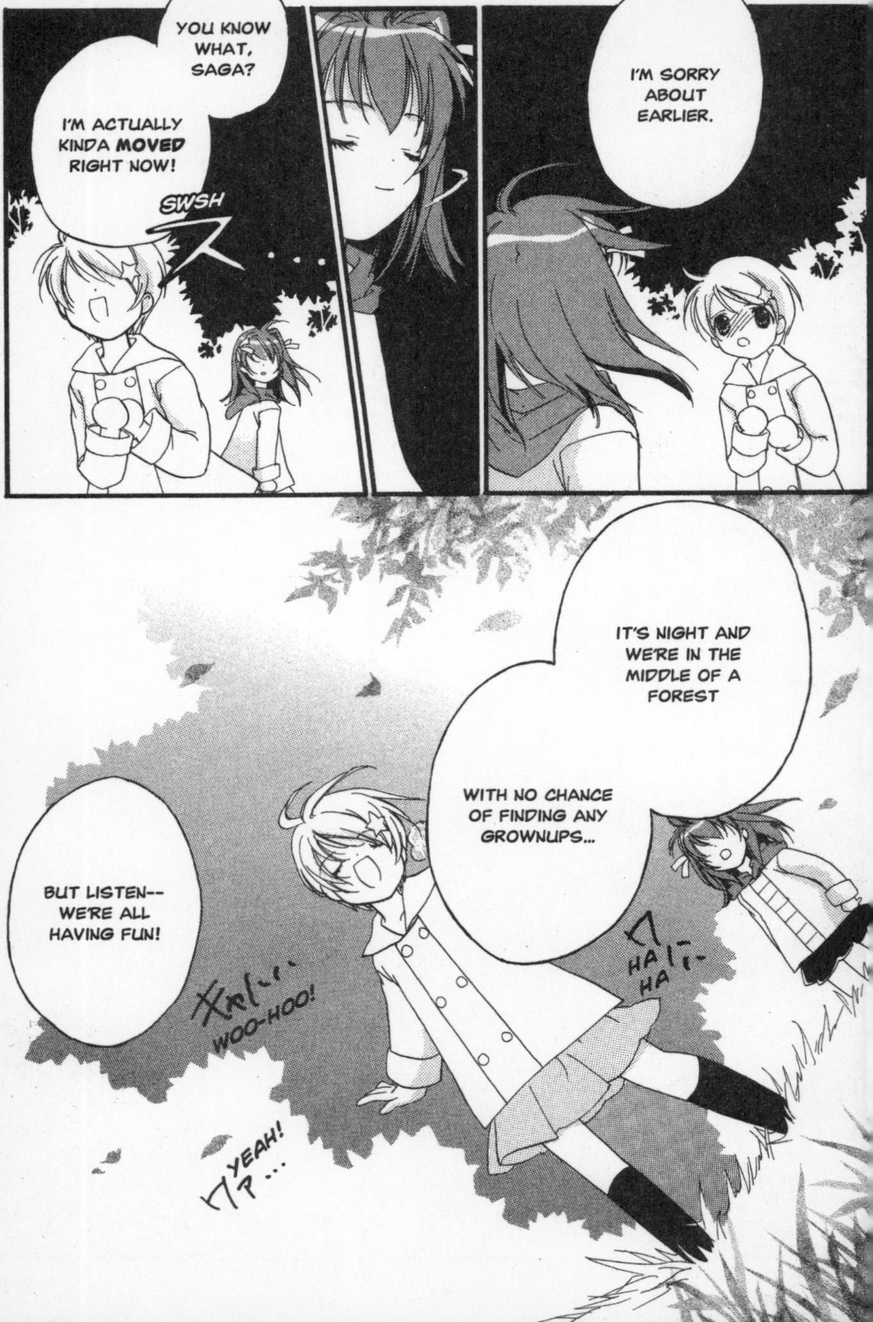
I'M SORRY ABOUT EARLIER.
YOU KNOW WHAT, SAGA?
I'M ACTUALLY KINDA MOVED RIGHT NOW!
SWSH
IT'S NIGHT AND WE'RE IN THE MIDDLE OF A FOREST
WITH NO CHANCE OF FINDING ANY GROWNUPS...
HA HA
BUT LISTEN-- WE'RE ALL HAVING FUN!
WOO-HOO!
YEAH! ...

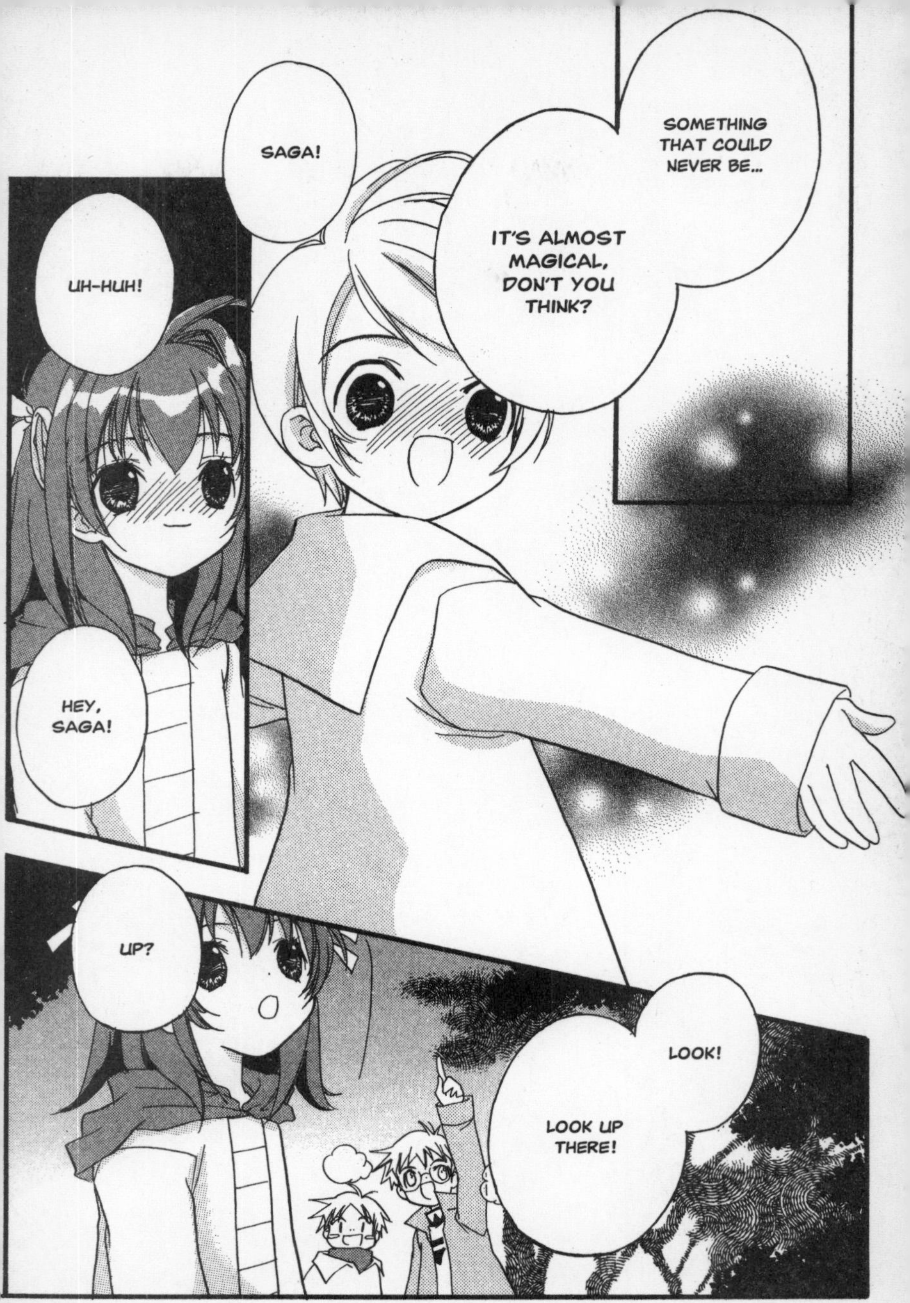

SOMETHING THAT COULD NEVER BE...
IT'S ALMOST MAGICAL, DON'T YOU THINK?
SAGA!
UH-HUH!
HEY, SAGA!
LOOK!
LOOK UP THERE!
UP?

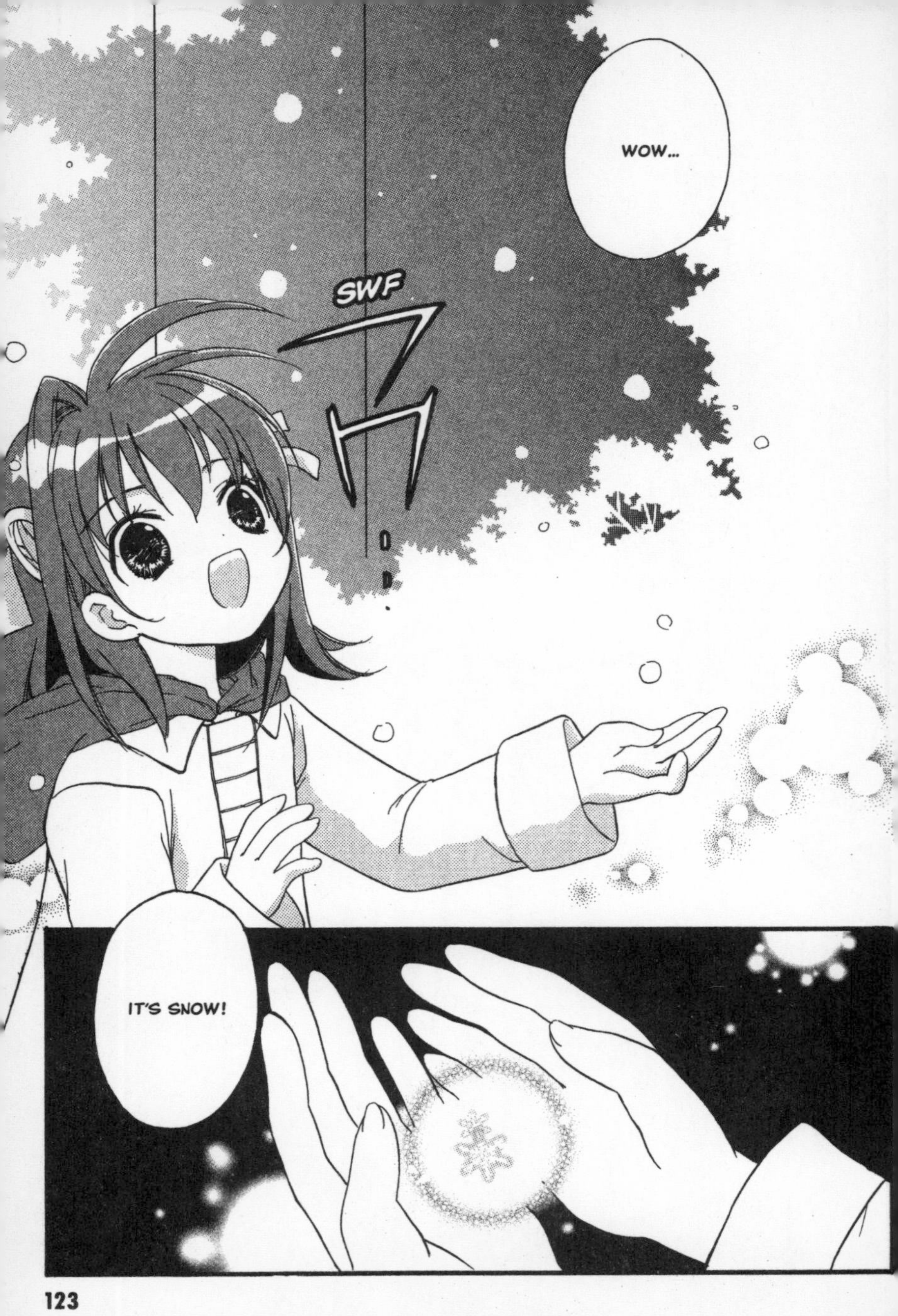
WOW...
SWF
IT'S SNOW!

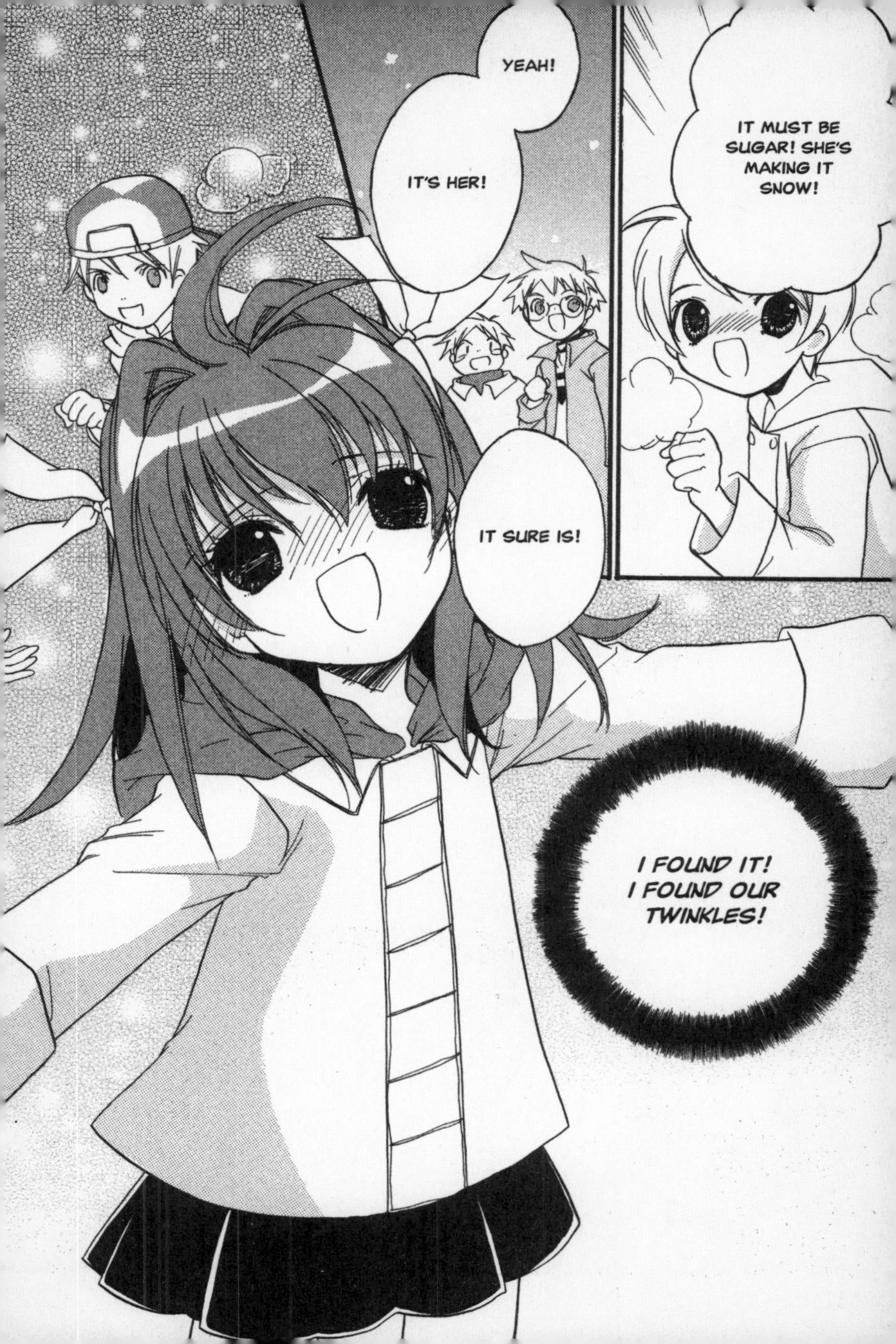
IT MUST BE SUGAR! SHE'S MAKING IT SNOW!
YEAH!
IT'S HER!
IT SURE IS!
I FOUND IT! I FOUND OUR TWINKLES!

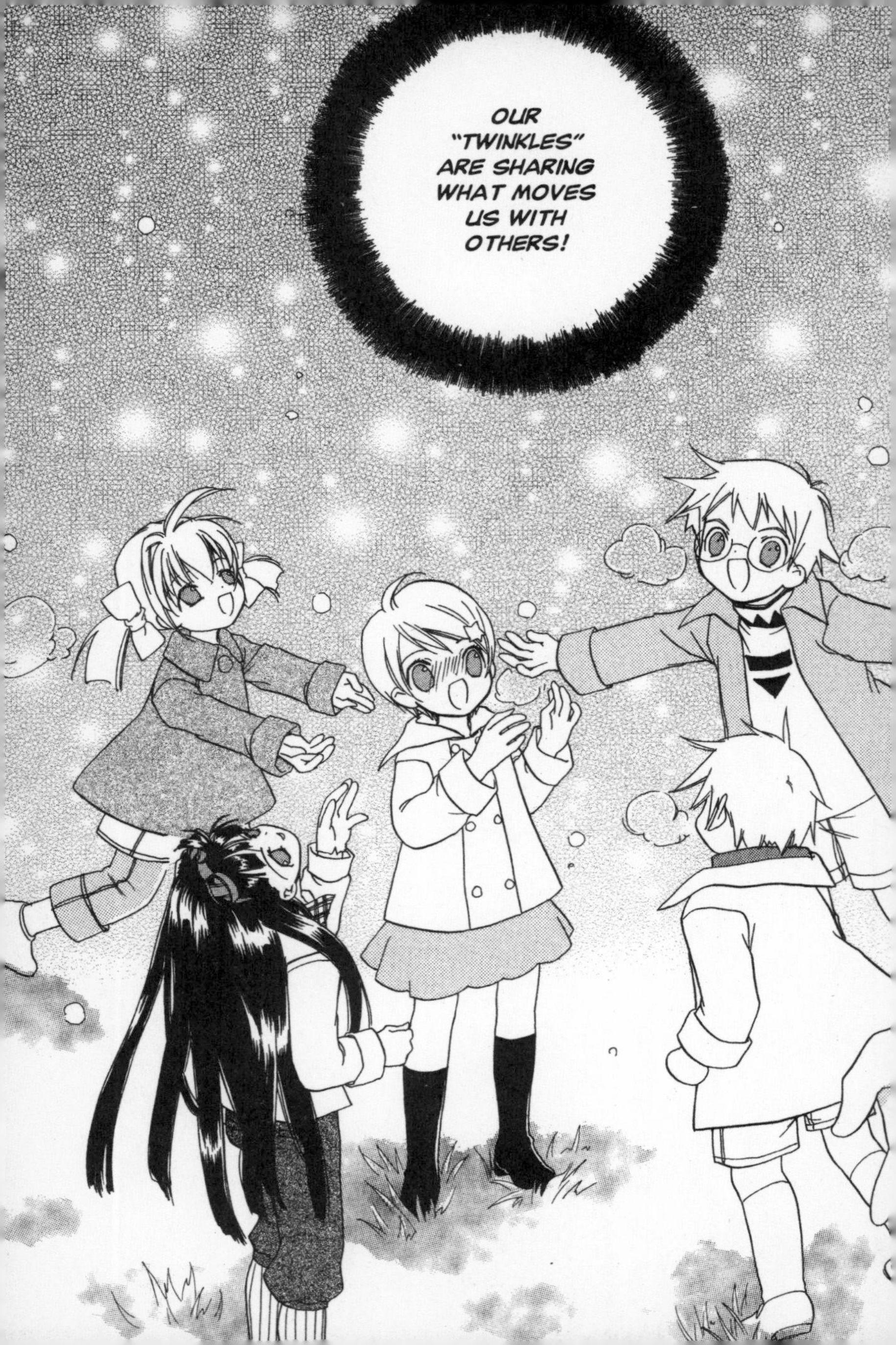
OUR "TWINKLES" ARE SHARING WHAT MOVES US WITH OTHERS!

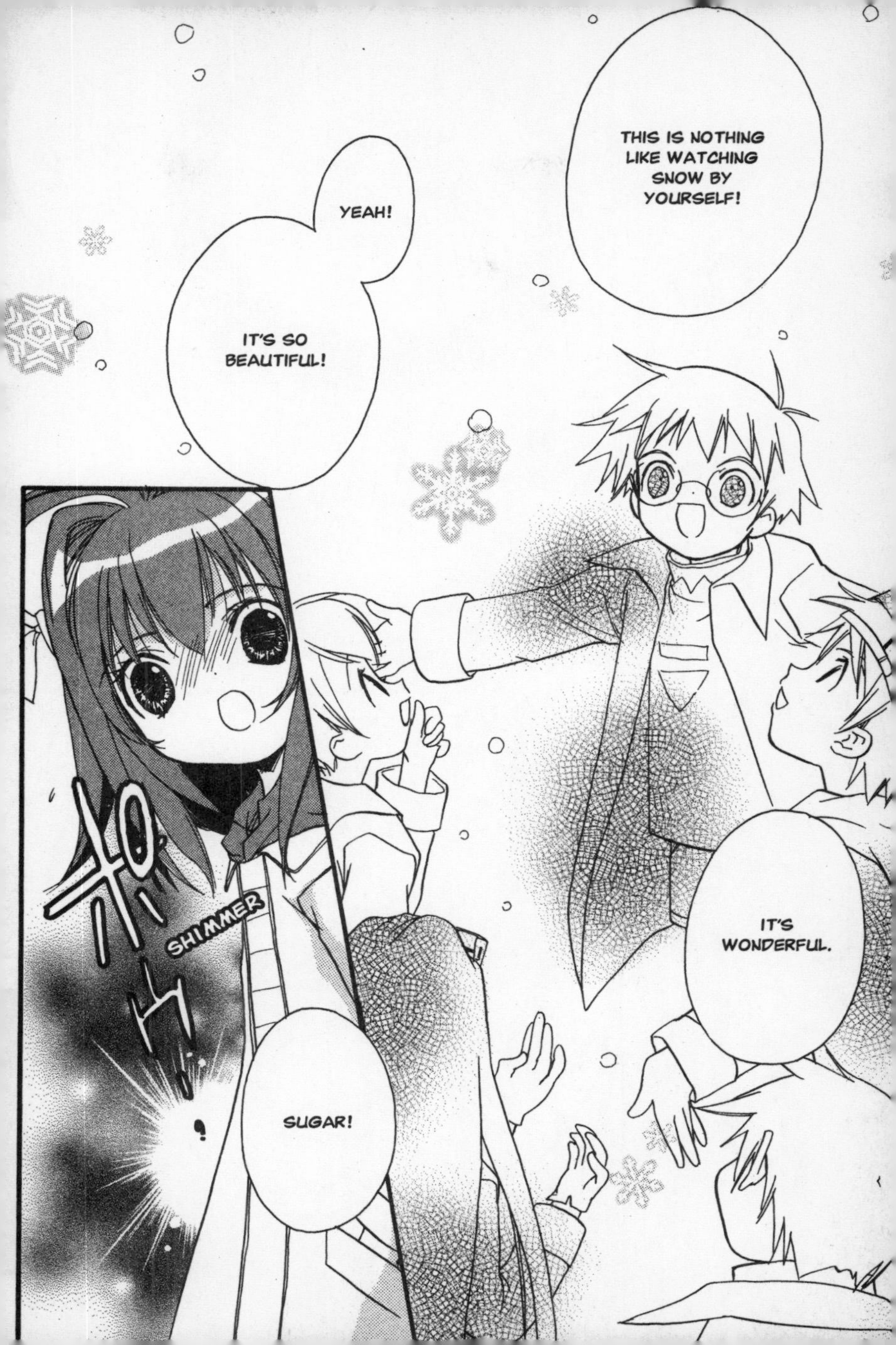
THIS IS NOTHING LIKE WATCHING SNOW BY YOURSELF!
YEAH!
IT'S SO BEAUTIFUL!
IT'S WONDERFUL.
SUGAR!
SHIMMER

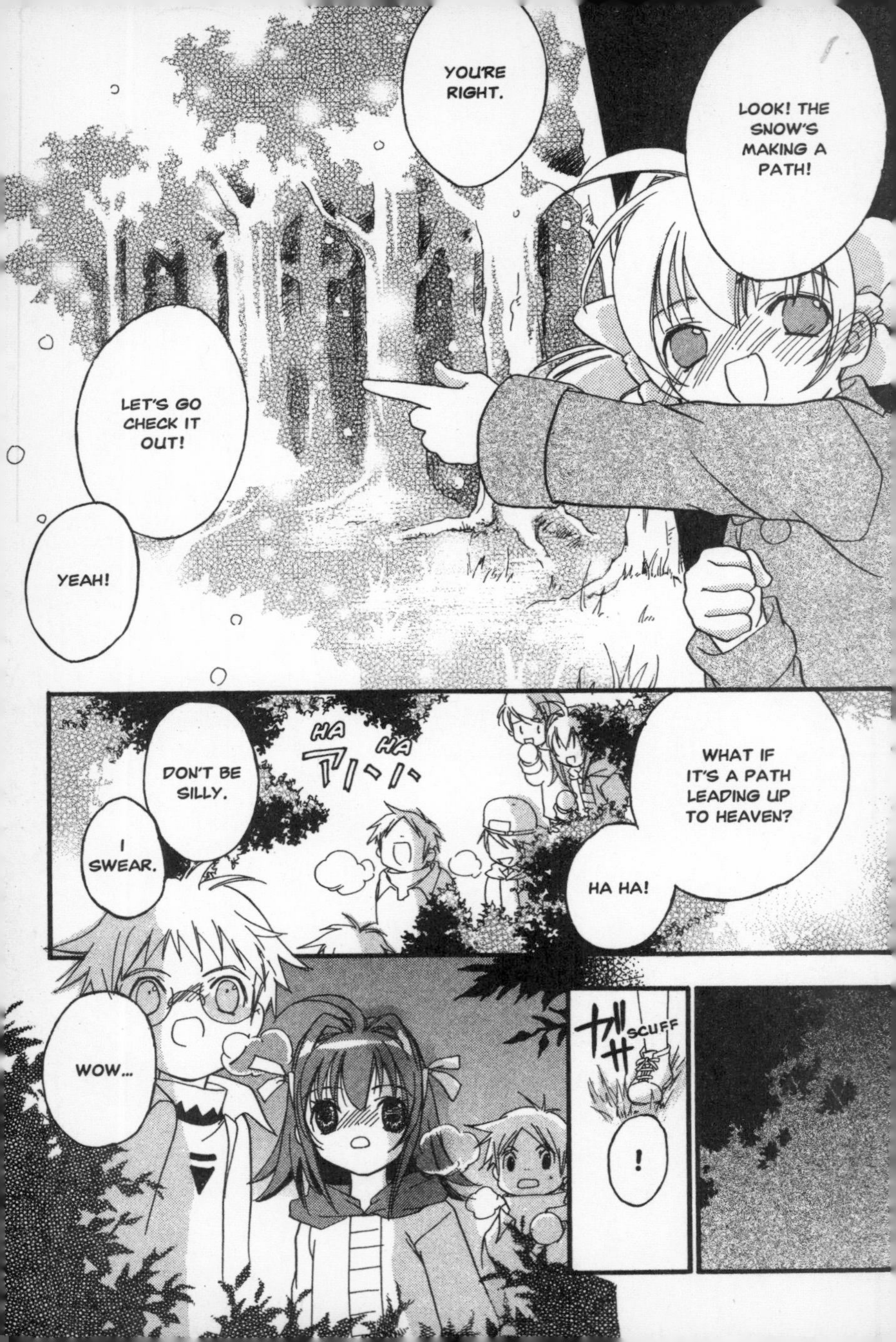
LOOK! THE SNOW'S MAKING A PATH!
YOU'RE RIGHT.
LET'S GO CHECK IT OUT!
YEAH!
WHAT IF IT'S A PATH LEADING UP TO HEAVEN?
HA HA!
HA HA
DON'T BE SILLY.
I SWEAR.
SCUFF
!
WOW...

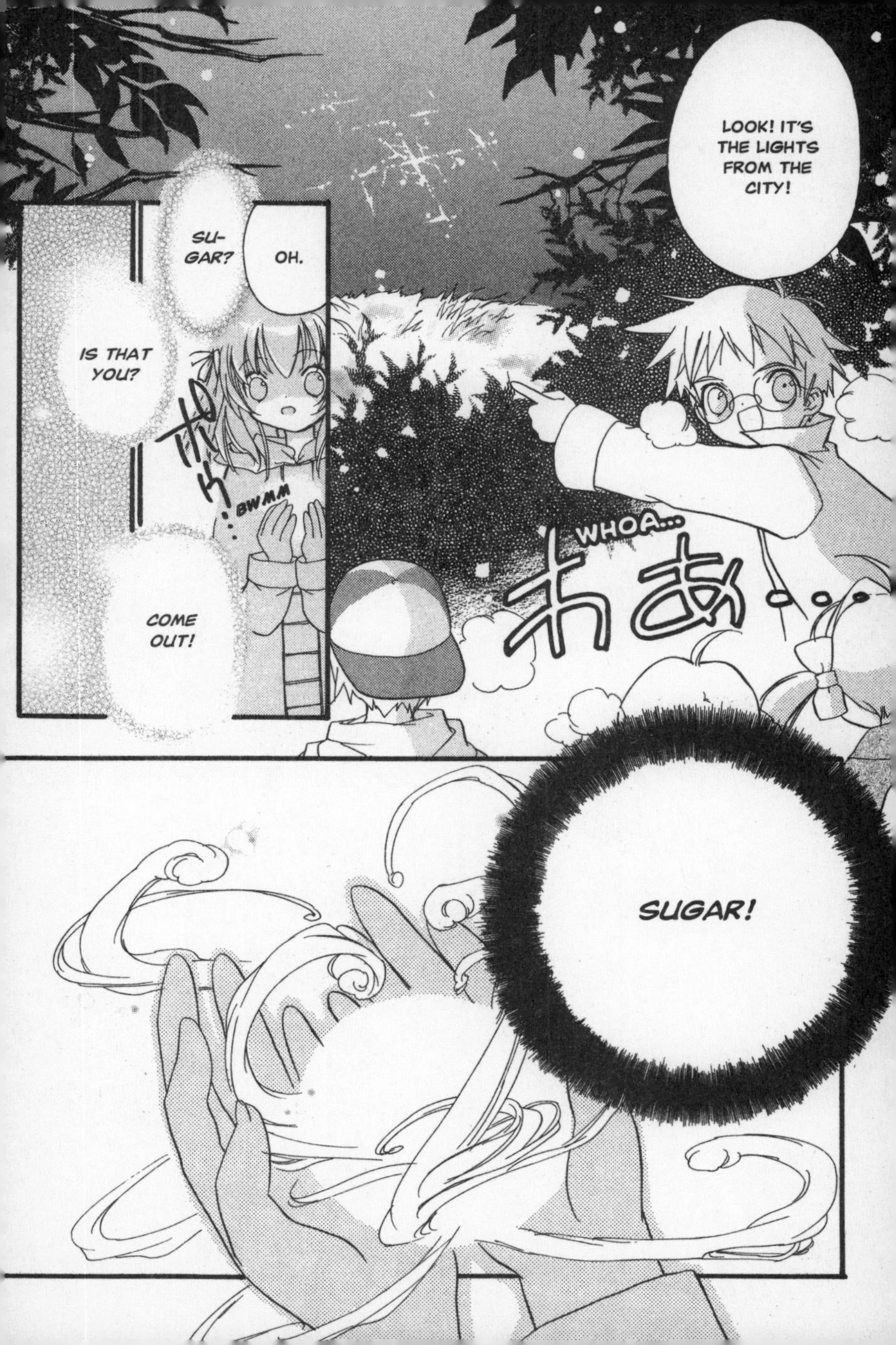
LOOK! IT'S THE LIGHTS FROM THE CITY!
WHOA...
わあ…
OH.
SU-GAR?
IS THAT YOU?
BWMM
COME OUT!
SUGAR!

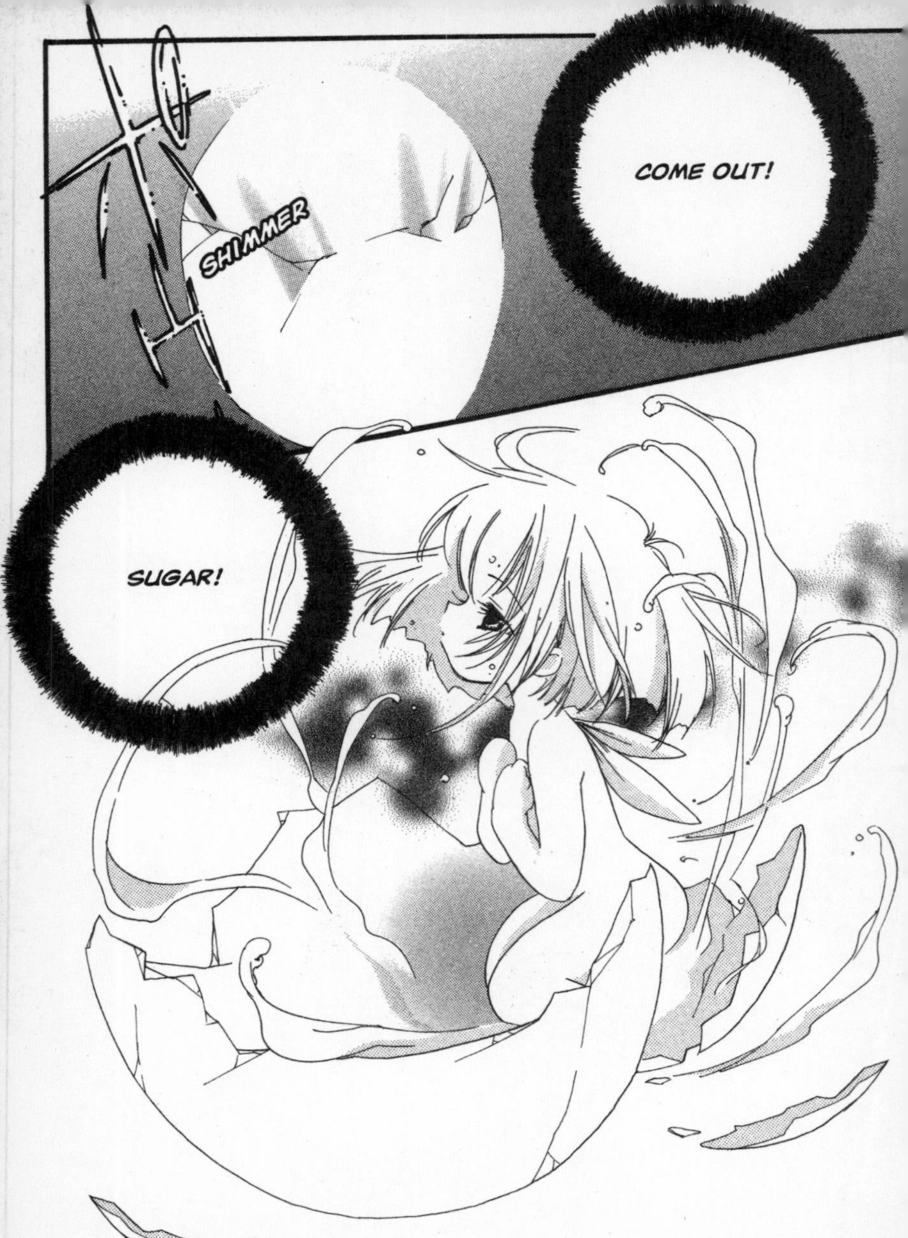
COME OUT!
SHIMMER
SUGAR!

CHAPTER 14 Sugar Baby Love

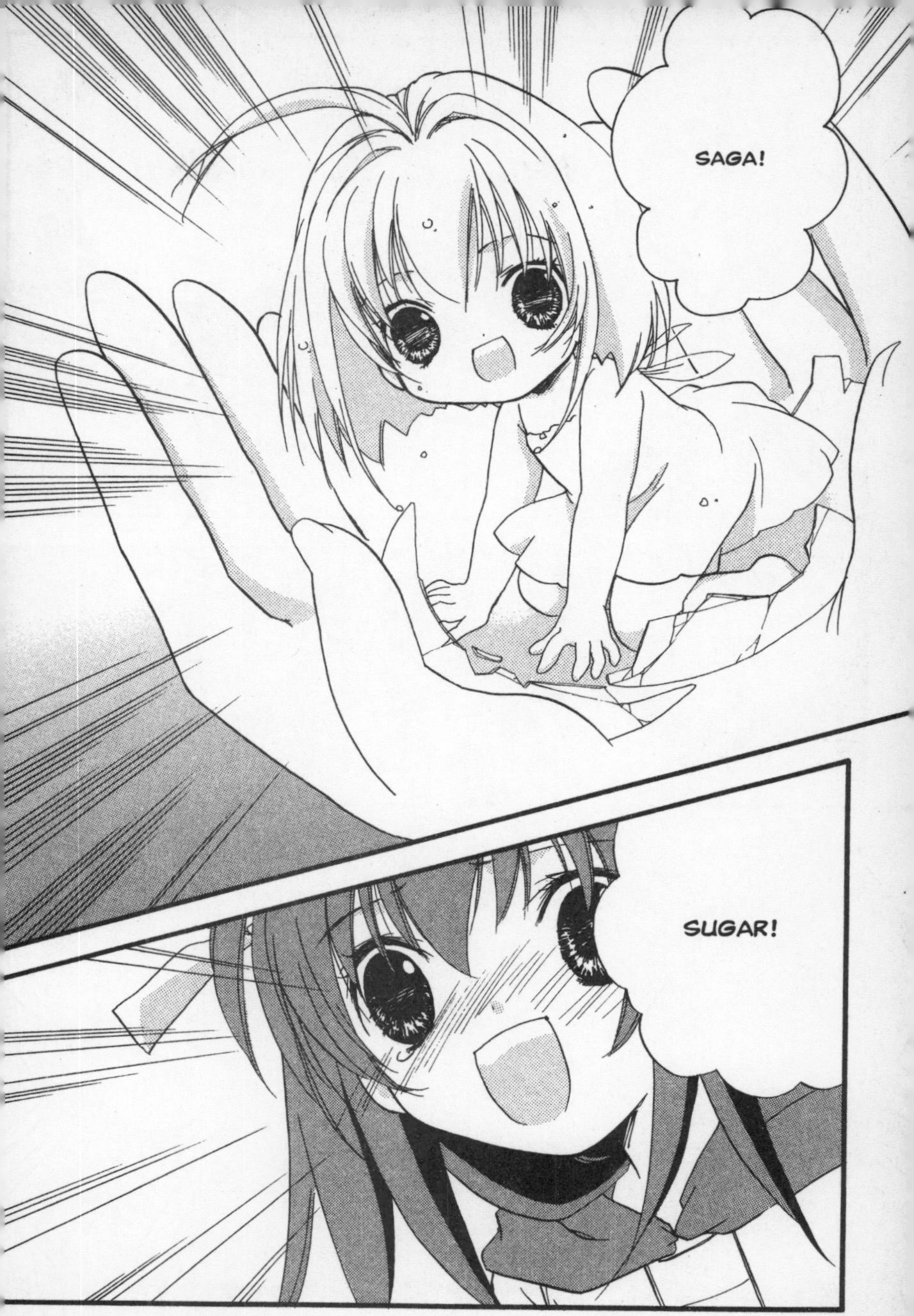
SAGA!
SUGAR!

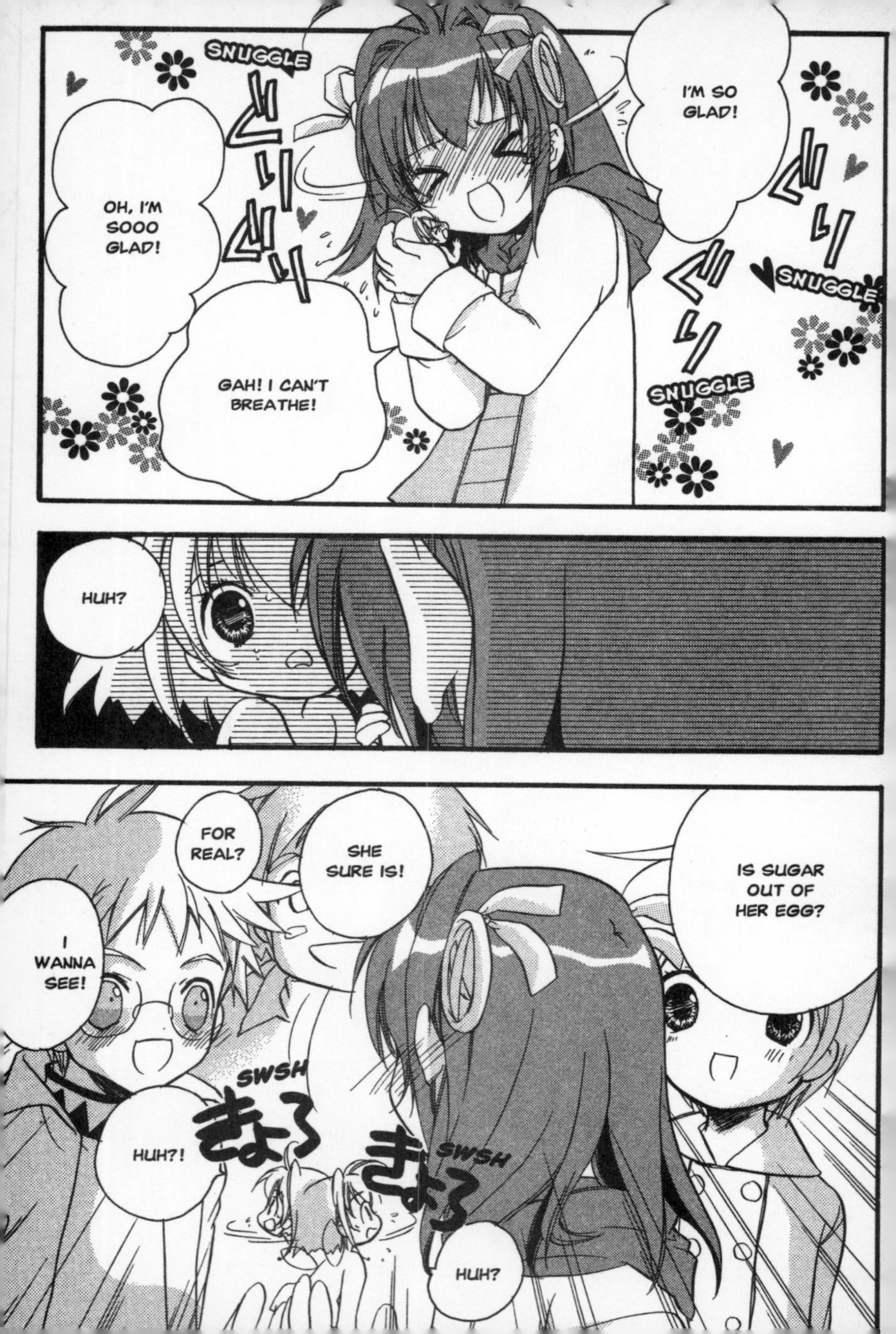
I'M SO GLAD!
SNUGGLE
SNUGGLE
SNUGGLE
OH, I'M SOOO GLAD!
GAH! I CAN'T BREATHE!
HUH?
IS SUGAR OUT OF HER EGG?
SHE SURE IS!
FOR REAL?
I WANNA SEE!
SWSH
SWSH
きょろ きょろ
HUH?!
HUH?

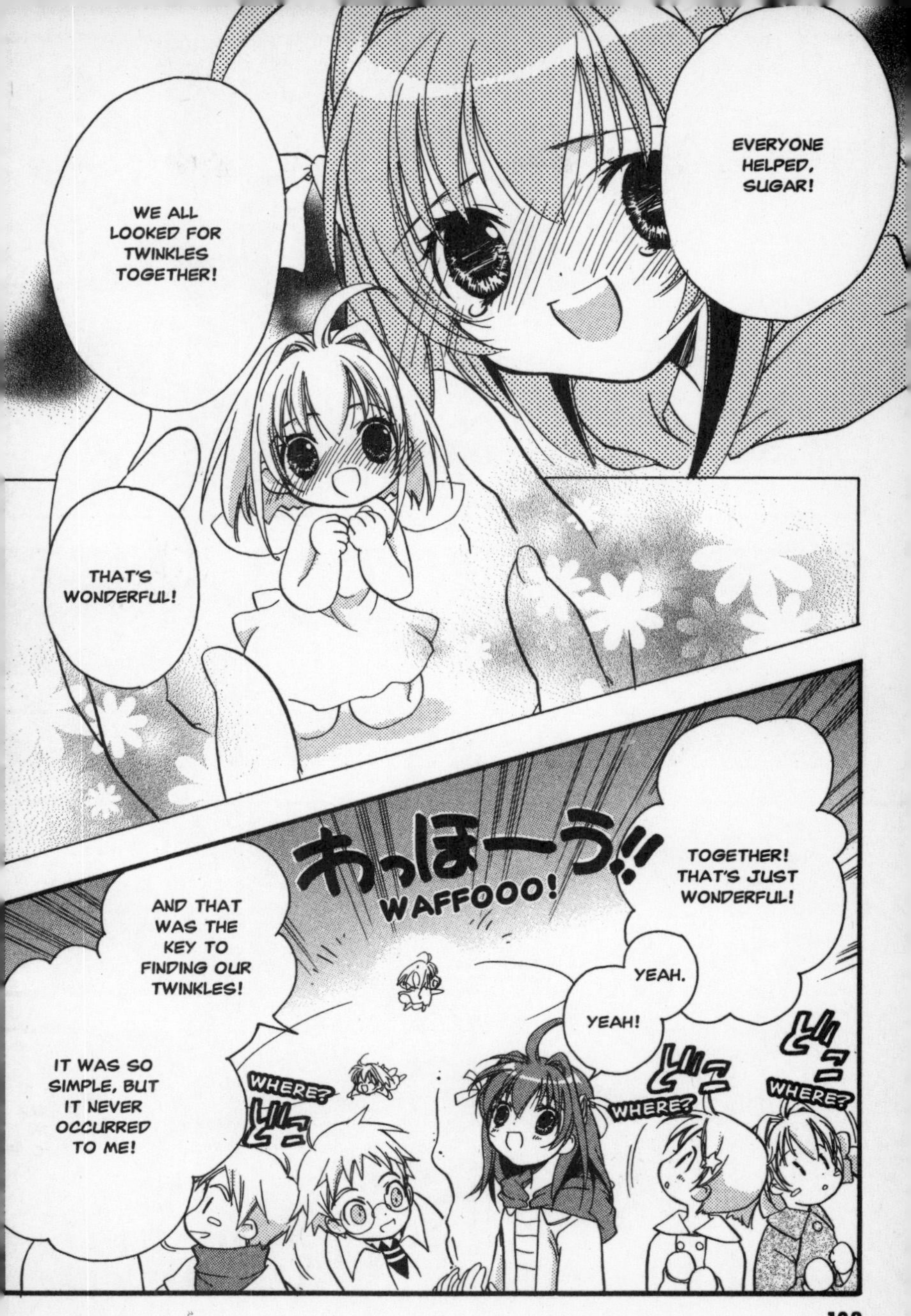
EVERYONE HELPED, SUGAR!
WE ALL LOOKED FOR TWINKLES TOGETHER!
THAT'S WONDERFUL!
TOGETHER! THAT'S JUST WONDERFUL!
わっほーう!!
WAFFOOO!
AND THAT WAS THE KEY TO FINDING OUR TWINKLES!
YEAH.
YEAH!
どこ
WHERE?
どこ
WHERE?
IT WAS SO SIMPLE, BUT IT NEVER OCCURRED TO ME!
WHERE?
どこ

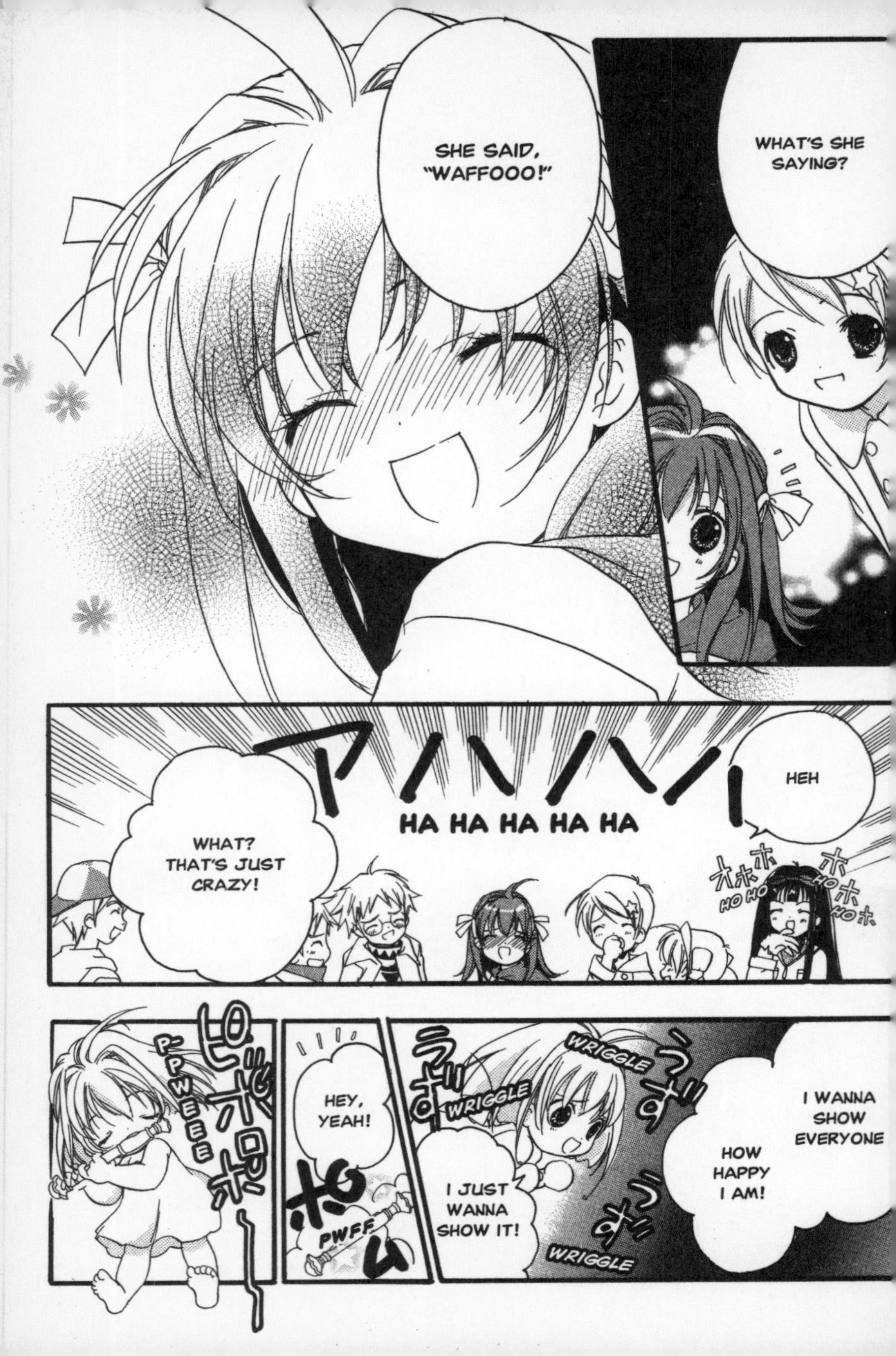
WHAT'S SHE SAYING?
SHE SAID, "WAFFOOO!"
HEH
HO HO HO HO
HA HA HA HA HA
WHAT? THAT'S JUST CRAZY!
I WANNA SHOW EVERYONE
HOW HAPPY I AM!
WRIGGLE
WRIGGLE
I JUST WANNA SHOW IT!
WRIGGLE
HEY, YEAH!
PWFF
P-PWEEE

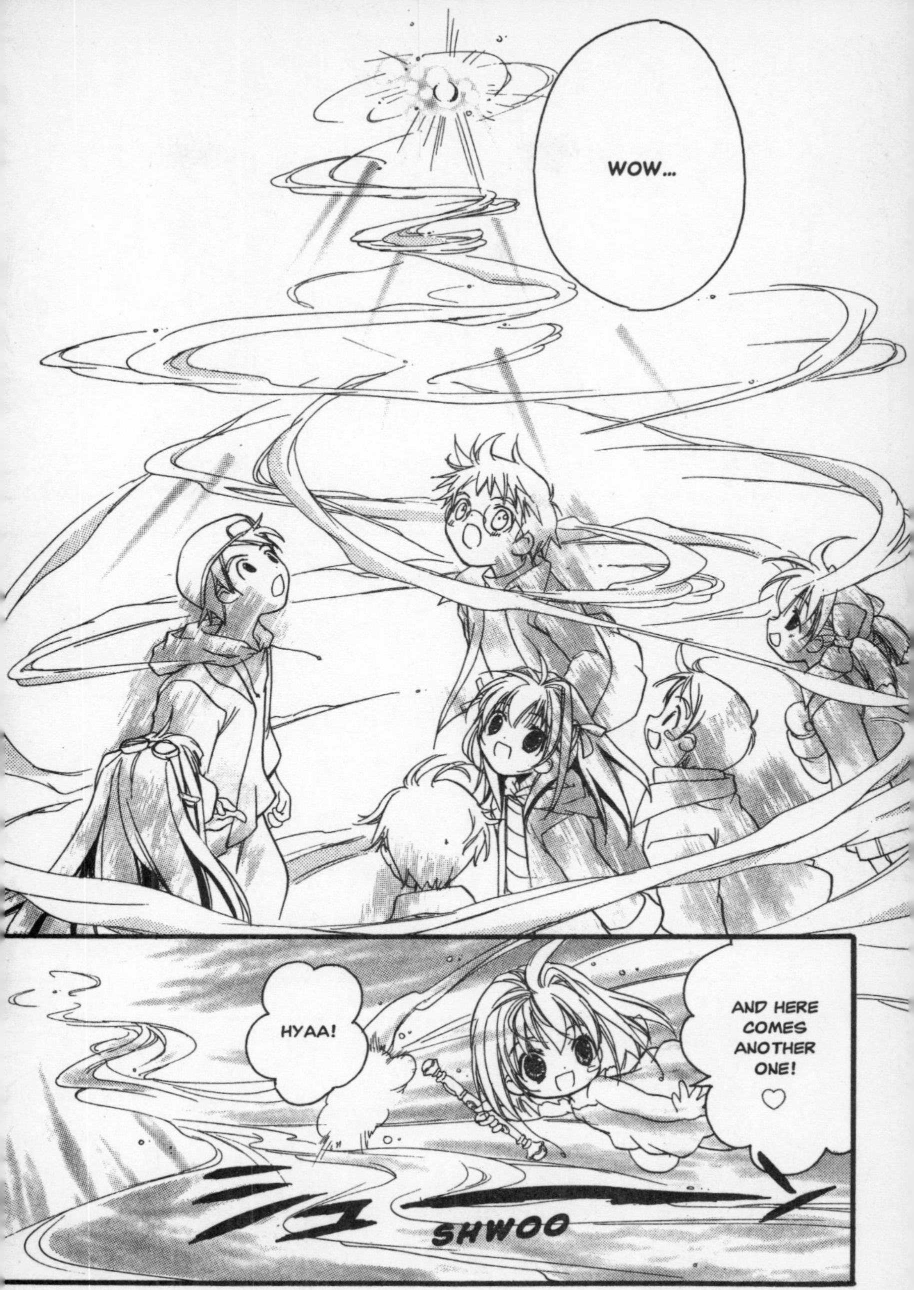
WOW...
AND HERE COMES ANOTHER ONE! ♡
HYAA!
SHWOO

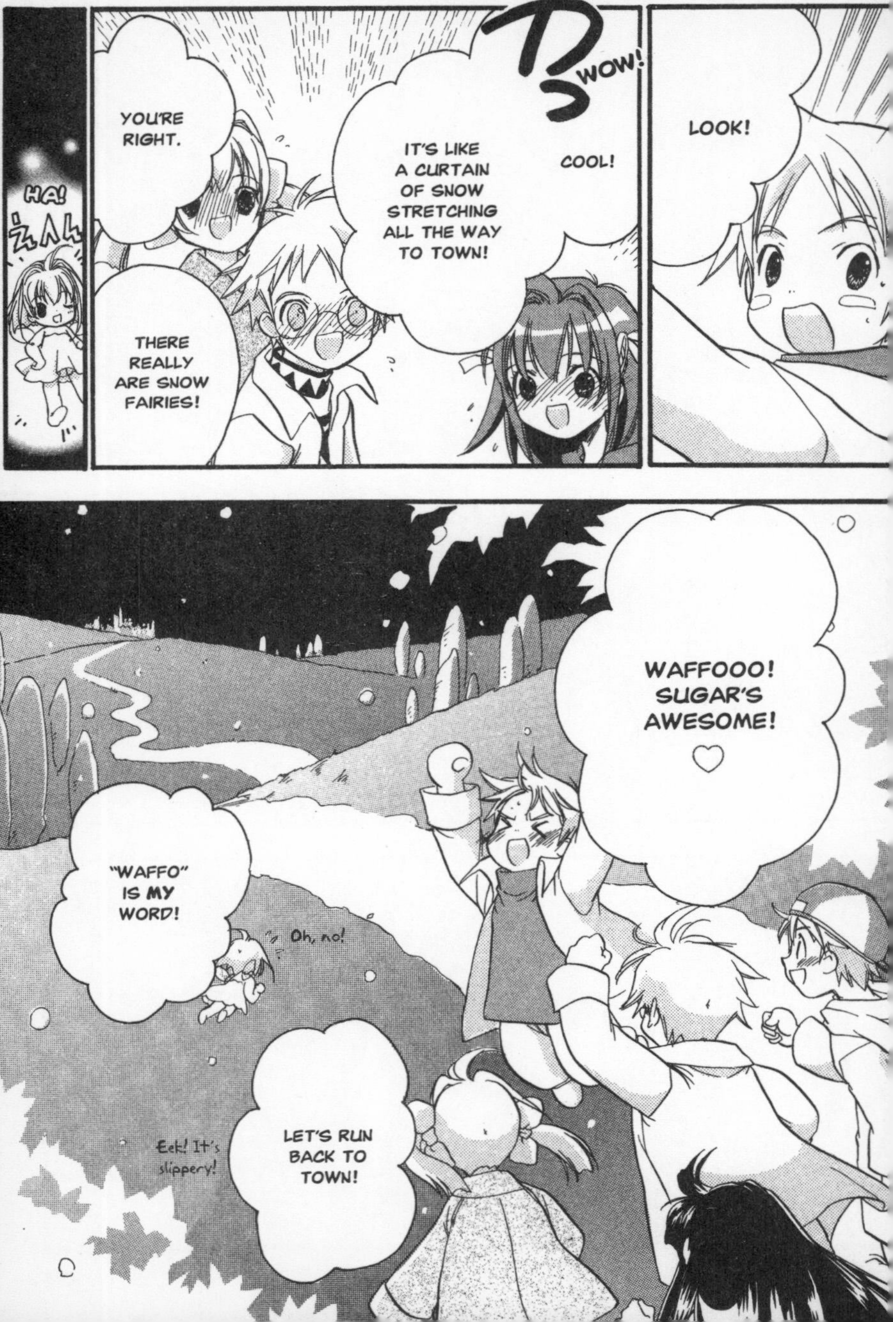
LOOK!
わっ
WOW!
COOL!
IT'S LIKE A CURTAIN OF SNOW STRETCHING ALL THE WAY TO TOWN!
YOU'RE RIGHT.
THERE REALLY ARE SNOW FAIRIES!
HA!
えへん
WAFFOOO! SUGAR'S AWESOME! ♡
"WAFFO" IS MY WORD!
Oh, no!
LET'S RUN BACK TO TOWN!
Eek! It's slippery!

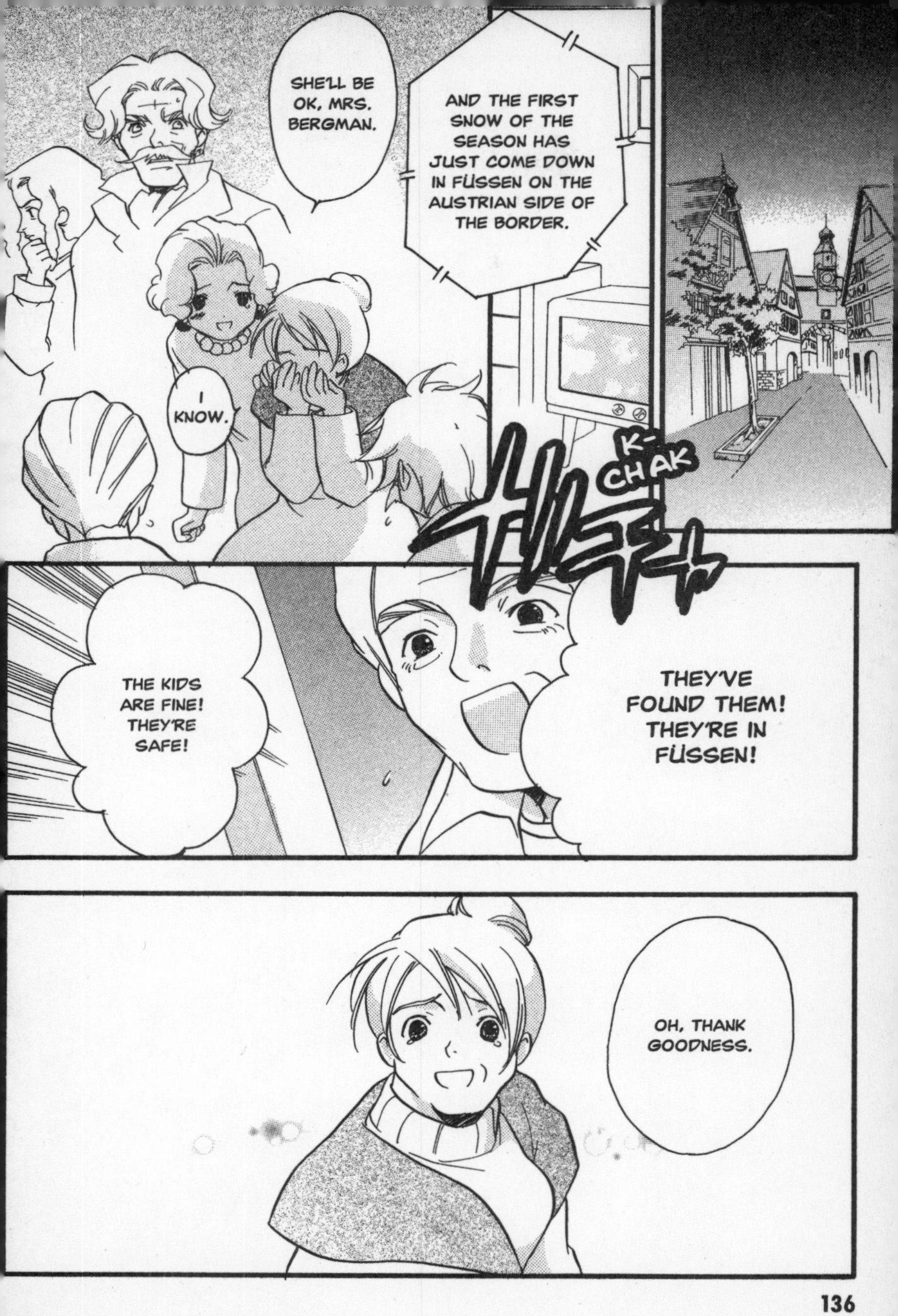
AND THE FIRST SNOW OF THE SEASON HAS JUST COME DOWN IN FÜSSEN ON THE AUSTRIAN SIDE OF THE BORDER.
SHE'LL BE OK, MRS. BERGMAN.
I KNOW.
K-CHAK
THEY'VE FOUND THEM! THEY'RE IN FÜSSEN!
THE KIDS ARE FINE! THEY'RE SAFE!
OH, THANK GOODNESS.

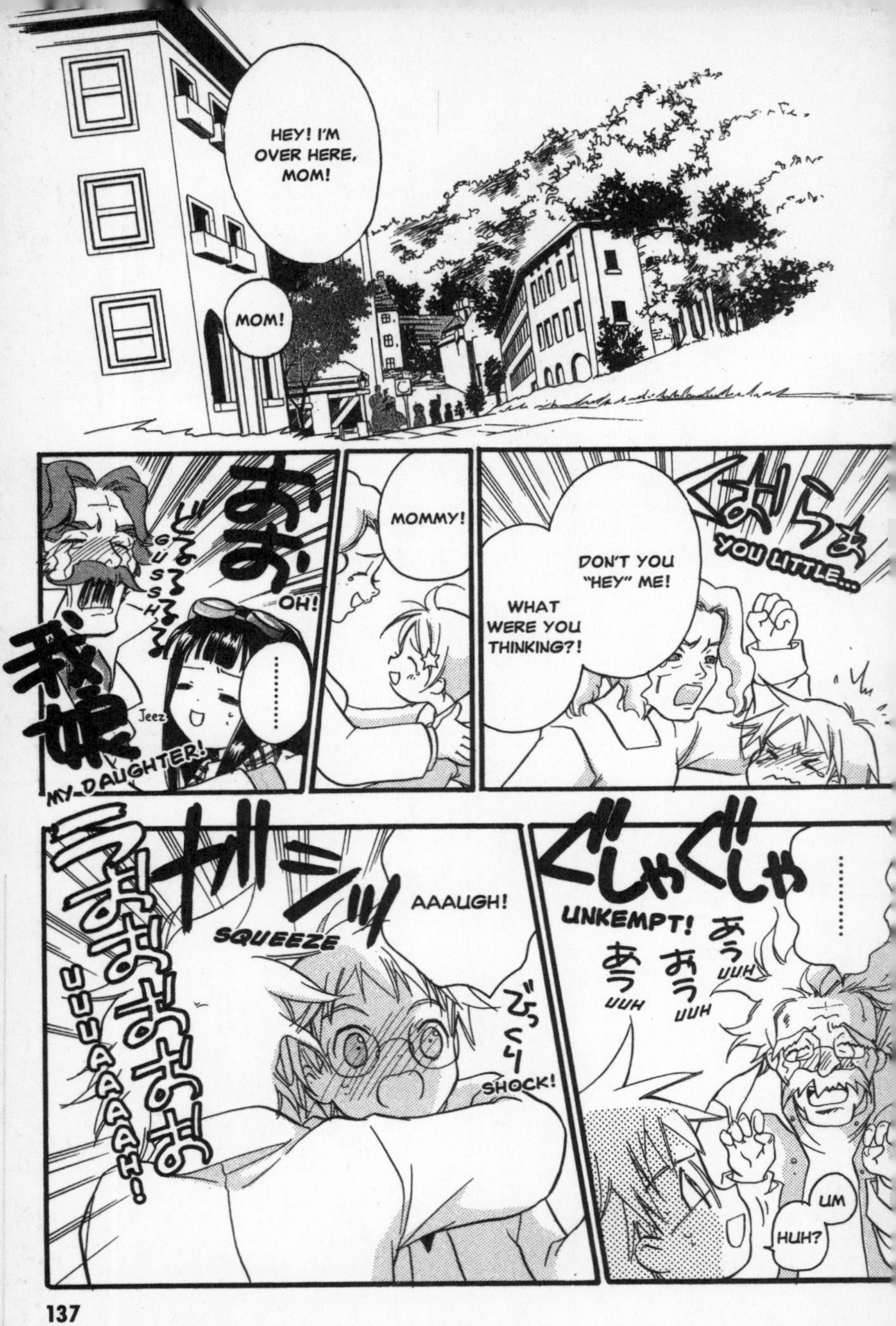

HEY! I'M OVER HERE, MOM!
MOM!
YOU LITTLE...
DON'T YOU "HEY" ME!
WHAT WERE YOU THINKING?!
MOMMY!
OH!
GUSSSH
......
Jeez
MY DAUGHTER!
......
UNKEMPT!
UUH
UUH
UUH
UM
HUH?
AAAUGH!
SQUEEZE
SHOCK!
UUUUAAAAAH!

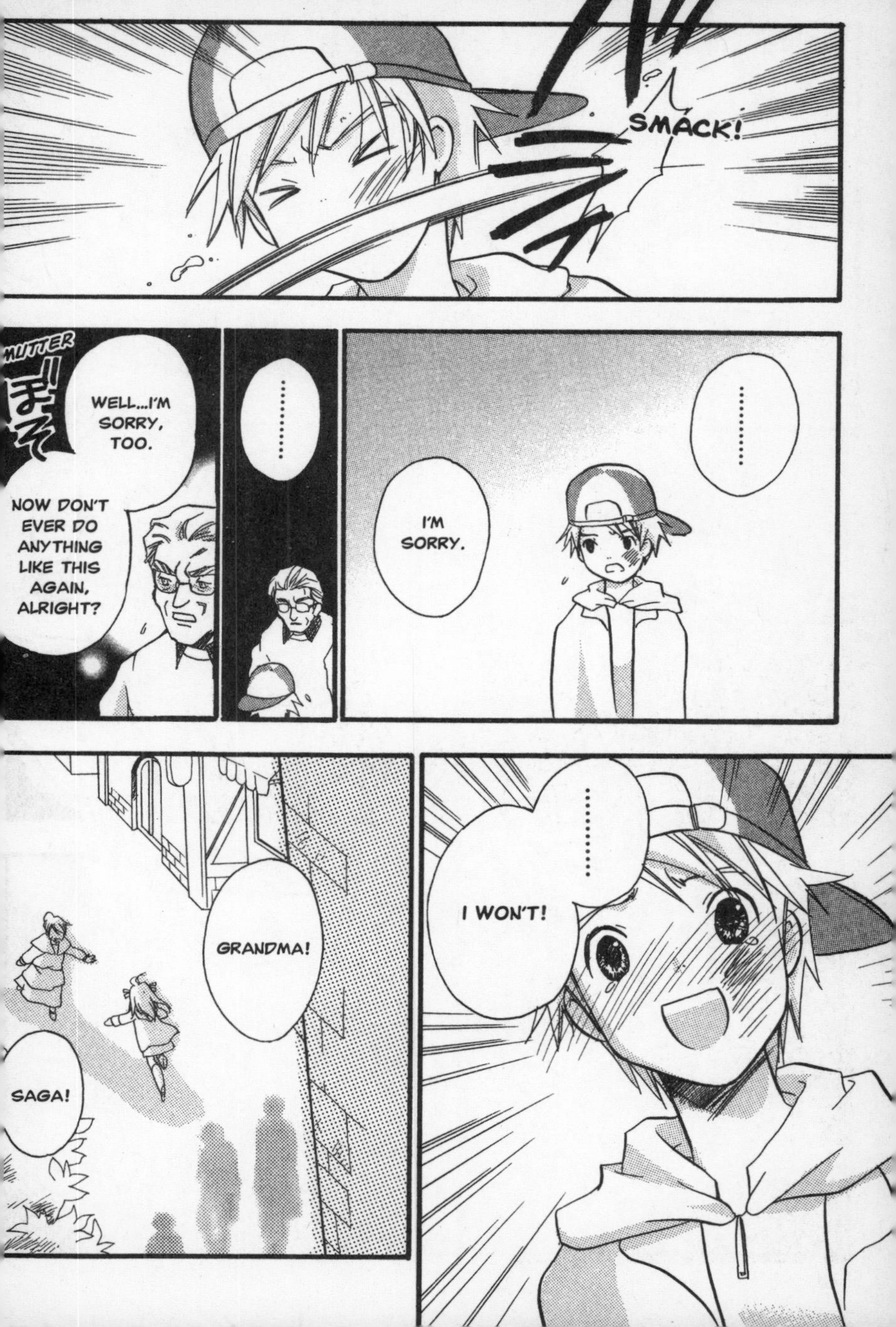
SMACK!
......
I'M SORRY.
......
MUTTER
ぼそ
WELL...I'M SORRY, TOO.
NOW DON'T EVER DO ANYTHING LIKE THIS AGAIN, ALRIGHT?
......
I WON'T!
GRANDMA!
SAGA!

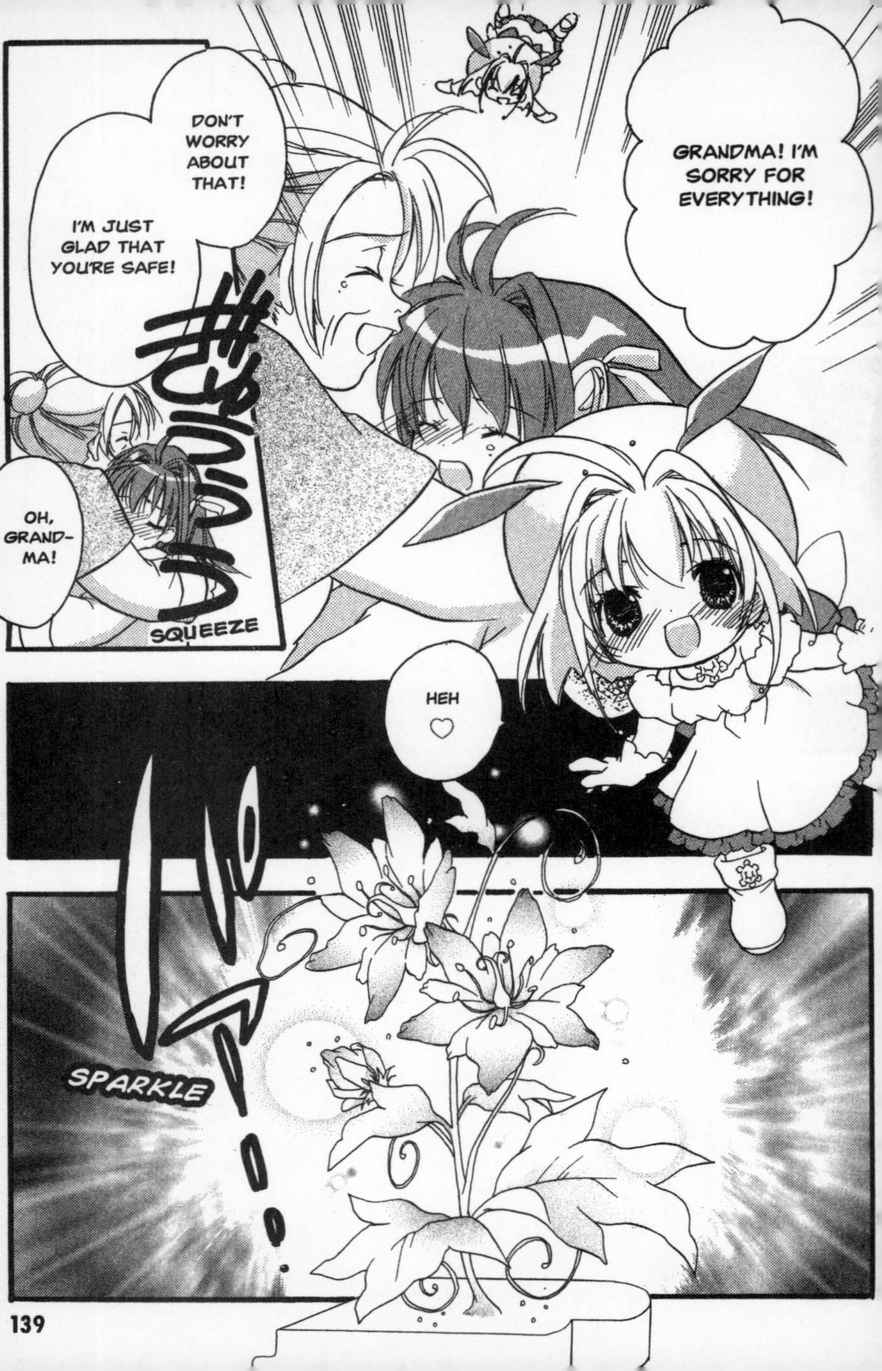
GRANDMA! I'M SORRY FOR EVERYTHING!
DON'T WORRY ABOUT THAT!
I'M JUST GLAD THAT YOU'RE SAFE!
OH, GRAND-MA!
SQUEEZE
HEH ♡
SPARKLE

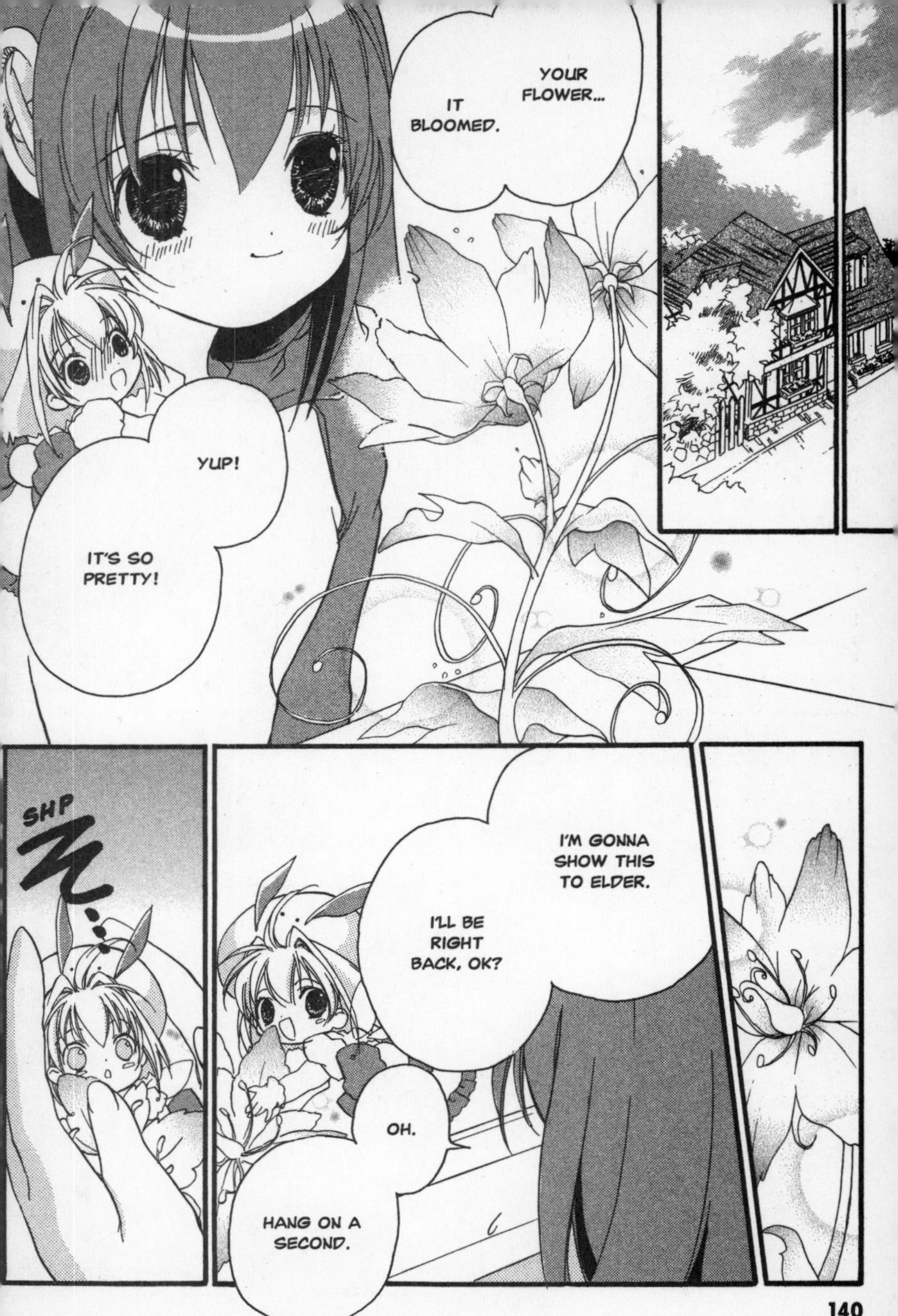
YOUR FLOWER... IT BLOOMED.
YUP! IT'S SO PRETTY!
I'M GONNA SHOW THIS TO ELDER. I'LL BE RIGHT BACK, OK?
OH. HANG ON A SECOND.
SHP

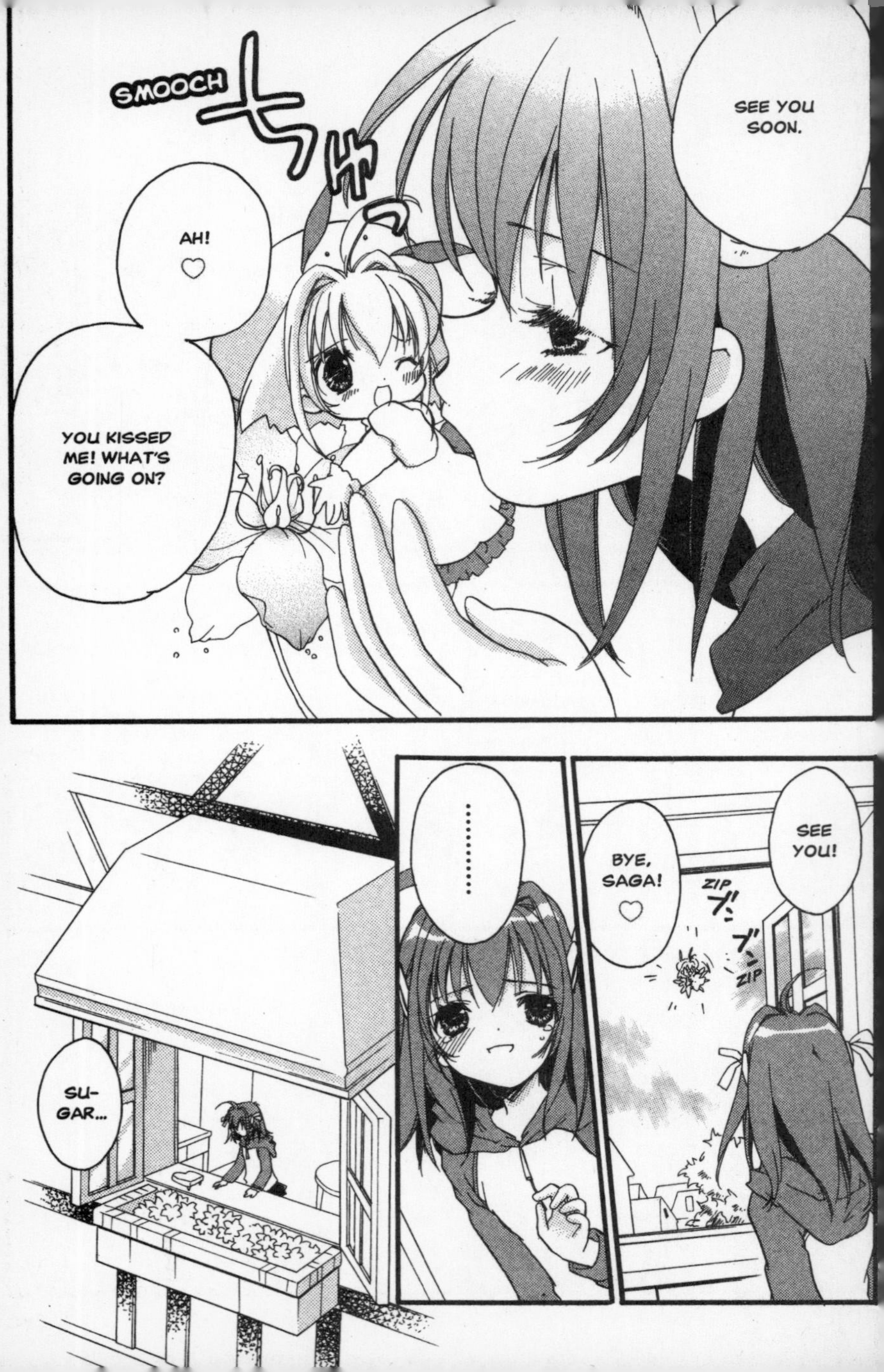
SEE YOU SOON.
SMOOCH
AH! ♡
YOU KISSED ME! WHAT'S GOING ON?
SEE YOU!
BYE, SAGA! ♡
ZIP
ZIP
……
SU-GAR...

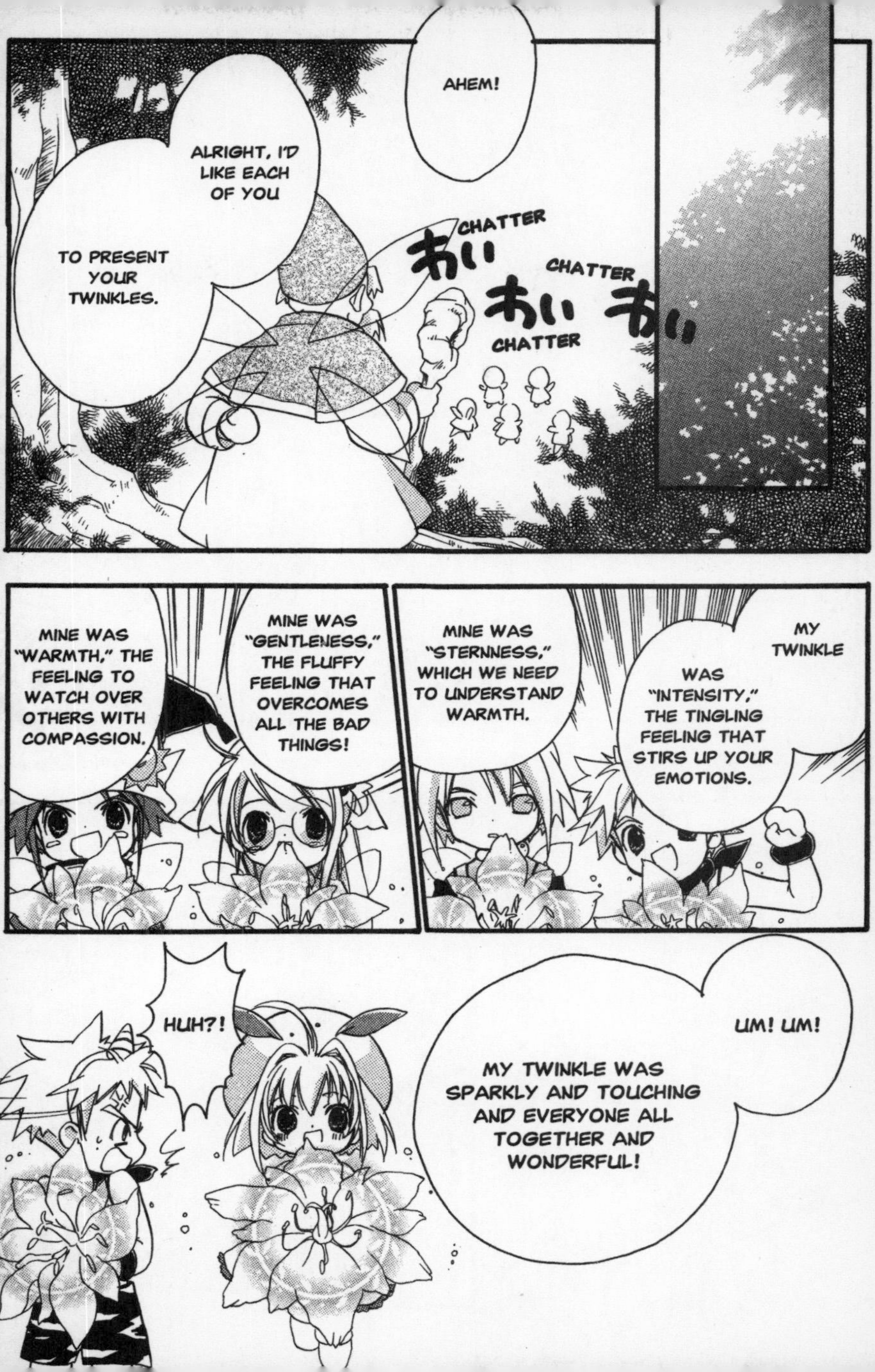
AHEM!
CHATTER
おい
CHATTER
おい
おい
CHATTER
ALRIGHT, I'D LIKE EACH OF YOU
TO PRESENT YOUR TWINKLES.
MY TWINKLE WAS "INTENSITY," THE TINGLING FEELING THAT STIRS UP YOUR EMOTIONS.
MINE WAS "STERNNESS," WHICH WE NEED TO UNDERSTAND WARMTH.
MINE WAS "GENTLENESS," THE FLUFFY FEELING THAT OVERCOMES ALL THE BAD THINGS!
MINE WAS "WARMTH," THE FEELING TO WATCH OVER OTHERS WITH COMPASSION.
UM! UM!
MY TWINKLE WAS SPARKLY AND TOUCHING AND EVERYONE ALL TOGETHER AND WONDERFUL!
HUH?!

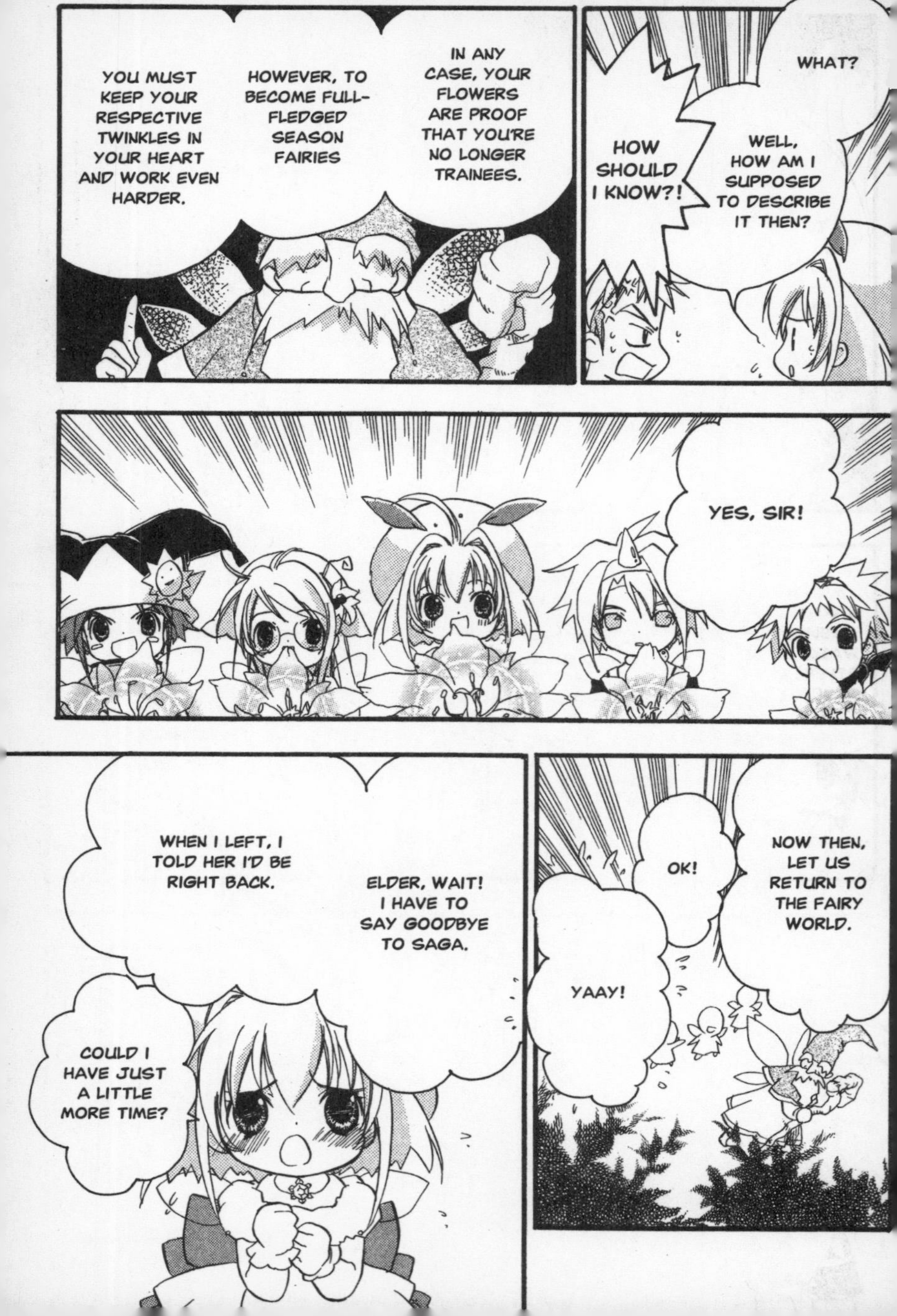
WHAT?
WELL, HOW AM I SUPPOSED TO DESCRIBE IT THEN?
HOW SHOULD I KNOW?!
IN ANY CASE, YOUR FLOWERS ARE PROOF THAT YOU'RE NO LONGER TRAINEES.
HOWEVER, TO BECOME FULL-FLEDGED SEASON FAIRIES
YOU MUST KEEP YOUR RESPECTIVE TWINKLES IN YOUR HEART AND WORK EVEN HARDER.
YES, SIR!
NOW THEN, LET US RETURN TO THE FAIRY WORLD.
OK!
YAAY!
ELDER, WAIT! I HAVE TO SAY GOODBYE TO SAGA.
WHEN I LEFT, I TOLD HER I'D BE RIGHT BACK.
COULD I HAVE JUST A LITTLE MORE TIME?

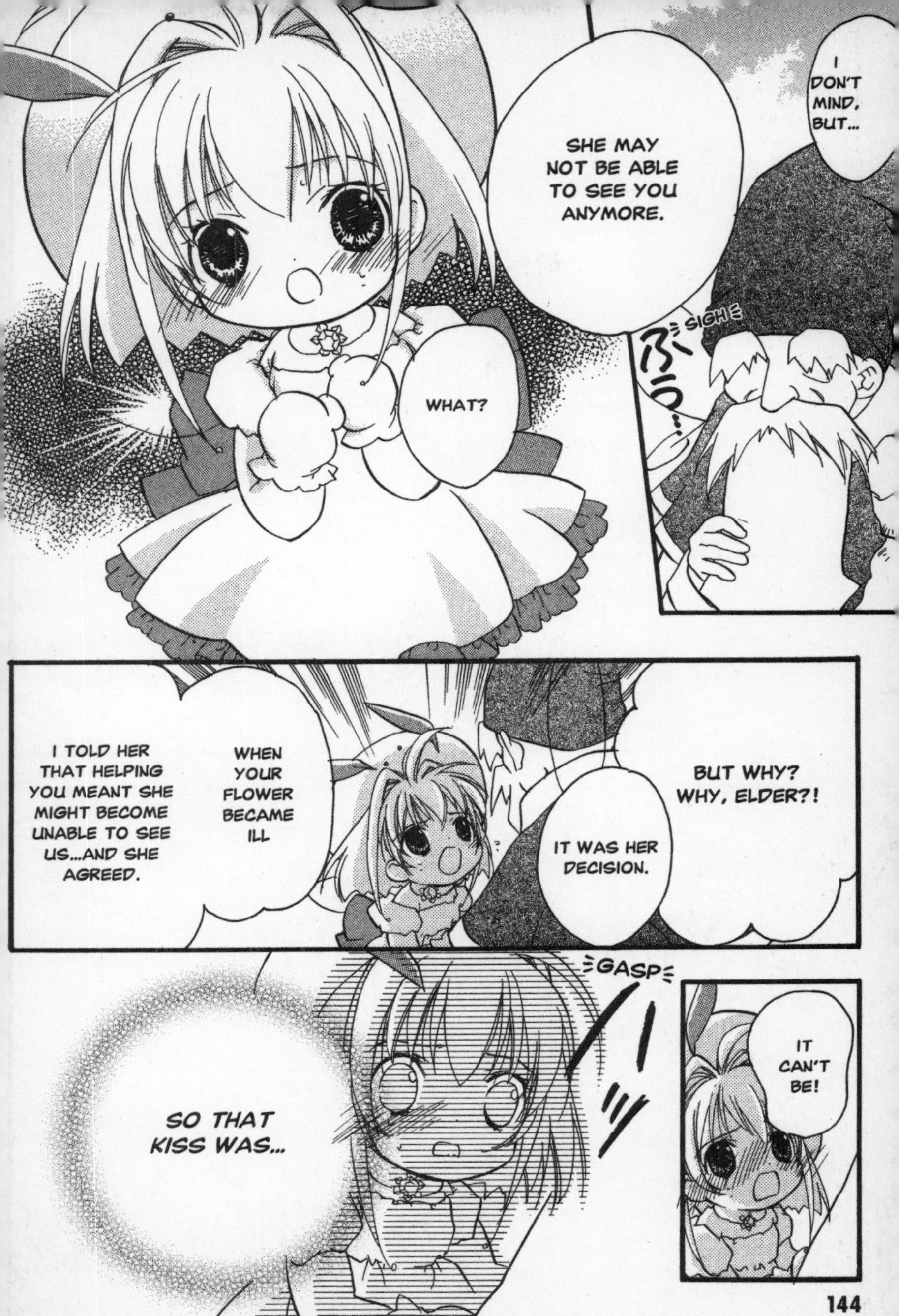
I DON'T MIND, BUT...
SHE MAY NOT BE ABLE TO SEE YOU ANYMORE.
SIGH
ふう…
WHAT?
BUT WHY? WHY, ELDER?!
IT WAS HER DECISION.
WHEN YOUR FLOWER BECAME ILL
I TOLD HER THAT HELPING YOU MEANT SHE MIGHT BECOME UNABLE TO SEE US...AND SHE AGREED.
IT CAN'T BE!
GASP
SO THAT KISS WAS...

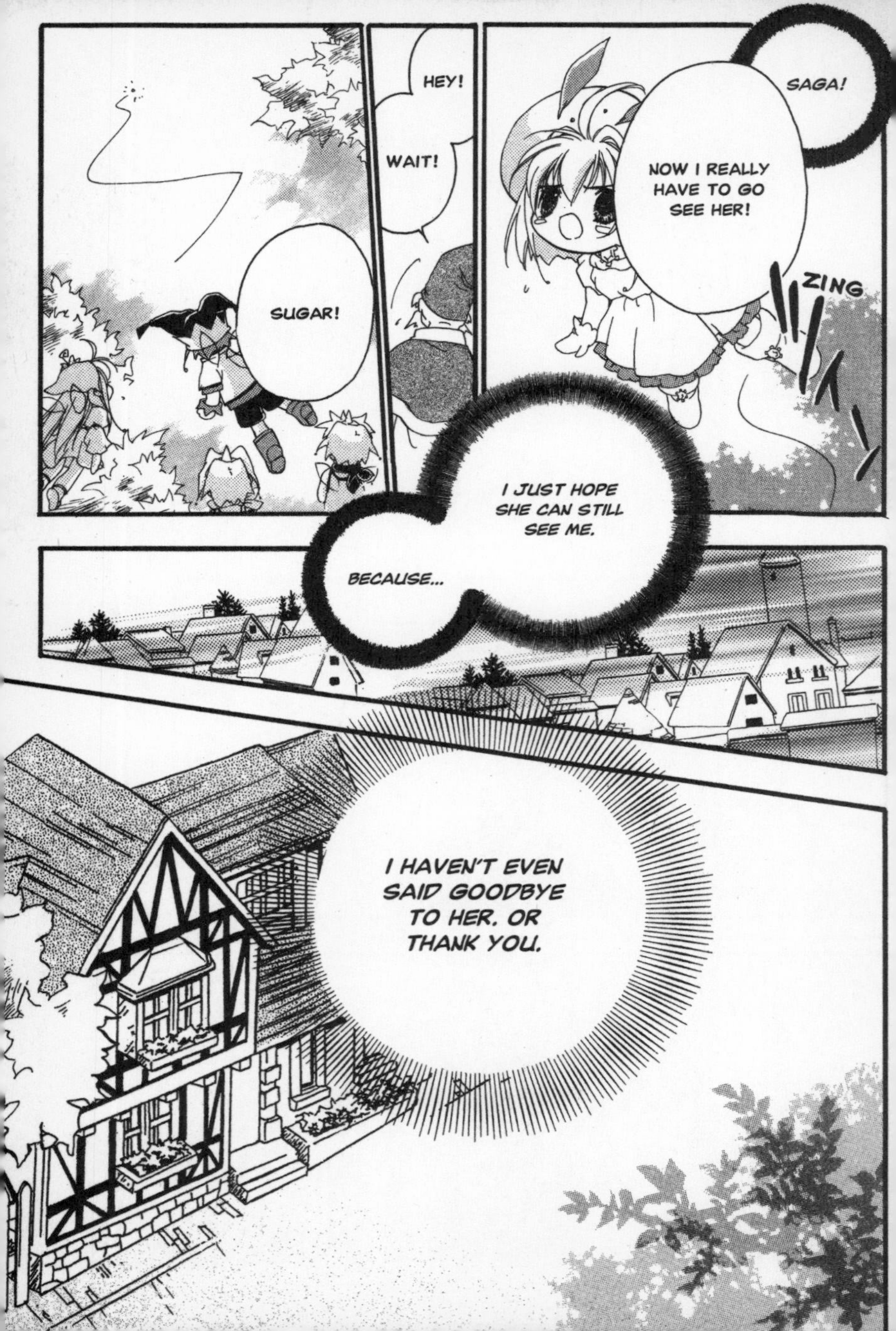
SAGA!
NOW I REALLY HAVE TO GO SEE HER!
ZING
HEY!
WAIT!
SUGAR!
I JUST HOPE SHE CAN STILL SEE ME.
BECAUSE...
I HAVEN'T EVEN SAID GOODBYE TO HER. OR THANK YOU.

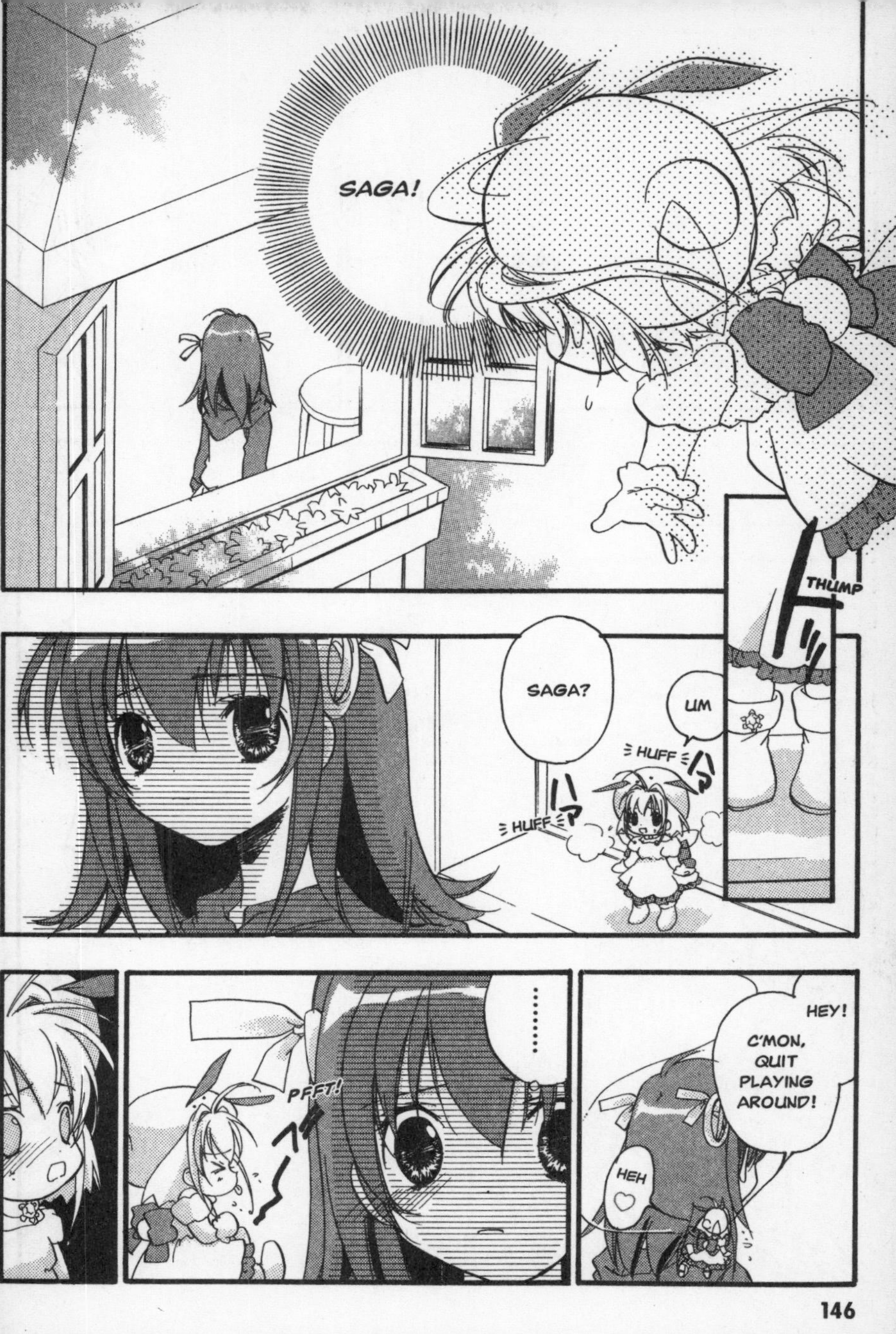
SAGA!
THUMP
SAGA?
UM
HUFF
HUFF
HEY!
C'MON, QUIT PLAYING AROUND!
HEH
......
PFFT!

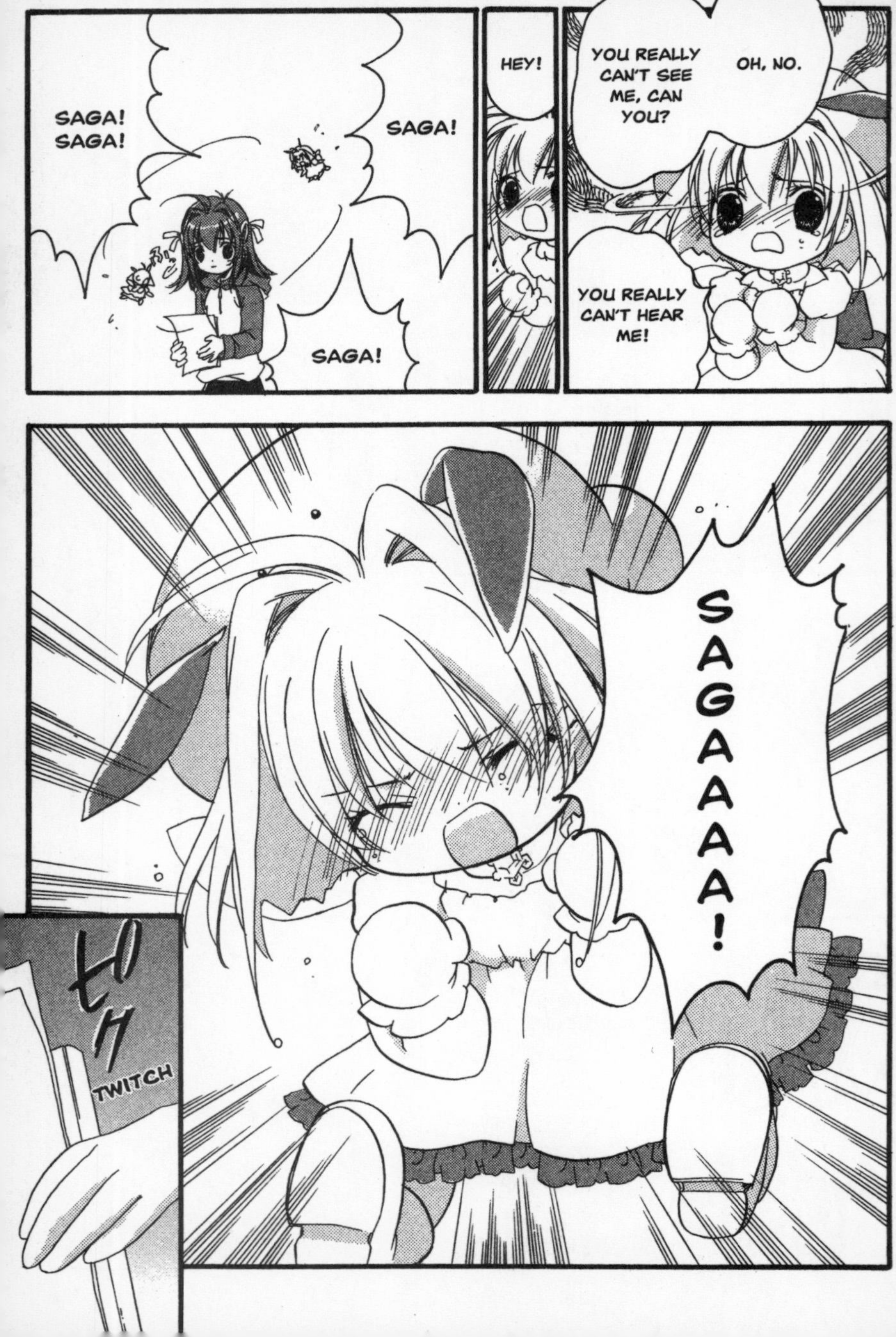
OH, NO.
YOU REALLY CAN'T SEE ME, CAN YOU?
YOU REALLY CAN'T HEAR ME!
HEY!
SAGA!
SAGA! SAGA!
SAGA!
SAGAAAAA!
ビク
TWITCH

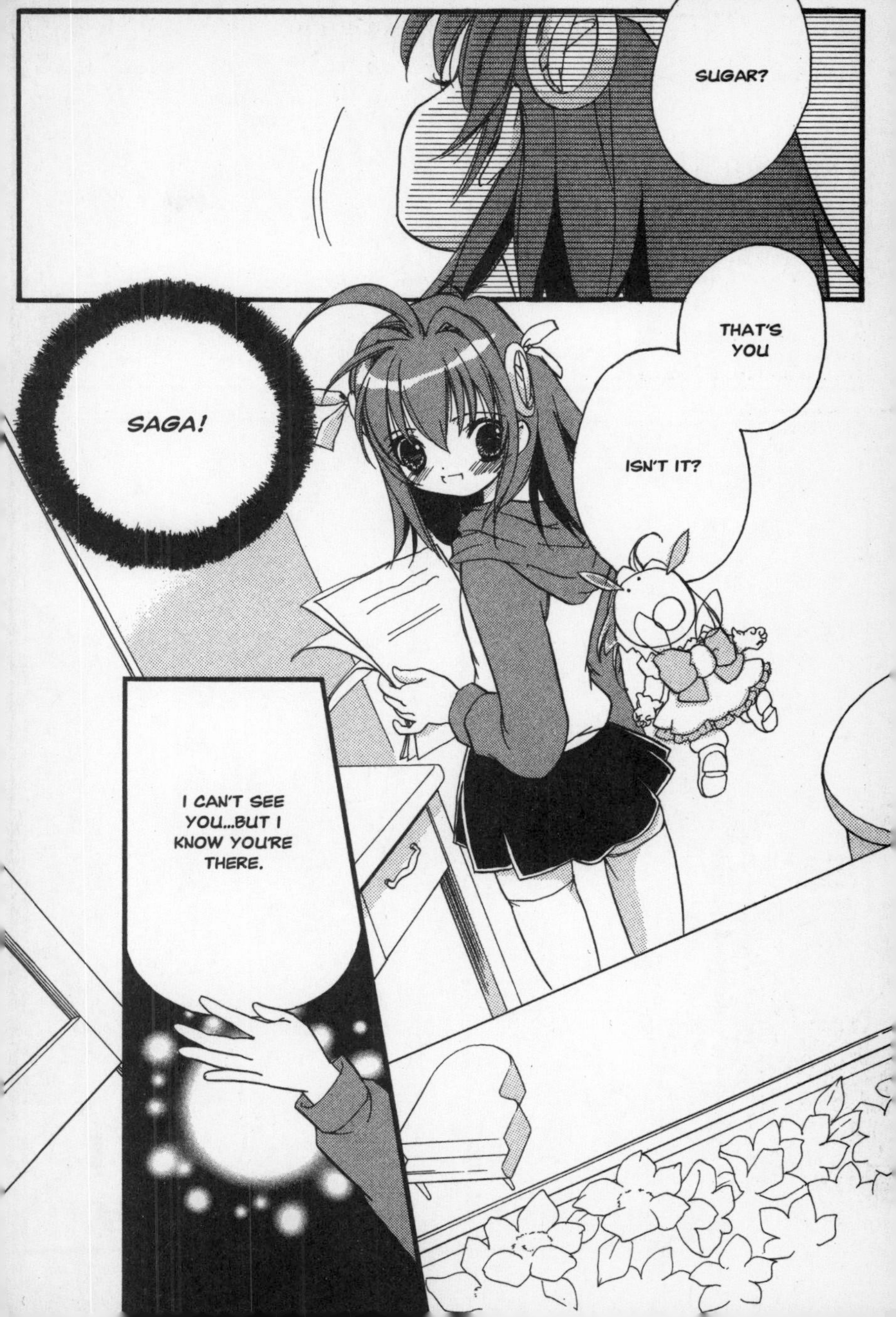
SUGAR?
THAT'S YOU
ISN'T IT?
SAGA!
I CAN'T SEE YOU...BUT I KNOW YOU'RE THERE.

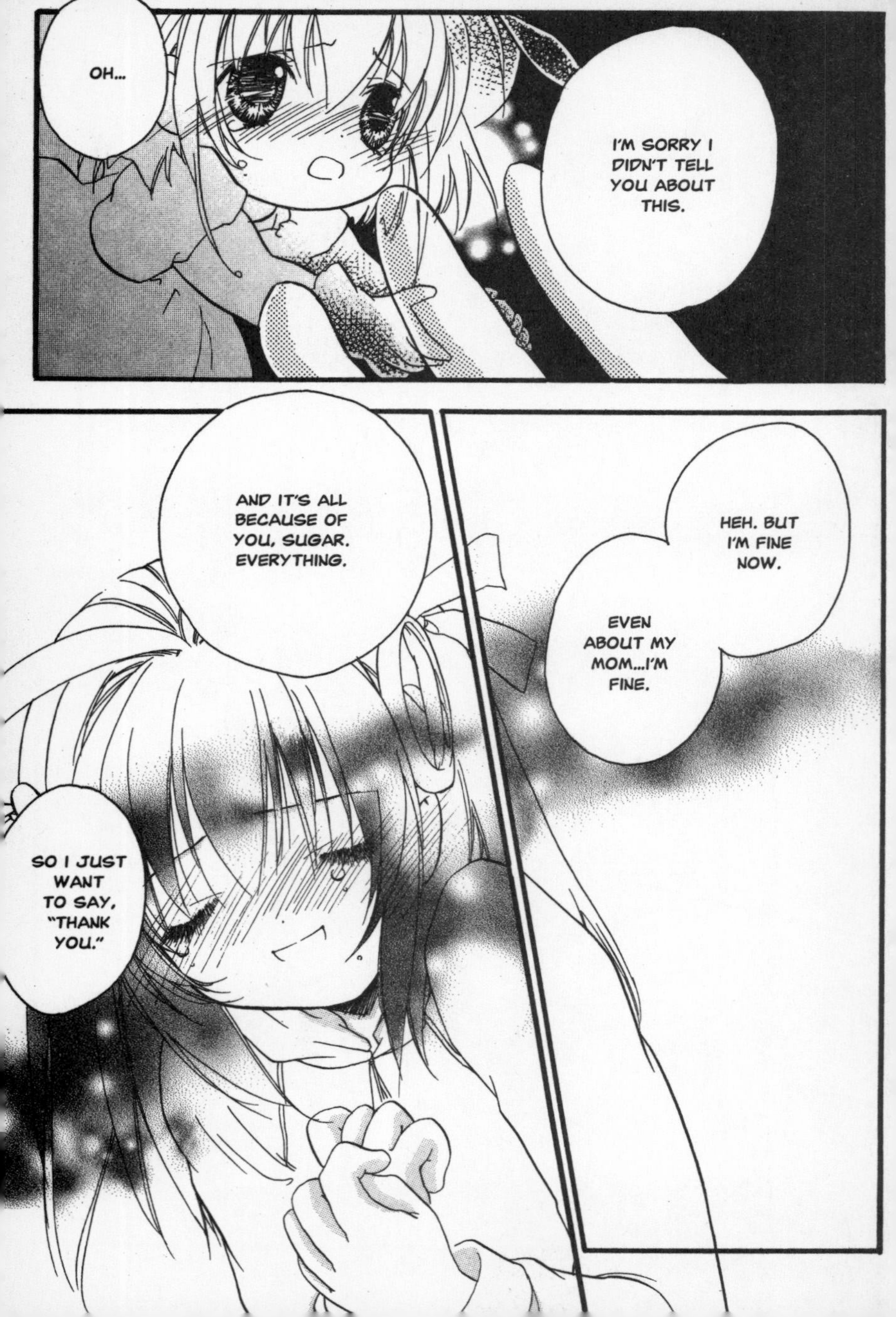
I'M SORRY I DIDN'T TELL YOU ABOUT THIS.
OH...
HEH. BUT I'M FINE NOW.
EVEN ABOUT MY MOM...I'M FINE.
AND IT'S ALL BECAUSE OF YOU, SUGAR. EVERYTHING.
SO I JUST WANT TO SAY, "THANK YOU."

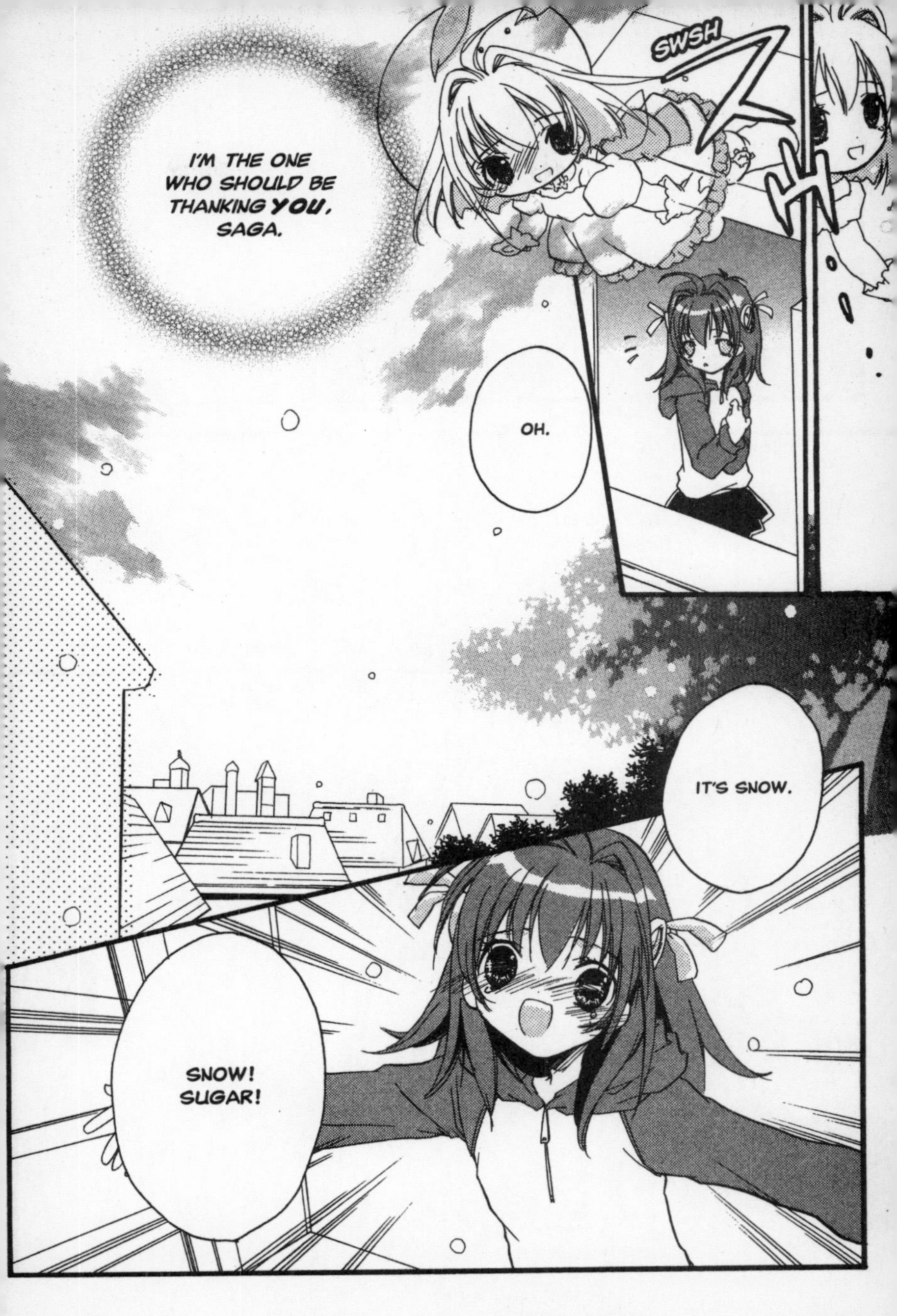
SWSH
I'M THE ONE WHO SHOULD BE THANKING YOU, SAGA.
OH.
IT'S SNOW.
SNOW! SUGAR!

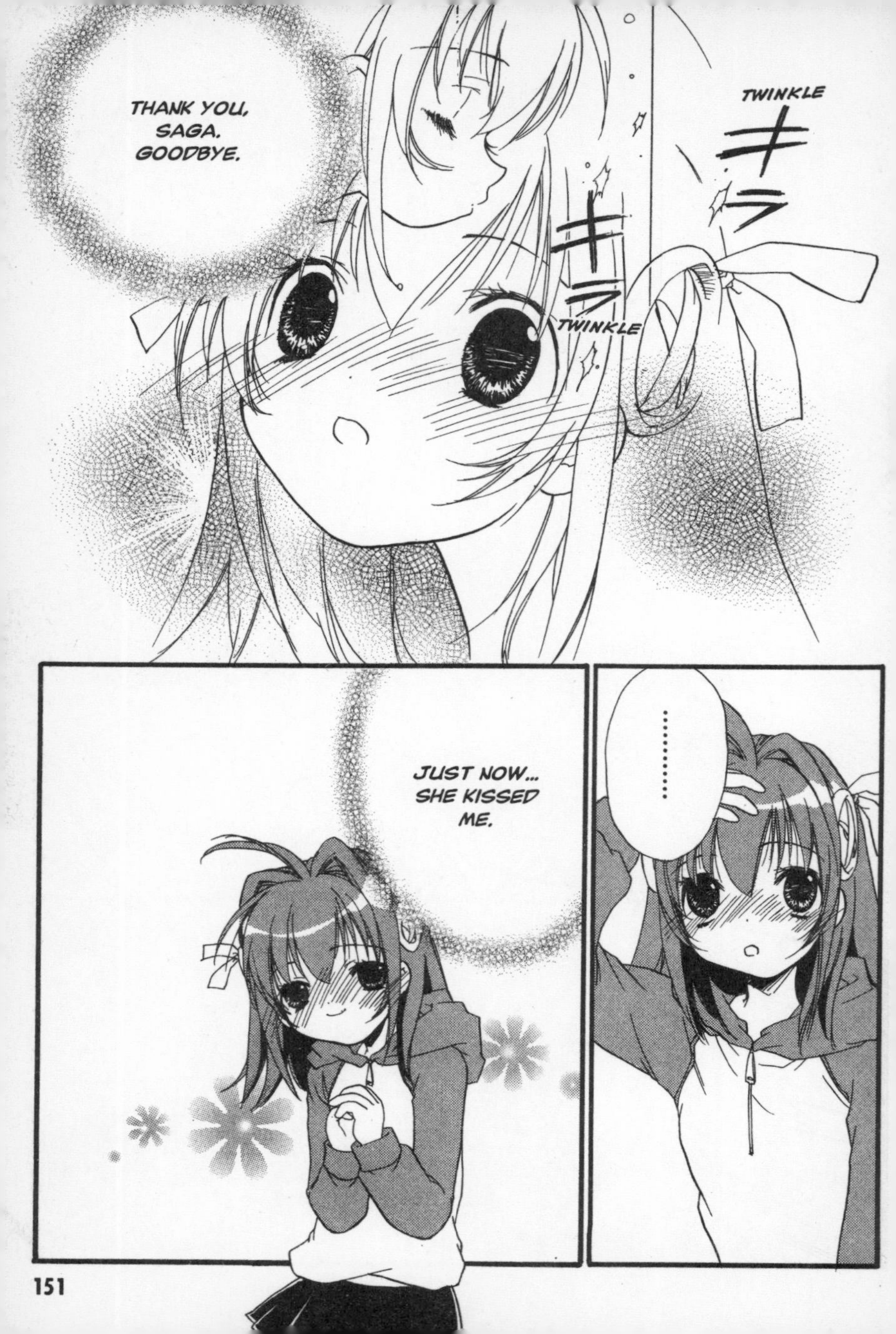
THANK YOU, SAGA. GOODBYE.
TWINKLE
キラ
キラ
TWINKLE
……
JUST NOW... SHE KISSED ME.

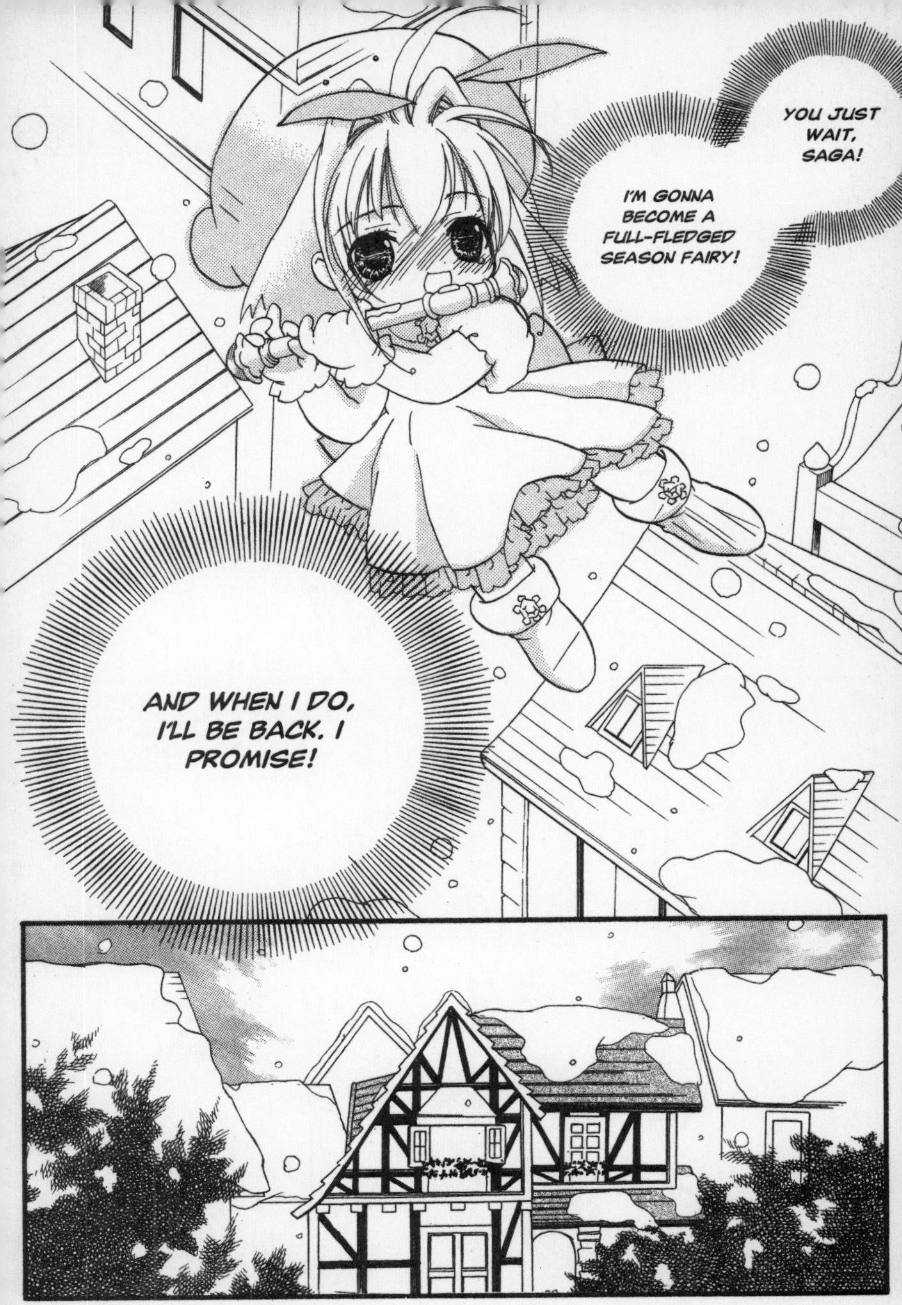
YOU JUST WAIT, SAGA!
I'M GONNA BECOME A FULL-FLEDGED SEASON FAIRY!
AND WHEN I DO, I'LL BE BACK. I PROMISE!

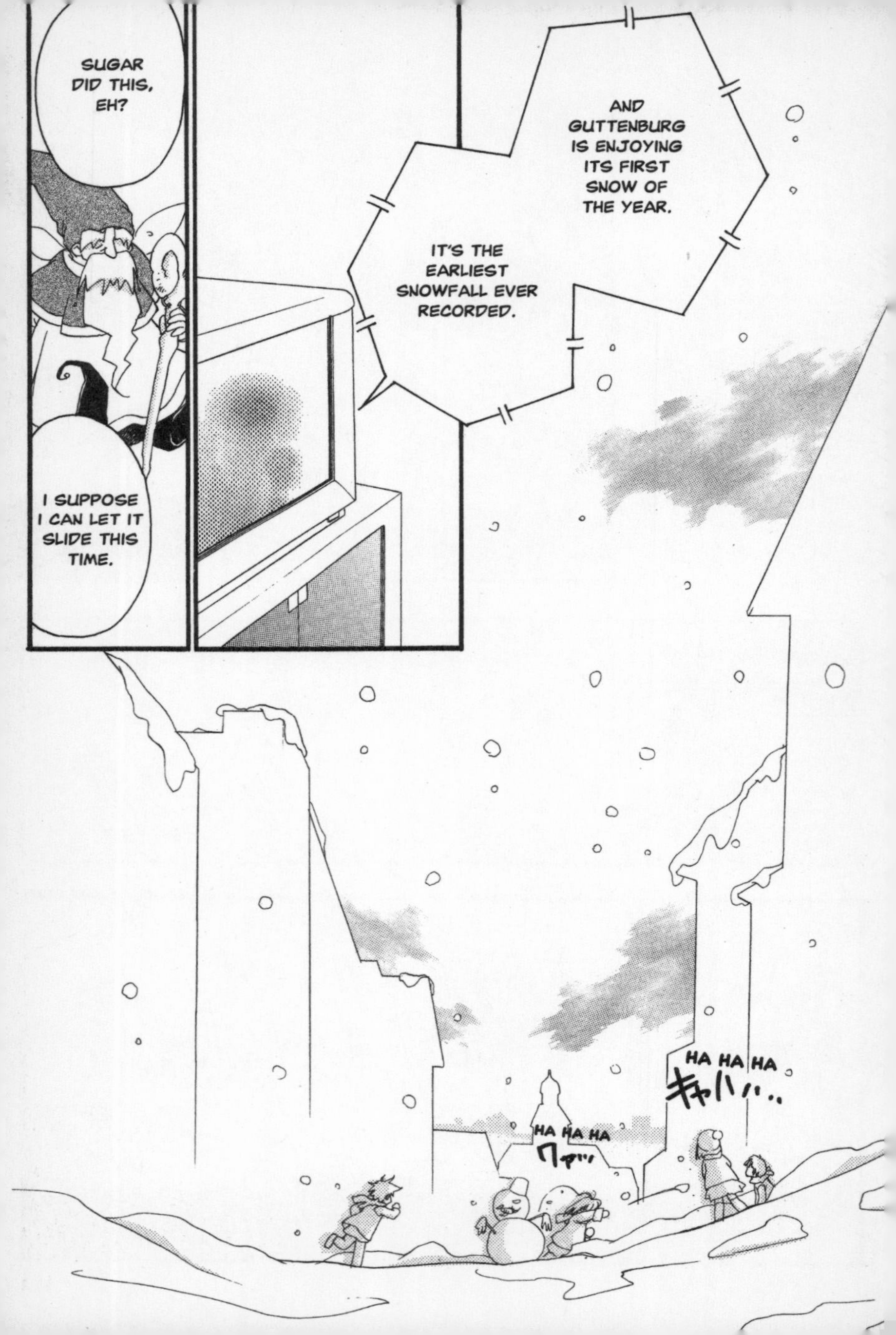
IT'S THE EARLIEST SNOWFALL EVER RECORDED.
AND GUTTENBURG IS ENJOYING ITS FIRST SNOW OF THE YEAR.
SUGAR DID THIS, EH?
I SUPPOSE I CAN LET IT SLIDE THIS TIME.
HA HA HA
キャハハ..
HA HA HA

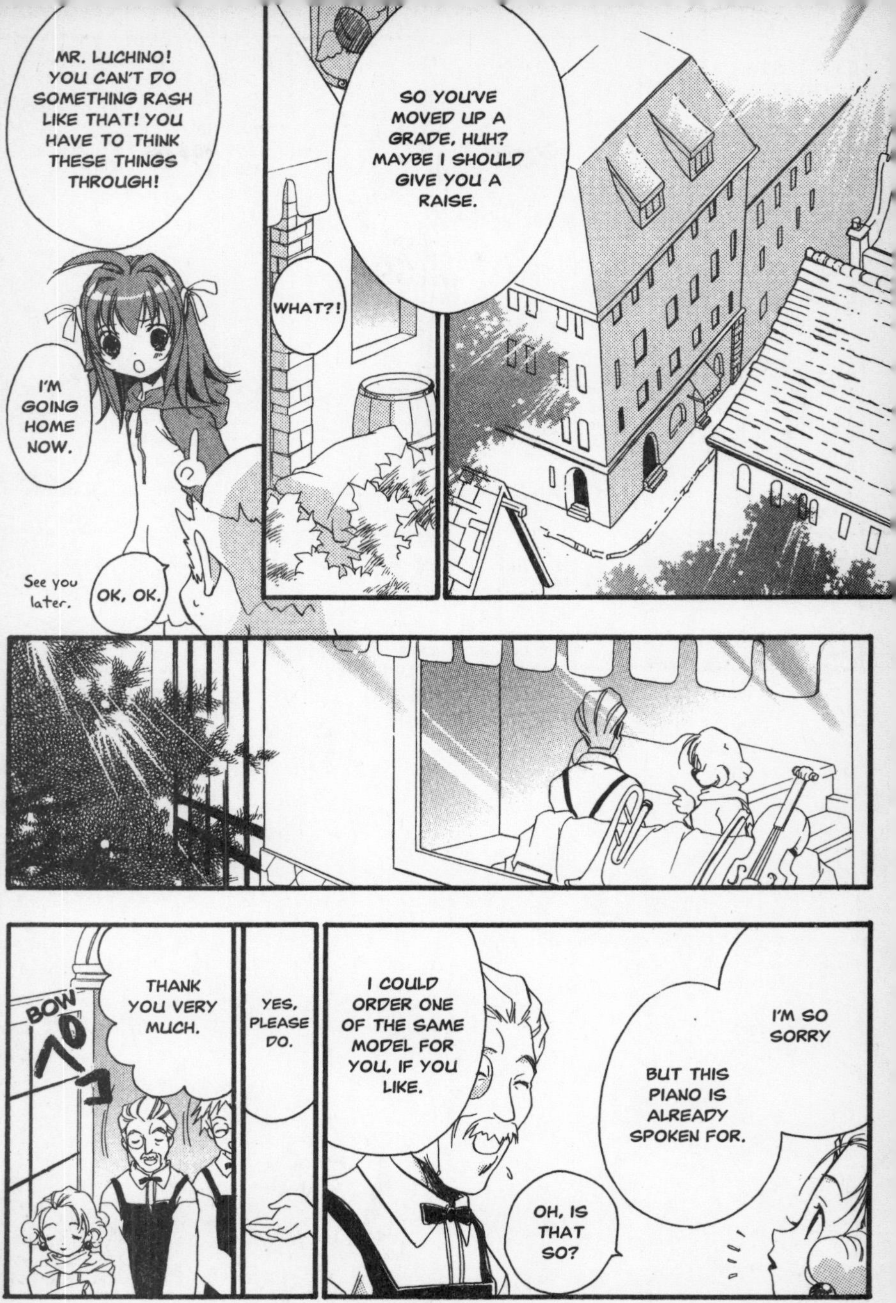

SO YOU'VE MOVED UP A GRADE, HUH? MAYBE I SHOULD GIVE YOU A RAISE.
WHAT?!
MR. LUCHINO! YOU CAN'T DO SOMETHING RASH LIKE THAT! YOU HAVE TO THINK THESE THINGS THROUGH!
I'M GOING HOME NOW.
OK, OK.
See you later.
I'M SO SORRY
BUT THIS PIANO IS ALREADY SPOKEN FOR.
OH, IS THAT SO?
I COULD ORDER ONE OF THE SAME MODEL FOR YOU, IF YOU LIKE.
YES, PLEASE DO.
THANK YOU VERY MUCH.
BOW

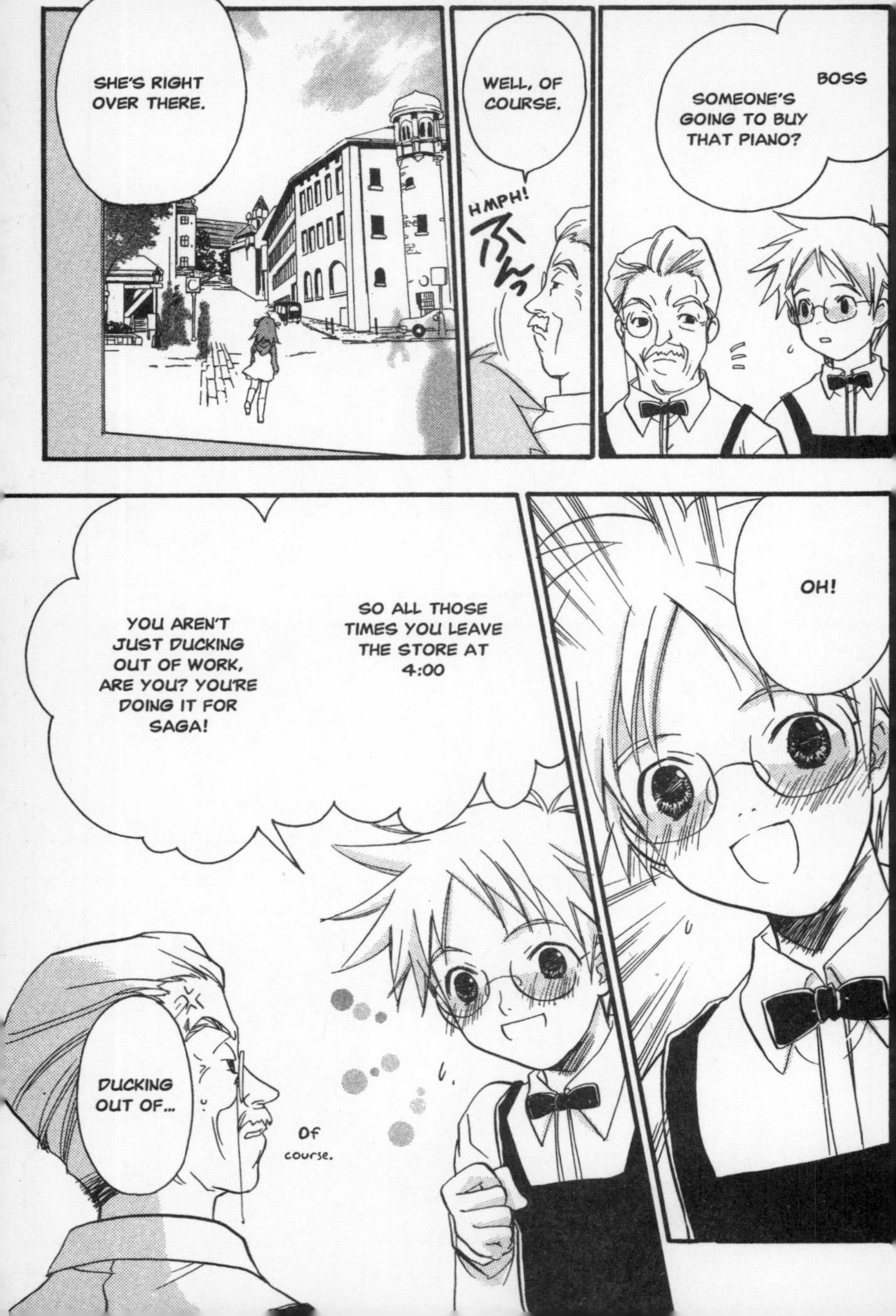
BOSS
SOMEONE'S GOING TO BUY THAT PIANO?
WELL, OF COURSE.
HMPH!
ふんっ
SHE'S RIGHT OVER THERE.
OH!
SO ALL THOSE TIMES YOU LEAVE THE STORE AT 4:00
YOU AREN'T JUST DUCKING OUT OF WORK, ARE YOU? YOU'RE DOING IT FOR SAGA!
DUCKING OUT OF...
Of course.

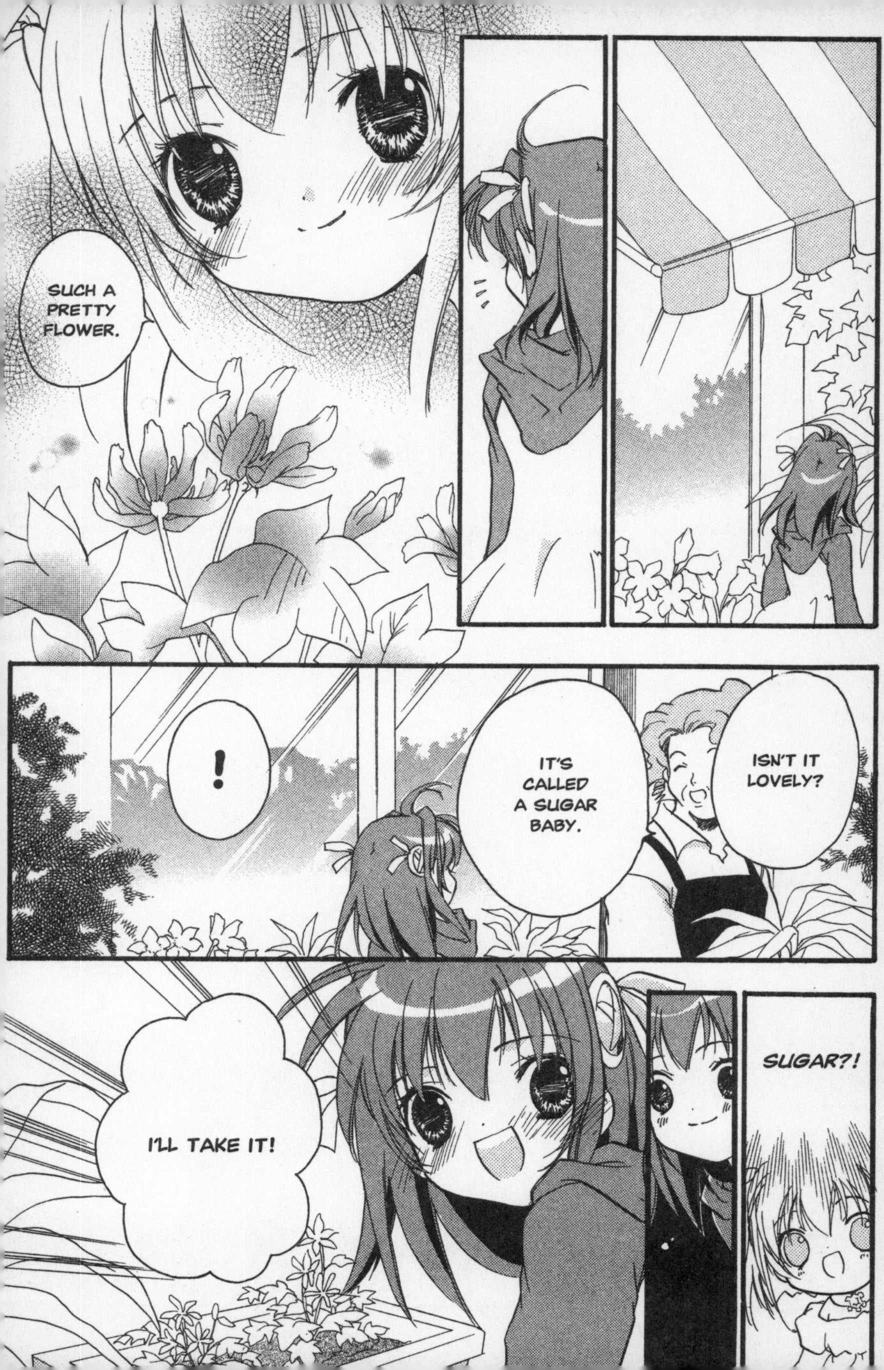
SUCH A PRETTY FLOWER.
ISN'T IT LOVELY?
IT'S CALLED A SUGAR BABY.
!
SUGAR?!
I'LL TAKE IT!

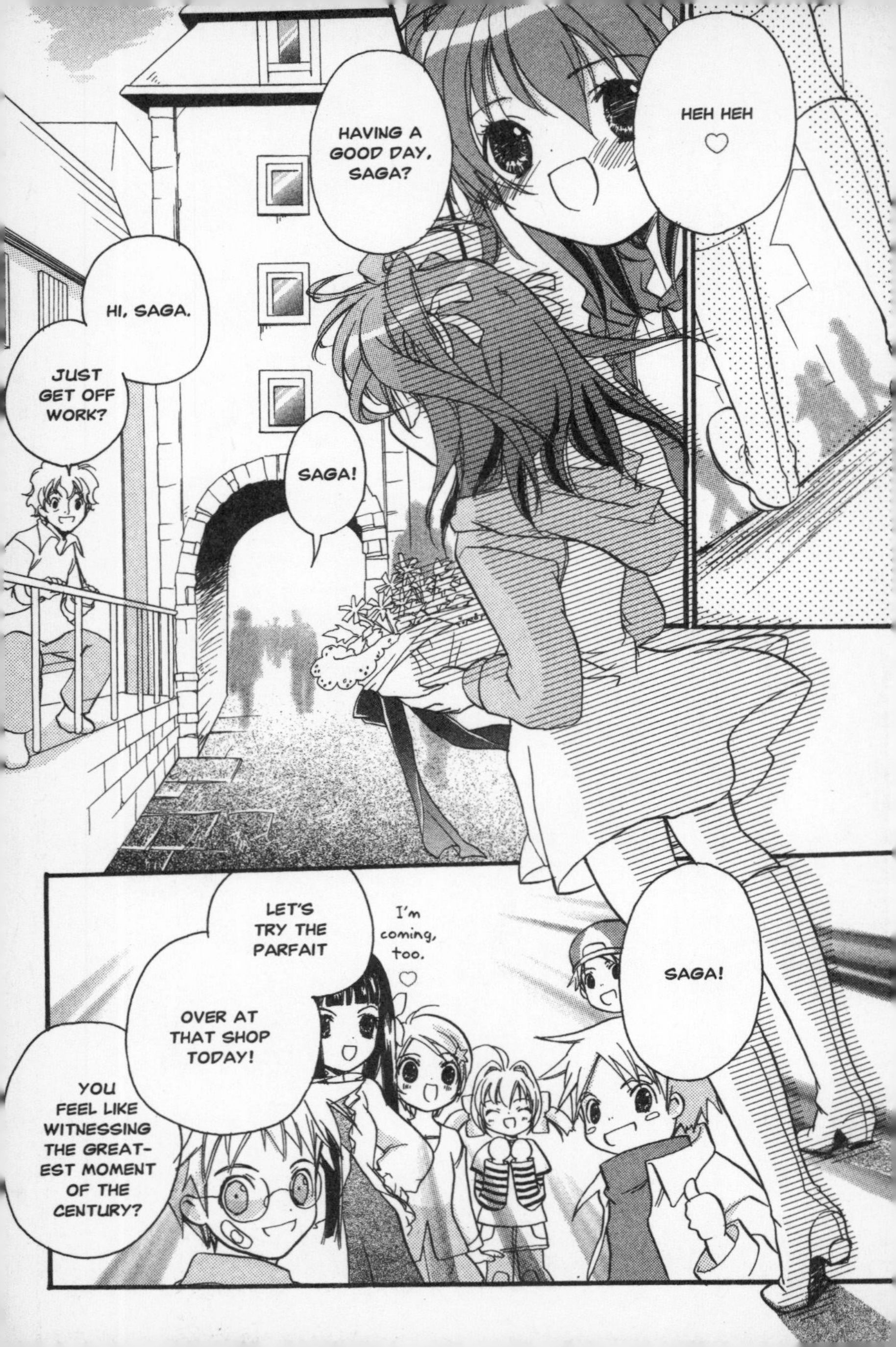
HEH HEH ♡
HAVING A GOOD DAY, SAGA?
SAGA!
HI, SAGA.
JUST GET OFF WORK?
SAGA!
I'm coming, too. ♡
LET'S TRY THE PARFAIT
OVER AT THAT SHOP TODAY!
YOU FEEL LIKE WITNESSING THE GREAT-EST MOMENT OF THE CENTURY?

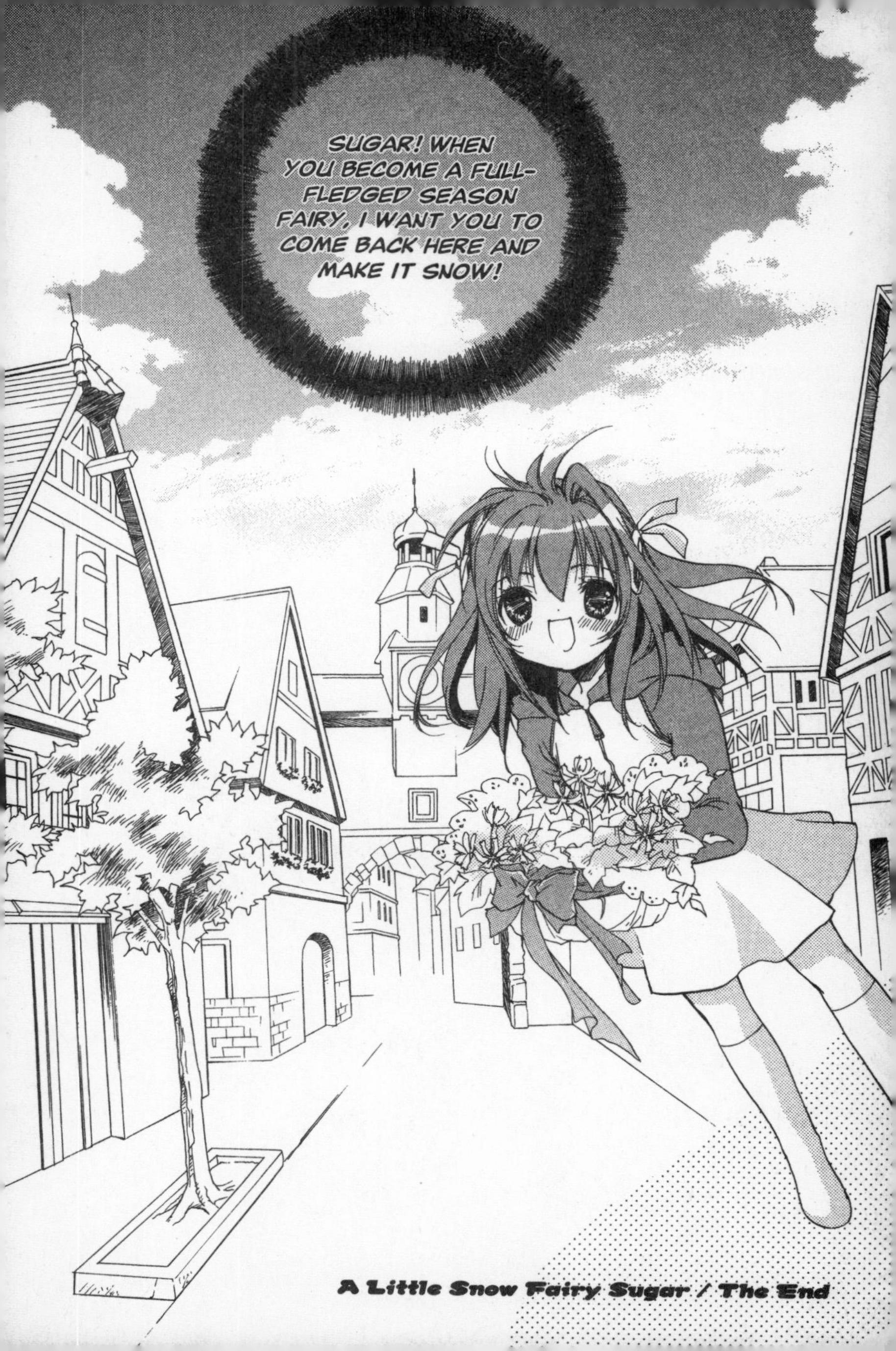
SUGAR! WHEN YOU BECOME A FULL-FLEDGED SEASON FAIRY, I WANT YOU TO COME BACK HERE AND MAKE IT SNOW!
A Little Snow Fairy Sugar / The End

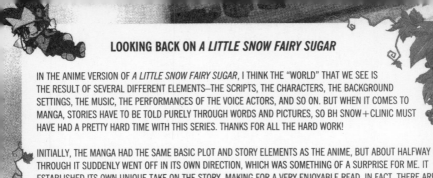

LOOKING BACK ON *A LITTLE SNOW FAIRY SUGAR*

IN THE ANIME VERSION OF *A LITTLE SNOW FAIRY SUGAR*, I THINK THE "WORLD" THAT WE SEE IS THE RESULT OF SEVERAL DIFFERENT ELEMENTS—THE SCRIPTS, THE CHARACTERS, THE BACKGROUND SETTINGS, THE MUSIC, THE PERFORMANCES OF THE VOICE ACTORS, AND SO ON. BUT WHEN IT COMES TO MANGA, STORIES HAVE TO BE TOLD PURELY THROUGH WORDS AND PICTURES, SO BH SNOW+CLINIC MUST HAVE HAD A PRETTY HARD TIME WITH THIS SERIES. THANKS FOR ALL THE HARD WORK!

INITIALLY, THE MANGA HAD THE SAME BASIC PLOT AND STORY ELEMENTS AS THE ANIME, BUT ABOUT HALFWAY THROUGH IT SUDDENLY WENT OFF IN ITS OWN DIRECTION, WHICH WAS SOMETHING OF A SURPRISE FOR ME. IT ESTABLISHED ITS OWN UNIQUE TAKE ON THE STORY, MAKING FOR A VERY ENJOYABLE READ. IN FACT, THERE ARE SO MANY ELEMENTS IN THE MANGA THAT WEREN'T PRESENT IN THE ANIME THAT THE COMIC VERSION CAN BE ENJOYED AS A SORT OF PARALLEL-WORLD VERSION OF *SUGAR*. I REALLY LIKED THE LITTLE SIDE STORIES WE SAW INVOLVING GINGER AND TURMERIC, WHICH, AGAIN, WAS SOMETHING THAT WASN'T IN THE ANIME. IT WAS ALSO INTERESTING TO SEE THE DIFFERENCES IN HOW THE CHARACTERS INTERACTED WITH ONE ANOTHER.

BH SNOW+CLINIC TOLD ME THAT, TO AVOID BEING UNDULY INFLUENCED, SHE WOULDN'T WATCH THE ANIME UNTIL HER COMIC SERIALIZATION HAD FINISHED ITS RUN. I WONDER IF SHE'S WATCHED IT BY NOW. I'D LOVE TO ASK WHAT SHE THOUGHT OF IT!

I HOPE THAT FANS OF *SUGAR* CAN ENJOY THE COMIC AND ANIME VERSIONS ON THEIR OWN MERITS, AND APPRECIATE THE DIFFERENCES IN TONE BETWEEN THE TWO. THINGS HAVE QUIETED DOWN NOW THAT THE MANGA SERIES HAS COME TO AN END, BUT I HOPE YOU'LL KEEP THESE VOLUMES (AS WELL AS THE OVA AND DVD) CLOSE AT HAND UNTIL SUGAR RETURNS TO ONCE AGAIN DELIGHT US ALL.

- HARUKA AOI

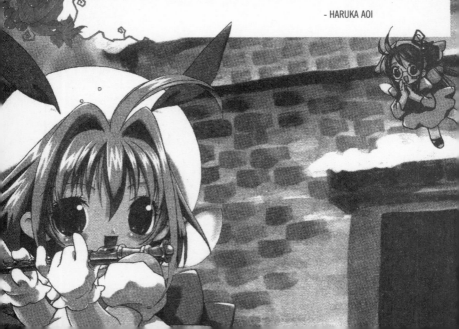

THANKS TO OUR FAITHFUL READERS!

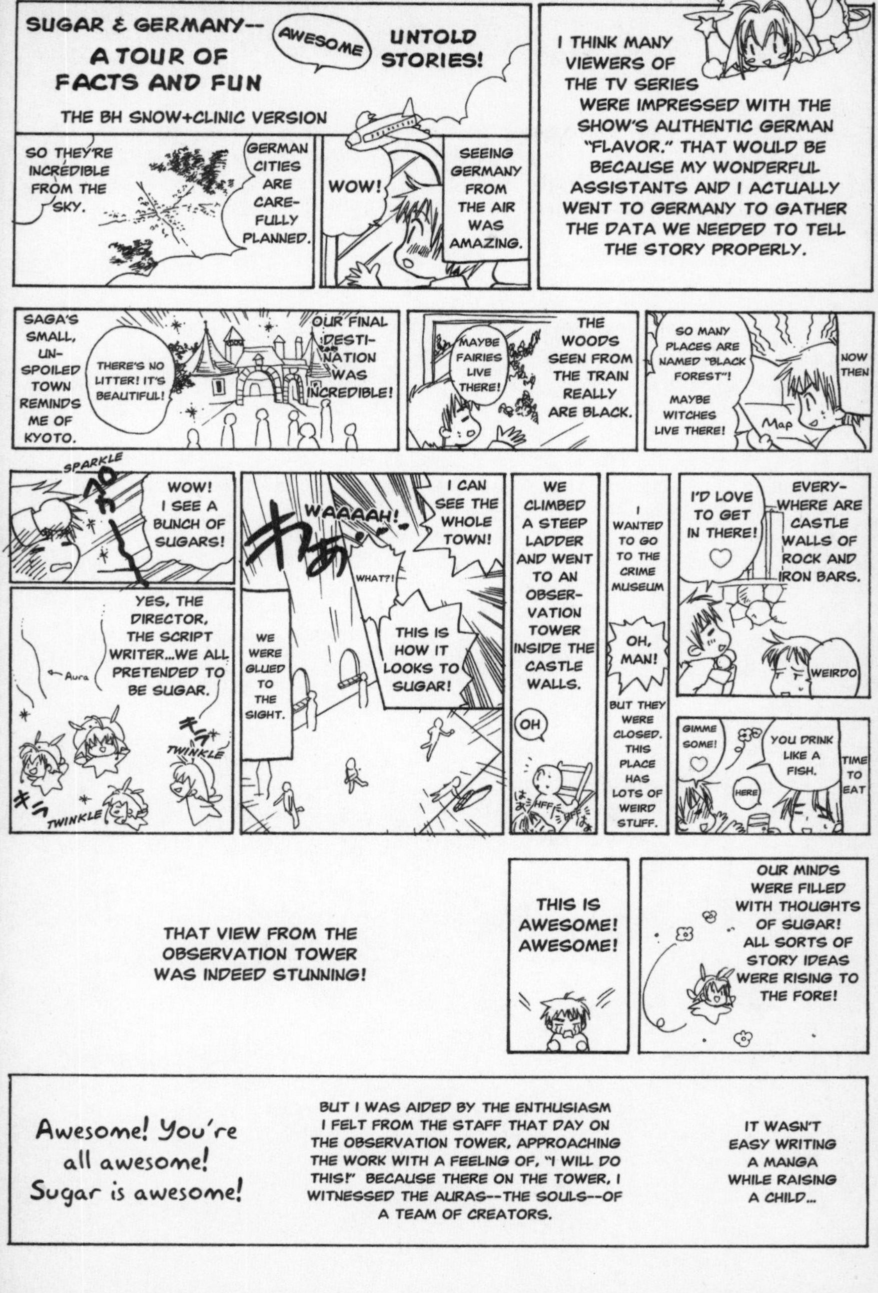
I THINK MANY VIEWERS OF THE TV SERIES WERE IMPRESSED WITH THE SHOW'S AUTHENTIC GERMAN "FLAVOR." THAT WOULD BE BECAUSE MY WONDERFUL ASSISTANTS AND I ACTUALLY WENT TO GERMANY TO GATHER THE DATA WE NEEDED TO TELL THE STORY PROPERLY.
SUGAR & GERMANY-- A TOUR OF FACTS AND FUN
AWESOME
UNTOLD STORIES!
THE BH SNOW+CLINIC VERSION
SEEING GERMANY FROM THE AIR WAS AMAZING.
WOW!
GERMAN CITIES ARE CAREFULLY PLANNED.
SO THEY'RE INCREDIBLE FROM THE SKY.
NOW THEN
SO MANY PLACES ARE NAMED "BLACK FOREST"!
MAYBE WITCHES LIVE THERE!
Map
THE WOODS SEEN FROM THE TRAIN REALLY ARE BLACK.
MAYBE FAIRIES LIVE THERE!
OUR FINAL DESTINATION WAS INCREDIBLE!
THERE'S NO LITTER! IT'S BEAUTIFUL!
SAGA'S SMALL, UNSPOILED TOWN REMINDS ME OF KYOTO.
EVERYWHERE ARE CASTLE WALLS OF ROCK AND IRON BARS.
I'D LOVE TO GET IN THERE!
WEIRDO
TIME TO EAT
YOU DRINK LIKE A FISH.
GIMME SOME!
HERE
I WANTED TO GO TO THE CRIME MUSEUM
OH, MAN!
BUT THEY WERE CLOSED. THIS PLACE HAS LOTS OF WEIRD STUFF.
WE CLIMBED A STEEP LADDER AND WENT TO AN OBSERVATION TOWER INSIDE THE CASTLE WALLS.
OH
HFF
HFF
I CAN SEE THE WHOLE TOWN!
WAAAAH!
WHAT?!
THIS IS HOW IT LOOKS TO SUGAR!
WE WERE GLUED TO THE SIGHT.
SPARKLE
WOW! I SEE A BUNCH OF SUGARS!
YES, THE DIRECTOR, THE SCRIPT WRITER...WE ALL PRETENDED TO BE SUGAR.
Aura
TWINKLE
TWINKLE
OUR MINDS WERE FILLED WITH THOUGHTS OF SUGAR! ALL SORTS OF STORY IDEAS WERE RISING TO THE FORE!
THIS IS AWESOME! AWESOME!
THAT VIEW FROM THE OBSERVATION TOWER WAS INDEED STUNNING!
IT WASN'T EASY WRITING A MANGA WHILE RAISING A CHILD...
BUT I WAS AIDED BY THE ENTHUSIASM I FELT FROM THE STAFF THAT DAY ON THE OBSERVATION TOWER, APPROACHING THE WORK WITH A FEELING OF, "I WILL DO THIS!" BECAUSE THERE ON THE TOWER, I WITNESSED THE AURAS--THE SOULS--OF A TEAM OF CREATORS.
Awesome! You're all awesome! Sugar is awesome!

A LITTLE SNOW FAIRY SUGAR VOLUME THREE

© 2002 HARUKA AOI/TBS
© 2002 BH SNOW + CLINIC
Originally published in Japan in 2002 by
KADOKAWA SHOTEN PUBLISHING CO., LTD., Tokyo.
English translation rights arranged with
KADOKAWA SHOTEN PUBLISHING CO., LTD., Tokyo.

Editor **JAVIER LOPEZ**
Graphic Artist **SCOTT HOWARD**
Translator **KAORU BERTRAND**

Editorial Director **GARY STEINMAN**
Print Production Manager **BRIDGETT JANOTA**
Production Coordinator **MARISA KREITZ**

International Coordinators **TORU IWAKAMI & MIYUKI KAMIYA**

President, CEO & Publisher **JOHN LEDFORD**

Email: editor@adv-manga.com
www.adv-manga.com

www.advfilms.com

For sales and distribution inquiries please call 1.800.282.7202

ADV MANGA™ is a division of A.D. Vision, Inc.
5750 Bintliff Drive, Suite 210, Houston, Texas 77036

English text © 2006 published by A.D. Vision, Inc. under exclusive license.
ADV MANGA is a trademark of A.D. Vision, Inc.

ISBN: 978-1-4139-0354-6
First printing, February 2007
10 9 8 7 6 5 4 3 2 1
Printed in Canada

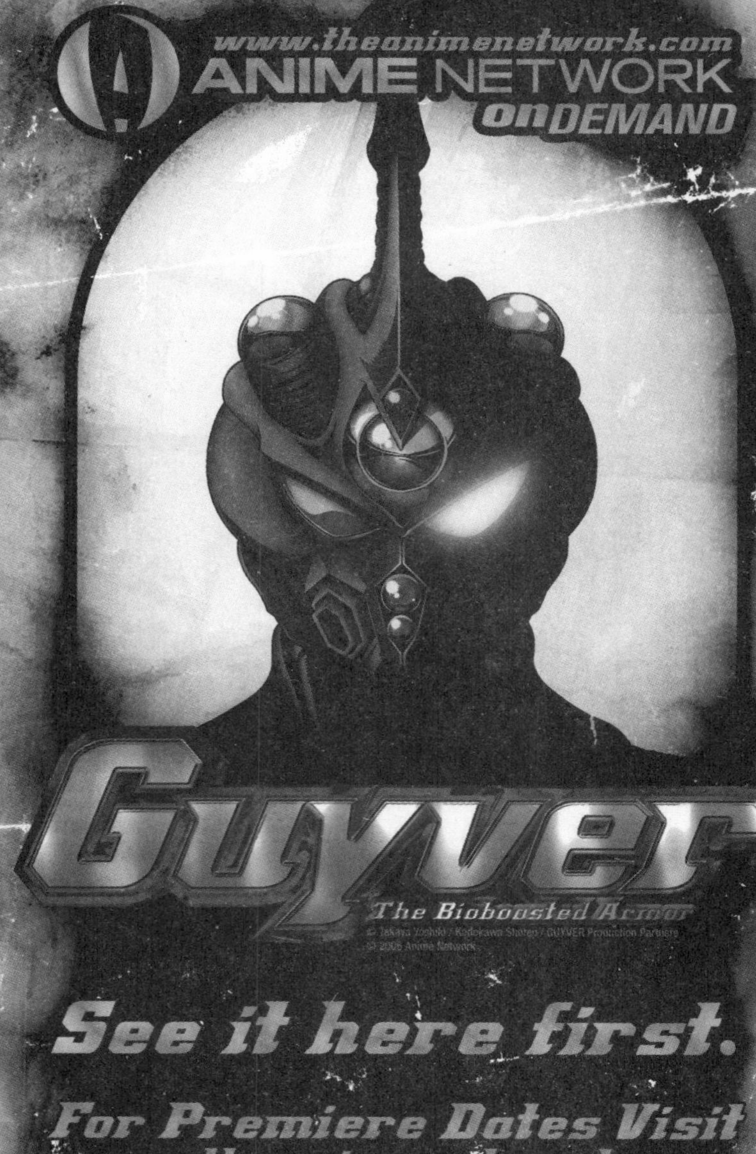

www.theanimenetwork.com
ANIME NETWORK
onDEMAND
Guyver
The Bioboosted Armor
© Takaya Yoshiki / Kadokawa Shoten / GUYVER Production Partners
© 2006 Anime Network
See it here first.
For Premiere Dates Visit
www.theanimenetwork.com

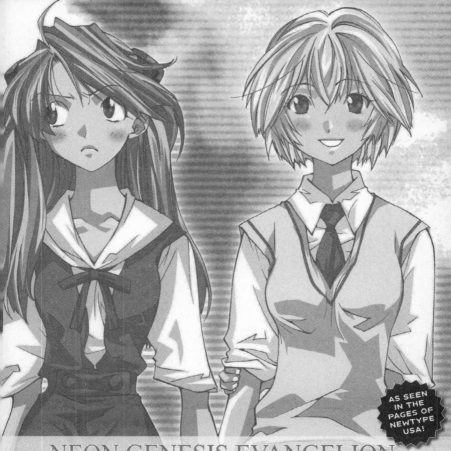

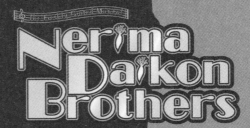

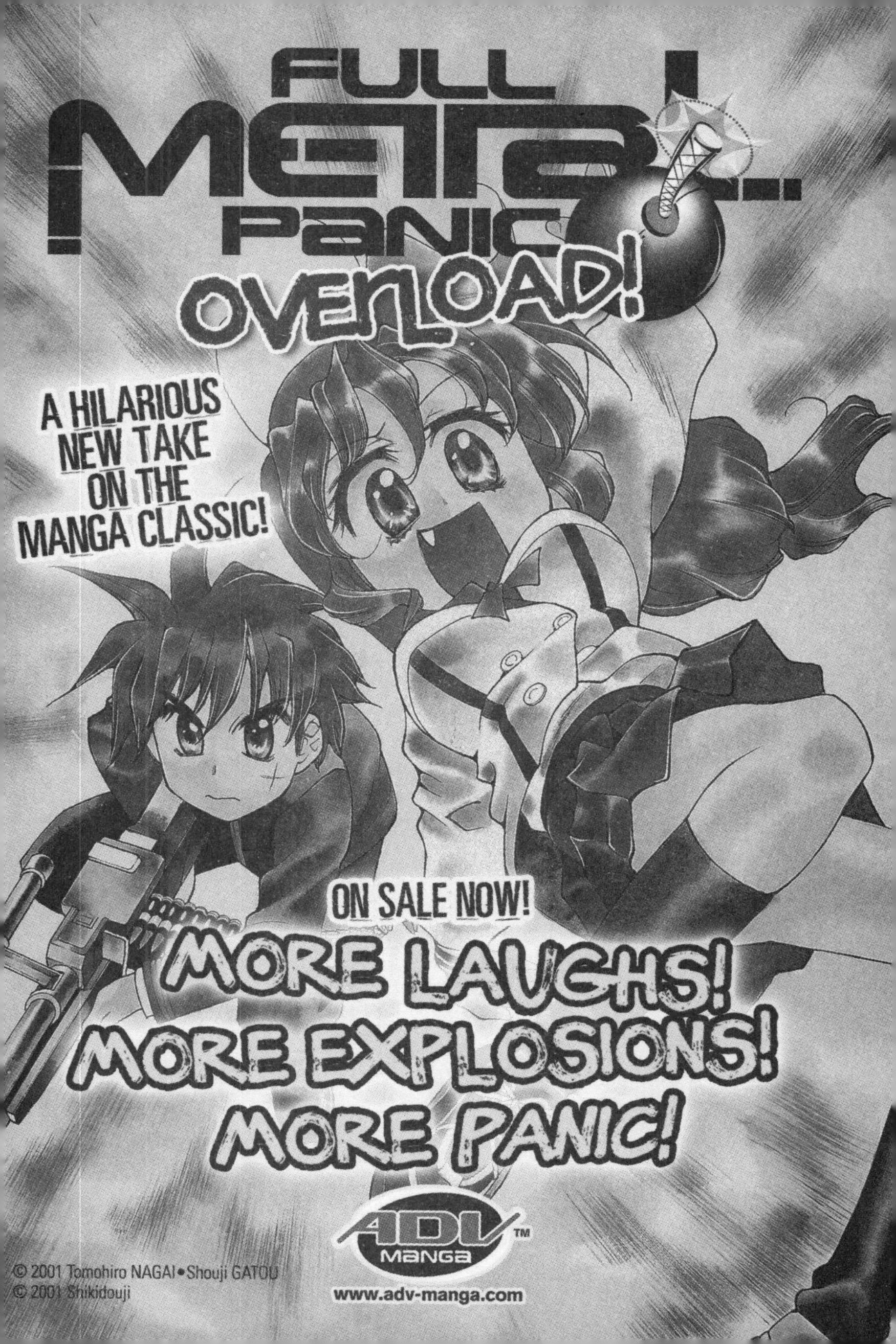

FULL METAL PANIC
OVERLOAD!
A HILARIOUS NEW TAKE ON THE MANGA CLASSIC!
ON SALE NOW!
MORE LAUGHS!
MORE EXPLOSIONS!
MORE PANIC!
ADV Manga ™
© 2001 Tomohiro NAGAI•Shouji GATOU
© 2001 Shikidouji
www.adv-manga.com

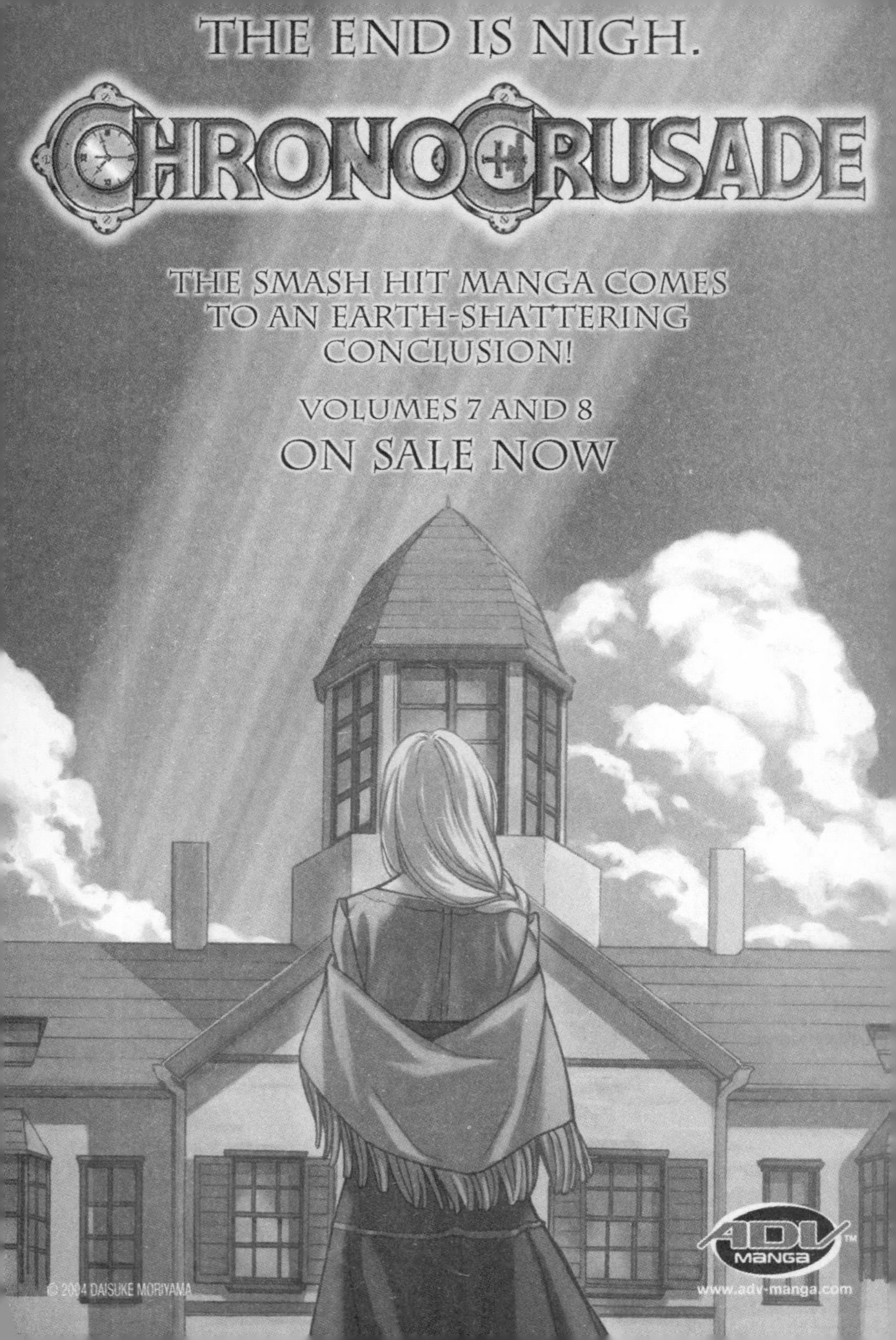
THE END IS NIGH.
CHRONO CRUSADE
THE SMASH HIT MANGA COMES TO AN EARTH-SHATTERING CONCLUSION!
VOLUMES 7 AND 8
ON SALE NOW
© 2004 DAISUKE MORIYAMA
ADV MANGA™
www.adv-manga.com

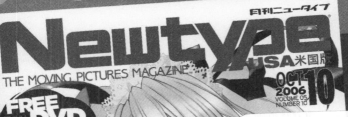